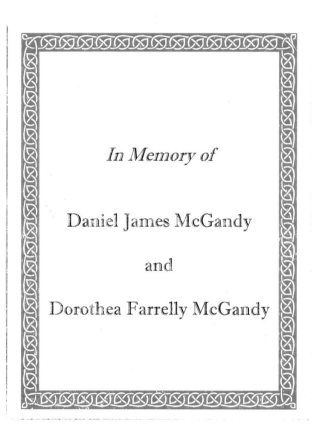

In Memory of

Daniel James McGandy

and

Dorothea Farrelly McGandy

❧ THE TEMPLARS,
THE WITCH, AND
THE WILD IRISH

THE TEMPLARS,
THE WITCH,
AND THE
WILD IRISH

VENGEANCE AND HERESY
IN MEDIEVAL IRELAND

MAEVE BRIGID CALLAN

CORNELL UNIVERSITY PRESS
Ithaca

First published 2015 by Cornell University Press

Printed in the United States of America

Library of Congress Cataloging-in-Publication Data

Callan, Maeve Brigid, 1970– author.
    The Templars, the witch, and the wild Irish : vengeance and heresy in medieval Ireland / Maeve Brigid Callan.
        pages cm
    Includes bibliographical references and index.
    ISBN 978-0-8014-5313-7 (cloth : alk. paper)
    1. Ireland—Church history—600–1500. 2. Trials (Heresy)—Ireland—History—To 1500. 3. Trials (Witchcraft)—Ireland—History—To 1500. I. Title.
    BR794.C35   2015
    282′.41509023—dc23   2014022145

Cornell University Press strives to use environmentally responsible suppliers and materials to the fullest extent possible in the publishing of its books. Such materials include vegetable-based, low-VOC inks and acid-free papers that are recycled, totally chlorine-free, or partly composed of nonwood fibers. For further information, visit our website at www.cornellpress.cornell.edu.

Cloth printing   10 9 8 7 6 5 4 3 2 1

For Seth, Finnian, and Hunter

As you well know, heretics have never been found in Ireland; rather, it is customarily called the isle of saints. Now, however, some foreigner comes from England and says we are all heretics and excommunicants, claiming for himself some papal constitutions that we have never heard of before now. And since defamation of this land touches every one of us, you all ought to unite against this man.

—Arnold le Poer at the Dublin Parliament, May 1324

❧ Contents

Acknowledgments   xi

Abbreviations   xiii

Chronology of Key Events   xvii

Map   xxii

Introduction   1

1. Heresy Hunting Begins in Ireland:
   The Trial of the Templars and the
   Case against Philip de Braybrook   31

2. The Dawn of the Devil-
   Worshipping Witch   78

3. The Churlish Tramp from England:
   Richard de Ledrede Tries the
   Alice Kyteler Case   117

4. Moments of Lucidity Dedicated
   to Malice: Ledrede's Continuing
   Conflicts in the Colony   149

5. The Heresy of Being Irish:
   Adducc Dubh O'Toole and
   Two MacConmaras   188

Conclusion   235

*Appendix A: The Articles against
the Templars in Ireland   243*

*Appendix B: The Charges against
Alice Kyteler and Associates   247*

Bibliography   249

Index   273

❧ ACKNOWLEDGMENTS

My debts are many and deep, matched only by my profound gratitude and appreciation for all who have helped with this fifteen-year project. Great thanks to the scholars who have shared their wisdom so generously, including Barbara Newman, Robert Lerner, Peter Schermerhorn, Helen Nicholson, Stuart Kinsella, Colleen Bos, David Collins, Matthew Slepin, Matthew Hussey, Michael Bailey, Michael Ryan, Shannon McSheffrey, Alan Forey, Dáibhí Ó Cróinín, Theodore de Bruyn, Dermot Moran, Niav Gallagher, Ciarán Parker, Katharine Simms, Anne Neary Lawes, Bernadette Williams, the late James Lydon, and especially the late Philomena Connolly. Librarians throughout the world are my heroes; I am particularly grateful to those at the Bodleian Library, the British Library, the Representative Church Body Library (Ireland), the National Library of Ireland, Trinity College Dublin, Northwestern University (especially Victoria Zahrobsky), and Simpson College (especially Kristen Graham). I have been blessed with outstanding teachers throughout my life, including Bob Turansky, Jennifer Rycenga, and the late Bill Whedbee; profound thanks to you all. The support I received at Northwestern University and the community I have found at Simpson College have been tremendous assets to my work and to me personally; my thanks to my colleagues, including Stephanie Neve, Jan Everhart, Mark Gammon, Steve Griffith, Daryl Sasser, Judy Walden, Shelly Priebe, Peg Pearson, and especially Nancy St. Clair, and to the students who continue to inspire me, particularly those who help cultivate greater interfaith understanding and engagement, such as Annie Fullas, Amanda Mackey, Madison Fiedler, and T. J. Hiatt.

Michael Larsen's brilliant expertise greatly enhanced my photographs, and Lia Mills's and Isaac and Millicent Warham's company made the taking of them all the more entertaining and enjoyable. Great thanks to all who help care for medieval sites, especially those who facilitated my visits, like the Perceval family, Pierce McAuliffe, and Tommy Halton. My friends and family in North America and Europe have been invaluable to me in countless ways, not least in letting me talk about my beloved medieval heretics (or mystics or saints or . . .), so here's to you, Anne, Hilary, Buzzy, Lisa, Jessica, Stu, Stryder, Nicole, Sophie, Michael, Virginia, Andrew, Collin, Fred, Alexis, Tiffany, Nathalie, Barbara, Trisha, Peggy, Jill, Hema, Katie, Michelle, Laura, Karen, Mike, Steve, Eric, Timm, Steve, Matthew, Liz, Jackie, David, Trudi, Simon, Bernadette, John, Danya, Róisín, Danielle, Robin, Alec, Donna, Clark, Adam, Jeff, Cris, Kitty, Christine (my legs in London), Phillip, Lenore, Mary Elizabeth, Jodi, Grainne, Norm, Eoin, Geneva, Colm, Julie, and above all my parents, Clair and Sean, whose love, support, and personal examples have made everything possible.

Sean Field read multiple drafts of my manuscript and gave invaluable advice, seasoned with his characteristic humor and perspicacity. Richard Kieckhefer has been instrumental at every stage of this book's development; my debt to and gratitude for his guidance and friendship are inestimable. Peter Potter's gifts as an editor, and the whole Cornell University Press team (including the anonymous readers), have vastly improved my work. My profound thanks to you all. For any errors that remain, my sincere apologies.

To my husband, Seth, my travel partner, muse, sounding board, and at long last index assistant, whose support in countless ways (not least those fabulous Indian feasts!) has helped make these years so rewarding; to my son Finnian, who was the greatest internal motivation a woman could have when this work was a dissertation and whose penetrating insights and wry perspective have been integrated into it; and to my son Hunter, whose love of life embraces all he encounters and whose enthusiasm for the book, even when it kept me from playing with him, buoyed my own: you inspire and delight me, and my love for you knows no bounds. I am deeply grateful for your patience and the entertainment and joy you provide every day. I dedicate this book to you.

❧ Abbreviations

AC	*Annála Connacht: The Annals of Connacht (A.D. 1224–1544).* Edited by A. Martin Freeman. 1944. Reprint, Dublin: Dublin Institute for Advanced Studies, 1996.
ACl	*The Annals of Clonmacnoise, Being the Annals of Ireland from the Earliest Period to A.D. 1408.* Translated by Conell Mageoghan [1627]. Edited by Denis Murphy. 1896. Reprint, Felinfach: Llanerch, 1993.
AI	*Annals of Inisfallen.* Edited by Seán Mac Airt. 1944. Reprint, Dublin: Dublin Institute for Advanced Studies, 1988.
Berry, *Early Statutes*	H. F. Berry, ed. *Statutes and Ordinances and Acts of the Parliament of Ireland: King John to Henry V.* Dublin: Alexander Thom, 1907.
CCR	*Calendar of the Close Rolls Preserved in the Public Record Office . . . 1272–1509.* 61 vols. 1892–1963. Reprint, Nendeln: Kraus, 1970–80.
CDI	*Calendar of Documents Relating to Ireland . . . , 1171–1307.* Edited by H. S. Sweetman and G. F. Handcock. 5 vols. 1875–86. Reprint, Nendeln: Kraus, 1974.
CFR	*Calendar of the Fine Rolls Preserved in the Public Record Office.* 22 vols. London: His Majesty's Stationery Office, 1911–62.
CJR	*Calendar of the Justiciary Rolls or Proceedings in the Court of the Justiciar of Ireland, Preserved in the Public Record Office of Ireland.* Vols. 1–2, *1295–1307*, ed. James Mills. Vol. 3, *1308–14*, ed. Herbert Wood and Albert E. Langman, rev. Margaret C. Griffith. Dublin: Alexander Thom, 1905–52.
Clyn	John Clyn, *The Annals of Ireland by Friar John Clyn and Thady Dowling, Together with the Annals of Ross.* Edited

	by Richard Butler. Dublin: Irish Archaeological Society, 1849.
CPL	*Calendar of Entries in the Papal Registers Relating to Great Britain and Ireland: Papal Letters.* Vols. 1–2, *1198–1342,* ed. W. H. Bliss. Vol. 3, *1342–1362,* ed. W. H. Bliss and C. Johnson. London: His Majesty's Stationery Office, 1893–97.
CPR	*Calendar of the Patent Rolls Preserved in the Public Record Office . . . 1232–1509.* 53 vols. 1891–1971. Reprint, Nendeln: Kraus, 1971–72.
CSM	*Chartularies of St. Mary's Abbey, Dublin.* Edited by J. T. Gilbert. 2 vols. Rolls Series 80. London: Longman, 1884.
CT	Sean MacRuaidhrí Mac Craith. *Caithréim Thoird-healbhaigh.* Edited and translated by Standish Hayes O'Grady. 2 vols. Irish Texts Society 26–27. London: Irish Texts Society, 1929.
IEP	*Irish Exchequer Payments, 1270–1446.* Edited by Philomena Connolly. 2 vols. Dublin: Dundalgan for the Irish Manuscripts Commission, 1998.
IHD	*Irish Historical Documents, 1172–1922.* Edited Edmund Curtis and R. B. McDowell. 1943. Reprint, London: Methuen, 1968.
NHI	*A New History of Ireland.* Vol. 2, *Medieval Ireland, 1169–1534,* ed. Art Cosgrove (1987; repr., Oxford: Clarendon Press, 2001). Vol. 9, *Maps, Genealogies, Lists,* ed. T. W. Moody, F. X. Martin, and F. J. Byrne (1984; repr., Oxford: Clarendon Press, 2002).
Prynne	William Prynne. *An Exact Chronological Vindication and Historical Demonstration of Our British, Roman, Saxon, Danish, Norman, English Kings' Supream Ecclesistical Jurisdiction over all Prelates, Persons, Causes, within Their Kingdomes and Dominions.* 3 vols. London, 1665–68.
RC	Record Commission.
RCB	Representative Church Body Library. Churchtown, Co. Dublin.
Rymer	Thomas Rymer, ed. *Foedera, conventiones, litterae, et cujuscunque generis acta publica, inter reges Angliae et alios quosvis imperatores, reges, pontifices, principes, vel*

communitates, ab ineunte saeculo duodecimo. 10 vols. 3rd ed. 1745. Reprint, Farnborough: Gregg Press, 1967.

Theiner   Augustinus Theiner, ed. *Vetera Monumenta Hibernorum et Scotorum.* Rome: Typis Vaticania, 1864.

Tresham   Edward Tresham, ed. *Rotulorum Patentium et Clausorum Cancellarie Hibernie Calendarium.* Vol. 1, part 1, *Hen. II – Hen. VII.* Dublin, 1828.

✶ CHRONOLOGY OF KEY EVENTS

431	Pope Celestine I sends Palladius as Ireland's first bishop
432	traditional date of Patrick's return to Ireland
615	death of Columbanus
ca. 633	Cummian writes *De controversia Paschali*
1022	first medieval execution of heretics (Orléans)
1066	Norman invasion of England
1096	First Crusade
1101	First Synod of Cashel
ca. 1119	Order of Knights Templar founded
1148	
November 2	Malachy of Armagh dies, and Bernard of Clairvaux writes his *Vita Sancti Malachiae* soon thereafter
1154	Henry II becomes king of England
1155	*Laudabiliter* issued
1165/66	Oxford heresy trial
1169	traditional date of start of Anglo-Norman invasion of Ireland
1170	murder of Thomas Becket
1171	arrival of Henry II in Ireland
1172	Second Synod of Cashel
1208–29	Albigensian Crusade
1256	complaints about immoral idol-worshippers by Maol Pádraig O'Scannell, bishop of Raphoe
1261	Battle of Callan
ca. 1280	Alice Kyteler weds William Outlaw
1291	fall of Acre
1300–1301	feud between the cathedral chapters of Holy Trinity and St. Patrick's, Dublin, comes to a head

1302	William le Kiteler and Fulk de la Freyne attempt to steal £3,000 from Alice Kyteler and her (presumably) second husband, Adam le Blund, then falsely accuse Alice and Adam of murder
1303	
September	Philip IV's agents imprison Boniface VIII with intention of trying him for heresy
October 11	Boniface dies
1306	Philip IV expels Jews from France
1307	
February and April	Adam le Blund quitclaims all his property to William Outlaw
July 8	Edward II becomes king
October 13	Templars arrested in France
1308	
January 10	Templars arrested in England
February 3	Templars arrested in Ireland
1309	Alice Kyteler wed to Richard de Valle
1309–78	Avignon Papacy
1310	
January/February to June	Templars tried in Dublin
May 12	fifty-four Templars burned at the stake in Paris
by September	trial(s) of Philip de Braybrook
1311	
June–July	three Templars tortured in London
July	Templar trial ends in England
October–May (1312)	Council of Vienne
1312 (March)	Templar order dissolved
1315–18	Bruce invasion of Ireland
1316	Alice Kyteler sues stepson Richard de Valle for her widow's dower
September	John XXII becomes pope
1317	Irish Remonstrance issued
April 24	Richard de Ledrede appointed bishop of Ossory
September	Ledrede arrives in Ireland
October 6	Ledrede holds synod in Kilkenny

1318 (May 10)	Battle of Dysert O'Dea
1320	John XXII expands definition of heresy to include demonic magic with actions as sufficient evidence
August	John XXII writes to Ireland's justiciar about Ledrede's abuse and imprisonment by secular officials
1324	
March–January (1325)	trial of Alice Kyteler and associates in Kilkenny
March?	Ledrede cites Alice Kyteler
March?	Arnold le Poer arrests Ledrede
April 23	Ledrede's procession to Arnold le Poer's court
late April/early May	Alice's countersuit
May	Dublin Parliament
late May/early June	poorer people arrested and Alice escapes
June 6	Ledrede requests that Walter de Islip arrest Alice and her now eleven named accomplices
June	Ledrede accuses William Outlaw of thirty-four separate counts, including heresy, aiding heretics, adultery, usury, and clericide
July 2	Alice convicted in absentia and her belongings burned
July–November	William Outlaw confesses to aiding heretics and is imprisoned, but Ledrede pardons him, setting his penance as hearing three masses per day for a year, feeding paupers, and reroofing St. Canice's with lead
November 3	Petronilla de Midia executed and William Outlaw returned to prison
November 10	Ledrede visits William in prison
November	Ledrede implies Roger Outlaw may face future accusations of heresy and Roger arranges William's further penance
1325	
January 17	William Outlaw's absolution
January 25	Roger Outlaw and others pay Ledrede £1,000
1325–29	Desmond–le Poer feud
1326 (July 7)	Maurice fitz Thomas's alleged conspiratorial meeting at Kilkenny to proclaim himself king

1327 (January 20)	Edward II deposed by Queen Isabella and Roger Mortimer
1328	
by February	Dónal mac Airt MacMurrough crowned king of Leinster
	Leinster Irish defeated by colonists
April 11	Adducc Dubh O'Toole executed for heresy in Dublin
1329	
January	Roger Outlaw clears his name at Dublin parliament
March 14	Arnold le Poer dies in prison awaiting trial for heresy charges brought by Ledrede
	Ledrede accuses Robert de Caunton then Alexander de Bicknor of heresy
	Bicknor accuses Ledrede of heresy
by June 14	Ledrede flees Ireland
1329–47	Ledrede's exile from Ireland
1330 (October 19/20)	Edward III assumes control of kingship of England
ca. 1330	Counter-Remonstrance issued
1332	Bunratty Castle destroyed by O'Briens and MacConmaras
1334 (December 4)	death of John XXII
1335 (January 8)	Jacques Fournier consecrated as Benedict XII
1340 (April)	death of Robert de Caunton
1341 (February)	death of Roger Outlaw
1342	
April 25	death of Benedict XII
May	Clement VI becomes pope
1347 (by September)	Ledrede returns to Ireland
1349 (July 14)	death of Alexander de Bicknor
1352 (December 30)	Innocent VI consecrated as pope
1352/53	Thomas de Rokeby's campaign against Munster Irish, including MacConmaras
1353	execution of two MacConmaras for heresy at Bunratty Castle
October 10	Ralph O'Kelly, archbishop of Cashel, allegedly attacks his suffragan and the MacConmaras' apparent inquisitor, Roger Cradock

1355	Ledrede's involvement in attack on Inistioge Priory
1356 (January)	death of Maurice fitz Thomas
ca. 1360	Ledrede dies
1366	Statute of Kilkenny

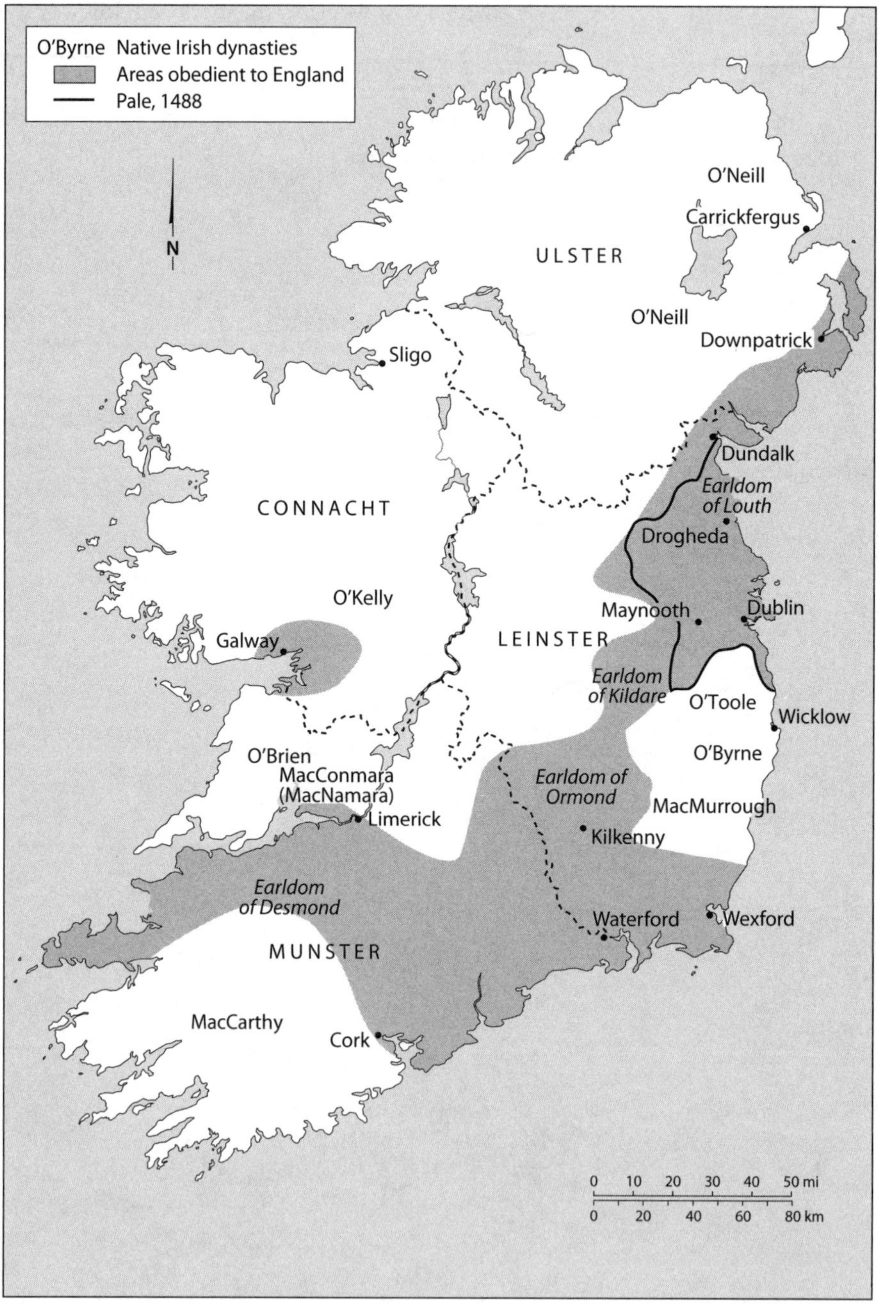
O'Byrne Native Irish dynasties
Areas obedient to England
Pale, 1488
N
ULSTER
O'Neill
Carrickfergus
O'Neill
Downpatrick
Sligo
CONNACHT
Dundalk
Earldom of Louth
Drogheda
O'Kelly
Maynooth
Dublin
Galway
LEINSTER
Earldom of Kildare
O'Toole
Wicklow
O'Brien
MacConmara (MacNamara)
O'Byrne
Earldom of Ormond
Limerick
MacMurrough
Kilkenny
Earldom of Desmond
Waterford
Wexford
MUNSTER
MacCarthy
Cork
0 10 20 30 40 50 mi
0 20 40 60 80 km

Late medieval Ireland. Adapted from Sean Duffy, ed., *Atlas of Irish History*, 2nd ed. (Dublin: Gill & Macmillan, 2000), 47.

THE TEMPLARS,
THE WITCH, AND
THE WILD IRISH

Introduction

In the early Middle Ages Ireland was better known as a sanctuary of saints and scholars than a haven of heathens and heretics. The Irish practiced a form of Christianity distinctly different from the Roman, which won them both the admiration and the suspicion of those outside of Ireland. By the twelfth century, however, suspicion had begun to eclipse admiration as an array of internal and external forces worked to bring Ireland into closer conformity with the rest of Western Christendom. The turning point came around the year 1170, with the invasion of Henry II's Anglo-Norman forces. Henry came with the blessing of Rome, which had sanctioned invasion as a means to return Ireland to orthodoxy, in keeping with a common contemporary opinion that the Irish were, in the words of Bernard of Clairvaux, "Christians in name, pagans in fact."[1]

Yet specific allegations of heresy or Irish apostasy did not surface during the Anglo-Norman conquest, and they are largely absent from the historical record until much later. Indeed, it isn't until the fourteenth century, a time of great upheaval, that reliable records attest to heresy trials in Ireland. Only one of these trials has received any significant scholarly attention: the sensational case of Alice Kyteler and her associates, prosecuted in 1324 by

---

1. Bernard of Clairvaux, *Opera*, 325. All translations from Latin and French are my own, unless otherwise noted.

Richard de Ledrede, bishop of Ossory. Remembered today for its brazen accusations of heretical devil-worshipping witches, the Kyteler trial is regularly referenced by historians of European witchcraft, but due to its isolation in time and place (the witch hunts of Europe began in the fifteenth century, with few trials occurring in Ireland), they rarely offer it more than cursory consideration. Historians of Ireland, meanwhile, have been wary of placing much emphasis on the Kyteler case, as it seems so exceptional and did not provide a paradigm for witchcraft prosecutions in Ireland. Yet the trial stands at the center of several heresy trials on the island, all of which occurred within a fifty-year period in the fourteenth century. Two trials occurred in 1310, one involving the Templars and the other a canon of Holy Trinity Cathedral. Four heresy proceedings followed in the five years after the Kyteler case, three of them also initiated by Bishop Ledrede. The fourth, prosecuted against Adducc Dubh O'Toole for a heresy that amounted to systematic denial of the Catholic faith, was ultimately a tool used by colonists to try to persuade the pope to call a crusade against the native Irish, in their hopes of completing the conquest begun in the twelfth century. Despite this plea, and despite three successive popes' repeated instructions that the investigation of heretics Ledrede claimed to have discovered in Dublin and Ossory be continued, no more trials occurred in Ireland until 1353, and then in the diocese of Killaloe against two men of the MacConmaras (MacNamaras), tried like Adducc Dubh by colonists who had recently defeated them in war.

This book returns the celebrated Kyteler case to its original context of late medieval Ireland by considering it in relation to the island's other verifiable medieval heresy trials during the fourteenth century. It is my contention that exploring these trials together in one study brings significant issues to the forefront, such as the relations between the "three nations"—the English, the Irish, and the Anglo-Irish—and the role of the church in these relations; tensions within the ecclesiastical hierarchy and between secular and spiritual authority; Ireland's position within its European context; and the political and cultural aspects of the heresies. Gender also played a crucial role as revealed most notably in the *Narrative of the Proceedings against Dame Alice Kyteler*, which is heavily biased in Ledrede's favor and was probably written by him. Because the Kyteler case has been studied primarily in terms of its relevance to the Continent, its differences from and influence on Ireland's other heresy trials have not yet been sufficiently examined, nor have the trials been used as a means for approaching fourteenth-century Irish religious and gender history or for exploring the impact of heresy and witchcraft prosecution on a land that previously had little experience of either.

In the remainder of this introduction I set the context for my accounts of these heresy trials by providing some necessary background. First, I give an overview of Ireland's distinctive Christianity and cultural codes, considering how these differences became increasingly divisive after the Gregorian Reform and the Norman Conquest of England. I discuss issues of ethnic identity among and between the native Irish, the English, and those who would come to be known as the Anglo-Irish. I then consider heresy prosecution in medieval Europe more generally, highlighting Ireland's similarities with and contrasts from its broader European context.

Returning Ireland to Christendom

Ireland earned the epithet "isle of saints" through the devotion to Christian faith and learning exemplified by the Irish both at home and abroad.[2] By the seventh century, however, questions were repeatedly raised about Irish orthodoxy, primarily concerning the date of Easter, for which Irish and Roman calculation differed. The Irish eventually conformed to the Roman observance of Easter, but they continued to practice a form of Christianity that varied significantly from the Roman, as Ireland had never been part of the Roman Empire. Before the turn of the millennium, the Irish church was more monastic than diocesan in organization, and bishops could be subject to abbots in administrative matters. Monastic discipline varied from house to house, a diversity generally accepted and even promoted by the Irish. Neither religious nor secular power was centralized in Ireland but was spread throughout a network of ruling families. The monasteries that dominated Irish religious life were often dominated in turn by these families; kinship to provincial kings was a virtual requirement for many abbots and abbesses, and abbacies frequently passed from father to son. The Viking raids, which began at the end of the eighth century, increased monastic dependence upon secular power and further isolated Ireland from the Continent; eventually what had been tolerated as differences became regarded as dangerous divisions.[3] Abrupt changes came in the twelfth century as the Gregorian Reform movement took hold and Ireland was swept up in a broader effort to centralize and standardize the church throughout Western Christendom. Irish reformers, in

---

2. See Gougaud, "Isle of the Saints," and Sharpe, *Medieval Irish Saints' Lives*, 1–3.

3. I have simplified complex issues. For studies of the early Irish church, see Hughes, *The Church in Early Irish Society*; Hughes, *Early Christian Ireland*; Sharpe, "Some Problems Concerning the Organization of the Church"; Bitel, *Isle of the Saints*; de Paor, *Saint Patrick's World*; Kenney, *Sources for the Early History of Ireland*; Ó Cróinín, *Early Medieval Ireland*; and Charles-Edwards, *Early Christian Ireland*.

concert with the English and Rome, worked to reshape Ireland in the mold of England and the Continent; in so doing, they initiated the history of heresy in Ireland.[4]

The Gregorian Reform, named after Pope Gregory VII (1073–85) but extending beyond his reign, was abruptly introduced to Ireland by Archbishop Lanfranc of Canterbury (1070–89). He claimed his primacy included Ireland as well as Britain, a claim that speaks volumes about the changing fortunes of the two islands in the eleventh century. The Ostmen, the Hiberno-Norse who had established the cities of Dublin, Wexford, Waterford, and Limerick, accepted his claim, as did the O'Brien kings, who believed that a centralized church would help their faltering kingship, established earlier in the century by Brian Boru. Lanfranc lambasted the Irish church for its clerical abuses and the immorality and unspecified "pagan" offenses it tolerated among the laity, accusations continued by his successor Anselm and that thereafter remained the general impression of the Irish among English and Continental Christians.[5] Indigenous Irish religious not initially associated with Canterbury, such as Saints Malachy (Máel-máedóc Ó Morgair) and Laurence O'Toole (Lorcán Ó Tuathail), also worked to bring their church into closer alignment with the Roman ideal. The twelfth century began with a reforming synod, the Synod of Cashel in 1101, and several more synods followed in the ensuing decades as the Irish voluntarily restructured their church according to the diocesan system, adopted foreign religious orders, and vowed to purge their church of secular influence and immoral practices.

Despite these reforming efforts, Ireland's reputation did not fare well during the twelfth century, thanks in part to a French Cistercian monk who had never been to Ireland, Bernard of Clairvaux. Bernard's influential work *The Life of St. Malachy* is heavily biased against the Irish, maintaining, among other things, that they "brought in paganism under the label of Christianity."[6] Much of his information probably came from the reformer Malachy himself, whom he met in 1140 at Clairvaux. The two were briefly reunited again eight years later, also at Clairvaux, where Malachy died, and Bernard composed Malachy's *Life* shortly thereafter. Bernard portrays the Irish as an ignorant and lawless race who claim the Christian name but whose lives, with notable exceptions, mock and offend the Christian faith. Yet he tells us only of one instance of heresy, that of a cleric of

---

4. For earlier references to heresy relating to Ireland, see chapter 5.
5. Lanfranc, *Letters*, Letters 9–10, pp. 69–71.
6. Bernard of Clairvaux, *Opera*, 330.

Lismore, "good in his character but not in his faith."[7] The cleric held views concerning the eucharist similar to Berengar of Tours, maintaining that it did not contain Christ's body.[8] According to Bernard, Malachy repeatedly tried to correct him in private, but the cleric was obstinate. Consequently Malachy convened two assemblies of clerics; both times the erring cleric was condemned but impenitent, and at the end of the second he was publicly declared a heretic.[9] Shortly after he left the second assembly, the cleric was overcome by a paralyzing illness; he returned to Malachy with the aid of a madman, repented of his heresy, was absolved, and then died. This occurred around 1130, making it Ireland's first known heresy trial and the only one prosecuted against an Irishman by Irishmen. It is also the only trial free from clear political motivations, although Bernard may not have been adequately aware of its dynamics. Given that a hagiographic work written far from Ireland and with a pronounced anti-Irish bias provides the only evidence of the trial, however, it cannot be counted among Ireland's reliably recorded heresy trials.

Bernard of Clairvaux, the archbishops of Canterbury, and Irish reformers themselves laid the groundwork for the Norman invasion of Ireland. In 1155 Pope Adrian IV, the first and only English pope, issued the bull *Laudabiliter* in which he encouraged Henry II to invade Ireland "in order to expand the boundaries of the church, declare the truth of the Christian faith to an ignorant and barbarian people, and weed out the new growth of vices from the field of the Lord."[10] Henry did not act on this support until fifteen years later, and then he did so out of greater concern for the threat his subject Strongbow's power might pose than for the state of the faith in Ireland. In 1172, Pope Alexander III reaffirmed *Laudabiliter*, echoing St. Bernard's opinion that the Irish were Christians in name only who had renounced their faith for monstrous abuses.[11] Yet, despite heresy's increasing prominence on the Continent, Alexander and his successors did not

---

7. Bernard of Clairvaux, *Life and Death of Saint Malachy*, 71 (Meyer's translation); see also Bernard of Clairvaux, *Opera*, 360.

8. See Murphy, "Eleventh or Twelfth Century Irish Doctrine Concerning the Real Presence." John Ryan has connected Lismore with French theological schools in the first half of the twelfth century ("Historical Background," 16).

9. Thus conforming to Titus 3:10–11.

10. Giraldus Cambrensis, *Expugnatio Hibernica*, 144. The authenticity of *Laudabiliter* has been debated, but it was regarded as genuine by multiple factions in medieval Ireland, especially in the fourteenth century, as discussed below. Furthermore, Alexander III's 1172 letters share many of its sentiments. For doubts about its authenticity, see Sheehy, "The Bull *Laudabiliter*"; Duggan, "*Totius christianitatis caput*"; and Duggan, "Power of Documents."

11. *IHD*, 21.

identify heresy as one of the Irish vices, at least not until the pontificate of Benedict XII in the fourteenth century, and then it was the Anglo-Irish the pope had in mind.

Laudabiliter and the ensuing English invasion of Ireland point to "one of the most fundamental ideological shifts in the history of the British Isles," in which the Celtic cultures of Ireland, Scotland, and Wales were identified as barbarous and in need of civilizing by the Normans and their heirs.[12] This same attitude served as part of the justification for the Norman invasion of England in 1066, which was done with the pope's blessing and banner and with the aim of reforming the English church to bring it into closer conformity with Rome.[13] Not two centuries before, the Normans themselves had been the hated heathen Norse, the Vikings, but after settling in France they converted not only to the religion of the Franks but to virtually every facet of their society, playing a dominant role in developments such as feudalism and the Gregorian Reform. They became "more French than the French," a trend that would also be noted of their descendants in Ireland centuries later.[14] The Norman victory in England was near total, but the following century the French-speaking, Norman-blooded conquerors of England identified themselves as English and even acknowledged the Anglo-Saxon past as their own, thus marking the beginnings of English imperialism.[15] The same pride with which they embraced their Englishness translated into scorn and contempt when they considered their Celtic neighbors, which incited and justified acts of aggression against them, including the invasion of Ireland, its first major foreign attack since the Viking age.

The origins of the English invasion of Ireland are complex and occasionally obscure. With reason, warring Irish kings, and in particular Diarmaid MacMurrough, king of Leinster, who enlisted the aid of English lords against other Irish kings, are often held responsible; the English, however, were independently considering invading the island before Diarmaid proffered his daughter's hand in marriage and his kingdom as her dowry to the earl of Pembroke, Richard de Clare, better known as Strongbow. Within a year of becoming king, Henry II discussed such an attack with his advisors.

---

12. Gillingham, "English Invasion of Ireland," 24.

13. Stenton, *Anglo-Saxon England*, 586, 658–79; Brown, *Normans and the Norman Conquest*, 13, 28, 128–29.

14. Brown, *Normans and the Norman Conquest*, 19.

15. Gillingham, "Beginnings of English Imperialism." Note, however, that "Englishry," which recognized two ethnicities in England, the Normans and the English, with a fine to be paid only in the murder of the former, was not abolished until 1340 (Stephen, *History of the Common Law*, 3:31, 40).

The bishops and clergy argued in favor of the idea, perhaps influenced by Pope Eugenius III's recent rejection of Canterbury's claims of lordship over the Irish church, but Henry followed the counsel of his mother and decided against it.[16] The proposal did not end with Henry's decision, however, for John of Salisbury, chief advisor of the archbishop of Canterbury and close friend of Bernard of Clairvaux as well as of Nicholas Breakspear, then Pope Adrian IV, soon won papal support for the project. According to John, he convinced Adrian to grant Ireland to Henry as a hereditary fief, on the grounds that all islands of Christendom belonged to the pope by right of the Donation of Constantine.[17] This text, an eighth-century forgery then generally regarded as genuine, purported to be a grant from the Roman emperor Constantine to Pope Sylvester of various properties and authority in his domain, yet Ireland was never part of the Roman Empire; thus, even if the Donation had been legitimate, Adrian's subsequent granting of Ireland on such a basis would not be.[18]

If John were referring to *Laudabiliter*, he seriously misrepresented its nature, as Adrian does not offer Ireland to Henry as a hereditary possession but merely sanctions Henry's intention of adding Ireland to his domains, though here too it is claimed that all the islands of Christendom belong to papal jurisdiction.[19] Yet even this claim is immediately called into question, as *Laudabiliter* portrays the Irish as barbarians who are no longer Christian, which would thus make the island no longer part of Christendom. This image of the Irish, found also in Bernard of Clairvaux's *Life of St. Malachy* and frequently repeated in the text that provides the earliest copy of *Laudabiliter*, Gerald of Wales's *Conquest of Ireland*, as well as his *History and Topography of Ireland*, reflects a return to a fifth-century understanding of the term "barbarian," exemplified by the anonymous author of the *Opus Imperfectum*'s characterization of the newly converted German peoples as

16. *NHI*, 2:56–57; Martin, "Ireland in the Time of St. Bernard, St. Malachy, St. Laurence O'Toole," 13–15; O'Doherty, "Rome and the Anglo-Norman Invasion of Ireland," 140; Sheehy, *When the Normans Came to Ireland*, 10–11.

17. O'Doherty, "Rome and the Anglo-Norman Invasion of Ireland," 131–32, and Martin, "Ireland in the Time of St. Bernard, St. Malachy, St. Laurence O'Toole," 14.

18. For the Donation, see Bettenson, *Documents of the Christian Church*, 135–40. Note Arnold of Brescia's or his supporter's condemnation of the Donation as a "heretical fable" in 1151 in a letter to Emperor Frederick I (quoted in Moore, *Birth of Popular Heresy*, 7).

19. John might be describing the actual grant, and *Laudabiliter* is simply an accompanying letter of exhortation that Gerald of Wales and thus subsequent historians misidentified as the grant; see Gwynn, *Irish Church*, 298–301. The claim about the islands of Christendom is also found in Alexander III's letter to Henry II (*IHD*, 21).

"barbarian[s] . . . who have the name of Christians but the manners of pagans."[20]

Yet in the twelfth century, the Irish had been Christian for centuries; they had served as missionaries and beacons of the faith in Britain and on the Continent; they had taken to the Latin and Greek languages and learning with great fervor, though they had not abandoned their own traditions and culture; and their libraries had preserved a considerable number of classical works that would have otherwise been lost. As the title of one popular book has overstated it, the Irish could be said to have saved Western Christian civilization. That they could be portrayed as non-Christians, as barbarian and ignorant, reflects more on the increasing conformity and centralization on the Continent and its most recent outpost, England, as well as on Ireland's ambiguous and fairly powerless position in the new Europe than on the state of the faith and learning in Ireland.[21]

Twelfth-century Ireland may have paled in comparison with the island's golden age in the fifth through eighth centuries, but it was also a time of renewed commitment to the religious life, as attested by the indigenous reform movement and the spread of new religious orders and houses. Moreover, virtually any area of Europe at this time would suffer from close scrutiny. Ireland was hardly the only country in which divorce and remarriage, clerical marriage, and battles between religious occurred. Henry II, whom Alexander III hailed in 1172 as Ireland's conquering Christian hero, is a case in point: in addition to his arguably adulterous marriage to Eleanor of Aquitaine, the former wife of the still living Louis VII of France, and further acts of adultery with the many women whom he used to warm his bed after Eleanor had fallen from his favor, he was responsible for the murder of the archbishop of Canterbury, St. Thomas Becket, less than two years before. For this act, the "Remonstrance of Irish Princes" proclaimed in 1317, Henry should have been deprived of his kingdom.[22] Instead Alexander presented Henry's conquest of Ireland as part of his penance, evidence of his profound Christian devotion, and the product of divine inspiration.[23]

The bitter irony that the Irish should be perceived as needing to be restored to the faith by men such as Henry was not lost on the Irish at the time, as Gerald of Wales himself reports. At a Dublin synod in 1186, the Irish

---

20. See Bartlett, *Gerald of Wales*, 158–77. Quotation (in English) in Jones, "Image of the Barbarian in Medieval Europe," 382.

21. Bartlett, *Making of Europe*.

22. Bower, *Scotichronicon*, 386; see chapter 5.

23. *IHD*, 20–21.

Cistercian abbot of Baltinglass, Ailbe Ua Máel Muaid, berated the Welsh and English clergy who had come over in the wake of the invasion for bringing all sorts of abuses, including clerical marriage, a guilt that was immediately substantiated, and claimed that they had infected the Irish church with their abuses.[24] Gerald replied with a sermon that recognized that Irish religious were exemplary, particularly with regard to reading, praying, abstinence, and asceticism, but he also criticized them for acting too much like monastics and failing in their clerical duties, especially correcting the laity, and he denounced the Irish generally for their rudeness and for failing to produce martyrs. Archbishop Muirges O'Heney of Cashel responded that Gerald spoke truly, for the Irish were a rude and ignorant people, yet they had ever honored the church, the religious, and the saints; though they had not yet produced martyrs, Muirges continued, "now a people has come to the kingdom which knows how, and is accustomed, to make martyrs. From now on Ireland will have its martyrs, just as other countries."[25] Gerald's rather convoluted criticism sets up Muirges's condemnation of the English for killing their own clergy (as they did Becket) and to lament the imminent martyrdom of the Irish at their hands as well. Gerald's inclusion of this exchange in a work that strives to discredit, mock, and condemn the Irish is curious, but its opposition to his overall message enhances its authenticity and provides us with a rare Irish response to the propaganda against them. Clearly Irish clerics such as Ailbe Ua Máel Muaid and Muirges O'Heney thought little of the claim that the invaders came as reformers who would restore Christianity to Ireland; rather, they celebrated the state of the faith among the indigenous Irish and bemoaned their fate in the hands of morally depraved martyr-makers.[26]

Ironically, Henry's conquest is one of the most peaceful moments in twelfth-century Irish history and saw less bloodshed in Ireland than the so-called Bloodless Revolution of 1688–89. He arrived in 1171, in part to escape temporarily the repercussions of Becket's murder, in part to restrain his subjects who had begun the invasion before him, lest they set up a rival kingdom in Ireland. With few exceptions the Irish kings soon peacefully

24. Giraldus Cambrensis, *Opera*, 1:66–72; Gwynn, *Irish Church*, 273. This synod's constitutions officially praise Irish clergy for their chastity and recognize that the colonial clergy may well corrupt them with their own crimes; see Gwynn, "Provincial and Diocesan Decrees," 42.

25. Giraldus Cambrensis, *History and Topography of Ireland*, 112–16, quote at 116 (O'Meara's translation).

26. Their remarks have added significance, given that Ailbe Ua Máel Muaid, who was made bishop of Ferns in the same year as this synod, became King John's "favourite bishop in Ireland" (Warren, "Church and State in Angevin Ireland," 7), and Muirges O'Heney, who was appointed papal legate in 1191, also served John in various capacities until his death in 1206.

submitted to him as their overlord, including those whose lands had not been immediately threatened by the invaders, and the bishops followed suit at the Second Synod of Cashel in 1172. Various theories have been proposed to explain the Irish kings' prompt and peaceful acceptance of Henry as their overking, from Irish reverence for Roman emperors and Henry's epithet "fitz Empress" to terror induced by the brutality of the invaders and the hope that Henry could control them.[27] The most convincing explanations stem from the ambiguous concept of the *ard rí* (high king), whose power was quite limited over his subkings and subjects, which undoubtedly shaped the manner in which the Irish kings regarded their submission.[28] Regardless of what they ultimately wanted or expected from this arrangement, however, they did not get it and warfare resumed following Henry's departure.

Pope Alexander wrote three letters following this bloodless coup, one to Henry himself, one to the religious leaders of Ireland, and one to its secular rulers. More clearly than Adrian's bull fifteen years earlier, Alexander's letters acknowledged Ireland's Christianity but asserted that it had become diseased or that, in some cases, it had been renounced. The symptoms of this infection or apostasy were not heterodox understandings of Christianity, however, but lax mores, primarily marital and sexual mores, which in Ireland, as in much of pre-Gregorian Europe, were considered more of a secular than an ecclesiastical concern. The only examples of religious misconduct among the Irish provided in Alexander's three letters are that they occasionally eat meat during Lent and do not pay tithes or offer those in religious orders the respect they deserve, exceptionally weak grounds for the holy war Alexander's predecessor had sanctioned against the Irish and for which he had commended Henry II. If such were the most severe sins against Christianity of which the Irish could be found guilty, virtually anywhere in Europe could be similarly targeted, although other Western Christian lands did not occupy such an ambiguous and peripheral position, geographically, politically, and culturally. Moreover, the conduct of colonists even when considered solely in the religious sphere evinced a "barbarism that makes a mockery of any claim that [they] came as reformers," including severe beatings and attempted assassinations of clergy, clerical marriage and ecclesiastical hereditary succession, and other offenses that make meat eating in Lent seem pious by comparison.[29] Even the invaders' primary propagandist ultimately realized the hollowness of the pretense of reform: Gerald of Wales reports that he rejected an offer

---

27. *NHI*, 2:88–89; Lydon, "Problem of the Frontier," 7.
28. See Byrne, *Irish Kings and High-Kings*.
29. Watt, *The Church and the Two Nations*, 62.

of an Irish bishopric because he did not trust the intentions of John, named lord of Ireland by his father, Henry II, toward the Irish church, having seen for himself "that the state of Ireland was every day the worse for [John's] coming."[30] Similarly, the monk William of Canterbury, a witness to Becket's martyrdom, thought that English casualties in Ireland deserved what they got, as there was "no reason for the disquieting of a neighbouring nation, who, however uncivilised and barbarous, were remarkable and noteworthy practisers of the Christian religion."[31]

The perspective of *Laudabiliter* and its like was apparently convenient cant rather than an actual concern of the church. For example, although all four archbishops and half of the bishops of Ireland attended Lateran IV in 1215, a council deeply concerned with matters of heresy, such issues seem to have had nothing to do with the matters the bishops brought with them or the letters they brought back.[32] While many of the abuses condemned in the canons of the council were found in Ireland along with the rest of Europe, Irish lawlessness and pagan Christianity, so frequently decried just a few decades previously, do not seem to have been mentioned either by the pope or the bishops, one-quarter of whom were Anglo-Norman. Indeed, the only canons that seem thoroughly alien to the Irish context are those that deal with heresy.[33]

Yet the portrayal of the high and late medieval Irish as pagans has received some support from one of the foremost scholars of the period. Katharine Simms argues that a pagan resurgence occurred in the twelfth and thirteenth centuries, citing bardic poetry and Gerald of Wales's portrait of Ireland.[34] Bardic poets often invoked Ireland's pre-Christian past and pagan sources of prophecy, such as druids, the Lia Fáil (the sacred stone at Tara that cries out at the touch of the rightful king), and nature itself, in keeping with larger Christian tradition that recognized the Hebrew Prophets, the Greek Sibyl, and other non-Christian soothsayers as legitimate prophets. Arguably "more than any other literary mode," bardic poetry draws intently from myth and legend.[35] Yet, as Francis John Byrne has noted, claims that medieval Irish poets and *brehons* (judges) were "crypto-pagans" are "wrong";

---

30. Giraldus Cambrensis, *Autobiography*, 90 (Butler's translation); Giraldus Cambrensis, *Opera*, 1:65.

31. Quoted (in English) in Bethell, "English Monks and Irish Reform," 125; Robertson, *Materials for the History of Thomas Becket*, 1:364–65.

32. Dunning, "Irish Representatives."

33. Rothwell, *English Historical Documents*, 643–76.

34. Simms, *From Kings to Warlords*, 26–27. For additional discussion of the relevant poems, see Quiggin, "O'Conor's House at Cloonfree," and Finan, "Prophecies of the Expected Deliverer."

35. Ó Buachalla, "Aodh Eanghach and the Irish King-Hero," 220.

their offices required them to transmit the *senchas* (traditional teachings and law), which included aspects of earlier Irish culture, but no evidence suggests they shared the pagan beliefs or practices of their predecessors.[36] Ireland's poets used the heroic pagan past to proclaim the immediate and inherently Christian future, celebrating contemporary native kings' opposition to the English and predicting their imminent success. As for Gerald, his clear biases against the Irish and his ardent support for the island's invasion by his own kin render his testimony suspect. The specific claims made by Gerald that Simms cites in support of her theory, a ritual in which a horse is raped, sacrificed, and eaten, and an encounter with some Connachtmen who had never heard of Christ or Christianity and took back bread and cheese as a wonder, are perhaps more accurately read as "blatant propaganda . . . in justification of the English conquest of Ireland."[37]

Similarly, Simms's final source for a purported pagan revival, which has been read as referring not only to paganism but also to heresy, derives from a hostile witness. In 1256, Maol Pádraig O'Scannell, Dominican bishop of Raphoe, complained to Alexander IV about idol worshippers in his diocese who practiced incest, plotted episcopal assassinations, and infected the faithful with their errors. The pope's reply refers to the offenders as "the messengers and ministers of the antichrist" and authorizes O'Scannell to use the secular arm against them, but it identifies them neither as pagans, as Simms suggests, nor as "grotesque heretics," as MacInerny labels them.[38] Clearly considerable tension existed between the bishop and denizens of his diocese, but its precise nature cannot be discerned, particularly as the pope's letter is the only extant account of the troubles.[39] Thus, I find little to support Simms's notion of revived or continued paganism in twelfth- and thirteenth-century Ireland. Since its inception Irish Christianity synthesized the indigenous culture with the new religion, sometimes to an extent that alarmed others, both Irish and otherwise, cultivating a faith that in ways diverged from the dominant Roman form. As the Irish came to terms with the invaders in the twelfth century and onward, they may have looked more fondly to and identified

---

36. Byrne, *Irish Kings and High-Kings*, 13.

37. Giraldus Cambrensis, *History and Topography of Ireland*, 110–12; Flanagan, "Reformation of the Irish Church," 80.

38. Theiner, 71; see also Sheehy, *Pontificia Hibernica*, 2:251–52, and *CPL*, 1:329. O'Scannell regularly had conflicts with others; see Watt, *Church in Medieval Ireland*, 65. For Simms's analysis, see *From Kings to Warlords*, 27–28. MacInerny labels them heretics in *History of the Irish Dominicans*, 178; see also 180. Williams repeats MacInerny's assessment ("Heresy in Ireland," 341–42).

39. The pope concurrently sent a letter to the head of the Dominicans in Ireland asking him to assist O'Scannell, but it does not elaborate on the nature of the dispute.

more deeply with their pre-Christian past and its heroes, but that does not mean they returned to their pre-Christian religion, and no solid evidence suggests otherwise; moreover, none of the heresy trials indicates paganism was a component of the alleged heresies.

The other slander against the Irish, that they were ignorant, has a touch more truth to it. While they still retained a vibrant scholarly culture, as indicated by their own contributions and the variety of works translated into Irish, university culture never took root in medieval Ireland.[40] The twelfth and thirteenth centuries saw the rise of both the university and the city in Britain and on the Continent, but later medieval Ireland's cities were mainly colonial. Various efforts were made by colonists, most notably Alexander de Bicknor, to found a university in medieval Ireland, but all ultimately failed, and education in Ireland remained essentially as it had in the sixth century, in monastic schools and secular apprenticeships.[41] Native Irish and Anglo-Irish also traveled outside of the country to attend universities such as those at Oxford and Montpellier. The absence of an enduring university exacerbated Ireland's differences from the rest of Europe as well as the opinion and perhaps the reality of their ignorance, but it also "helped to spare Ireland the type of atmosphere in which conventional 'heresy' could have arisen."[42] In addition, the lack of cities, an urban elite, and centralization associated with universities proved to be critical for the survival of the Irish and their culture, for there was no one king to conquer, no cities to capture that would ensure their defeat. Gerald of Wales derides what he portrays as their stunted development, their "primitive habits of pastoral living."[43] Though the Irish did have larger settlements, their comparative lack of urbanization facilitated their retreat to bogs, forests, and mountains, whence they could continue their attacks on the colonial settlements and win back their land, little by little.

Attitudes toward ethnic identity such as those espoused by Gerald played a critical role in the English invasion of Ireland, colonial policies, and the heresy trials that are the subject of this study. The image of the Irish painted by outsiders in the twelfth century portrayed them as almost irredeem-

---

40. See Flower, *The Irish Tradition*; Ó Cuív, *Seven Centuries of Irish Learning*; *NHI*, 2:688–814; McGrath, *Education in Ancient and Medieval Ireland*; and Simms, "Literacy and the Irish Bards."

41. A university was established in 1321, with William de Rodyerd, who was involved in both the Kyteler case and the case of Adducc Dubh O'Toole, as its chancellor, but it faltered when Alexander de Bicknor fell from favor. For the charters of the fourteenth-century university, see Mason, *History and Antiquities*, app. 7.

42. Burrows, "Fifteenth-Century Irish Provincial Legislation," 63.

43. Giraldus Cambrensis, *History and Topography of Ireland*, 101 (O'Meara's translation).

ably other, and colonial legislation continued to pronounce them as such. The Irish apparently returned the favor, as suggested by references in texts such as the fourteenth-century *Caithréim Thoirdhealbhaigh*, which repeatedly refers to the English and the Anglo-Irish as gentiles, indicating that the native Irish saw *them* as the non-Christians.[44] Another fourteenth-century text, the "Remonstrance of Irish Princes," deemed "the first trumpet blast of Irish nationalism," presents the Irish as one people who differ in every conceivable way from the English while arguing for an ethnic identity with the Scots on the basis of shared ancestry and language.[45] Yet less than a decade later, Arnold le Poer, the seneschal of Kilkenny whose ancestor had come over at the start of the invasion, argued before an audience of colonial leaders for an Irish nationalism that arose from the island itself, laying claim to Irish history that predated 1169 and defining this identity in opposition to England and the papacy. Evidence for nationalism in Ireland stretches back essentially to the dawn of Ireland's recorded literature in the seventh century, though this sense of nationhood did little to prevent the political fragmentation that both enabled medieval Ireland's colonization and prevented its full conquest.[46] Boyce's argument, that the Irish possessed a strong sense of cultural identity that under the impact of colonization was transformed into national identity and by the end of the Tudor period into ethnic nationalism, seems the most helpful in understanding the sense of communal self that developed in medieval Ireland and after, yet the perspective Arnold le Poer articulated in the early fourteenth century ill fits such an analysis.[47] Such is the fate of his people, the Anglo-Irish, about whose identity countless studies have been written and a few words must here be said.

The acknowledged ambiguity of the Anglo-Irish position began remarkably early in their history. In 1171, two years into the invasion and only a year after he himself had landed in Ireland, Maurice fitz Gerald made a remark that

---

44. E.g., *CT*, 2:30, 57, 92, 95. Medieval Christians adopted Jewish terminology, so that gentiles came to signify non-Christians, as opposed to non-Jews; see for example Thomas Aquinas, *Summa contra gentiles.*

45. Quotation from Watt, *Church in Medieval Ireland*, 80. For further discussion of the Remonstrance, see chapter 5. Significantly, the Declaration of Arbroath, written a few years after the Remonstrance, with which it shares many similarities, and often hailed as the charter text of Scottish nationalism, deliberately omits reference to Ireland in its romantic reconstruction of the Scottish past (Fergusson, *Declaration of Arbroath*, 6–7). Ironically, Loyalists in Northern Ireland have repeatedly drawn on the Declaration of Arbroath in their murals but substitute the Irish for the English as the oppressors; for some examples, see Rolston, *Drawing Support 2*, 9, 11, 50.

46. Ó Corráin, "Nationality and Kingship."

47. Boyce, *Nationalism in Ireland*, 19.

would echo throughout the ages. According to his nephew, Gerald of Wales, writing about twenty years later, Maurice exhorted his men to continue their invasion by declaring that they could rely only on themselves, for "just as we are regarded as English by the Irish, so we are Irish to the English. And the inhabitants of this island and the other pursue us with equal hatred."[48] The accuracy of his remark, with echoes even to this day, is unmistakable, with the crisis of 1341–42 providing the most profound fourteenth-century example of the hostile suspicion with which the English back in England regarded the colonists. Clearly tensions remained twenty-five years later, as the Statute of Kilkenny, infamous mainly for its hostility to the Irish and any colonists who acted like them, also demanded that the English born in Ireland should not call the English born in England "yokels," and the yokels were not to call the Irish-born English "Irish dog."[49] But it was the hatred with which the "two nations," that is, the Irish and the Anglo-Irish, assailed each other that aroused the most comment: in 1242, Archbishop Albrecht Suerbeer of Armagh characterized it as "insatiable"; to his successor Richard fitz Ralph a century later it was "traditional and inborn."[50] The vulnerability of the Irish under English law further exacerbated the relations; as fitz Ralph had to remind the Anglo-Irish of his diocese, "killing native Irish people might not be a felony in English law, but [it] was nevertheless a sin in the eyes of God."[51] The records attest to ethnic enmity in virtually every facet of life, and in particular the religious sphere. The attempted systematic exclusion of the Irish from episcopal office, cathedral churches, and religious houses, of which the Remonstrance bitterly complained in the fourteenth century, began in 1217. Honorius III immediately denounced "such a rash and unjust abuse," but in 1253 Innocent IV had to condemn this "detestably common vice" again, and similar policies were used throughout the Middle Ages.[52] The hostilities could rip apart religious orders as well, as happened with the Cistercians in the first half of the thirteenth century and the Franciscans in the first half of the fourteenth.

The relations between the Gaelic Irish and the Anglo-Irish were not entirely poisoned, however. The Remonstrance lists a variety of crimes committed by

---

48. Giraldus Cambrensis, *Expugnatio Hibernica*, 80.

49. Berry, *Early Statutes*, 436; see also *NHI*, 2:388.

50. Suerbeer quoted (in English) in Smith, *Colonisation and Conquest*, 74. Fitz Ralph quoted (in English) in Walsh, *Richard FitzRalph*, 289.

51. Frame, "Exporting State and Nation," 151. This relates to the Irish Remonstrance's claim in 1317 that the Anglo-Irish preached the "heresy" that it was no sin to kill an Irish person; see chapter 5.

52. Theiner, 16, 56; Sheehy, *Pontificia Hibernica*, 1:225.

the Anglo-Irish upon the Irish, but in so doing it reveals that members of the rival ethnicities frequently visited with each other in friendly fashion and entered into intimate relations, such as godparent-godchild.[53] Intermarriage between colonists and native Irish was as old as the conquest itself, as the marriage between Strongbow and Aífe, the daughter of Diarmaid MacMurrough, provided a primary justification for the transference of leadership in Diarmaid's lands to Strongbow, in a major departure from both Irish and English inheritance laws. Intermarriage furthered allegiances between the given colonial and native Irish families and created children with ties to both sides of the ethnic divide; bonds between ethnicities were further strengthened by the native Irish custom of fosterage, in which children would be raised by another, carefully chosen family. Gaelic Irish and Anglo-Irish also entered into political alliances with each other and against other members of their ethnicities, as one faction of the O'Briens and the de Burghs did against another faction of the O'Briens, the de Clares, and Gerald of Wales's Geraldines.[54] *Caithréim Thoirdhealbhaigh* offered the de Burghs, or Burkes in the hibernicized form, high praise when it described them as "English-born but Irish-natured," but the tendency of some Anglo-Irish to become "more Irish than the Irish themselves" seems to have struck as much if not more fear into the colonial consciousness as the armed resistance of the native Irish.[55]

Colonial fear of gaelicization did not arise solely from contempt of all things Celtic; it was a response to an increasingly tenuous hold on the island. The unity of the colonists did not survive the first year of their arrival, and divisions continued to grow among them, especially after the lordship of John.[56] Their infighting, which the feud between Arnold le Poer and the Geraldine Maurice fitz Thomas discussed in chapter 4 exemplifies, the absenteeism that in the fourteenth century reached near epidemic proportions, Ireland's relative insignificance in the overall royal agenda, and colonial acculturation to native Irish customs, law, dress, and language helped to facilitate what is known as the Gaelic Resurgence. This resurgence could be said to have begun with the Battle of Callan in 1261, the first major military victory of the native Irish over the colonists, and to have ended in 1603, with the submission of Hugh O'Neill and the Treaty of Mellifont. Since the end of the thirteenth century, the king and his colonial administration attempted

---

53. Bower, *Scotichronicon*, 394; see chapter 5. For discussion of intermarriage between the ethnicities, see Kenny, *Anglo-Irish and Gaelic Women*, 85–91.

54. See chapter 5.

55. *CT*, 1:73, 2:66; I have adapted O'Grady's translation, "aboriginally English but now Irish-natured."

56. Orpen, *Song of Dermot and the Earl*, 80–87, 92–103.

to address the situation, legislating against absenteeism and demanding that the colonists defend their land, that truces or wars with the native Irish be universally observed, and that the "degeneration" of the Anglo-Irish who adopt Irish appearance come to a stop, since they might be taken for Irish and unwittingly killed, a telling statement on the value of native Irish life in the colony, but the frequency of such condemnations attests to their impotence.[57] That the parliament of 1541, which acknowledged Henry VIII as "king of Ireland" (rather than "lord of Ireland," as his predecessors were called), was conducted in Irish, as only one of the lords present knew English, further emphasizes the point.[58] The best-known medieval attempt to prevent Gaelic Irish military and cultural encroachment was the Statute of Kilkenny of 1366, but this merely repeats earlier legislation, forbidding the Anglo-Irish from marrying or associating with the Irish, from acting like them, from employing them, from speaking their language and using their law, and in general serving the same function as the Penal Laws promulgated against Catholics in the seventeenth to nineteenth centuries. Although the statute remained in place until James I ascended the throne, the Geraldine third earl of Desmond, Maurice fitz Thomas's son, who was justiciar the year following the passing of the statute, got a license in 1388 to foster his son among the Irish, one of the prohibitions of the statute, and he was known for his Irish verse.[59] By the fifteenth century colonial holdings had been pushed back to "the Pale," roughly counties Dublin, Kildare, Meath, and Louth, and the situation was not reversed until England's king was a queen and its religion Protestant.

It was against such a beleaguered background as this that the heresy trials occurred, yet only two of the cases were the product of ethnic tensions. The trials can be separated into three categories. In the first stand the Templars and Philip de Braybrook, a canon of Holy Trinity. The former was primarily an offshoot of the trial begun in France and conducted throughout Western Christendom on the orders of the pope. It was also purely a colonial affair, as all of the Templars examined (and perhaps all Templars ever in Ireland),

---

57. Berry, *Early Statutes*, 194–213; degeneration discussed 210–11.

58. Ó Cuív, "Era of Upheaval," in *Seven Centuries of Irish Learning*, 140.

59. Tresham, 139. The native *Annals of Clonmacnoise* offered him great praise in an obituary, including celebrating him as "a witty & Ingenious composer of Irish poetry" (*ACl*, 319–20). His poetic skill strengthens the basis of Arnold le Poer's alleged slander of his father; see chapter 4. He is said to have had magical abilities as well, but this legend may have arisen from confusion with his homonymous descendant, the sixteenth earl of Desmond; see Seymour, *Irish Witchcraft and Demonology*, 53, 69–75. According to tradition, another Geraldine, an unnamed prioress of St. Catherine's in Limerick with ties to the earls of Desmond, practiced witchcraft and divination and "had wrought much evil in the district." At the dissolution, she refused to leave the convent, which then became known as the Black Hag's Cell (Wardell, "History and Antiquities," 50–52, quotation at 50).

the witnesses, and other participants in their trial, with the exception of one of their three inquisitors (an Italian), were English or Anglo-Irish. As Ireland's first verifiable heresy trial, it sheds considerable light on the understanding of heresy in the colony at the time and its attitude to such allegations.[60] The colonists' receptivity is indicated both by the unanimously negative testimony of outside witnesses, which also demonstrates that they had little concrete evidence against the Templars and a fairly feeble grasp of heresy, and by the trial of Philip de Braybrook, which seems to have been concurrent with the trial of the Templars and shared the same inquisitor, Thomas de Chaddesworth. While evidence concerning Philip's case is limited, it probably resulted from a ten-year feud between the two men, which itself derived from the rivalry between their cathedral chapters, Holy Trinity and St. Patrick's.

Ledrede's prosecutions constitute the second category. Like the first, they involved only colonists, although they offer a wider perspective on the fourteenth-century colony than the first two trials, which were largely restricted to Dublin and the religious. Also like the first category, these trials were essentially the products of personal enmity. The Kyteler case began as a family feud that took on qualities unknown in Ireland or elsewhere when prosecuted by the English Franciscan bishop of Ossory. His subsequent proceedings against some of the most powerful men of the colony, including his own metropolitan, were the religious face of the infighting that greatly weakened the colony. As in the first category, little suggests that genuine heretical beliefs or practices were behind Ledrede's prosecutions, and the same is equally true for the third category, the trials and executions of Adducc Dubh O'Toole and two MacConmaras.

These three men fell victim to the sort of anti-Irish propaganda articulated in *Laudabiliter*, that the Irish were not really Christian, but while they had been labelled pagan in the twelfth century, in the fourteenth they were denounced as heretical. Their alleged heresies demonstrate that their accusers or at least those who recorded their cases did not fully grasp the concept: Adducc Dubh's heresy was more accurately apostasy, and the MacConmaras' apparently blasphemy. This same confusion surfaces in a petition from the citizens of Dublin that described the pre-Christian Irish as "eretiks," yet a non-Christian, especially one who has not even heard of Christianity, cannot be a heretic.[61] Moreover, while some medieval Europeans may have been

---

60. The only source for the trial of the cleric of Lismore is Bernard of Clairvaux; thus it is foreign hearsay likely shaped by Bernard's own assumptions and agenda.

61. Sayles, *Documents*, 99–100. This petition was issued sometime between 1317 and 1319.

atheists, the manner in which Adducc's alleged apostasy came to light and its exceptional usefulness for the colonists' agenda render his unbelief highly suspect.[62] The colonists presented Adducc as the incarnation of the notions of *Laudabiliter*, to which they added a few more, in their request to the pope that a crusade be called against the Gaelic Irish to finish what *Laudabiliter* had started, to complete the conquest, which the colonists could not do on their own. Fortunately for the Irish, however, popes took a more cautious view of English activities in Ireland after the twelfth century. Though the kings of England could count on considerable papal support for most of their policies in Ireland, Irish complaints of English and Anglo-Irish injustice did not fall on deaf ears, and no pope called a crusade, at least not while England was a Catholic country. Perhaps for this reason, the colonists decided not to pursue this tactic, and after the execution of the MacConmaras references to heresy in the records are little more than intracolonial episodes in name-calling with virtually no basis in religious belief, and none is known to have reached trial. Those that did reach trial between 1310 and 1353 were not a reflection of the state of the faith in Ireland, however, but a mask for other agendas. As the representatives of the Irish church declared at the Council of Vienne and as the "Remonstrance of Irish Princes" pointed out in 1317, the English used religion as a pretense for conquest; Edward III offered a similar appraisal of Ledrede's conduct in 1329 and again ca. 1357; and such a dynamic is clearly evident in the trials and executions of Adducc Dubh O'Toole and the MacConmaras.[63]

The Concern over Heresy in Medieval Europe

A common theme underlies all three categories of trials—Dublin's 1310 trials, Ledrede's prosecutions, and the two cases against the native Irish—and serves as a central thesis of this study: heresy trials in medieval Ireland did not involve actual alternative understandings of Christianity but were used to discredit one's opponents and to attack groups or individuals whom the accusers feared and resented. This does not mean that alternative and even heretical understandings of Christianity did not exist in medieval Ireland; individual medieval Irish Christians may well have held deviant understandings of the faith that have escaped both the records and potential inquisitors. Heresy, however, does not exist in the abstract; it must be identified as such

---

62. See Arnold, *Belief and Unbelief*, and Reynolds, "Social Mentalities."

63. Ehrle, "Ein Bruchstück," 370–71; Bower, *Scotichronicon*, 388; see chapters 1 and 5. Rymer, vol. 2, pt. 3, p. 28; Raine, *Historical Papers and Letters*, 403–6; see chapter 4.

by authoritative ecclesiastics and, for the label to stick, have that identification upheld by an *inquisitio*, a legal investigation, that after 1252 had papal permission to use torture to compel accused heretics to confess. Deriving from the Greek *hæresis* (choice), heresy hinges upon issues of control and authority; the church denied choice to its faithful in matters of doctrine and church structure. Religious views that differed from official teachings would be heterodox unless authoritatively declared as heresy, but merely advancing heretical views ought not suffice to have one deemed a heretic; "error became heresy when, shown his deviation, the obstinate refused to obey and retract."[64] Persisting in deviant belief after authoritative attempts at correction, the heretic chose her own understanding rather than submit to the authority of the church, and it is this choice—of the self over authority, as Lucifer was said to have done, as Adam and Eve were said to have done—that constituted heresy in the eyes of the church.[65]

Alternative understandings of Christianity became an increasing concern for the church in the eleventh century, as it strove to centralize its authority, and a constant challenge from the twelfth century on. Sects such as the so-called Cathars, alleged dualists who maintained that Christ was pure spirit and the physical world evil and against whom the church called a crusade in the early thirteenth century, and the Waldensians, who were initially quite similar to their later orthodox brethren, the Franciscans, but came to challenge Catholic customs and corruption as much as they extolled the ideals of the *vita apostolica* (apostolic life), spread throughout the Continent in the high and late Middle Ages. Though deeply opposed to each other, both Cathars and Waldensians were shaped by a twelfth-century movement in which itinerant preachers called people to follow a life of apostolic perfection, to renounce material possessions and return to the simplicity and commitment of the early church. Occasionally this religious fervor led to (and arose out of) condemnation of clerical abuses and a rejection or qualification of the ecclesiastical hierarchy, which did not know how to respond to this movement. The Waldensians serve as "the classic example of the would-be reform movement drawn into heresy by the inadequacies of ecclesiastical authority."[66] Like Francis of Assisi, Valdès of Lyon had a conversion experience that inspired him to put into practice Jesus's advice to the rich man to sell all his possessions, give the proceeds to the poor, and follow him.[67] Forbidden to preach

---

64. Lambert, *Medieval Heresy*, 5.

65. For useful overviews, see Lambert, *Medieval Heresy*, and Deane, *History of Medieval Heresy*.

66. Lambert, *Medieval Heresy*, 70.

67. Mark 10:17–31; Matthew 19:16–30; Luke 18:18–30. Franciscan similarites may be due to later influences (Moore, *War on Heresy*, 221–22).

by his bishop, Valdès went to Rome to plead his case to the pope during the Third Lateran Council (1179). Alexander III admired Valdès's piety, but he sided with the bishop on the matter of preaching, primarily due to issues of control and authority. Walter Map, Henry II's representative at the council, mocked the humble piety of Valdès and his followers but also perceived it as a potent threat to the ecclesiastical hierarchy, declaring, "If we admit them, we shall be driven out."[68]

Valdès and his followers initially accepted the papal position and remained orthodox, but five years later the Waldensians were condemned as heretics by Alexander's successor, Lucius III, in his bull *Ad abolendam*, apparently for their refusal to renounce preaching. The problem was not *what* they were preaching but *that* they, laypeople, were preaching, which was a jealously guarded clerical privilege. Once labelled heretics, the Waldensians eventually came to act like it, challenging conventional Christian practices and beliefs that did not have a solid scriptural foundation, like purgatory and clerical ordination.[69] This did little to stem the growth of the movement, which became increasingly hostile to the church that it initially had sought to strengthen. Fortunately for Francis, and perhaps for the church, a pope with greater vision than his predecessors was on the throne when he came to the curia in 1209 for papal approval, which he received, possibly on two conditions, promptly performed: he and his followers had to become tonsured as clerics, and he had to swear obedience to the pope and his followers to him.[70] Further illustrating the shifting line between "heresy" and "orthodoxy," the same pope who approved Francis and his order, Innocent III, reconciled a branch of Waldensians with the church, conceding them "precisely that for which they had been excommunicated and persecuted. In this case the true 'convert' was the curia."[71]

At the same time, however, Innocent was merciless toward heretics in southern France known as Cathars or Albigensians but who called themselves Friends of God or simply Good Christians. Regarding them as agents

---

68. Wakefield and Evans, *Heresies of the High Middle Ages*, 204 (all quotations from Wakefield and Evans use their translation).

69. See Alain of Lille's *De fide catholica contra haereticos sui temporis* (in Wakefield and Evans, *Heresies of the High Middle Ages*, 217–20); see also Cameron, *Waldenses*, 26, 33–34, 45–48, 75–78, 84–86, and 92–95; cf. Moore, *War on Heresy*, 224.

70. According to Bonaventure, Innocent III tonsured Francis and his followers; according to the *Legend of the Three Companions*, Cardinal John of Santa Sabina wanted them tonsured and made the arrangements; about these conditions Thomas of Celano is silent (Lawrence, *The Friars*, 47). The percentage of clerics among early Franciscans was quite small; the claim of clerical tonsuring could represent later Franciscan attempts to make sense of Innocent's approval of lay preachers.

71. Grundmann, *Religious Movements*, 48.

of the apocalypse that threatened the very existence of Christendom, Innocent called a crusade against them in 1208, "merg[ing] a century or more of Latin Christian thought on heresy and holy war."[72] As with most medieval heretics, their portraits were painted primarily by their opponents, making the accuracy of their representation questionable. The hostility came overwhelmingly from outsiders who, as in Ireland, wished to claim their land and remake the region over in their own image.[73] Like the Waldensians and others the church labelled heretics, these Good Christians took their inspiration from the same scriptures as the church, but they sharpened the dualistic dimensions so that the material world and the spiritual realm were diametrically opposed, with God in control solely of the latter.[74] The "elect," the priestly class of the faith, were to abstain from entanglements with the corrupting material world, especially in their (pesco-vegan) diet and human relationships, which would be much like those of orthodox clergy and monastics. Their faithful, the believers (*credentes*), were to listen to, honor, and care for the elect, but each believer also had the potential to become elect, an honor primarily reserved for those on their deathbed, achieved through the rite of *consolamentum*, which purified them of material pollution and filled them with the Spirit.[75] The Good Christians were enmeshed within the fabric of southern France; even those who did not share their theology respected them for their pious and moral conduct as well as family connections. Their theological differences from conventional orthodoxy could seem somewhat subtle, at least prior to the crusade, but their differences in ecclesiastical hierarchy were considerable, regarding holiness as something shared within the network of Good Christians, as opposed to the orthodox system of apostolic succession.[76]

The pope, the pinnacle of apostolic succession, saw them not as Good Christians but as a threat to good Christians everywhere and called a crusade against them, turning the full force of the weapon the papacy had developed to wrest the Holy Land from Muslims against European Christians for the first time.[77] Innocent fanned the flames of apocalyptic vengeance against heretics and the thirst for conquest among the northerners of France's

---

72. Pegg, *A Most Holy War*, 60.

73. Moore, *War on Heresy*, 151, 203, 225–27.

74. The extent of actual dualist belief among the Cathars is somewhat suspect (Pegg, *A Most Holy War*, especially 46; Moore, *War on Heresy*, especially 197–201, 215–20, and 304–6).

75. Pegg, *Corruption of Angels*, 97, 105.

76. Pegg, *A Most Holy War*, 46–49.

77. Tyerman, *God's War*, 583–87, 894. While earlier examples share similarities, the Albigensian Crusade was "the first fully-authenticated crusade against Christians" (Housley, "Crusades against Christians," 28).

langue d'oïl, as opposed to the *lenga d'oc* (hence Languedoc to northerners and subsequently to history) in the south.[78] The northerners and other crusaders brutally pursued the pacifist Good Christians and their allies, laying waste the cities of Languedoc and massacring their inhabitants. According to Caesarius of Heisterbach, just before the massacre at Béziers in 1209, the crusaders asked Arnau Amalric, papal legate and leader of the Albigensian Crusade, how they should proceed. Since the heretics looked and acted much the same as Catholics, they could not be discerned as easily as Muslims in the Holy Land. Arnau's alleged response, "Kill them all! God will know his own," reflects "a homicidal ethic that . . . was an essential principle of the holy war on heresy."[79] The shared Christian basis of the heretics made them an even greater danger than Muslims. The subtlety of the differences posed a more intimate threat; if the crusaders left any standing, they might eventually be enticed down the heretical path as well. They had to kill them all so they could save themselves.[80]

This genuine fear of heresy combined with northern French territorial ambitions; "the Albigensian Crusade was at heart a crusade of conquest," with the primary victor the French monarchy, which absorbed much of Languedoc.[81] The Good Christians were decimated by the crusade, which officially ended in 1229; by a century later, they had essentially disappeared. The Waldensians managed to survive centuries of persecution, the sole heresy of the high Middle Ages to "link hands with the Protestant Reformation" in the sixteenth century, and continuing even to the present day.[82] Neither sect had direct links with medieval Ireland, yet both illuminate key aspects of Ireland's medieval heresy trials. The Waldensians demonstrate how a deeply orthodox group such as Valdès and his followers could be pushed into heresy by ecclesiastical mismanagement and insistence on control. Valdès felt called by God to preach primarily so he could combat heretics and repeatedly demonstrated that the content of his preaching and beliefs was orthodox. The church, however, refused to allow laypeople to preach, in part because of fear of potential error by the uneducated but also because preaching was a privilege reserved for clerics. Despite their profoundly pious and orthodox origin, doctrinal differences emerged between Waldensians and Catholics within a few years of the church labelling them heretics. The Irish, however, were

---

78. The two regions had different dialects: in the north the word for "yes" in the native tongue was *oïl*; in the Languedoc it was *oc*.

79. Pegg, *A Most Holy War*, 77.

80. Ibid., 78.

81. Deane, *History of Medieval Heresy*, 54.

82. Lambert, *Medieval Heresy*, 2nd ed., 147.

portrayed as apostates, heretics, and worse by Catholic ecclesiastical leaders for centuries. To the extent that it had authority to do so, the papacy handed their homeland over to the English, whose brutality toward and oppression of them at times met with papal indifference if not encouragement. As the words of the Irish Remonstrance in 1317 and Muirges O'Heney in 1186 attest, the Irish realized that the papacy's blessing on the conquest had subjected them to slavery and martyrdom at the hands of the English. Yet they remained committed to the pope and the church, playing Griselda to the papacy's Walter, although their sacrifices were real, not illusory.[83]

The Albigensian Crusade provides a more obvious parallel with the Irish context, with religion used to sanction a conquest of European Christians by other European Christians who were favored by the papacy. The Good Christians were clearly categorized as heretics by the standards of the time, whereas the Irish were not, but the Good Christians were not alone in Languedoc. Catholics and Good Christians had peacefully coexisted there for decades, and the nobles who held the lands and led the armies to defend them against the invaders/crusaders were Catholics (as were most of the warriors, given that Good Christians abhorred violence and espoused pacifism), although family members may have been Good Christians. These Catholics, denounced as *fautors*, or supporters and enablers of heresy, were nearly as hated by the church as the heretics themselves. Ultimately, however, it mattered little what an individual who lived in the lands between the Garonne and the Rhône actually believed or did. "All persons between these rivers were pestiferous (or soon would be)," and the pope sanctioned their annihilation, which he presented as a matter of self-defense.[84] Heresy was a contagion, and proximity to it could be a death sentence, both according to papal paranoia and to the invaders'/crusaders' vengeance. Reversing the clemency God offered to extend to Sodom or Jerusalem, sparing a city if ten righteous people or even a single virtuous person could be found among the inhabitants, the legal scholar Johannes Teutonicus asserted in 1217 that "all the inhabitants can be burnt" if even a few heretics were found in a city.[85] Location did not suffice to officially condemn an individual as a heretic, but the invaders'/crusaders' genocidal policies, endorsed by the papacy, amounted to the same thing.[86] Fortunately for the Irish, though the similarities between the Albigensian Crusade and the papally endorsed Anglo-Norman invasion

---

83. Chaucer, "The Clerk's Tale," in *Canterbury Tales*, 154–85.

84. Pegg, *A Most Holy War*, 61.

85. Genesis 18:32; Jeremiah 5:1. Johannes Teutonicus quoted (in English) in Pegg, *A Most Holy War*, 77.

86. For the Albigensian Crusade as genocide, see Pegg, *A Most Holy War*, 188–91.

to reclaim Ireland for Christianity are unmistakable, Ireland's conquest was not a true crusade. The colonists tried to make it one, sacrificing Adducc Dubh O'Toole to that cause and begging the pope to call a crusade against the native Irish and those infected with their heresy—the heresy, that is, of being Irish, by blood or culture. But, perhaps due to the absence of genuine heretical sects or to the perception of Ireland as a marginal country with little strategic significance, they failed, and the Irish survived to fight their invaders and reclaim their land, if incrementally.

Identifying heresy where none existed was not unusual in the high and late Middle Ages. One did not need to be a "Good Christian" to see Satan stalking this earth and good and evil locked in a desperate struggle. The devil and his minions, humans swayed by lies, lust, and greed, ceaselessly sought to overthrow Christ and his church, according to ecclesiastical leaders such as John XXII, as discussed in chapter 2. Heresy was a key weapon in the devil's arsenal, and the church required constant vigilance to identify his cunning agents. Fear and paranoia at times put the cart before the horse, however, as when the Council of Vienne, which also decided the fate of the Templars, issued the decree *Ad nostrum*, "the birth certificate of the heresy of the Free Spirit." *Ad nostrum* alleged that members of this sect claimed they could reach a state of perfection so that they surpassed the church and became God's own self. "But, as if it were in the theater of the absur[d], there is a birth certificate without it being fully clear whether there was any child."[87] As Robert Lerner has shown, the Free Spirit was not an organized heretical sect but part of a larger orthodox and heterodox mystical quest for spiritual perfection. By its very nature, mysticism tests the boundaries of orthodoxy and ecclesiastical authority, but the sect of the Free Spirit that *Ad nostrum* and subsequent scholars saw never existed. Inverting this example, the Templars were clearly an organized group to whom their persecutors and others imputed a heresy where none existed, as discussed in chapter 1. Their trial provided a poor example of what constitutes heresy and how to try it, and its deficiencies marked the subsequent cases Ireland experienced in the fourteenth century. Their "inquisitorial extermination . . . on outrageously bogus charges" perversely provided Ireland's most rigorous example of a proper trial.[88] Unlike the Continent, the island had no tradition of heresy to draw upon, even in its fabrications.

Heresy was thus a fluid and frequently shifting concept, virtually limitless in its forms, but it was in its essence a label applied to others, not the self; a

---

87. Lerner, *Heresy of the Free Spirit*, 83.
88. Kelly, "Inquisition and the Prosecution of Heresy," 448.

modern analogy could be the term "terrorist"—individuals to whom it is applied often regard themselves as fighters for righteousness, justice, and freedom, seeing their opponents as the terrorists.[89] The defining element was the ability to support such a label with authority and often with force. To some extent, heresy was simply a matter of being defined as such by authoritative ecclesiastical leaders after a thorough investigation. As Ignatius of Loyola famously declared in the sixteenth century, a good Catholic "ought always to hold that the white which I see, is black, if the Hierarchical Church so decides it," a pithier expression of Thomas Aquinas's teachings in the thirteenth century.[90] If the church declared something heretical, ipso facto it was heretical and clinging to it made one a heretic; one must not substitute one's own opinion for the church's authority. Yet the church was far from monolithic, and it reflected a tremendous range of opinions of what, specifically, constituted heresy. For the concept to have any coherence as analyzed by modern scholars, claims of heresy need to be rigorously examined: who made them, why, with what authority, when, who benefited from such claims, if others who shared such views were celebrated by the church, what was the political, ethnic, economic, and cultural context, et cetera. An examination of the heresy claims made in medieval Ireland's trials demonstrates that none can be sufficiently supported, especially since apparently only the Templars underwent anything approximating a thorough investigation, and reveals the ways in which heresy was wielded as a weapon against one's opponents, particularly in a fractious climate with vicious local politics, severe ethnic tensions, and an apparent dearth of actual heretical beliefs. This antagonistic application takes on even greater importance in light of the fact that these heresy trials included one of the earliest witchcraft trials, a precursor to the persecution that would later consume tens of thousands of women and their male associates on the Continent and in Britain; again, however, Ireland proved largely immune.

As the Kyteler case helps illuminate later developments, so does this later persecution illuminate the case and its contemporary trials in Ireland. Scholars generally agree that the victims of the witch craze were killed more for their persecutors' fears and hostilities than for their own actions. They commonly concede that few if any victims were actually practicing witchcraft, let alone performing the supernatural feats or diabolical devotions attributed

---

89. Deane, *History of Medieval Heresy*, 6.
90. Ignatius of Loyola, *Spiritual Exercises*, 92 (Mullan's translation); Thomas Aquinas, *Summa Theologiae*, 157–61.

to them.[91] A similar skepticism is in order when examining the trials in Ireland, yet as discussed in the following chapters, scholars have too often sided with the ecclesiastical authorities who condemned these individuals as heretics, ultimately with no greater evidence than that the authorities said so. This implicitly perpetuates the logic advanced by the medieval church, that heresy is decided by authority and submission (or lack thereof) to that authority alone. The medieval church itself did not fully support these condemnations, however, as Archbishop Ralph O'Kelly's alleged attack on Bishop Roger Cradock after he burned the MacConmaras for heresy forcefully attests. Even when inquisitors succeeded in obtaining confessions, others were not so quick to accept them. Though individual Templars outside of Ireland confessed after torture, they generally renounced their coerced confessions, and those who went to the stake persisted in defending their order's innocence and proclaiming their devotion to the church with their last breaths, unlike actual heretics who followed their alternative understandings of the faith into the flames, insisting on the righteousness of their views and proclaiming the church the true heretics. The Council of Vienne ultimately decreed that the order should be dissolved due not to guilt but to suspicion, and many churchmen spoke out against those who targeted the Templars and their wealth.[92] Moreover, no evidence indicates that the Templars of Ireland were guilty of the supposed heresy imputed to the order. Similarly, Petronilla de Midia gave an equally dubious confession after being brutalized by Ledrede, and his findings were vigorously disputed by other ecclesiastical authorities, as discussed in chapters 3 and 4. No reliable evidence indicates that others condemned for heresy in Ireland ever confessed or that their accusers properly understood what heresy was, beyond something defined as such by ecclesiastical authorities, making it all the more puzzling when modern scholars echo the words of the would-be inquisitors against their victims. As Moore points out, "the only reparation that [scholars] can now offer to [the victims'] memory is to try to reach a better understanding of what it was they died for."[93] The more an individual stood to benefit from the prosecutions—as repeatedly was the case with

---

91. Certain Christian practices involved magical aspects, but this does not mean that practitioners understood this as witchcraft. For discussion of magical aspects of medieval Christianity, see Thomas, *Religion and the Decline of Magic*, 25–50, and Rider, *Magic and Religion*; Bailey's overview, *Magic and Superstition in Europe*, is also helpful. For examples from Ireland, see chapter 2.

92. Those accused of heresy could be convicted on a lesser charge of suspicion of heresy if heretical connections were proved but the evidence did not suffice for a conviction of the crime of heresy itself (Kelly, "Inquisition and the Prosecution of Heresy," 444; see also Lea, *History of the Inquisition*, 1:433–34, 454–56).

93. Moore, *War on Heresy*, 10.

Ledrede, as was the case with the colonists who sought a crusade against the native Irish, as was indeed the case of the English generally who claimed the Irish as false Christians so they could take their lands—the more suspect the intentions behind his claims must be.

As accusations of heresy became increasingly common in high and late medieval Europe, so too did the likelihood that such claims had little to do with actual dogmatic difference but were rather weapons wielded amid ongoing conflicts. Modern scholars of heresy differentiate between "real," doctrinal heresies and "artificial" heresies "in which unpopular groups or individuals were smeared with slanderous charges by authority at various levels or by local opinion."[94] Disobedience had always been a determining element in heresy, hinging on an individual's willingness to submit to church authority and renounce his or her own alternative understanding. Without concomitant deviant dogmatic views, however, an alleged heresy most likely was artificial, as opposed to real. By the early fourteenth century papal pronouncements attest that "*the* heresy par excellence had become disobedience instead of disbelief."[95] The deciding factor was who had greater ability to compel obedience. Significantly, though, Ireland's inhabitants made use of this weapon only in the chaotic fourteenth century, when the colony was in decline and after the concept had been abruptly introduced by international proceedings in which the colonists were compelled to play a part. Moreover, the weapon apparently held little interest for the native Irish, who conducted no known trials apart from Bernard of Clairvaux's twelfth-century claim about the cleric of Lismore. Bernard's report, while suspect, indicates that this would be Ireland's only trial to arise from genuine doctrinal differences, rather than political ones, though Malachy's commitment to reform and greater standardization must also be considered. The absence of trials among the native Irish and after the mid-fourteenth century among the colonists stands in stark contrast to their contemporary medieval Europeans, who provide ample examples of heresy trials based on both actual doctrinal deviation and political conflicts. The conclusion considers some of the potential reasons for this difference, such as greater tolerance of diversity and syncretism among the Irish, the relative decentralization of the Irish church prior to the twelfth century, and hostility toward heresy prosecution among Ireland's leading metropolitans in the fourteenth century.

---

94. Lambert, *Medieval Heresy*, 8–9.
95. Patschovsky, "Heresy and Society," 27.

A Note on Time and Terms

This book explores all of medieval Ireland's reliably recorded heresy trials, beginning with the trials of the Templars and Philip de Braybrook in 1310 and ending with the MacConmaras' execution in 1353. It focuses on two groups of people, the native Gaelic Irish and the colonists, to whom I usually refer as the Anglo-Irish. Much ink has been spilled on the accuracy of such a label. They identified themselves as "English" or "the English of Ireland," but to distinguish them more clearly from their compatriots in England I have favored the use of "Anglo-Irish." Even more debate has raged regarding the terms used to describe the early invaders and settlers; Normans, Anglo-Normans, Cambro-Normans, Anglo-French, English, and Angevins are some of the more popular choices. As contemporary sources most commonly refer to them as English, I have done likewise. Occasionally I have used the term "Anglo-Norman," which can also be applied to the inhabitants of the colony, particularly before 1216.[96] By their very nature, labels are inherently problematic, and none of the possibilities accurately describes every person within the group to which it is applied; by my use of the terms I am not necessarily making a statement about a person's or group's self-perception, length of time in a given country, degree of acculturation, language or law used, and so on, unless such matters are explicitly explored. The accuracy of referring to Ireland as a colony has also been challenged, particularly due to its proximity to England, but the policies adopted toward the native population and its secular and economic dependence on England attest to the term's aptness for the situation.[97] I have also used the term "lordship," but by both I mean only those areas that the royal government actually controlled.

As discussed above, heresy is a Christian's persistent belief in something contrary to officially defined doctrine after authoritative attempts at correction. A relapsed heretic has returned to a heresy that she has previously been convicted of and abjured. A fautor is one who supports and enables heresy by providing heretics with aid and assistance, but is not necessarily accused of sharing their heretical beliefs.[98] Witchcraft is considered here as a subset of heresy; since it surfaced solely in the Kyteler case, it is explored almost exclusively in chapter 2. *Maleficia* is literally evildoing but more narrowly means malicious magic that harms people or property. Apostasy is the renunciation of one's vows or faith: an apostate monk or nun has abandoned

---

96. *NHI*, 2:liii.

97. See Davies, "Lordship or Colony?"

98. For a summary of eleven categories of transgression in heresy, including heretics and fautors, as defined by the Council of Tarragona in 1242, see Arnold, *Inquisition and Power*, 42–43.

the religious life and returned to the secular world without dispensation; an apostate Christian has abandoned his Christianity, perhaps to convert to another faith. Blasphemy is conduct by word or deed that conveys contempt of God or other holy people or things. And lastly, although it could be said that the Middle Ages lasted in Ireland until the early seventeenth century, by the standards of this study the medieval period ended with the conversion of Henry VIII to Protestantism, itself a heresy in the eyes of the Catholic church.

❧ CHAPTER 1

Heresy Hunting Begins in Ireland

*The Trial of the Templars and the Case
against Philip de Braybrook*

According to John de Pembridge, writing in the second quarter of the fourteenth century, a moon of diverse colors shone on December 14, 1312, "in which it was divined that the Order of the Templars should be abolished for all eternity."[1] The evidence of the forty-two outside witnesses in the Irish trial, who offered the only unanimously negative assessment of the order in the British Isles, further indicates support for the order's suppression, by then a fait accompli.[2] Yet the trial passed virtually unnoticed by contemporary Irish or Anglo-Irish annalists. Pembridge himself, a Dominican of St. Saviour's Priory in Dublin, records their arrest and imprisonment in transmarine lands, England, and Ireland but says nothing about their subsequent fate apart from the marvelous moon and its implications.[3] Only "Chronicler A" of the "Kilkenny Chronicle" noted their trial in Ireland or elsewhere.[4] Friar John Clyn, who also composed his annals in the second quarter of the fourteenth

---

1. *CSM*, 2:341. For Pembridge as the author of these annals, see Williams, "Dominican Annals."

2. Nicholson numbers the witnesses at forty-nine (*Proceedings Against the Templars*, 2:xxxvi), but she apparently includes the seven observers in this number. The order was dissolved by the bull *Vox in excelso*, dated March 22, 1312; see below.

3. *CSM*, 2:336.

4. Flower, "Manuscripts of Irish Interest," 334–35. The chronicler also mentions the death of Roger de Heton (*s.a.* 1315), the warden of the Franciscans in Ireland who attended at least three of the examinations of the Templars and served as the first outside witness in their trial. For the different chroniclers who contributed to this text, see Williams, "The Kilkenny Chronicle."

century, mentions merely that the order was dissolved by the Council of Vienne in 1312.[5] The mid-fourteenth-century scribe of the *Annals of Inisfallen* discusses the council in relation to the refusal of several Irish bishops to attend "for fear that unpleasantness might befall them." He also fulminates against the Spiritual Franciscans who, "spreading the poison of their diabolical tricks under the semblance of religion and false piety, have wickedly submitted themselves, their sect, and their erroneous doctrine to the immediate protection of the Holy See and of certain people of the Curia who support them." Franciscan representatives, he tells us, requested of the pope and council that they condemn Spiritual Franciscan teachings, "lest from the deadly draught the Lord's flock contract the disease of heretical leprosy."[6] On the matter of the Templars, about whom similar remarks could have been made, the scribe is silent, as indeed are medieval Irish or Anglo-Irish annalists regarding Templars in general.[7]

Thus Ireland's first full-fledged heretical inquest seems to have aroused little interest among either colonists or the native Irish, at least in the records. This apparent apathy becomes all the more perplexing in light of the position of power and privilege Templars enjoyed in the lordship, as they did throughout Britain and western Europe prior to their precipitous fall from grace, and in light of the damaging testimony given by Templars themselves during their examination in Ireland, which has led one scholar to conclude that they were tortured.[8] Nor has the trial in Ireland garnered much interest among modern scholars, apart from Helen Nicholson's studies of the trial in the British Isles. It inspired one of its inquisitors, Thomas de Chaddesworth, however, to immediately adopt similar techniques against an old rival, Philip de Braybrook. The case against Braybrook was apparently tried in the same place (St. Patrick's), by the same man (Chaddesworth), and in the same year (1310) as the trial of the Templars. It illuminates the dynamics between Dublin's dueling cathedral chapters, St. Patrick's (represented by Chaddesworth) and Holy Trinity (Braybrook), and the ways in which accusations of heresy were promptly seized upon in medieval vendettas, yet it has been largely ignored by scholars. Both cases, and especially that of the Templars, set a standard that would be followed in the coming decades: trumped-up charges

5. Clyn, 11. He also noted the arrest of the Templars in Ireland on February 3, 1308.

6. *AI*, 410 (in the last passage I have closely followed Mac Airt's translation). The annalist calls them "Sarabites," i.e., degenerate religious; Clyn also mentions the "Soraboita" sect as flourishing during the papacy of Clement V in his entry for 1309.

7. The only reference to the Templars in the *Annals of Inisfallen* is indirect; under the year 1244 it says that many Christians were slaughtered by Saracens in Damietta. The *Annals of Multyfarnham*, under the same year, specifies that Templars and Hospitallers were killed.

8. Perkins, "History of the Knights Templar," 140, 143, 150, 151, 154, 159; Perkins, "Trial of the Knights Templars," 445, 447.

to discredit opponents without solid supporting evidence. As Chaddesworth copied the tactics used against the Templars in his own feud with Philip, so would colonists copy Ledrede's tactics in theirs with the native Irish.

Ireland had never witnessed anything like the Templar trial, but over the next fifty years it experienced a rash of heresy accusations and trials, more than in the rest of the Middle Ages combined. While the trial of the Templars in Ireland directly influenced only the case of Philip de Braybrook, their trial in France most likely shaped the perspective of the man responsible for most of Ireland's future trials and accusations, Richard de Ledrede, and it provided a context for participants in Ledrede's and other subsequent proceedings in Ireland. Moreover, the trial provides invaluable insight into the colony's initial response to and understanding of heresy, as well as into the development of that response and understanding throughout the following half century. The trial of the Templars in Ireland also enables exploration of the order and the accusations against them in a land in which they were almost entirely separate from their original purpose, the recovery of the Holy Land. The loss of that purpose after the fall of Acre was a primary cause of their demise, yet this dimension seems to have held little significance for those in Ireland, which was more of an object than an agent in the crusading movement.

Templar History in Ireland Prior to the Trial

The Knights Templar came to Ireland with the Anglo-Normans, possibly accompanying Henry II, who pledged to support Templars as part of his penance for the murder of the archbishop of Canterbury—a penance intertwined with his very conquest of Ireland.[9] His grant to them of lands in Ireland was confirmed by every king of England up to Edward II, who perhaps did not have time to confirm the grant before the events in France reached his ears.[10] Thirteen Templar preceptories have been identified in Ireland, only one of which lay outside colonial territory, and they may have had as many as forty-five other preceptories, houses, and churches.[11] The Irish Templars were a branch of the English province, and the preceptor of Ireland, though

---

9. Gervase of Canterbury, *Opera Historica*, 239; *IHD*, 21; see Introduction.

10. For Templar properties in Ireland, see Wood, "Templars in Ireland," 363–71; Perkins, "History of the Knights Templar," 230–32; Mac Niocaill, "Documents Relating to the Suppression of the Templars in Ireland"; Gwynn and Hadcock, *Medieval Religious Houses*, 327–31; and Lord, *Knights Templar in Britain*, 137–42.

11. Perkins, "History of the Knights Templar," 230–32; Gwynn and Hadcock, *Medieval Religious Houses*, 339–42. Loghnehely manor, also known as Teachtemple (Templehouse), in Co. Sligo lay outside colonial territory.

FIGURE 1. Templehouse/Loghnehely Manor. Photo by the author.

more often called master of Ireland, was subject to the English master.[12] Their experience in Ireland was similar to that of the order in England, particularly preceptories in the countryside, with greater engagement in agrarian activities than in military or political ones. One document attests that native Irish were involved in the order, at least in Clonaul in the early fourteenth century, but it cannot be determined if these were members or tenants.[13] Native Irish could have entered as sergeants or chaplains, but it seems unlikely given the usually rigid divide in Ireland between ethnicities in religious houses. All other known Templars in Ireland were almost certainly of English extraction and, judging from the Templars who were tried, most entered the order in England.

---

12. William de la More, master of England at the time of the trial, testified that he knew all the Templars of England, Ireland, and Scotland except for two Irish brothers whose names he did not know (Nicholson, *Proceedings Against the Templars*, 1:168).

13. Wood, "Templars in Ireland," 339, citing Plea Roll 76, 33 & 34 Ed I, m.27. Plea Roll 76 is no longer extant; the calendar (RC 7/11) does not include this entry about the Templars, but it has more entries omitted than included, according to Philomena Connolly (personal correspondence, April 2002). Among the items taken from Clontarf was a book of the Gospels in Irish (Mac Niocaill, "Documents Relating to the Suppression of the Templars in Ireland," 215). Family tradition associated with Templehouse in Co. Sligo also claims that Anthony O'Hara was a member of the order and donated his land to it (personal correspondence with Sandy Perceval, confirmed by Helena Perceval, December 2013). Lord asserts that Templar tenants in Ireland were mostly Irish (*Knights Templars in Britain*, 138), but cites only an unspecified plea roll from the time of Edward I, perhaps the lost Plea Roll 76.

The Templars had extensive rights and concessions in Ireland, as elsewhere. The papal privileges lavished on the order were legion: they were under the pope's direct authority and thus exempt from episcopal jurisdiction; they had their own clergy from whom they could receive the sacraments, but who were subservient, like all members, to the grand master; they did not have to pay tithes but instead could claim them, and alms given to the Templars were said to absolve donors of a seventh of their penances; they could not be placed under interdict or excommunication except by the pope, and if an area was under interdict when the Templars came to make their annual collections, the churches were to be opened, services held, and donations made. The kings of England further augmented these favors. They could not be tried before anyone in Ireland but the justiciar or the king, though after 1210 no king of England visited the island while Templars were still around to enjoy this privilege, and they had their own courts with full jurisdiction over their tenants. They were free from all amercements, aids, tallages, and tolls, as well as military service, an odd exemption for a military order and one the Hospitallers apparently did not share. Such generous grants, however, often proved difficult for the Templars to enforce, at least in England, where they were dependent upon the fickle favor of the king, who could at pleasure allow or withhold many of their privileges, both financial and jurisdictional. They do not seem to have served as bankers nearly to the extent the order did elsewhere, but the preceptors of Ireland often acted as auditors for the Irish treasurer and sometimes served as collectors of both secular and religious monies.[14] They also occasionally acted as mediators in important affairs, including for the king.[15] By the nature of the colony, the Irish Templars did not have as close a relationship with the king as did their English brethren, yet they were clearly well favored and their leaders high-ranking men.

Evidence for the resentment that played such a critical role in their downfall is slight and indirect in Ireland. They were at times prevented from making annual collections by local clergy who exacted their own collections before Templars could do so.[16] Though the colony was often at war with the native Irish and the king frequently enlisted colonists to fight in his wars elsewhere, the Irish Templars do not seem to have participated in such military activities, although Irish Hospitallers did, as did English Templars in

---

14. E.g., *CPR* (1232–47): 67, 277; (1247–58): 68, 212; (1272–81): 277, 379, 451.

15. Luard, *Chronica Majora*, 274–75; *CPR* (1232–47): 71; *CDI*, 1:313; *AC*, 49; *CDI*, 2:149; *IEP*, 1:1.

16. Wood, "Templars in Ireland," 336.

Edward I's campaign against Scotland.[17] Rather, when Irish Templars were assessed to supply soldiers and horses, they proved themselves exempt. One such occasion was in 1302, when the sheriff of Dublin seized and sold the Irish master's livestock to exact a fine levied on him by the Irish exchequer for failing to provide horses and men at arms to maintain peace in the land. The court awarded the master damages for the seizure and mistreatment of his property, since "he and his predecessors were always and ought to be free and quit of the finding of such horses and men, by charters of the Kings of England."[18] As Templars could be tried only before the justiciar or the king, they often successfully stalled suits made against them, as in the dispute over lands with the abbot of St. Mary of Dunbrody that began in 1278 and took thirteen years to resolve. The abbot complained that the delay had caused his house to fall into poverty and would lead it into ruin if he continued the case "against such powerful opponents as the Templars."[19] In the end his patience and perseverance profited him nothing; the master of Ireland paid him one hundred marks for recognition of Templar ownership of the lands, which did little to recoup the cost of the case for the abbot.[20]

The financial privileges enjoyed by the Templars, which intensified the burden that fell on others, may have been a source of ill will toward them, but it also made them attractive lords. Repeated references demonstrate that colonists were more likely to establish connections with or copy them than to clamor against them.[21] Templars shared with Hospitallers virtually every secular privilege they enjoyed in Ireland, the exemption from military service a notable exception, and all royal mandates that attempted to limit their role as landlords were directed at the Hospitallers along with the Templars. Thus it seems unlikely that Templars aroused any particular animosity among the laity or religious, especially since the latter often benefited from similar if less extensive privileges themselves. Even the non-Templar witnesses in the trial offered little against the Irish Templars in particular, though they claimed to have heard or known about a great many crimes committed by Templars elsewhere, including sodomy, murder, and appropriating lands unjustly.

---

17. For the Irish Hospitallers, see *CDI*, 2:200; MacInerny, "Templars in Ireland," 228–32; Prynne 3:174; Dublin, National Library of Ireland, NLI 1–4, *Collectanea de rebus Hibernicis*, comp. Harris, 1:279; see also Nicholson, "Hospitallers' and Templars' Involvement." For the English Templars, see Walsingham, *Historia Anglicana*, 1:76.

18. *CJR*, 1:409.

19. *CSM*, 2:lxxxvi.

20. *CDI*, 3:332.

21. *CCR* (1227–31): 548; *CDI*, 1:284, 470–71; Wood, "Templars in Ireland," 366; Gilbert, *Historic and Municipal Documents of Ireland*, 255.

FIGURE 2. Dunbrody Abbey, which lost an ongoing dispute with the Templars, and which may have been the house of Adducc Dubh O'Toole. Photo by the author.

Three troublesome Templars are known from the Irish branch prior to the trial, all of them masters. In 1235, Henry III ordered the justiciar of Ireland to arrest Ralph de Southwark, who had been master of Ireland but now was an apostate. Ralph's reasons and his fate are unknown, but his behavior clearly did not harm the king's relationship with the Templars; the same letter instructed the justiciar to receive the new master in Ireland, Roger le Waleis, and to protect him, his men, lands, rents, et cetera.[22] Roger le Waleis himself was later charged with the death of a man but pardoned because the victim's name was unknown and thus he was unprotected by the law.[23] The third miscreant was repeatedly mentioned in the trial of the Templars in Ireland, as well as in their trial in London. Walter le Bacheler, master of Ireland from 1295 to 1301, was excommunicated and imprisoned by the order for allegedly stealing some of its property. He was apparently starved to death in a four-and-a-half-by-two-and-a-half-foot cell at the New Temple in London.[24] He died after about eight weeks, shortly after confessing and receiving the viaticum.[25]

---

22. *CCR* (1234–37): 183. Another letter of protection was issued the next day for the master and brothers of the Templars in Ireland (*CDI*, 1:337).

23. *CPR* (1232–47): 404.

24. Wood, "Templars in Ireland," 361.

25. Nicholson, *Proceedings Against the Templars*, 1:104–5, 2:95–96; see also 1:28, 2:30.

Ten of the fourteen Templars examined in Ireland mentioned Walter's imprisonment and death, as did one outside witness. His case was one of very few examples offered in the British Isles in connection with the charges that the order killed or imprisoned its members for revealing the manner of or refusing to participate in their reception, yet none claimed those as the reasons for his punishment.[26] Of those who gave an explanation in Ireland, three said it was for disobedience and one for theft; none implied that the order was wrong for punishing him in such a manner. Two Templars tried in England testified to the use of torture on Walter; while both their testimonies could be regarded as suspect, his quick demise increases the plausibility.[27] Yet several Templars died during their trial in Britain, though they were almost certainly not tortured, and a few may have died while imprisoned in Ireland as well. The repeated yet singular references to Walter's case in the trial record suggest that, so far as was known, he was the only Templar to have died in England while being punished by the order, and thus the inquisitors seized on his death as the one possible proof that Templars killed their members, as was alleged of them in the papal bull and about which ample testimony was given in France.

The Rise and Fall of the Crusading Ideal

The arrival of the English in Ireland in the late twelfth century was part of an expansion of western Continental Europe that found its most sensational expression in the movement to reclaim the Holy Land for Christ and his church.[28] Jerusalem itself was captured in 1099 by the First Crusade and a kingdom set up under Frankish control soon after, yet pilgrims who wished to visit the lands most intimately connected to Christ and the early church had little to ensure their safety en route to or within the kingdom. From this need to protect pilgrims the Templars were born, providing a military counterpart to the Hospitallers, who offered pilgrims lodging and medical care,

---

26. Stephen de Stapelbrugge explicitly said that, although in transmarine lands Templars were killed for refusing to participate in the reception, that was not the reason for Walter's fate, which he describes as death by torture in prison, a fate with which Stephen could empathize all too well (Nicholson, *Proceedings Against the Templars*, 1:350–51; see below).

27. Stephen de Stapelbrugge may have embellished his testimony with details from his own experience (see preceding note, and below). Either Ralph of Barton (Nicholson, *Proceedings Against the Templars*, 1:28) or William Raven (Wilkins, *Concilia*, 337), a priest directly asked about Walter's fate, said that he knew nothing except that he had been placed in prison and died there and that he had heard that some force had been used, but as a priest he was not party to it, due to potential irregularity (i.e., priests are not to shed blood).

28. Bartlett, *Making of Europe*.

though they too added a military dimension. Early on, the Templars won the support of Bernard of Clairvaux, who advanced their cause at the Council of Troyes in 1129, resulting in papal recognition of the order. The Templars quickly became the favored sons of popes and kings and were showered with spiritual and secular privileges. Yet their meteoric rise to power, wealth, and fame would be eclipsed by their cataclysmic fall in the early fourteenth century.

Ireland was an object rather than an agent of this crusading ideology. The Celtic Christianity for which the Irish won fame throughout the early Middle Ages caused them to come under increasing suspicion during the eleventh and twelfth centuries. Distinctive practices cultivated in Ireland and its outposts became regarded as alien aberrations, an attitude that extended as well to their Anglo-Saxon neighbors. When William invaded England in 1066, he did so with the pope's blessing and banner and with the aim of reforming the English church to bring it into closer conformity with Rome.[29] Less than a century later, when Henry II began contemplating a similar conquest of Ireland, he promptly received papal approval in *Laudabiliter*, which portrayed Ireland as outside the boundaries of the church and praised Henry for his intention to return it to the Christian fold. When Henry acted on that permission fifteen years later, again a pope gave him thanks and praise. This religious justification for the Anglo-Norman presence in Ireland would resurface with a vengeance in the first half of the fourteenth century, when the colony's grasp on the island became increasingly tenuous.

Due to the ongoing attempts to subject the island to Anglo-Norman control and the concomitant efforts to resist such attempts, neither colonists nor indigenous Irish could afford much investment in battles fought against Muslims in distant lands.[30] Gerald of Wales eventually criticized Henry II for choosing colony over crusade, sending his son John to fight against Christians in Ireland when he should have been sent to help free the Holy Land from Saracens.[31] References to the wars waged in the Holy Land are rare in medieval Irish and Anglo-Irish annals, with few remarking upon the fall of Acre that proved so disastrous for the Templars. Only two of the fourteen Templars tried in Ireland referred to their engagements abroad, as did three of the

---

29. Stenton, *Anglo-Saxon England*, 586, and chap. 18, passim; Brown, *Normans and the Norman Conquest*, 13, 28, 128–29.

30. Relatedly, in 1320 John XXII instructed Alexander de Bicknor to absolve Edmund Butler, his wife, and their son of their vow to go to Compostella, which they could not fulfill "on account of the wars between the English and the Irish" (*CPL*, 2:196); instead they were to give an amount comparable to the cost of the trip to the Holy Land subsidy.

31. Giraldus Cambrensis, *Opera*, 1:61.

forty-two outside witnesses; a fourth severely criticized William de Warenne, a former master of Ireland, for his disdain of pilgrimage. Nor did the Templars tried in Ireland include defense of the Holy Land or pilgrims among their reception vows, and the extent of the military equipment seized at the time of the arrest was slight indeed.[32] Although Ireland contributed along with the rest of western Christendom to crusade tenths, neither the Templars in specific nor other inhabitants of Ireland evinced particular interest in the Crusades to which Templar fortunes were so closely tied. Indeed, the remarks of Laurence Somercote, a collector of crusade tenths in Ireland in the mid-thirteenth century who declared that he would rather go to prison than "go to Ireland again to be crucified for the sake of the crusade tax," suggest that at least some inhabitants were not only indifferent to the crusading effort but openly hostile.[33] A trial in the year following the Templars' (1311) indicates more support for the cause, as it concerns the theft of "money arising from oblations of divers people for the aid of the Holy Land" that was held at Holy Trinity; William de Clifford, a canon of Holy Trinity not mentioned in the dispute between the chapters discussed below, assisted Philip le Clerk in robbing those donations and other items from the church.[34]

The death throes of the Templars began with the fall of Acre in 1291; neither the order nor the crusading movement with which it was inextricably intertwined ever recovered from the defeat. Templars provided "the living justification of the crusade," and they served as scapegoat when the crusade movement lost its momentum and became associated with failure.[35] By the time their trial began, the Templars had been kept for over fifteen years from their raison d'être, and financial activities had replaced military ones as their primary function. An order cut off from its primary purpose is vulnerable; one with great wealth is dangerously so, especially when one of its greatest debtors was Philip IV of France. In 1306 he arrested then expelled the Jews (approximately one hundred thousand people), to whom he was also in considerable debt. He portrayed his confiscation of their wealth as purifying the realm; it also alleviated the constant strain on his coffers. He had already perfected his "signature techniques of defaming the crown's perceived enemies: paint the accused as a demonic heretic and threat to the Christian people of

---

32. Three swords, three lances, one hauberk, one iron helmet, a bow, and two baudreys.

33. Quoted in Watt, *Church in Medieval Ireland*, 135. Note that Clyn claims that in 1335 many people burned a cross into their flesh with an iron to signify their intention of going to the Holy Land, but such enthusiasm came too late for the Templars. For an overview of native Irish involvement in the Crusades, see Lawless, "Gaelic Ireland and the Crusades."

34. *CJR*, 3:221. The *Registrum Novum* does refer to a William of Kerry, but not of Clifford.

35. Barber, *Trial of the Templars*, 1st ed., 8.

France, convoke public assemblies to clamor in favor of these accusations, and pressure church and lay assemblies to formally support the king."[36] Before he devastated an order (the Templars) and a people (the Jews), he devastated the pope. Amid a heated dispute that has been described as the first medieval conflict between church and state over national sovereignty, Philip succeeded in winning over much of the French people, eventually including the clergy, to his propaganda proclaiming Boniface VIII a heretic, a sexual deviant, and above all an illegitimate pope.[37] The conflict culminated in September 1303 in Boniface's hometown of Anagni, where he was imprisoned by William de Nogaret, Philip's representative, and Italian allies. Their bickering as to whether Boniface should be killed on the spot or taken back to France to be tried for heresy bought papal supporters enough time to rescue Boniface, but he never recovered from the attack and died shortly thereafter. The reaction to these events in Ireland is unknown. Pembridge and the Kilkenny Chronicle record this outrage, but they do not remark upon it. Thus the Irish context seems little suited to, prepared for, or even interested in the events that transpired in France in the fall of 1307.

The Trial in France

According to princely propaganda, multiple reports had reached Philip of monstrous abuses within the order, which he at first found unbelievable, given the severity of the accusations and his personal regard for the Templars. His conscience demanded he investigate the matter, however, so he had a dozen men infiltrate the order. To his great shock and sorrow, their findings proved the initial reports too mild, not severe, for they revealed the Templars to be more dangerous and despicable than the heathens who had driven them from the Holy Land. They reported that, at his reception into the order, each Templar was made to deny Christ, spit or worse on the crucifix, promise to relieve his sexual desires with his brothers and to let them do the same with him, and swear to do whatever he could to promote the order's interests; after these diabolical vows, the initiate kissed his receptor on the lips, navel, and base of the spine or sometimes on the anus, then made offerings to the idols worshipped by the order; those who refused to take such vows or give such kisses were summarily executed, while those who acquiesced proved all too faithful to their promises. After consultation with William of Paris, papal inquisitor in France and Philip's personal confessor, and other leading men

---

36. Field, *The Beguine, the Angel, and the Inquisitor*, 14–15.
37. The description is Tierney's (*Crisis of Church and State*, 172).

of the realm, Philip ordered all the Templars in his lands to be rounded up and arrested. His commands were carried out with remarkable stealth and efficiency in the early hours of Friday, the thirteenth of October, 1307; the Templars seem to have been taken by surprise and few escaped, though Philip had issued the writ for arrest a month before.

Once imprisoned in France, the Templars were subjected to various tortures and nearly all of them confessed to at least some charges. Of the 138 extant depositions from the hearings in Paris in October and November 1307, only 4 offered a complete denial of guilt.[38] One hundred and five admitted the denial of Christ, though they said they did it *ore et non corde* (by mouth and not in their heart); 123 confessed to spitting at, on, or near a crucifix at the orders of their receptors; 103 said they had been indecently kissed; 102 explicitly or implicitly said homosexuality was encouraged among brothers, although only 3 admitted to personally practicing homosexuality; and 9 gave evidence about idol worship, though their testimonies differed considerably.[39] Hugues de Pairaud, the visitor of France who was the receptor in 15 of the 138 depositions, confessed to the denial of Christ and spitting at the crucifix; he stated further that though no obscene kisses had occurred at his own reception, he ordered those he received to kiss him on the base of the spine and navel as well as the mouth, and he also admitted participating in idol worship at Montpellier.[40] Denial of the charges was somewhat stronger in the provinces, but the basic pattern remained the same.[41] The grand master himself, Jacques de Molay, confessed to the denial of Christ and spitting at the crucifix both at his own reception and at those in which he had been the receptor. Nogaret had him repeat his testimony before a gathering of university men on October 25, 1307, and the following day, thirty-eight Templars representing all three classes within the order—knights, chaplains, and sergeants—confirmed his confession, declaring to the university assembly that they had been received in the manner described by Molay.[42]

Despite the many confessions that Philip ensured became widely known, other European rulers remained dubious, most notably the pope. Although Clement V and Philip had discussed the matter previously, Clement did not support the arrest of the Templars, nor did he know about it until after the fact. On October 27, 1307, he wrote a letter rebuking Philip for his presumptuous action in a matter under ecclesiastical jurisdiction and against

---

38. Barber, *Trial of the Templars*, 69, 73; Barber, *New Knighthood*, 301.
39. Barber, *Trial of the Templars*, 75–76.
40. Ibid., 81–83.
41. Ibid., 69, 76–77.
42. Ibid., 78–79.

an order under papal protection. Less than a month later, however, he issued *Pastoralis praeeminentiae*, which ordered the arrest of the Templars and seizure of their property in all Christian lands. He cited the "spontaneous" confessions of the grand master and other Templars that required that the matter be investigated, and he urged Christian rulers to assist him by "discreetly, cautiously, and secretly" arresting the members in their lands.[43] Recognizing that Philip's deeds could not be undone, Clement strove to retake the reins and sent two cardinals to Paris to interview the grand master and other Templars. Allowed a brief respite from the tortures employed by Philip's agents, Molay and Pairaud recanted their confessions before the cardinals, as did other Templars. Clement became increasingly uneasy about the affair and in February 1308 suspended the proceedings. Philip then turned his well-honed intimidation tactics against the pope, including implying that he was a fautor of the Templars' heresy, reapplying pressure regarding a posthumous trial of Boniface VIII for heresy, and bringing a considerable military force when he went to meet with the pope, but Clement remained intractable as long as the king held the Templars and their property. Any decisions regarding the order had to have at least a semblance of papal authority; they had to come from Clement's hand and mouth, even if he were issuing Philip's will and words. As a compromise, Philip selected seventy-two Templars who confirmed their confession before the pope and swore that their confessions had been freely made; apparently satisfied, Clement ordered the inquisition resumed, although this time on his, not Philip's, terms.

In August 1308, Clement issued a series of bulls concerning the Templars, their trial, and their future fate. *Faciens misericordiam* summarized the papal version of the events to date, decreed that diocesan inquests concerning the guilt and innocence of individual Templars were to be held throughout Christendom under the authority of the (arch)bishop assisted by canons, Dominicans, and Franciscans, and established a papal commission to investigate the order as a whole. Another bull, *Regnans in coelis*, called for a general council to consider the results of the inquests and determine the fate of the Templars both individually and as a whole. The provincial inquiries seem to have begun in France in the spring of 1309 and the papal commission in August, though the hearings did not begin until November 22, 1309.[44] Men with greater loyalty to the king than to the pope dominated the former and heavily influenced the latter, but at length the trickle of Templars who denied the charges became a torrent of hundreds, all vociferously declaring to

---

43. Rymer, vol. 1, pt. 4, p. 100.
44. Barber, *Trial of the Templars*, 292.

the papal commission the innocence of the order and the invalidity of their previous confessions, extracted by extreme torture. Their defense gathered such momentum that from February to April 1310 it seemed that they might succeed in exonerating themselves. The torrent was soon dammed, however, when fifty-four of the nearly six hundred Templars who had recanted their confessions went to the stake on May 12.[45] According to a contemporary chronicler, "all of them, with no exception, finally acknowledged none of the crimes imputed to them, but constantly persisted in the general denial, saying always that they were being put to death without cause and unjustly: which indeed many of the people were able to observe by no means without great admiration and immense surprise."[46] Several more Templars were sent to the stake in the days that followed. Those who maintained their innocence were sentenced to perpetual imprisonment, whereas those who confirmed their confessions were reconciled and released.[47] The last executions occurred in 1314, when the grand master himself and Geoffroi de Charney, the preceptor of Normandy, were burned at the stake on Philip's orders after insisting that their confessions were false and their order innocent.[48]

The Trial in Britain

While Philip engineered the trial in France, Edward II played a much more ambiguous role in the trial in his domains. His surprise and indignation rivaled the pope's when Philip informed him of the arrests in France. In his reply of October 30, 1307, Edward declared the accusations to be beyond belief; in a letter to other Christian kings issued December 4, he emphasized the Templars' excellent reputation, with nearly two centuries of courageous and honorable service of the faith, urged his fellow rulers to ignore detractors who were motivated more by greed and envy than by righteousness, and entreated them not to allow the brothers or their property to be harmed unless the allegations were justly proved; six days later, he wrote to Clement echoing the same sentiments and exhorting the pope to endeavor to clear the order.[49] But then Edward received *Pastoralis praeeminentiae* and quickly complied, beginning the process for the arrest the following day, December 15.

---

45. Barber notes that those burned at Paris may not all have recanted their confessions; rather, the burnings may have been indiscriminate (ibid., 179).

46. The continuator of Guillaume de Nangis, quoted (in English) in Barber, *Trial of the Templars*, 178.

47. Ibid., 178.

48. Ibid., 281–82.

49. Rymer, vol. 1, pt. 4, pp. 94–95, 101, and 102.

Five days later, he wrote to the justiciar and treasurer of Ireland, informing them that the arrests would be made in England on January 10 and ordering them to select a day for the arrests in Ireland, "taking care to execute it before the tidings of what has been done in England herein can reach Ireland." That same day he sent similar letters to his ministers in Scotland, Wales, and Chester, and the day after Christmas he wrote to the pope, declaring that he "fully understands the affairs connected with the Templars" and promising to promptly perform the papal will.[50]

When Edward received Philip's first report, he had occupied the throne only a few months, his wedding to Philip's daughter Isabella was imminent, and his father's wars, many of them against Philip, had drained the English coffers almost as dry as the French. Edward's defense of the Templars, brief though it was, showed considerable courage, integrity, and initiative for an untried king. But to oppose his future father-in-law in a matter of the faith was one thing; to oppose the pope took more loyalty to the order than Edward possessed. Once Clement had given qualified approval of the Templars' arrest and had ordered him to do the same, Edward availed himself of the opportunity to help his faltering finances by appropriating their wealth, as Philip had done. Besides the financial benefits he received from the seizure, which turned out to be less than he had anticipated, he received religious rewards from the pope, including absolution from deeds done in time of war and the preclusion of any papal legate placing him under excommunication or interdict.[51] Edward's rapid turnaround might not be laudable, but it is understandable, and the Templars in his lands were well treated—that is, until the summer of 1311.

Clement appointed Dieudonné, abbot of Lagny in the diocese of Paris, and Sicard de Vaur, a canon of Narbonne and papal notary, as the inquisitors of Britain in conjunction with the archbishops and bishops of the island; after they arrived in England, the trial commenced on October 20, 1309. Apart from some confusion about absolution among Templars in York and Scotland, which would also surface in Ireland, and some hostile but empty claims from outside witnesses, especially in Scotland, little damaging evidence was given before June 1311. Most Templars declared the testimonies given by their brothers in France to be untrue or claimed ignorance; less than a fifth accepted them, and those did so primarily out of respect for the pope, who in *Faciens misericordiam* asserted their validity. The inquisitors made extensive use of outside witnesses, as English common law did not allow for the use

---

50. *CCR* (1307–13): 48–49.
51. Rymer, vol. 1, pt. 4, p. 141.

of torture, nor did the English support its use in a religious trial, and confessions proved negligible without it. Edward repeatedly instructed his agents to allow the inquisitors to have free reign over the Templars and their bodies in accordance with ecclesiastical law, provided nothing was done against the crown or kingdom, and appointed William de Dien to assist the inquisitors to these ends in February 1310.[52] On June 16, 1310, however, the inquisitors issued a report to the archbishop of Canterbury decrying the lack of cooperation they had received regarding torture from the English, including William de Dien, and proposing eight ways in which the proceedings might be more successfully continued.[53] These included transferring the Templars and their trial to Ponthieu, which was part of Edward's realm yet outside of Britain, so torture could be more freely applied.

Clement took up the inquisitors' case the following August, admonishing the English bishops for failing to assist the inquisitors to effect torture and reprimanding Edward for refusing torture.[54] Shortly thereafter, Edward again repeated his commands that the inquisitors were to have free reign over the Templars in accordance with ecclesiastical law, which after 1252 included the use of torture to compel confessions from accused heretics, but these orders seem to have been as effective as his earlier ones, for two months later they were again reissued. Meanwhile, in September 1310, the provincial council decreed at Canterbury that if the Templars still would not confess after being placed in solitary confinement, they should at last be tortured, although not to the point of maiming, permanent disablement, or violent and profuse bloodshed.[55] Still, torture seems to have been avoided in England, for in December 1310 the archbishop of York noted that though other Templars have confessed elsewhere (presumably France), those in York will not do so without torture and no torturer can be found in England.[56] That same month Clement wrote to Edward once again, claiming the king's immortal soul was in peril due to his contempt of the papal will and offering him remission of sins and God's eternal mercy on the condition that he assist the inquisitors and arrange for the proceedings to be transferred to Ponthieu.[57]

The Templars, however, remained in Britain, and at last the inquisitors achieved the kind of confessions they had sought for so long in the southern

---

52. Powicke and Cheney, *Councils and Synods*, 2:1268; *CPR* (1307–13): 203, 208–9; Rymer, vol. 1, pt. 4, pp. 163, 165–66.

53. App. 1 in Perkins, "History of the Knights Templar," 243–47.

54. *Regestum Clementis Papae V*, 6376, year 5, pp. 433–36, and 6378, year 5, pp. 437–38.

55. Wilkins, *Concilia*, 314.

56. Perkins, "History of the Knights Templar," 170; Walter of Guisborough, *Chronicle*, 392.

57. *Regestum Clementis Papae V*, 6670, year 5, pp. 484–86.

province in June 1311, with three fugitive Templars who had recently been captured and were subjected to torture: Thomas de Thoraldeby, who had escaped two times before, once after bribing his jailor; John de Stoke, the treasurer of the New Temple who had carried Walter le Bacheler to his grave; and Stephen de Stappelbrugge, who may be the same Stephen de Stappelbrugge named among Templars receiving a royal allowance in Ireland in 1308.[58] On June 23, two weeks after his arrest in England, Stephen was brought before the inquisitors and confessed to two kinds of reception, one good and the other against the faith, involving denial of Christ and Mary as well as spitting on the cross, which he did with his mouth but not in his heart. He added that those who refused to participate in these heinous acts in transmarine lands were killed, but he did not know of such happening in England; though he was familiar with the case of Walter le Bacheler, he specifically said that this was not the reason for his fate.[59] He also attributed cat and idol worship to the Templars abroad but said this was not practiced in England. He admitted that homosexuality was permitted among the Templars, though he had never engaged in it, and claimed that no absolution was necessary apart from that bestowed by the master in chapter. At the end of his examination, "kneeling on the ground, with his eyes to heaven and his hands clasped together, he begged devoutly for mercy and the grace of Holy Church with tears, sighs, and lamentation. And he asked that wholesome penance be imposed upon him for his sins, saying that he did not care about the death of the flesh, nor about any other torment, but only about the salvation of his soul."[60] This was a response the inquisitors had been unable to elicit prior to the introduction of torture, and the inquisitors complained no more about English reluctance to allow its use.

A few days later, Thomas de Thoraldeby was examined and admitted little that was incriminating. Shortly thereafter, he was again interrogated and this time confessed to the double reception and the concomitant crimes. He further claimed that all in the order were guilty of illicit absolution or some other illicit act.[61] John de Stoke was examined next, on July 1. Though he had denied all charges when interrogated months before, this time he claimed he had been forced to deny Christ by the grand master himself in the presence of two foreign brothers; though he had at first refused, he had acquiesced after being threatened with imprisonment in a sack that would

58. Wilkins, *Concilia*, 385–86; Nicholson, *Proceedings Against the Templars*, 1:354, 2:403.
59. Wilkins, *Concilia*, 384; Nicholson, *Proceedings Against the Templars*, 1:350–51.
60. Wilkins, *Concilia*, 384; Nicholson, *Proceedings Against the Templars*, 1:351.
61. Wilkins, *Concilia*, 386–87; Nicholson, *Proceedings Against the Templars*, 1:357, 2:409.

be taken to a place "where he would never find a friend, nor would it be well with him ever again."[62] Like Stephen de Stappelbrugge before him, John ended his examination by prostrating himself, begging forgiveness, and submitting himself to the church's judgment. Having been induced by torture to a "saner spirit," all three were then received back into the church.[63] The inquisitors then turned their attention to William de la More, master of England, but again he refused to confess to the charges and insisted on his innocence until his death in the Tower on December 20, 1312.

True to the inquisitors' words, torture facilitated the end of the trial in England. Over the month of July, over a hundred brothers declared themselves unable to purge themselves of the order's alleged crimes, abjured all errors in general, a few abjuring the heresy of lay absolution in specific, and were reconciled with the church. The provincial councils then decreed that these brothers should be separated and sent to perform penance in various monasteries.[64] And so ended the trial of the Templars in England. By that point, however, the trial had been concluded in Ireland for over a year, and for ten days before the inquisitors issued their letter to the archbishop of Canterbury complaining at length of their inability to employ torture in Edward's realms. Intriguingly, the author of the account of the trial in Britain continues this antipathy to torture, as he ends with a summary of the terrors, specifically including bloodshed, inflicted on the three Templars by the bishops themselves, their clerics, and *severas et crudelas personas laicas* (harsh and cruel laypeople) in order to obtain confessions.[65] Yet torture was not requisite for confession, as a few of the Templars in Ireland admitted guilt all the same.

The Trial in Ireland

In conjunction with *Faciens misericordiam*, Clement issued a mandate to Ireland's four archbishops, as well as the archbishops of Canterbury and York, to cite before them the Templars in their archdioceses and to begin an inquisition into the charges against them.[66] The English archbishops played an active role once the trial began in England over a year later, but if any Irish

---

62. Wilkins, *Concilia*, 388; Nicholson, *Proceedings Against the Templars*, 1:358. The Latin is in second, not third, person and the future, not subjunctive, tense.

63. Wilkins, *Concilia*, 388–89; Nicholson, *Proceedings Against the Templars*, 1:359.

64. Perkins, "History of the Knights Templar," 167; Wilkins, *Concilia*, 314, 391–94; Nicholson, *Proceedings Against the Templars*, 1:363–70; Rymer, vol. 1, pt. 4, p. 202.

65. Oxford, Bodleian Library, Bodley 454, fol. 170r; Nicholson, *Proceedings Against the Templars*, 1:371.

66. *Regestum Clementis Papae V*, year 3, 3422, p. 291, 3488–91, p. 305, 3496–97, pp. 307–8, 3516, pp. 316–17; *CPL*, 2:48.

archbishops heeded the papal command the records have been lost.[67] Edward II had already followed papal commands and ordered the Templars' arrest throughout his lands in December 1307. Though the royal writ was not received in Ireland until two weeks after the arrests had occurred in Britain (January 25, 1308), the justiciar, John Wogan, allowed for no further delay. He followed the procedures outlined by the king with remarkable efficiency, and on February 3, the Templars were arrested and their property in all four provinces taken into the king's hand.[68]

The records documenting the arrest pay closer attention to Templar goods than to the brothers themselves, carefully detailing the property seized, its value, and its fate, but mentioning only eleven Templars, three of them solely in connection with the worth of their beds.[69] This material emphasis arises from the primary purpose of the extant accounts of the seizure, drawn up twenty years later as part of the audit of the former treasurer of Ireland and then archbishop of Dublin, Alexander de Bicknor. Four of the Templars mentioned are not included among the nineteen Templars named as receiving wages from the king beginning the day of their arrest, though two of those four were among the fourteen Templars examined in 1310.[70] Thus at least twenty-three Templars seem to have been arrested in Ireland, but the fate of two of those men after February 3, 1308 is unknown.[71] They may have died by Michaelmas 1308, when the pensions were recorded, as perhaps did Thomas of Rathenny and Michael of Sutton between then and February 1310, when the trial began.[72] Others may have fled Ireland prior to the arrest, as they were most likely aware of the events in France and perhaps of the arrests in England, but if so, they have eluded the records as well as the authorities.[73] Two of the nineteen seem to have been fugitives from England themselves: Stephen de Stappelbrugge, whose torture in June

---

67. The only named episcopal representative in the trial records is John le Marshall, a canon of Kildare, specially commissioned by the bishop of Kildare to attend the proceedings. The vicar of the archbishop-elect of Dublin, however, was one of the inquisitors.

68. *CCR* (1307–13): 49.

69. Mac Niocaill, "Documents Relating to the Suppression of the Templars in Ireland," 193–218. No Templars are mentioned in connection with the seizure of their property at Clontarf, Loghnehely, Rathbride, or Kilcork (ibid., 211, 214–17). Templar property was also seized in Drogheda and Meath, but they seem to have had only lands and tenants there (ibid., 218).

70. *IEP*, 1:204, 209.

71. Peter de Malverne (Mac Niocaill, "Documents Relating to the Suppression of the Templars in Ireland," 199, 202; Wood, "Templars in Ireland," 337) and Thomas le Palmer (Mac Niocaill, "Documents Relating to the Suppression of the Templars in Ireland," 207).

72. Nicholson, *Knights Templar on Trial*, 148.

73. The number is small for the thirteen manors they held at the time of their dissolution, but only Kilclogan seems to have housed more than one or two Templars.

of 1311 provided the inquisitors with the confession they had so ardently sought, and Thomas de Lindsey, who returned to England in 1312, submitted to the church, and received penance; the circumstances surrounding their departure from Ireland are unknown.[74] Templars in Ireland fared reasonably well during their imprisonment and received more generous financial support than did their brothers in Britain.[75] Henry Danet was released on bail in Michaelmas term 1312, with William de Hothum, who had observed Henry's interrogation and who earlier that year had been appointed chancellor of the Irish exchequer, as one of his pledges, and the others may have regained their freedom soon after.[76] The exchequer continued to pay their wages until April 7, 1314, after which point the burden of their support, now one-quarter of the original rate, fell on the Hospitallers.[77]

At the end of September 1309, Edward ordered Wogan to arrest any Templars still at large and to deliver them and those already imprisoned to the archbishop-elect of Dublin or his vicar. He also named the deputies selected by the English inquisitors: Thomas, dean of Dublin, Bindus de Bandinell, of St. Paul's in the diocese of Florence, and John Balla of Clonfert, canons.[78] Edward also sent a letter to the archbishop-elect of Dublin, Richard de Haverings, instructing him to be present in person or by his vicar at the inquisition of the Templars.[79] Haverings went beyond an absentee archbishop: provided to the see in July 1307, he resigned over three years later without seeking consecration or visiting Ireland, though he received the fruits of the office, and he does not seem to have responded to either the royal or papal commands regarding the Templars. His vicar was none other than the dean of Dublin, Thomas de Chaddesworth, who would put into practice what he learned as inquisitor in his own vendetta against Philip de Braybrook. Chaddesworth probably played a dominant role, as he was both an independent

---

74. Nicholson, "The Trial of the Templars in Ireland," 229–30; Nicholson, *Knights Templar on Trial*, 148–49.

75. *IEP*, 1:204, 209, 217, 220, 223; Tresham, 17; Memoranda Roll, Excheq., 4–5 Ed. II, m.66; Memoranda Roll, Excheq., 5–6 Ed. II, m.12, m.24; RC 8/5, 810; RC 8/6, 91–93, 164–65; Wood, "Templars in Ireland," 357.

76. Dr. Connolly located this reference to Danet, which Wood misidentified ("Templars in Ireland," 357). It is from the justiciary roll for 6–7 Edward I, which Dr. Connolly was preparing for publication at the time of her unexpected and much lamented death (personal correspondence, April 2002).

77. *IEP*, 1:223; Rymer, vol. 2, pt. 1, pp. 62–63.

78. Rymer, vol. 1, pt. 4, p. 157; *CPR* (1307–13): 192; *CCR* (1307–13): 179. A letter of safe conduct was also issued for "John de Solercio, going to Ireland as deputy to the commissioners appointed by the Pope to hold an enquiry in that country touching the Knights Templars" (*CPR* [1307–13]: 193). This is most likely a mistake, as Solercio was sent to Scotland as deputy to the inquisitors.

79. Rymer, vol. 1, pt. 4, p. 157.

FIGURE 3. St. Patrick's Cathedral, Dublin. Photo by the author.

inquisitor and the vicar of the archbishop-elect of Dublin, a position he had filled for various archbishops since 1271, and the trial was held in his home court, St. Patrick's Cathedral, from January or February until June, 1310.

The only extant account of the trial, Oxford, Bodleian Library, Bodley 454, folios 134–55, is incomplete, lacking the introductory material naming the inquisitors, the place of the trial, the defendants, and the date the proceedings began. Only fourteen of the twenty-three Templars arrested in Ireland were examined, and it seems unlikely that other Templars were involved, as only those fourteen appear among the list of Templars present on May 23, at which point their examinations had finished, and on June 6, when the trial as a whole was concluded in Ireland. In addition, each Templar was questioned at least three times, and two, Richard de Bustlesham and William de Kilros, were examined four times; no other Templars surface as witnesses amid these multiple interrogations.[80] At least seven other Templars were receiving allowances during the time of the trial, one of whom, William de Warenne, until recently the master of Ireland himself and the only other Templar identified as a knight, was accused of various misdoings by three of the forty-two outside witnesses. The records do not explain why these Templars were not

---

80. The name William de Cheneley is given on fol. 150r, but this seems a mistake for Walter de Choneby.

examined. Nicholson suggests that William de Warenne's family connections spared him the humiliation of interrogation, yet also engendered some of the hostility against him from outside witnesses. If Stephen de Stappelbrugge and Thomas de Lindsey were fugitives from England, the inquisitors may have felt their testimony lacked relevance for the Irish context; a third Templar, Walter le Lung, may have been a fugitive from York and may have been excluded for similar reasons.[81] In addition, ill health after two years of imprisonment may have been a factor. One of the imprisoned Templars may have died by Michaelmas 1311 and another by Michaelmas 1312, as the number of those receiving wages fell from nineteen to seventeen and then to fifteen for those periods.[82]

Nine preliminary questions preceded the eighty-eight articles in each Templar's first recorded examination.[83] The first three established guilt by association, for all fourteen verified that the same customs were practiced throughout the order, that the manner of reception and profession was identical wherever one entered the order, and that whatever the grand master decreed held true for all Templars everywhere. They were then asked where, when, by whom, and in whose presence they had been received into the order. Five entered in Ireland, including Adam de Langeport, who at nearly forty years had been in the order the longest and had been present at three of the other four receptions in Ireland. Eight brothers entered in England, and one, Richard de Bustlesham, was received in Tripoli in the presence of two future masters of England, Brian le Jay and William de la More. Only one other Templar among those examined had explicitly spent time overseas: Henry Danet had spent two and a half of his seven years in the order accompanying the grand master abroad before being chosen to be the master of Ireland three years previously. Some confusion exists about Henry's time in the order and in Ireland, however, but he likely arrived on February 1, 1307, just over a year before the arrests.[84] The average time spent in the order was

---

81. Nicholson, *Knights Templar on Trial*, 148–50; Nicholson, "The Trial of the Templars in Ireland," 229–30.

82. *IEP*, 1:217, 220, 223. Stephen's and Thomas's return to England in 1311 and 1312 respectively would account for the loss of one in each period.

83. Six of those questions also constitute article 86. For the articles, see appendix A.

84. Apparently on February 25, 1310, Henry testified that he had entered the order "seven years ago on the next vigil of the Purification of blessed Mary" and had been in Ireland for three years, also since the next February 1, having come from "transmarine lands" (Oxford, Bodleian Library, Bodley 454, fol. 139v; Nicholson, *Proceedings Against the Templars*, 1:301). If this is accurate, then he arrived in Ireland only two days before the Templars were arrested (February 3, 1308), having travelled throughout western Europe as Templars were rounded up and imprisoned, which seems improbable. No other evidence indicates that Henry's knowledge of Ireland and its Templars was confined to two days before arrest. Wood suggests that Henry was first interviewed in January 1310 and was stating

twenty-one years, though Ralph de Bradeley had entered the order less than three years before the arrest. Other than Henry Danet and Ralph de Bradeley, all the brothers had been in the order longer than ten years, and eight had been brothers for twenty years or more (that is, prior to the fall of Acre). The Templars were then asked at what time of night they had been received, to which they all responded they were not received at night but at dawn. The last question posed prior to the articles concerned the manner in which they were received, to which they all said they swore obedience, to live without property, and chastity. None of the Templars mentioned vows to aid the Holy Land, as their brethren did elsewhere, further evidence that the Templars in Ireland were less committed to the cause for which their order had been founded and upon which it floundered.[85]

Absolution

Though most of their brethren in Britain denied the validity of the French confessions, the Templars tried in Ireland unanimously accepted them on the basis of the papal bull. Yet all but Henry Danet denied any knowledge of blasphemous acts, apostasy, or idol worship, and William de Kilros provided the single admission of homosexual activity within the order, and then only after denying any such knowledge in three previous interrogations. Confusion did exist about the nature of absolution within the order, however. Several admitted articles 24–26 and 28, which stated that they believed and were told that the grand master, visitor, and preceptor, though laymen, could absolve members of the order, though all claimed them to be privileges (article 27). Thirteen Templars admitted article 74, that they were instructed not to confess to anyone who was not a member of the order, although nine of those added "provided they could have them" (i.e., provided they had access to Templars to confess to). The one exception, significantly the chaplain, claimed ignorance, though he also added the most information concerning absolution.

The problem of Templar absolution arose from their papal privileges compounded by distance from the development of sacramental theory in the thirteenth century.[86] Their Primitive Rule, to a large extent authored by Bernard

---

that he arrived in Ireland on February 1, 1307 (Wood, "Templars in Ireland," 352). I agree that Henry meant that he arrived in Ireland on February 1, 1307, but think it likely that either he or the scribe mistakenly used *proxime* (next) when the much nearer prior (*priore*) February 1 was intended.

85. For example, all twenty-three Templars examined in York in April and May 1310 included this promise about the Holy Land among their reception vows (Perkins, "History of the Knights Templar," 126n3).

86. See Lea, "Absolution Formula," in *Minor Historical Writings*, 97–112.

of Clairvaux, instructed brothers to confess their sins to the master, who in consultation with others decided the penance to be assigned.[87] The dynamics of confession within the order changed after the bull *Omne datum optimum*, given March 29, 1139, enabled the order to include its own clerics. According to the French Rule, Templars were to confess only to a Templar chaplain, who had "greater power to absolve them on behalf of the pope than [did] an archbishop."[88] They could, however, confess to another in times of great necessity and when no Templar chaplain was available.[89] When a Templar chaplain was not present, a secular priest could serve in his stead with regard to his penance or the master or chapter leader might do so before the other brothers, but no mention is made of alternative absolution.[90] William de la More admitted that at the close of chapter he forgave brothers as far as he was able according to the power granted to him by God and the pope for sins that remained unconfessed due to frailty of the flesh or fear of the order's justice, a statement supported by the testimony of several other Templars in England.[91] This practice was apparently common in France as well, and it seems to be an alteration of article 539 of the French Rule that declared that those who did *not* neglect to confess their sins due to shame or fear and were truly repentant shared in the forgiveness of the chapter.[92] Even so, the forgiveness offered both by More and by article 539 was done in the interests of harmony of the house and did not constitute absolution.

Although the inclusion of priests within the order could have alleviated what was presented as a heretical practice in their trial, chaplains never entered the order in great numbers. Only 8 of the nearly 150 Templars tried in Britain were chaplains, and the percentage was even smaller among those tried in France.[93] The honors they were accorded within the order, such as the finest robes, a privileged place at table, and exemption from menial labor, apparently could not compensate for the circumscription of their power and prestige within a military order.[94] William de Kilros, the only chaplain among the Templars arrested in Ireland, clearly resented the limitations placed upon priests in the order, claiming that "when any cleric [has entered the order],

---

87. Upton-Ward, *Rule of the Templars*, 30.
88. Ibid., 79, art. 269.
89. Ibid., 98, art. 354. See also 137, art. 525.
90. Ibid., 137, art. 525, and 137, art. 524. See also 138–39, arts. 532–34.
91. Perkins, "History of the Knights Templar," 131.
92. Lea, "Absolution Formula," 110; Upton-Ward, *Rule of the Templars*, 140.
93. For England, see Barber, *Trial of the Templars*, 229. For France, see Lea, "Absolution Formula," 108; see also Forey, *Military Orders and Crusades*, 145; Gilmour-Bryson, *Trial of the Templars in Cyprus*, 31; and Gilmour-Bryson, "Priests of the Order of the Temple," 337.
94. See Barber, *New Knighthood*, 197–98.

whether he has the first tonsure or is an acolyte, a subdeacon, or a deacon, he always remains in the grade in which he was received and will not be promoted to another grade in the order."[95] The practice of confessing exclusively to Templar priests was claimed by opponents as a means of keeping nefarious deeds hidden from outsiders, but the order in Ireland as elsewhere did not have enough priests to enable them to take advantage of this papal privilege. William de Kilros could not consistently serve his twenty-two brothers in their houses scattered throughout the island, and they must have often relied on outside priests, as is suggested by the testimony of outside witnesses. Three spoke of alleged Templar offenses in Ireland concerning the mass and confession, which two described as being administered by non-Templars; the third did not mention the priest. Nine Templars seem to be alluding to this sacerdotal shortage in their qualification, "provided they could have them," to article 74, that they were instructed not to confess to anyone who was not a member of the order.

Article 74 was almost universally affirmed by the Templars in Ireland; the one exception, significantly the chaplain, claimed ignorance, though he also added the most information concerning absolution. In his first examination, William de Kilros asserted that brothers confessed only venial sins to the chaplain; their other sins were confessed in chapter and absolved by the master and preceptor.[96] At his fourth interrogation, he added that after the grand master had heard a brother's confession, he ordered the chaplain to absolve him, although the chaplain had not heard his confession.[97] This, however, contradicts his earlier testimony, which alleged that the master absolved brothers in his own right. Perhaps from fear of the implications of his position, William pleaded ignorance as to whether or not Templars were required to confess only to their own chaplains, as their Rule clearly stipulated and as all other Templars in Ireland admitted.

Only four of the fourteen Templars consistently claimed that the order's officers could absolve brothers' sins, and the testimony of one, William de Kilros, is fairly suspect. Moreover, it is unlikely that any but Henry Danet and Richard de Bustlesham had any contact with a grand master, and thus would not know from direct experience what the grand master did or did not do in chapter (article 24). Visitors (article 25) may have been as unfamiliar

---

95. Oxford, Bodleian Library, Bodley 454, fol. 149v; Nicholson, *Proceedings Against the Templars*, 1:325.

96. Oxford, Bodleian Library, Bodley 454, fol. 148v; Nicholson, *Proceedings Against the Templars*, 1:323.

97. Oxford, Bodleian Library, Bodley 454, fol. 150r; Nicholson, *Proceedings Against the Templars*, 1:327.

as grand masters to the Templars of Ireland, if the testimony of Ralph de Bradeley is any indication. When asked the duties of a visitor, the only one to be asked such a question, he responded that he had never seen a visitor but he believed their responsibilities were selling Templar property, raising money, and bringing it to transmarine lands. While such may have formed part of visitors' activities, their chief responsibilities concerned regulating and reforming various Templar houses in a province, but Ralph mentioned nothing of this.[98] Ralph also was asked what kind of sins were confessed in chapter, to which he responded, "destruction of the houses and forests and the like."[99] If such sins were representative of the substance of capitular confession, it is little surprise that certain brothers believed that their officers could absolve them, as such offenses were more against the order and its rule than against God and his church.

Secrecy and Cords

The only other areas in which the Templars proved vulnerable, apart from the lurid hearsay reported by the master and the chaplain, were their loyalty to and the strictness and secrecy of the order. The first three defendants admitted to vowing to do whatever they could to benefit the order *per phas et nephas* (through licit and illicit means; article 78), though all three declared it a sin (article 79). One (Richard de Bustlesham) later recanted his confession of article 78, and the other eleven Templars all denied such an oath throughout their multiple examinations. Articles 34 through 37, which stated that receptions were secret and closed to outsiders, that they included a vow never to leave the order, and that after his reception each initiate was immediately regarded as a professed brother, were affirmed whenever included in the recorded testimony. The Templars also unanimously admitted article 71, that they were not to reveal the manner of reception. Two claimed that they were not to talk about their reception with other members of the order (article 72), though eleven declared that they could discuss their reception with other brothers but not with outsiders.[100] In response to article 73, that if any were found to have revealed these things, they were

---

98. If visitors rarely visited Templar houses, abuses and irregularities may well have become common in the order. The admittedly sparse records for the Templars in Ireland do not indicate that a visitation ever occurred there. According to Alan Forey, Templar records generally ignore visitations and their frequency cannot be determined (personal correspondence, September 2013).

99. Oxford, Bodleian Library, Bodley 454, fol. 144v; Nicholson, *Proceedings Against the Templars*, 1:312.

100. Richard de Bustlesham's testimony omits article 72.

punished by death or imprisonment, six said they had never known or heard of any Templar ever being punished by death or incarceration by the order, though three allowed for the exception of Walter le Bacheler. The other eight, however, said those who revealed the reception to non-Templars would be punished severely, five of those also mentioning Walter le Bacheler, though none attributed his fate to any disclosures about the manner of reception. Yet, apart from the confessions to article 78, nothing in these admissions is damaging unless one assumes that Templars were engaged in the alleged blasphemous, idolatrous, and homosexual acts, which all fourteen Templars denied participating in and of which only two admitted to having any knowledge independent of the papal bull.

Another Templar custom, that of constantly wearing cords, came under suspicion during their inquisition, which attributed the practice to idol worship (articles 58 and 60). Though they denied any connections with idol worship, all fourteen admitted that they were commanded to and did wear such cords (article 61). Two (Richard de Bustlesham and Robert de Pourbriggs) explained the custom as arising from veneration of the Virgin Mary and said that such cords were tied around a column in the chapel of Mary in Nazareth. This serves in a summary of the trial in the British Isles as the most common explanation, other than that they used the cords only for licit and good purposes.[101] As Nicholson has noted, this explanation, which was also offered by brothers tried in France, probably arose within the context of the legend of Mary's upbringing in a temple in Nazareth, where the Annunciation had taken place.[102] Ironically, contemporary heretical sects criticized Marian devotion as idolatry, but in a Catholic context this practice and its origin should have been regarded as orthodox. Henry Danet said the cords were worn so that the brothers could always be ready for war against the Saracens; similarly, William de Kilros asserted that they were worn so that brothers could always be ready for service of the order, though it is not clear how such cords lent themselves to perpetual preparedness. John de Faversham claimed the practice was adopted so that a brother would not touch his flesh with his hands, which is another obscure explanation since these cords were said to be small and worn above clothes. The other nine brothers said that they did not know why they were commanded to wear them, and such ignorance was also common among their brothers in France. *Les*

---

101. "Deminutio," in Schottmüller, *Der Untergang des Templerordens*, 2:65, 93; see also Stubbs, *Annales Londonienses*, 195; Wilkins, *Concilia*, 366, Nicholson, *Proceedings Against the Templars*, 1:220, 2:245.

102. Nicholson, *Knights Templar*, 143.

Grandes Chroniques de France, a roughly contemporary semiofficial history of the Capetian kings from the Abbey of Saint-Denis, had a ready explanation, however: the cords were proof of Templar treason with Muslims.[103] To this theory Barber adds another: the church believed that such a practice was indicative of Catharism, as they thought it was a sign of having received the *consolamentum*.[104] Yet this seems a stretch, as the wearing of cords, particularly those that had touched venerated relics, was a common devotional practice of the time.

Testimony of the Preceptor and the Priest

Two Templars provided evidence that was particularly damaging to the order while studiously avoiding self-incrimination: Henry Danet, the master of Ireland, and William de Kilros, the chaplain. Whereas the other twelve brothers said they did not know if the secrecy of the order had aroused suspicion against it (article 38), these two acknowledged such suspicion and added their own allegations against members of their order. According to Henry, he had heard a rumor common among the laity that the Templars ate one of their brothers during chapter, which he asserted was not true.[105] During his fourth examination, William theorized that the order's rapid exaltation as well as its friendship and business with the Saracens had led to such suspicion. At this time he also claimed to have heard that a brother whose name he did not know was a sodomite and consequently confined at Killofan, where he had later died.[106] This is the single admission in Ireland of homosexual acts within the order, and it significantly was given after William had endured three previous interrogations in which he had denied any knowledge of such acts. At his first examination, on March 24, 1310, he offered incriminating evidence regarding absolution alone, though he apparently admitted having heard of suspicion against the order. Four days later, he added his statement concerning limitations placed upon clerics within the order. On April 12, he affirmed what he said on March 28. Then at his fourth examination he added his theory about the source of suspicion against the order, his claim that the master commanded the chaplain to absolve brothers for sins he

---

103. Barber, *Trial of the Templars*, 206.

104. Ibid., 213. Barber also suggests that the Templars did not actually wear these cords.

105. A like allegation was repeated and then denied by Thomas de Broghton, an outside witness who had formerly served the Templars (Oxford, Bodleian Library, Bodley 454, fol. 153v; Nicholson, *Proceedings Against the Templars*, 1:336; see below).

106. Nicholson tentatively identifies Killofan with Kilsaran in Co. Louth (*Knights Templar on Trial*, 154).

had not heard, his awareness of the fate of Walter le Bacheler, whom he had not mentioned previously, and finally his allegation that an anonymous Templar sodomite had been imprisoned and died at Killofan. While torture could have induced William to relate such tales, brutal force was probably not applied in Ireland, as discussed below. Perhaps repeated interrogations combined with long imprisonment helped William to disclose, remember, or invent certain information that he thought would please the inquisitors.

While it took William four examinations to offer seriously incriminating evidence against the order apart from the matter of absolution, Henry Danet made his allegations against foreign brothers right from the start. His first examination apparently occurred on February 25, and in response to the first article, regarding the denial of Christ et cetera, Henry offered two separate accusations against brothers in Syria.[107] Though he maintained that he had never done or been advised to do such things, he claimed to have heard of a Templar marshal at Tortosa who had abandoned his faith as well as his castle to the sultan of Babylon.[108] He added that he had heard of a certain preceptor of Castle Pilgrim in Syria who received many brothers whom he required to make such denials, though Henry did not know the names either of the preceptor or of those he had received.[109] To article 16, which stated that Templars did not believe in the sacrament of the altar, Henry maintained that he deeply believed in the sacrament and always had, but in Cyprus he had seen a brother named Hugh de la Roche who did not believe in the sacraments and for which disbelief he had been imprisoned. He continued that he had seen many brothers of the order, and especially those from Catalonia, who shared Hugh's unbelief. In his reply to article 26, he blamed Burgundian preceptors alone for misleading those they received regarding their abilities to absolve. His initial response to article 46, that brothers in every province had idols or heads, was that he had never known or heard of Templars having such things, yet he immediately contradicted this denial, stating that he had heard of a Catalan brother who had a double-faced oracular bronze head, which he had

---

107. Henry's first examination may have occurred over two days, but February 25 is the only date given. Wood theorizes that he was first interrogated in January ("Templars in Ireland," 352); see above.

108. The tale might be a distortion of an incident at Gaston, where an unnamed Templar brought the castle's keys to the sultan, Baybars (Upton-Ward, *Catalan Rule of the Templars*, section 180; Vogel, "Templar Runaways and Renegades," 322). Nicholson connects it with Brother Hugh of Ampurias's advice to surrender the island of Ruad, also known as Tortosa, to the Muslims ("Testimony of Brother Henry Danet," 418).

109. For Castle Pilgrim (aka Pelerinus Castle and 'Atlit), see Nicholson, *Knights Templar*, 60–61, 82, 86, 143, 146, 187.

heard was a common possession among the laity in those parts.[110] In response to articles 47 and 48, Henry declared that he had never heard or known of any Templar adoring such heads, but he added to his reply to article 48 "except the aforesaid preceptor and Brother Hugh and brothers received by them," a reference to those he incriminated in his answers to articles 1 and 16, though he had then alleged only denial of the faith and had not referred to idols.[111]

Other contradictions are evident in Henry's testimony. Although he provided multiple examples of errors practiced by brothers from Catalonia to Syria, some of which he claimed to have personally witnessed, in his reply to articles 75 and 77 he asserted that he had never known nor heard of such errors and thus had not left the order.[112] In the context of articles 66–68, that those who refused to participate in the alleged obscenities at the reception were murdered or imprisoned, he said that he had never heard that any Templar had ever been punished by death or incarceration except Walter le Bacheler, who he said was punished on account of theft, yet in his answer to article 16 Henry spoke of having been witness to Hugh's imprisonment for rejecting the sacraments. It is unlikely that torture was used to extract such evidence, and the inquisitors apparently did not pursue the inconsistencies that riddle his testimony, as one would expect in an exacting court. Henry garnered the greatest number of outside observers during at least the first part of his first examination, one of whom, William de Hothum, the future chancellor of the Irish exchequer, proved his friendliness to Henry when he served as his pledge in his release from prison two years later. William was joined by John le Marshall, a canon of Kildare who was acting as his bishop's representative; Peter Wylyby, the rector of the church of Ballygriffin; the Franciscans Roger de Eton, then warden of his order, and Walter (here mistakenly named William) Prendregest, the order's lector, both of whom also witnessed the examinations of Henry de Haselakeby and Adam de Langeport; and the Dominicans Philip de Slane, then lector of his order and the future bishop of Cork, and Hugh de Saint Leodegario, who along with Roger and Walter also observed the trials of Henry de Haselakeby and Adam, and with Richard de Balybyn, described as the former minister of the Dominicans, witnessed

---

110. Catalonia and Iberia generally had a reputation for the occult, due in part to its combination of Jewish, Muslim, and Christian cultures. See Ryan, *Kingdom of Stargazers*, and Rider, *Magic and Religion*, 121–23.

111. Oxford, Bodleian Library, Bodley 454, fol. 141r; Nicholson, *Proceedings Against the Templars*, 1:304.

112. Article 76 is omitted from Henry's recorded testimony.

the trial of Richard de Bustlesham.[113] Their presence perhaps increased the pressure put upon Henry, causing him to contradict himself and embellish his testimony. As the highest ranking Templar with respect to both his office and his camaraderie with Jacques de Molay, in whose entourage he had spent two and a half years overseas, he may well have been aware of rumors against the order and of misdeeds committed by its members to a greater extent than his brethren in Ireland. Not once, however, did Henry incriminate himself, the order in Ireland or Britain, or his friend Jacques de Molay, who he knew had already confessed to many of the charges.

Torture and Confession

Though the degree of guilt established in Ireland was marginal compared to that obtained in France, on significant points the Templars themselves provided more damaging evidence there than they did elsewhere in the British Isles before the summer of 1311, particularly in the statements about apostasy, idol worship, and homosexuality made by Henry Danet and William de Kilros. This has led Perkins to conclude that they were tortured, but such a conclusion seems far from certain.[114] Though half of the Templars in Ireland admitted to articles involving lay absolution at one point in their interrogation, a significant number of Templars in Britain made similar admissions, and such confusion has been adequately addressed by Lea.[115] Many of these admissions came from York, where it was unlikely that torture was employed, given their lax imprisonment and their vehement denial of other articles; furthermore, the archbishop himself declared in December 1310 that the Templars were not tortured there. The confessions obtained in England in the summer of 1311 demonstrate the effects of torture; if Templars in Ireland had been subjected to such treatment, one would expect more elaborate evidence that more closely conformed to the articles upon which the Templars were tried, rather than the hearsay reported by Henry Danet and William de Kilros. The three tortured Templars all incriminated themselves as well as other members of their order and tearfully begged the forgiveness of the church from its representatives, the inquisitors. Henry and William, however, directed their allegations against others; though William approached an admission of guilt when he claimed the master ordered chaplains to absolve brothers for sins they had not heard, he did not admit to obeying such orders,

---

113. Observers are mentioned only in connection with these four examinations.
114. Perkins, "History of the Knights Templar," 140, 143, 150, 151, 154, 159.
115. Lea, "Absolution Formula."

and to the one article that could have implicated him in particular (article 74), William alone of the fourteen responded *ignorat* (he does not know). Henry's initial deposition is riddled with inconsistencies that could suggest that he testified untruthfully from fear of torture, but these inconsistencies were not pursued by the inquisitors as they surely would have been in a court that applied torture in order to extract confessions.

Richard de Bustlesham, Henry de Haselakeby, and Robert Pourbriggs also made some incriminating admissions, but as they were the first three interrogated, they may have been more intimidated by the process, and one of them later retracted the more damaging statements. One of the articles admitted by at least two of them, that they were not to discuss their manner of reception with another brother, may have been a Templar custom, since receptions occurred in chapter and revealing the chapter's affairs to another brother not present was considered a serious offense.[116] As to their admission of vowing to do whatever they could to benefit the order through licit or illicit means, which they all considered a great sin, they may have interpreted one of their vows in such a fashion, an interpretation Richard later reconsidered and found incorrect. None confessed to actually doing anything illicit either for or within the order, and if the inquisitors had asked leading questions after they had been subjected to brutal treatment, they surely would have provided the inquisitors with at least one sinful act, performed by either themselves or their brothers. All of the Templars were aware of the confessions extracted from French Templars, though most had never heard of them before their imprisonment, yet only Henry Danet and William de Kilros offered testimony that compared even slightly to the French confessions.

The most persuasive evidence against Perkins's theory that torture was used on the Templars in Ireland is the inquisitors' repeated complaints about their inability to effect torture in Edward's realm in the British Isles. The Irish lordship was equally subject to English common law, and no evidence suggests that its denizens would have looked more favorably upon the use of torture in a religious trial than their compatriots in England. Although Edward repeatedly ordered his agents in England to comply with the inquisitors' requests regarding torture, the inquisitors in Ireland do not seem to have made such requests, nor did Edward instruct his agents in Ireland to facilitate the inquisitors should they wish to employ torture.[117] When the inquisitors made their most detailed report about the need for torture, significantly

---

116. See the section "Reception into the Order" in Upton-Ward, *Rule of the Templars*, 168–74, arts. 657–86, and ibid., 73, art. 225; 106, art. 390.

117. Powicke and Cheney, *Councils and Synods*, 2:1268; Rymer, 3:100, 195, 202–3; see above.

issued ten days after the trial in Ireland had finished, they advised relocating the trial to outside of the British Isles in the hopes that at long last they could find somebody who would apply torture to the Templars. About a year later, they succeeded in introducing torture into the trial and obtained confessions of a caliber unknown previously in the British Isles.

Although according to the archbishop of York the Templars would not confess without torture, neither torture nor guilt is required for confession; sometimes fear, confusion, and long imprisonment will suffice. In addition, Henry Danet may have hoped that by offering evidence against brothers in distant lands he would obtain better treatment for himself and his brothers in Ireland. William de Kilros may have felt genuinely at odds with the rest of the brothers as the only chaplain, and he clearly resented the lack of respect accorded to priests within the order. Even still, he offered little incriminating against the order apart from the matter of absolution and the incident at Killofan. His theories as to why suspicion arose against the order have been echoed by subsequent historians: their rise was too rapid and they were too familiar with Muslims for the comfort of others. Significantly, however, William did not suggest that such suspicion was deserved. The overall impression produced by the testimony of the Templars in Ireland was that their primary fault was ignorance. As Lea has argued, this explains the confusion regarding absolution, but it also surfaces in other practices, such as the wearing of cords. Only two of the twenty-three arrested in Ireland were knights, and only one a priest. The order still enjoyed considerable privileges, but the brothers apparently offered little to justify that position; they seem for the most part simple men living on borrowed glory in an order that prized its secrecy in Ireland as elsewhere. When forces outside of Ireland combined to bring about the order's downfall, the members in Ireland seem to have acquiesced to their fate. Though all asserted their own individual innocence, and only two offered specific allegations concerning other members, none rose to defend the order, as several brothers did in England; rather, all fourteen accepted the statements contained in the papal bull about the French confessions, though those confessions were used to condemn them all.

Outside Witnesses

Associative guilt was sufficient for the vast majority of outside witnesses in the trial in Ireland to find Templars there as culpable as those in France. Over three-fourths of the forty-two outside witnesses testified that they vehemently suspected Ireland's Templars due to the universal profession and reception and since the same statutes and ordinances were observed through out the order. Only about a third offered any additional "evidence" against the Templars, most of it little more than rumor, prejudice, and presumption. Walter Waspayl told the inquisitors that a friend told him of witnessing a Templar's confession of their nefarious profession to the king and his clergy in Paris and thus all Templars must be guilty.[118] Three witnesses (Richard de Balybyn, O.P., Ralph Kilmainham, F.M., and Roger, the prior of the Augustinian friars) said that they especially suspected Henry Danet due to his time in transmarine lands and his close relations with the grand master, who had appointed him preceptor of Ireland; one, Richard de Balybyn, characterized Henry as Jacques de Molay's "sidekick and roommate" (*socius collateralis et concubilaris*).[119] Nicholson interprets this as an insinuation that the two committed sodomy together.[120] While the alleged intimacy may not have extended so far, clearly Henry was regarded as too close to a renowned reprobate for his and his order's own good. Ireland's previous preceptor, William de Warenne, was the target of more substantial accusations. Adam le Latimer claimed that he had heard William scorning pilgrimage and saying that he wished the crosses of Holy Trinity and St. Patrick's as well as images of the Virgin Mary would be burned.[121] According to Philip de Kenefek', William called Jesus a whore's son.[122] Hugo de Lummour said that at Clontarf he had seen William look at the ground when the host had been elevated.[123] Hugo would later do what none of the tried Templars had apparently done, travel from Ireland to the Holy Land, though like Moses he died before he could enter, and he was buried in the Church of St. Martin in Old Cairo in 1323.[124]

The last three witnesses offered the most specific and trustworthy testimony about the Templars, yet all three focused on overseas lands and in particular Cyprus. Thomas de Broghton, who had formerly served the Templars, did not state his opinion of their guilt; instead he talked mainly about suspi-

---

118. Oxford, Bodleian Library, Bodley 454, fol. 151r; Nicholson, *Proceedings Against the Templars*, 1:330. The witnesses' testimony to the gossip spread about the Templars indicates that the trial was of greater interest to Dublin's denizens than annals would indicate.

119. Oxford, Bodleian Library, Bodley 454, fol. 151v; Nicholson, *Proceedings Against the Templars*, 1:331.

120. Nicholson, "Testimony of Brother Henry Danet," 417.

121. Oxford, Bodleian Library, Bodley 454, fol. 153v; Nicholson, *Proceedings Against the Templars*, 1:335.

122. Oxford, Bodleian Library, Bodley 454, fol. 153r; Nicholson, *Proceedings Against the Templars*, 1:334. Similar allegations were made against Adducc Dubh and the MacConmaras; see chapter 5.

123. Oxford, Bodleian Library, Bodley 454, fol. 151r; Nicholson, *Proceedings Against the Templars*, 1:329.

124. Ó Clabaigh, *Friars in Ireland*, 194–98; Marios Costambeys, "Symon Simeonis," in Matthew and Harrison, *Oxford Dictionary of National Biography*, 53:589.

cions against them, which he attributed to the order's secrecy. He often heard in overseas lands that Templars engaged in indecent kisses at their reception, or that members were placed in sacks and submerged under water, or that one brother was killed during each chapter. He did not respond to the first rumor; to the second he said that he had never been told what the purpose of such a practice might have been nor did he know of anyone to whom it had happened; the third he rejected outright, since the same number of brothers always exited the chapter as had entered it. He also told of a brother who had been imprisoned in Cyprus and had escaped to the Hospitallers, with whom he had died and who had paid for his body to be returned home. Thomas, however, did not criticize the Templars with this tale, but said simply that he did not know why the man, whom he had seen but whose name he did not know, had been imprisoned and that so far as he knew the man had never returned to the Templars again.[125]

The last two witnesses, Robert de Hereford and Michael de Bras, are not identified by order or house and may be laymen, but laymen who had spent time in Cyprus.[126] Robert informed the inquisitors that nine years ago he had heard it commonly said in Cyprus that the Templars were of bad faith and that they denied Christ and engaged in indecent kisses at their clandestine receptions.[127] When asked if the Templars of Ireland were the same, he answered yes, due to the universal profession. He then described part of the reception, without explaining how such supposedly jealously guarded information became *fama publica* (public opinion) in Cyprus and elsewhere; he claimed these features of the reception demonstrated that one could not leave the order without being killed. Michael agreed with Robert in everything, and also added the authority of a knight named Hugo de Hylibi, who he said told him the same things. Michael was the only one of the forty-two witnesses to raise the spectre of sodomy, which he said was commonly imputed to Templars overseas. He then recounted a tale that foreshadows the confession of John de Stoke a year later and echoes the information provided by Thomas de Broghton, that when a Templar wished to leave the order he was drowned; he also claimed that those who did not consent to their crimes were

---

125. Oxford, Bodleian Library, Bodley 454, fol. 153v; Nicholson, *Proceedings Against the Templars*, 1:336.

126. Nicholson identifies them as merchants ("The Trial of the Templars in Ireland," 234).

127. In contrast, non-Templar witnesses in Cyprus spoke quite favorably about the order (Gilmour-Bryson, *Trial of the Templars in Cyprus*, 55–74, 409–36; Nicholson, *Proceedings Against the Templars*, 2:378n73). As Barber points out, outsiders who interacted with Templars regularly as in Cyprus "had no doubts about the brothers' beliefs and probity, while the hostile secular witnesses in England" (and all the more so in Ireland) could only report rumor and hearsay (*Trial of the Templars*, 284).

killed. Among the crimes Michael mentioned were trampling the cross on Fridays, which formed part of articles 10 through 13, and engaging in what he presents as illicit financial dealings, which he said he knew of firsthand in Cyprus, adding that he believed all Templars would behave in the same way throughout the world.[128] He then repeated the ultimate underlying cause of the trial, that it was commonly said that the Holy Land had been lost because of the Templars, and concluded with one last bit of hearsay and conjecture: that what the grand master did and ordained for his order should be and was observed by all members throughout the world on pain of death.

Nearly all of the outside witnesses were religious, with Franciscans forming the majority (thirteen).[129] Nine were Dominicans, six were Augustinian canons of St. Thomas the Martyr, two Augustinian canons from All Hallows, six Augustinian friars, and two Crutched friars.[130] One witness, Thomas de Broghton, was identified as a former servant of the Templars, and three (Adam le Latimer, Robert de Hereford, and Michael de Bras) were not connected with any house or order and were presumably laymen. One might expect that members of a religious order such as the Franciscans or Dominicans, who together constituted more than half of the witnesses, who themselves benefited from and depended on papally bestowed privileges that not infrequently aroused the resentment of the secular clergy and others, who were more skilled in the detection of and defense against heresy than other religious, and who had experienced decades of tension within their own orders in Ireland, would be less likely to accept such a blanket condemnation of an order and on such weak grounds. Furthermore, the Franciscans were simultaneously undergoing their own investigation for heresy within their order, which could have strengthened their opposition to the Templars (in order to distance themselves further from any heretical taint), but also could have made them more sympathetic to the Templars' plight: condemned as a whole for what a portion of their order stood convicted in other lands. Yet virtually all the Franciscans and Dominicans

---

128. Oxford, Bodleian Library, Bodley 454, fol. 154r; Nicholson, *Proceedings Against the Templars*, 1:336–37.

129. William le Botiller is not identified by order or house, but his testimony clearly indicates that he is religious, he is listed in a group of Franciscans, and the witness after him, Henry de Stone, is said to be of the same order (Oxford, Bodleian Library, Bodley 454, fol. 153r; Nicholson, *Proceedings Against the Templars*, 1:333).

130. All Hallows is the same priory to which Philip de Braybrook was to be sent later that year. Two of the Augustinian friars are identified as canons, but see Gwynn and Hadcock, *Medieval Religious Houses*, 298. Seventy years later their house would suffer its own scandal; see Martin, "Murder in a Dublin Monastery." Interestingly, neither the Augustinian canons of Holy Trinity nor their rivals, the canons of St. Patrick's, numbered among the witnesses, although the trial was held in St. Patrick's cathedral, its dean served as inquisitor, and Peter Wylyby, one of its canons, observed the trial.

accepted the guilt of the Templars of Ireland simply because the Templars in France had confessed and been found guilty and because the Templars of Ireland acknowledged the universality of their reception, observances, et cetera.[131] Not one of the outside witnesses drew upon the incriminating testimony of the Templars themselves, such as Henry Danet's tales of Cyprus or Syria and William de Kilros's allegations of the sodomite at Killofan, although three friars—a Dominican, a Franciscan, and an Augustinian—cited Henry's admission of his time spent overseas as if that alone condemned him. Two witnesses testified to the blasphemous if not heretical remarks of William de Warenne, but he himself was not among the Templars examined in 1310. One of those witnesses was a Dominican, but the other was presumably lay, and those witnesses who were probably lay gave more substantial and informed testimony than did the religious. Apart from the reference to William de Warenne, however, that testimony also constituted little more than hearsay against the Templars of Cyprus, incriminating the Templars of Ireland only on the loosest and most biased terms. The one witness who had the most familiarity with Templars, Thomas de Broghton, was also the one witness to dispel nearly all of the allegations against Templars that he recounted. While he did not state his personal opinions as to the order's guilt or innocence, he demonstrated much greater equanimity on the matter than did the other forty-one witnesses, who were prepared to condemn the Templars in Ireland almost entirely on the bases of association and presumption. Even the inquisitors of England apparently recognized just how little such unsubstantiated testimony helped their cause, as they wholly disregarded it in their summaries of the trial in the British Isles, though they made considerable use of the testimonies of the Templars of Ireland as well as equally dubious hearsay and conjecture provided by outside witnesses in England and Scotland.[132]

The Council of Vienne and the Suppression of the Order

On October 16, 1311, the general council called by the bull *Regnans in coelis* convened at Vienne to decide the Templars' fate.[133] While the full list of

---

131. Nicholson suggests that hostilities toward the English and Anglo-Irish could have been a factor in the friars' condemnation of an order seen as closely connected to the colonial government ("Testimony of Brother Henry Danet," 423); the witnesses' own affiliation with the colonial establishment makes this possibility unlikely.

132. Stubbs, *Annales Londonienses*, 179–98; Schottmüller, *Der Untergang des Templer-Ordens*, 2:78–102.

133. *Regnans in coelis*, issued in August 1308, called the council to meet in October 1310, but a subsequent bull, *Alma mater*, postponed the council for a year.

Irish ecclesiastics in attendance is not known, it included the archbishops of Armagh (Roland Jorz) and Dublin (John Lech), as well as Lech's successor, Alexander de Bicknor, who was then treasurer of Ireland and would later face charges for his mismanagement of Templar property.[134] Wood says that the archbishop of Cashel and the bishops of Emly, Killaloe, and Cloyne attended, but the *Annals of Inisfallen* states that though they and the bishop of Lismore were summoned, they refused to go or to send competent representatives "for fear that unpleasantness might befall them."[135] Finke lists all four archbishops as attending, each accompanied by a suffragan; if this is accurate, at least four of the ecclesiastics were native Irish, the archbishops of Tuam and Cashel and their suffragans.[136] Whatever the identity of the Irish or Anglo-Irish in attendance, though, according to Ptolemy of Lucca they all declared that the order should be allowed further defense, as did the prelates of England, Scotland, Spain, Germany, and Sweden, as well as the majority of those from Italy and even France.[137] Two contemporary English witnesses relate how nearly all attendees spoke in the Templars' favor except those of France who feared their king, an apprehension shared by the pope himself.[138] Philip arrived at the council with a vast army in March of 1312 and pressured Clement to suppress the order; within days it was done. The bull *Vox in excelso* dissolved the Templar order due to the presumption against and scandal associated with it, and *Ad providiam*, issued two months later, transferred the bulk of their property to the Hospitallers. *Ad providiam*'s provisions no doubt infuriated Philip, whose success in destroying the Templars was near complete, yet Clement denied him at least official sanction in his appropriation of the Templar wealth that had motivated his mission against them.

While no firsthand opinions on the matter from Irish or Anglo-Irish attendees are extant, Walter of Guisborough's comments on the council may provide a rough approximation of the estimation of representatives of the British Isles. Walter attributed "that entire scandal" to Philip, and he also criticized Clement's handling of the affair, declaring that the Council of Vienne "did not deserve to be called a council, since the lord pope did everything

134. Watt, "Negotiations between Edward II and John XXII," 10n43; Müller, *Das Konzil von Vienne*, 75; *CPR* (1307–13): 400; Rymer, vol. 1, pt. 4, p. 190; Maxwell Lyte, *Calendar of Chancery Warrants*, 365–66. Hand does not think Bicknor actually attended the council ("Two Cathedrals of Dublin," 100–101).

135. *AI*, 410.

136. Finke, *Papsttum und Untergang*, 2:304. The bishops are of Meath (Armagh), Ferns (Dublin), Cork (Cashel), and Achonry (Tuam). One of the suffragans, Benedict O'Brogain of Achonry, died before the council ended (March 19, 1312; *NHI*, 9:321).

137. Barber, *Trial of the Templars*, 264.

138. Walter of Guisborough, *Chronicle*, 396; Barber, *Trial of the Templars*, 264.

from his own head, neither responding to nor consulting the holy council."[139] Perhaps the Irish and Anglo-Irish likewise felt that the order had been treated unfairly, that the scandalous behavior was not the Templars' but Philip's. Evidently they believed that the order deserved a fairer hearing than it received, an opinion that perhaps they first formed in Ireland, unswayed by the empty gossip and prejudiced opinion the outside witnesses had offered in Dublin.[140] Perhaps they saw little difference between Philip and Edward, as most of their concerns recorded from the Council of Vienne focus on Edward's appropriation of ecclesiastical jurisdiction, including using ecclesiastical courts to serve secular interests. The English prelates levelled similar accusations against their king, but the Irish representatives had the additional grievance that "before the arrival of the English in Ireland, the Irish church was free, so that it did not recognize a superior in temporal matters, having every manner of jurisdiction and exercising it with regard to both spiritual and temporal affairs." Though they did not take issue with the papal right to grant lordship of Ireland, they presented *Laudabiliter* as a pretext on which Henry II entered Ireland; in the part that he had managed to subjugate to him, he and his successors had little by little usurped the clergy's rights and so vilely mistreated them that, "with cathedral communities and sites abandoned, they hide in caves and lead a miserable life."[141] Such a portrait of Henry and his successors, in particular Edward II, would be reiterated by the native Irish five years later in the Remonstrance of Irish Princes and suggests that native Irishmen did number among the attendees at Vienne, or that Anglo-Irish leaders enlisted Ireland's pre-Norman past in their efforts to rid themselves of unwanted English interference, as Arnold le Poer would do during the Kyteler case.[142]

The fate of the order's property in Ireland after the Council of Vienne has been far better documented than the fate of its members.[143] By 1314, the Hospitallers had received at least some of the Templars' lands and goods, and that February the prior of the Hospitallers was instructed to take over payment of their daily allowance.[144] Henry Danet, the preceptor of Ireland,

---

139. Walter of Guisborough, *Chronicle*, 396.

140. Barber, *Trial of the Templars*, 264; see above.

141. Ehrle, "Ein Bruchstück," 370–71. This assessment of the effects of the colony on the church in Ireland echoes that of Gerald of Wales roughly a century earlier (Giraldus Cambrensis, *Opera*, 1:61).

142. Phillips suggests that the dossier of colonial abuses that formed the basis of the "Remonstrance of Irish Princes" may have been originally prepared for the Council of Vienne ("The Remonstrance Revisited," 20); see chapter 5.

143. See Mac Niocaill, "Documents Relating to the Suppression of the Templars in Ireland," 193–218, and Wood, "Templars in Ireland," 357–60.

144. Rymer, vol. 2, pt. 1, pp. 62–63. Four years later, however, the allowance may have become the responsibility of the clergy; see Wood, "Templars in Ireland," 359.

was released on bail in 1312, but history does not record what became of his brethren, or of him subsequently.[145] Templars elsewhere often entered other orders, but no evidence attests that such occurred in Ireland. Wood contends that Henry's fellow Templars were probably released from prison when he was and that almost a decade after the dissolution "the Templars were still tenaciously clinging to their ancient rights in some parts of the country."[146] While this seems a fairly radical reading of the record, a remark made by Clyn does give one pause. In his entry for 1331, Clyn relates how the O'Tooles killed about thirty colonists, including *unus templarius de Geraldinis* (a Templar of the Geraldines).[147] Bernadette Williams suggests that Clyn's meaning might be that one or many of the earl of Desmond's entourage may have been former Templars who continued to use their weapons.[148] While it is tantalizing to envision renegade Templars continuing to fight with "MacThomas's Rout," a simpler explanation may be in order. Pembridge, who wrote his annals at approximately the same time as Clyn, offers a more detailed account of this attack, which he says took its greatest toll on the family of Alexander de Bicknor. Here the knight in question is identified as Brother Maurice fitz Gerald and his order as the Hospitallers.[149] It seems most likely, then, that Clyn simply made a mistake, although his slip shows that Templars were not as forgotten decades after their suppression as the historical record might suggest.

The Case against Philip de Braybrook

The three inquisitors of the Templar trial in Ireland received letters of safe conduct the month after the hearings finished in Dublin, probably in connection with a visit to the inquisitors in England to inform them of the Irish proceedings.[150] It is unlikely that Thomas de Chaddesworth made the journey, however, as he had tried to excuse himself from travelling to England due to bodily infirmity in 1308 and similar complaints had been a cause of

---

145. Wood, "Templars in Ireland," 357, citing Memoranda Roll, Excheq., 6 Ed. II, m.2.

146. Wood, "Templars in Ireland," 357 and (quote) 359; it is not clear if the country to which he is referring is England or Ireland.

147. Clyn, 22. All four manuscripts use the term *templarius* (Williams, "Annals of Friar John Clyn," 69).

148. Williams, "Annals of Friar John Clyn," 69, 75n69.

149. *CSM*, 2:374. Perhaps Maurice was a former Templar who became a Hospitaller after the order's suppression.

150. Rymer, vol. 1, pt. 4, p. 171; *CPR* (1307–13): 267.

concern for him since 1302.[151] Moreover, a letter sent to him from the as ever absent archbishop-elect of Dublin, Richard de Haverings, on September 4, 1310, indicates that he was otherwise occupied with another heresy case, one he had brought against a longtime rival, Philip de Braybrook.[152] Haverings's letter, written in Gascony while he attended to royal business, as he did throughout his time as archbishop-elect of Dublin, provides the only extant account of Philip's heresy, and it reveals extreme irregularities in the case. Haverings informed his vicar Chaddesworth that, after having the process Chaddesworth had sent him concerning Philip, a canon of Holy Trinity (now Christ Church), examined by men expert in human and in divine law, he would have found him guilty of heresy had Chaddesworth not reported that Philip had confessed and abjured his heresy previously to Chaddesworth; given this claim, Haverings decreed that Philip was guilty of relapsed heresy, apparently for refusing to accept the sacrament in both forms.[153] Thus, Philip was condemned and convicted by a judge in another country based exclusively on an adversary's written allegations against him.[154] Haverings's letter offers few details, but an account describing events of ten years previously provides requisite context, revealing the rancor with which Chaddesworth pursued the canons of Holy Trinity, with Philip a particular source of frustration for him.[155] Philip's conviction for relapsed heresy stands as a final chapter in Chaddesworth's feud with the canons of Holy Trinity, which itself developed out of a near century-long dispute between Dublin's cathedral chapters, and to which Chaddesworth applied allegations of heresy only after the trial of the Templars had alerted him to the efficacy of such allegations against opponents.

Chaddesworth was an exceptionally powerful man in the Dublin diocese, repeatedly ruling it in all but name during the frequent vacancies and absences of archbishops from 1271 until his death in early 1311. He was a pivotal figure in both the secular and ecclesiastical administration of the lordship, serving as the first known chancellor of the Irish exchequer, as justice of the common bench since 1276, and as dean of St. Patrick's since 1284. He had been twice (1294 and 1299) elected and twice rejected as archbishop of

151. Connolly, "List of Irish Entries," 169; Richardson and Sayles, *Administration of Ireland*, 236–37; Prynne, *Exact Chronological Vindication*, 3:943.

152. Callan, "Dublin's First Heretic?"; Callan, "Case of the 'Incorrigible' Canon."

153. RCB, *Liber Niger*, fol. 209r; Callan, "Dublin's First Heretic?," 4, 9, 11.

154. The letter in Haverings's name could have been a forgery by Chaddesworth; see Callan, "Case of the 'Incorrigible' Canon," 177, 185, 188.

155. RCB, *Registrum Novum*, 1:339–74; Callan, "Case of the 'Incorrigible' Canon."

FIGURE 4.   Christ Church (formerly Holy Trinity) Cathedral, Dublin. Photo by the author.

Dublin himself by the time the feud with Holy Trinity erupted in 1300.[156] Two cathedral chapters in one diocese was uncommon in medieval Christendom; two in one city was virtually unprecedented, and their relationship had been tense since the recently elevated St. Patrick's first participated with Holy Trinity in archepiscopal elections in 1228. The rancor between them grew particularly vicious after Chaddesworth's contested and ultimately overturned election as archbishop in 1299, in which some of Holy Trinity's canons had voted for their own prior, Adam de Balsham. In his vengeance against the canons of Holy Trinity Chaddesworth demonstrated the ruthless and duplicitous facets of his character that facilitated his rise to and maintenance of power. He abused his position as the archbishop's vicar by holding Holy Trinity's first known visitation, without obtaining the necessary commissions to do so as the archbishop's deputy, and when the canons of Holy Trinity had repudiated his authority to do so, as they had litigation pending against him. He also repeatedly confiscated (or, according to the narrator of these events, an unnamed canon of Holy Trinity, "robbed") donations made at Holy Trinity.[157] He was on the verge of exiling three canons leading the

---

156. For various references to Chaddesworth's role in the civil administration of the lordship, see Richardson and Sayles, *Irish Parliament*, and Richardson and Sayles, *Administration of Ireland*.

157. RCB, *Registrum Novum*, 1:372.

opposition to him before he turned his animosity upon their prior, Adam de Balsham, whom he excommunicated and forced to resign. Conflict between Chaddesworth and the canons of Holy Trinity continued in the following decade, and a letter of papal protection from Clement V issued to Philip on November 1, 1305, instructing the bishop, dean, and archdeacon of Clogher (in the province of Armagh) to undo any actions of Archbishop Richard de Feringes against Philip, suggests that Chaddesworth may have been using his absent metropolitan to harm Philip, as he would again five years later.[158]

As Chaddesworth abused his position as vicar in the 1300 conflict with Holy Trinity, so too does he appear to have abused his position as inquisitor, to which he had been appointed solely in connection with the Templars. He apparently lost little time applying these newly learned techniques in his vendetta against Philip, who was "the most authoritative and knowledgeable" of Holy Trinity's canons, according to the narrator of the 1300 conflict.[159] Certain commonalities between Haverings's letter and words and actions attributed to Chaddesworth in the account of the 1300 conflict further indicate that the case was orchestrated entirely by Chaddesworth.[160] The punishment that Haverings decreed for Philip in 1310 echoes the punishment Chaddesworth had attempted to impose upon the leaders of Holy Trinity's opposition to him in 1300: a year under custody in another monastery, with Wednesdays and Fridays spent fasting, a remarkably lenient fate for an allegedly relapsed heretic. Since Philip's previous offense(s) had apparently included preaching, the archbishop-elect surprisingly ordered him to return to preaching and teaching in the same places where he had preached and taught before, although this time the subject was to be his own error and the truth of the Catholic faith. Considering that a common punishment for relapsed heresy was death, and on such grounds scores of Templars had gone to the stake in May 1310, as Haverings was well aware, the verdict seems all the more suspect. Moreover, no evidence supports Chaddesworth's claim of a previous trial to justify his allegation that Philip had relapsed.[161] Perhaps as Bishop Ledrede would do fourteen years later, Chaddesworth fabricated the claim of relapse to prevent a possible appeal, in accordance with Boniface VIII's *Ut inquisitionis*. Yet Haverings showed more mercy than did Ledrede,

---

158. RCB, *Registrum Novum*, 1:391; McEnery and Refaussé, *Christ Church Deeds*, 177.

159. RCB, *Registrum Novum*, 1:349; Callan, "Case of the 'Incorrigible' Canon,"

160. E.g., "ut dum nonulli virus suum in alios seminant modico fermento totam massam corrumpi faciunt" (RCB, *Registrum Novum*, 1:359–60); "quia fermento parue commistionis solet cum suis masse puritas infici" (RCB, *Liber Niger*, fol. 209r). These passages echo Galatians 5:9, which is often related to heresy, but these are the only instances I have encountered within Ireland.

161. Indeed, the only evidence for this supposed second trial is this letter itself, which could have been forged by Chaddesworth; see Callan, "Case of the 'Incorrigible' Canon," 177, 185, 188.

and his letter ends on a note of further clemency: "we do not intend to deny ourselves the option of acting more graciously with him without offense to the law if he remains steadfast in the Catholic faith from now on, if the judgments of his merits demand it."[162]

Philip apparently received such mercy, as no evidence indicates he ever served his sentence. This may be because within three months of this letter's issue, on November 21, 1310, Clement V accepted Haverings's resignation, said to be brought on by a nightmare shaming him for taking the Dublin diocese's financial benefits while doing nothing to earn them.[163] Perhaps his irregular conviction of a well-respected canon for relapsed heresy on exceptionally flimsy grounds, the "only one matter of note in connection with the diocese, with which [Haverings's] name is associated," helped him see his shame.[164] Even if Chaddesworth was in Dublin, rather than in England testifying about the Templars, when he received Haverings's letter and immediately attempted to implement its instructions, he himself was dead by March 1311, and it is unlikely that others felt as strongly about the matter. The letter's survival in the *Liber Niger* indicates that Philip's prior, Henry La Warr, who had been elected toward the end of the 1300 conflict, was aware of Haverings's verdict, however, as the book belonged to him.[165] Whatever opinion Henry may have had of Philip and his "heresy," the man elected to succeed him as prior in 1313, John Pekok, one of Chaddesworth's main opponents in the conflict whom he had tried to subject to a fate similar to the one Haverings decreed for Philip, apparently disregarded Philip's conviction, as he allowed him to serve as the chapter's only representative when they sought license to elect another archbishop of Dublin in 1313. Philip clearly died in good standing; he was one of only three canons involved in the 1300 conflict to have his death commemorated in the *Book of Obits of Holy Trinity*, the other two being the priors Henry la Warr and John Pekok.[166]

While it is possible that Philip de Braybrook's heresy was a matter of an isolated canon repeatedly challenging the orthodox position on the eucharist, as the only document directly related to the case indicates, the events of ten years previously, Philip's unique role in them, and Chaddesworth's tendency to abuse his position in his vendetta against Holy Trinity and its canons strongly suggest otherwise. Philip's case conforms to the general trend found in Ireland's heresy cases, resulting from personal vengeance in ongoing

---

162. RCB, *Liber Niger*, fol. 209r; Callan, "Dublin's First Heretic," 10–12.
163. Theiner, 182; *CSM*, 2:334.
164. Ronan, "Anglo-Norman Dublin and Diocese," 46:506.
165. Gwynn, "Some Unpublished Texts," 285.
166. Crosthwaite, *Book of Obits*, 51.

disputes rather than actual doctrinal or practical deviations. It exhibits even more extreme irregularities, however, as he seems to have been tried and convicted by letter, solely on the basis of a report Chaddesworth could have fabricated. The circumstances surrounding his conviction as well as his quick return to grace indicate that his alleged heresy was little more than the product of a feud with a powerful and bitter man that was dismissed after (or even before) his prosecutor died and the archbishop-elect whom he represented renounced office. Chaddesworth's abuse of his position as inquisitor to pursue old grievances befits both the nature of the trial of the Templars and the trials Ireland would endure in the next forty-odd years.

As the overwhelming majority of prelates recognized at the Council of Vienne and as the grounds for the dissolution given in *Vox in excelso* attest, the trial of the Templars did not prove the case against them. The evidence against them derived almost entirely from torture-induced confessions or from the malice and presumption of outsiders. While it is possible that some members may have engaged in or subscribed to some of the practices and beliefs imputed to them, the evidence does not demonstrate that they did in fact do so, let alone that the entire order was complicit in such acts or beliefs.[167] Contemporary accounts attest that participants and witnesses were no less aware of Philip IV's centrality in and the impact of the failure of the Crusades on the trial than are modern historians. To Walter of Guisborough, the trial was a scandal caused by Philip of France; Michael de Bras testified that it was common belief that the Holy Land had been lost because of them and detailed their alleged sins that made them unworthy defenders of Christianity; during his fourth and final interrogation, William de Kilros attempted to come to terms with the fate of his order by explaining the source of suspicion against them as their too rapid rise to power and wealth as well as their friendly relations with Muslims.

Furthermore, the evidence indicates that Templars were highly unlikely to have actually espoused or engaged in heretical views or practices. As Barber has noted, the heretical accusations represent an attempt to play on deep-seated fears of contemporaries that were calculated to exploit hostility toward the order after the loss of Acre.[168] Inventories of Templar goods attest that their deeds "did not take place under the gaze of 'Baphomet' or some

---

167. Jonathan Riley-Smith offers a particularly thoughtful argument concerning Templar guilt ("Were the Templars Guilty?"). See also Alan Forey's solid response to recent scholarship (including Riley-Smith's) that argues in favor of Templar guilt ("Alleged Templar Malpractices").

168. Barber, *Trial of the Templars*, 290.

other idol. Rather it was the *ymago Beate Marie supra altare*—the image of the Blessed Virgin Mary (mentioned in several inventories)—that silently witnessed the fall of the Templars."[169] The argument has been made particularly forcefully by Lea: for powerful and prestigious men such as the Templars to have propagated an alternative faith that sought to invert the established order they benefited from would have been an enterprise in insanity that would require "a spiritual exaltation and a readiness for martyrdom which we might expect from the asceticism of a Catharan or a Dolcinist," but not from worldly Templars; the inconsistency of the confessions, the lack of discrimination in reception, and the facts that the confessions themselves were overwhelmingly obtained by force and that none of the Templars were willing to die for their alleged heresy but preferred "to be burned in scores rather than submit to the stigma of having it ascribed to them" all attest to the innocence of the order.[170]

The confused image of heresy that emerges in the articles against the order, the flimsiness of the evidence used to condemn it, the exaction of torture and death at the stake, and the areligious and political origins of the Templars' trial make it an accurate representative of those that followed in fourteenth-century Ireland. It likely instigated the case of Philip de Braybrook, which occurred at the same time, in the same place, and with the same inquisitor. Like all other known heresy trials and accusations in fourteenth-century Ireland, Philip's case resulted from a feud, this time between Dublin's cathedral chapters, of which Chaddesworth and Philip represented opposing sides. While the case contains at least a veneer of doctrinal impropriety, little specific about it is known, and it seems probable that, even if deemed a convicted heretic, Philip never actually served his sentence or was regarded as such once the archbishop-elect resigned and Chaddesworth died within months of the sentencing. Whether he served it or not, the sentence was remarkably lenient and closely corresponded to the punishment decreed for Chaddesworth's main opponents in Holy Trinity ten years earlier, who were not accused of heresy. Later defendants would not be so lucky; of the four other cases known to have undergone something approximating a trial, three resulted in death at the stake.

Two of those four cases were instigated by Richard de Ledrede, bishop of Ossory, as were two others that never reached trial, one of which also claimed the life of the defendant. Though the Templar trial in Ireland was unlikely to have influenced Ledrede, the trial in France almost certainly

---

169. Burgtorf, "Trial Inventories," 115.
170. Lea, *History of the Inquisition*, 3:265–77, quotations at 268 and 265.

did. Like French inquisitors, he used torture to obtain confessions in the Kyteler case and sentenced his victim to the stake. As did the articles against the Templars, he equated apostasy and diabolism with heresy and focused on practice rather than belief. The hostilities and resentment that were the original source of the trial sprang from Alice's stepchildren, but Ledrede's own animosities eventually consumed him and the case, causing him to direct most of his energy against Alice's son and, later, her two powerful defendants and relations by marriage; his feud with one of those defendants seems likely also to have been the source of the fourth heresy case he is known to have initiated. None of his allegations of heresy, however, suggests that the accused actually espoused an alternative, heretical understanding of Christianity. Ireland's Templar trial, which occurred approximately fifteen to twenty years before Ledrede's prosecutions, may have caused his colonial audience to extend greater tolerance to Ledrede and his accusations than they otherwise might have, although such tolerance proved limited indeed.

The alleged heresies of the other two cases that resulted in deaths at the stake are even more problematic. One man was burned in Dublin for what amounts to apostasy from Christianity that, if true, would technically render him a non-Christian and thus not a heretic.[171] Two other men were burned at Bunratty Castle for having insulted the Blessed Virgin; while such slander would be blasphemous, it does not constitute heresy. These three men were also the victims of feuding and vendettas, but this time ethnic rather than personal or political in nature. The trial of the Templars as well as Ledrede's prosecutions laid the groundwork for colonial authorities to execute members of troublesome native Irish families for heresy after they had defeated them in battle. It imparted to the authorities in colonial Ireland an incoherent image of heresy that was exacerbated by Ledrede's accusations. When those authorities chose to wield that most potent religious weapon against their Irish enemies they demonstrated their own ignorance of the nature of heresy, an indication of an apparent paucity of actual heretical beliefs and practices in fourteenth-century Ireland. In ways, the history of heresy in Ireland is a fitting legacy of the trial of the Templars: a rash of irregular and illegitimate cases in the fifty years that followed, and empty accusations hurled in various feuds for another twenty-odd more.

---

171. Apostasy could be considered heresy, however. See, for example, Nicholas Eymeric's claim in 1376 that consulting demons was "apostasy from the faith, and as a consequence, heresy" (quoted, in English, in Bailey, "From Sorcery to Witchcraft," 974).

✄ CHAPTER 2

The Dawn of the Devil-Worshipping Witch

Seven years after the trials of the Templars and Philip de Braybrook, three separate fronts saw developments in the history of heresy in Ireland: native Irish attributed to Anglo-Irish colonists propagation of "the heresy that it is no more sin to kill an Irishman than a dog or any other brute"; the "meen poeple Dirland," that is, the Anglo-Irish, described the pre-Christian Irish as "eretiks"; and Richard de Ledrede arrived in Ireland as the new bishop of Ossory and quickly demonstrated that accusations of heresy would be his weapon and shield in the unfamiliar and chaotic politics of the colony.[1] The first two instances are part of the intense ethnic rivalry between the native Irish and the colonists, but this played a marginal role in Ledrede's prosecutions, which focused on prominent Anglo-Irish citizens.

Born in England, trained in France, polished at Avignon, Ledrede was far more familiar with French heresy and sorcery trials and John XXII's paranoia than the piety or politics he found in Ossory. He welcomed himself to his new diocese by convening a synod at which he made heated allegations of clerical abuses and rigorously exhorted the faithful to perform their Christian duty of reporting heresy. Accusations and evidence of the former repeatedly surfaced in Ireland as elsewhere, but Ledrede's stance on heresy

---

1. *IHD*, 43 (Curtis and McDowell's translation); Sayles, *Documents*, 99–100.

FIGURE 5.   Richard de Ledrede's effigy and tomb, north side of altar, St. Canice's Cathedral, Kilkenny. Photo by the author.

was *novum et inauditum* ("new and unheard of," a common medieval expression conveying disdain and suspicion), as was the face he eventually put on that heresy, that of the devil-worshipping witch. Before he was finished with the first stage of his crusade against evil, Ireland would kill its first "heretic," Ledrede himself would be imprisoned, the chancellor of Ireland would be labelled a fautor of heresy until he allegedly tearfully begged Ledrede's pardon, and Alice Kyteler, the primary defendant, would disappear from Ireland, to remain only in legend.

Unlike Ireland's other heresy trials, the case of Alice Kyteler has received considerable scholarly attention due to its pivotal role in the prosecution of witchcraft as heresy, the political importance of the participants, and the wealth of detail about life in the fourteenth-century lordship provided in *The Narrative of the Proceedings against Dame Alice Kyteler*, which is heavily biased in Ledrede's favor and was likely written by him. Several historians of witchcraft and heresy have discussed the significance of the trial, yet due to its isolation in time and space it rarely receives more than a cursory analysis in their studies. Experts on medieval Irish history have also commented upon the case, but because of its isolation in nature few have offered more than a passing reference. Anne Neary and Bernadette Williams have published particularly useful articles on the subject, but their work considers the case largely in isolation from the other heresy trials and accusations.[2] Williams raises important points regarding the role of gender in the trial, as has Eithne Massey in her study of Roger Outlaw, but significant aspects remain unaddressed, including the *Narrative*'s gender inconsistencies and its representation of heresy as a diabolical inversion of Catholicism, marriage, and motherhood.[3] This chapter focuses on the accused and the charges with particular attention to the role of gender within the trial, *Narrative*, and colony and also considers its significance in the history of heresy and witchcraft; the opposition to the proceedings, Ledrede's eventual if qualified success, and the legal conflicts in the case are examined in chapter 3.

Ledrede's prosecution of the Kyteler case offers a classic representation of the witch craze in many of its aspects. An older woman who deviates from the norm is charged with outrageous crimes against God and decency in a deliberate subversion of Christian ritual and patriarchal order.[4] Another woman so accused is tortured into confessing before being burned at the stake. Alice and her named accomplices reflect the ratio thought to most accurately depict the gender imbalance in the witch trials of 1300–1500, two-thirds female, one-third male, and the fate of these accomplices is unclear, due to the imprecision of the *Narrative*.[5] If anyone besides Petronilla de Midia lost their lives to this persecution, their names have also been lost to history, as have those of countless victims of the witch craze. Other significant elements in the history of the prosecution of Christian witchcraft emerge in this trial: an identification of sorcery and natural magic with demonic magic; an identification of magic with heresy; the witches' sabbath; a pact between a demon and a witch in which sex and money were exchanged; a group of twelve witches who, together with their demon, Robert or Robin son of Art, formed the number for a coven; torture; and death at the stake. Yet the very traits found in the Kyteler case that seem standard of witchcraft render it a far

---

2. Neary, "Origins and Character" and Neary, "Richard Ledrede"; Ms. Neary also generously shared with me her BA thesis, "Richard de Ledrede," which, though by an undergraduate and over thirty years old, remains the most solid study of the bishop to date. Bernadette Williams has been equally generous, repeatedly providing me with unpublished versions of her articles; see her "The Sorcery Trial of Alice Kyteler" and "'She Was Usually Placed with the Great Men.'" She recently published an article that considers the other trials as well ("Heresy in Ireland"). The introduction and notes to Davidson and Ward's English edition of the *Narrative* are also indispensable, as is Wright's commentary in the Latin edition.

3. Massey, *Prior Roger Outlaw*, esp. 34–35.

4. Alice married for the first time around 1280, over forty years before the trial. A child from this marriage, William Outlaw, was an adult by 1302, and his penance in 1324 takes into account obstacles that old age might cause.

5. Kieckhefer, *European Witch Trials*, 96. Alice had seven alleged female accomplices and four male.

more striking anomaly, particularly as the Kyteler case is Ireland's only known medieval witchcraft trial and one of very few in its entire history.[6]

In the Kyteler case, "a new image of the witch begins to emerge" in which the witch merged with the heretic and the heretics were overwhelmingly lay and mostly female.[7] This development has been read mainly in terms of the Continent but is no less significant for Ireland, where previous heresy trials had involved only male religious. While the case provides a fairly precise prototype of what witchcraft on the Continent would become, Ireland seems an alien birthplace for such a prototype. The island was relatively untouched by the developments that enabled the witch craze to reach the depths it did on the Continent, with little experience of heresy or its prosecution, and little troubled by witchcraft. Although hagiography and penitentials testify to belief in witches, they depict a markedly different kind of witch, primarily a powerful practitioner of the pre-Christian religion in the former and an apparently Christian individual who practices mainly love or reproductive magic in the latter.[8] Perhaps as early as the fifth century, however, the so-called First Synod of Patrick vigorously denounced any who believed in witchcraft and declared that those who so believed or accused anyone of practicing witchcraft were to be anathematized.[9] The island remained reluctant to accept such accusations even after the Kyteler case, as the next known allegation of witchcraft led to a declaration by the parliament to the king in 1447 that "no such art was attempted at any time in this land."[10]

The precise chronology of the Kyteler case remains somewhat unclear, partly because the Narrative's main objective is to defend the precedence of ecclesiastical over secular authority, not to provide a clear and accurate account of the trial's development. Only one medieval copy of the Narrative

---

6. Ireland would not see another death for witchcraft until 1578, also in Kilkenny, and apparently none of its other half dozen witchcraft cases claimed lives, with the possible exception of Florence Newton in 1661. See Seymour, Irish Witchcraft and Demonology, and Lapoint, "Irish Immunity to Witch-Hunting." The case of Bridget Cleary, killed by her husband at the end of the nineteenth century, is occasionally identified as a witchcraft case, but it was more properly the product of faerie and changeling beliefs; see Bourke, Burning of Bridget Cleary.

7. Cohn, Europe's Inner Demons, 141.

8. Plummer, Bethada Náem nErenn, 2:28; Bieler, Irish Penitentials, 78–79, 100–101. The qualities ascribed to heroes, saints, and denizens of the "Otherworld" in Irish myth, legend, and hagiography share similarities with those ascribed to witches, but their analysis falls outside the scope of this study. Borsje, "Love Magic," considers some examples. Sneddon theorizes that such beliefs inhibited Gaelic Irish (as opposed to Anglo-Irish) witch prosecution in the early modern era (Possessed by the Devil, 84; see also Conclusion).

9. Bieler, Irish Penitentials, 56–57.

10. Berry, Statute Rolls, 100–101.

exists, and it is impossible to tell how far removed it is from the original.[11] Contradictions run rampant within it, and it often reads more like a novel than a reliable history. It is permeated by the perspective of the protagonist, Richard de Ledrede, and its similarities with a letter written in 1328 by Ledrede regarding Arnold le Poer further suggest that Ledrede himself was the author.[12] As the *Narrative* makes no mention of Ledrede's prosecution of Arnold le Poer for heresy or Roger Outlaw as a fautor of heresy, a composition date between 1325 and 1328 seems probable. The extant copy may be an abbreviation of the original or an occasionally jumbled compilation from various sources.[13] It starts by summarizing a visitation that included a customary inquest during which Ledrede claimed to have discovered "that in the city of Kilkenny there had been for a long time and still were a great many heretical sorceresses (*hæretici sortilegæ*), skilled in diverse sorceries and knowing many heresies," and then details the seven charges ultimately brought against Alice and her accomplices.[14] Six of these charges, however, appear to be based on Petronilla de Midia's confession several months after the case had begun and were almost certainly composed after many of the events described in the *Narrative* had occurred.

Though the exact chain of events is unclear, Ledrede's hunt for heretics clearly began within weeks of his arrival in Ireland. He was in Avignon when John XXII appointed him bishop of Ossory on April 24, 1317, and in London as of August 7.[15] Two months later he convened a synod in Kilkenny to celebrate his inauguration and begin regulating the affairs of his diocese. The first article of the synod's constitution instructed members of the diocese to report within a month any knowledge of anyone teaching anything contrary to the faith, though previous bishops had not expressed concern about heresy in Ossory.[16] Ledrede's episcopate between 1317 and 1324 was far from serene, as his temporalities had already been seized by Michaelmas 1318, he complained about extortion from the sheriff of Dublin, and he had been arrested by 1320, yet those events pale beside those that occurred from approximately March 1324 to January 1325.[17] By 1324 Ledrede decided to intensify his efforts against suspected heretics in his diocese, summoning

---

11. London, British Library, Harley 641, fols. 186v–206v (rectos of fols. 186–205 blank).
12. Clarke, *Fourteenth Century Studies*, 24; Neary, "Richard de Ledrede," v.
13. Davidson and Ward, *Sorcery Trial*, 33–34, n27.
14. Wright, *Contemporary Narrative*, 1. This inquest may have been regarded as illegal by common lawyers; see Davidson and Ward, *Sorcery Trial*, 26n4. See Appendix B for the charges.
15. Clyn, 13; Theiner, 197; *CPL*, 2:148; Fitzmaurice and Little, *Materials for the History*, 102.
16. Gwynn, "Provincial and Diocesan Decrees," 58.
17. RC 8/10, 118–20; Sayles, *Documents*, 88; *CPL*, 2:206–7.

five knights and several other nobles to the inquest for this purpose. At what point he specifically focused on Alice Kyteler as "the mother heretic" is unclear.[18] The first date given in the *Narrative*, the Monday following the octave of Easter, 1324, occurs about a third of the way through the *Narrative* and apparently fell within a few months of Ledrede's first citation of Alice for heresy.[19]

The occasion for Ledrede's focus on Alice was a complaint made by her stepchildren that she had used *maleficia*, including murder, to appropriate their fathers' wealth unjustly, an accusation that could have been brought to Ledrede's notice very early in his episcopate, as in 1316 Alice had to sue one of her stepsons for her widow's dower.[20] According to the *Narrative*, Ledrede first cited Alice alone, although the evidence gathered against her is attributed to "her accomplices."[21] It is almost certain, however, that most of the charges brought against her were composed later and Ledrede initiated his proceedings against Alice solely on the basis of her stepchildren's allegations. Alice's son, William Outlaw, sprang to his mother's defense, enlisting the aid of Roger Outlaw, the prior of the Hospitallers at Kilmainham, the chancellor of Ireland, and kin to Alice's first husband, William's father, and Arnold le Poer, seneschal of Kilkenny and kin to her current husband, whom Ledrede and apparently her stepchildren claimed she was killing through her sorcery.[22] This accusation did nothing to deter Arnold from remaining one of her staunchest allies, an allegiance that cost him dearly in the end. Arnold and Roger refused to proffer Ledrede the secular assistance he needed, and shortly thereafter Ledrede expanded his accusations to include William as a heretic and a fautor of heretics.[23] Throughout the first half of the *Narrative*, only Alice and William specifically had been cited for heresy, although the charges provided at the beginning clearly apply to a group of women.[24]

When Ledrede at length succeeded in attaining secular assistance in his prosecution, Alice and six associate sorcerers were publicly denounced, sur-

---

18. Wright, *Contemporary Narrative*, 35.

19. Ibid., 13. Shortly before describing Ledrede's arrest on a Tuesday in Lent (ibid., 4–5), the *Narrative* asserts that Alice had been excommunicated "for forty days and longer" (ibid., 4), though this claim is suspect; see below.

20. RC 8/11, 475–76.

21. Wright, *Contemporary Narrative*, 3.

22. The *Narrative* describes Roger as William's blood-kin (ibid., 3), but the exact relation is unclear. Roger and Arnold have been assumed to be Alice's brothers-in-law, but the records do not specify.

23. Ibid., 4.

24. The first mention of Alice's accomplices, apart from the initial remark that her *comparticipes* had provided much of the evidence against her (ibid., 3), occurs more than halfway through the account (ibid., 22).

prisingly with the help of William Outlaw acting in an official capacity. Only *pauperiores* (poorer people) were arrested, however, while Alice, "the mistress of all," was allowed to escape freely.[25] According to the *Narrative*, all of the imprisoned quickly confessed before Ledrede to an almost infinite number of crimes and maintained that Alice was and had been their mother and mistress. The bishop then wrote to Roger Outlaw, asking him to arrange secretly for the investigation's continuation, lest other accomplices be allowed to escape. On the same day (June 6), he wrote to Walter de Islip, the treasurer of Ireland and keeper of Kilkenny, asking for his help in the arrest of twelve people: Alice; William; Robert of Bristol, a cleric apparently in minor orders; John Galrussyn; William Payn de Boly; Petronilla de Midia; her daughter Sarah; Alice, the wife of Henry the smith (*uxorem Henrici Fabri*); Annota Lange; Elena Galrussyn; Syssok Galrussyn; and Eva de Brounestoun.[26] Nine of the additional ten defendants surface solely in this letter and the subsequent warrant for their arrest; the tenth, Petronilla de Midia, next appears in the *Narrative* at her execution and offered the only confession provided in the account. Judging by the *Narrative*'s often confused and ambiguous chronology, the *pauperiores* who had been arrested did not include these ten. The *Narrative* does not clarify when or if these people were arrested or imprisoned, nor is it known what connection these people had to Alice Kyteler or why suspicion arose against them. Petronilla is often identified as Alice's maid, presumably because of the claim that an unnamed maid helped Alice's husband open her chests and Petronilla's admission that she cleaned up after Robert and Alice had sex.[27] No such identification is made in the *Narrative* and annals, however; nor is it known what if any interaction Petronilla previously had with Alice. The account mentions only her torture, confession, and

---

25. Ibid., 21–22.

26. Wright, *Contemporary Narrative*, 23. Robert of Bristol may have been the Robert of Bristol appointed justice of the Common Bench in 1320, a position he held until Easter Term, 1324 (Richardson and Sayles, *Administration of Ireland*, 155). He was dead by the following Michaelmas, which could suggest that he was one of those the *Narrative* claims to have been executed. As Neary has argued, however, such a conclusion seems unlikely, as his wife and son continued to receive payment of his arrears after his death ("Richard de Ledrede," 36). Given the number of men from Bristol in the colony, however, many men likely had that name. William Payn de Boly acted as the attorney of John de Fresingfeld, whose manor was Boly in Ossory, in 1306 (*CJR*, 2:273), and fifteen years later acknowledged a debt of two silver marks (Davidson and Ward, *Sorcery Trial*, 53n93). "De Midia" means "of Meath" but was a well-established family name in the Cork area; little is known about Petronilla beyond the information provided in the *Narrative*, except that her husband, Nicholas de la Montayn, died by 1316 (Neary, "Richard de Ledrede," 35–36). Pembridge identifies Petronilla's daughter as Basilia; she likely was the same daughter the *Narrative* claims as Alice's accomplice, as Pembridge makes the same claim (*CSM*, 2:362).

27. E.g., Davidson and Ward, *Sorcery Trial*, 6, 9; Williams, "'She Was Usually Placed with the Great Men,'" 81; Wright, *Contemporary Narrative*, 2, 32.

execution, which Clyn tells us occurred on November 3, 1324.[28] According to the *Narrative*, "she was the first heretical sorceress among a great many ever burned in Ireland," but it does not name any who met a similar end.[29] In its conclusion, the account describes various fates met by the other heretics and sorcerers of the pestiferous sect of Robin son of Art: death at the stake, public confession and abjuration of heresy with the front and back of their clothes being marked by a cross "as the custom is," whippings through the town and market place, exile, and excommunication; others fled Ledrede's persecution, including Alice Kyteler.[30] It seems unlikely, though, that any of the other accused shared Petronilla's punishment, as closely contemporary chroniclers from Kilkenny and Dublin mention her execution alone.[31]

Petronilla's Confession and Ledrede's Charges

Like the three Templars tortured in England in the summer of 1311, Petronilla provided her inquisitor with all that he desired to hear after being repeatedly whipped. Her confession, no doubt largely shaped by Ledrede, combines *maleficia* with diabolical sorcery and ritual and love magic with apostasy. She declared that, at Alice's instigation, "she had denied her faith in Christ and the church completely," a claim that was curiously altered in the charges ultimately brought against Alice and her accomplices.[32] The first charge states that the culprits denied their faith in Christ and his church for a month or a year, depending on their sorcery's needs.[33] This suggests a temporary and eminently practical motivation, rather than the more permanent rejection indicated by Petronilla's confession. She also admitted sacrificing to demons thrice on Alice's behalf, at least once with three cocks at the crossroads outside the city to Robert son of Art, *ex pauperioribus inferni* (from the dregs of hell), which is repeated in the second charge. She then poured out the cocks' blood, chopped up the carcasses, and combined the intestines with insects and herbs, which she boiled with the brains and clothes of an unbaptized boy in a pot made from a thief's skull.[34] In addition to this foul brew, she

---

28. Clyn, 16.

29. Wright, *Contemporary Narrative*, 33.

30. Wright, *Contemporary Narrative*, 40. While wearing crosses was a common punishment in heresy cases, I have not found evidence of a prior use in Ireland.

31. Clyn, 16; *CSM*, 2:362–64.

32. Wright, *Contemporary Narrative*, 32.

33. Ibid., 1.

34. Petronilla's confession claims she mixed the ingredients "cum cerebro et pannis pueri decedentis sine baptismo" (with the brain and clothes of a boy who died without baptism); the charges allege Alice and her accomplices did so "crebro et pannis puerorum decendentium sine baptismo"

had made many "brews, potions, and powders" that were used to inspire love or hatred and to generally harass good Christians; by adding incantations to these concoctions, she could make certain women's faces appear like horned goats.[35] This portion of her confession constituted the fifth charge, with minor changes.[36]

Petronilla continued that she had often consulted demons and received answers at Alice's prompting and once in her presence (charge 3). Furthermore, she said she had made a pact to play the mediator between Alice and the demon Robert, her "friend."[37] She declared that she had seen Robert take the form of three Ethiopian men each carrying an iron stick in their hands in broad daylight. Then, while she watched, Alice and Robert fornicated, and Petronilla cleaned up after them. Ledrede omitted this last detail in the seventh charge, but he otherwise expanded Petronilla's testimony. He claimed that Alice herself had admitted that, in exchange for her submission and sexual services, she received the entirety of her considerable estate from her incubus, Robert or Robin son of Art, who might come to her as a cat, a hairy black dog, or a black man with two big friends holding an iron rod.[38] Alice, however, successfully evaded Ledrede's prosecution and thus never admitted any such thing. Petronilla's confession, though undoubtedly heavily influenced by Ledrede's leading questions, makes no reference to Alice's wealth or how she attained it. Alice's stepchildren postulated a connection between her *maleficia*, marriages, and money, but the association of her wealth with her sexuality and witchcraft, as well as Robert's identification with an incubus, cat, or dog, seem to be products of Ledrede's own mind, most likely shaped by slander made against other heretical sects and alleged sorcerers, and perhaps occurred to him as something of an afterthought.

The last element in Petronilla's confession is among the most fascinating, that she and Alice often uttered curses against their husbands by lighting wax candles and spitting "exactly as their rite required." Petronilla identified herself as the *magistra* (leader) in this ritual, but maintained that she was nothing compared to Alice, from whom she had learned all and whom she described as

---

(ibid., 32, 2). This difference could be deliberate, but *crebro* (repeatedly) seems likely to be a mistake for *cerebro* (brain) and may indicate Ledrede's or his scribe's sloppiness in copying the charges from Petronilla's confession. I thank Christine Donnelly for helping me confirm that *crebro* is faithful to the manuscript (London, British Library, Harley 641, fol. 186v). See Appendix B.

35. Wright, *Contemporary Narrative*, 32.

36. Ibid., 2. The charge omits the specific reference to women as victims.

37. Ibid., 32.

38. Ibid., 2–3.

the most skilled witch "in all the realm of the king of England," and possibly in the world.[39] The fourth charge, like the seventh, augments Petronilla's confession and makes more explicit the connection between subversion of the church and subversion of patriarchal marriage, accusing the heretics of usurping the instruments and prerogatives of the church and inflicting them upon their husbands, without clarifying how such charges could apply to the male members of the sect:

> In their nightly conventicles, they usurped the jurisdiction and keys of the church, when with waxen candles burning they would fulminate sentences of excommunication even against their own husbands, naming one by one every part of their body from the soles of their feet to the top of their head, and in the end they would extinguish the candles as they said, "fiat, fiat, fiat, amen."[40]

This description echoes that invoked by Ledrede during the general sentence of excommunication at the end of his synodal constitutions, discussed in chapter 3, and furthers the sense of Ledrede's understanding of sorcery as inverted Catholicism.[41]

An interesting addition to Petronilla's confession is found in Pembridge's annals: "when she was close to death, she said that William Outlaw deserved death just as much as she did, and she also asserted that he wore a diabolical belt around his naked body for a year and a day."[42] If Petronilla had made such an accusation as the flames began to engulf her, the *Narrative* would almost certainly reference it, as it would have bolstered Ledrede's claims against William. Pembridge presents William's inclusion among Alice's accomplices as arising from Petronilla's last words and asserts that Ledrede then had William arrested, but according to the *Narrative*, William was imprisoned before the time of Petronilla's execution; moreover, he had been cited along with his mother long before Petronilla ever appeared in the *Narrative*. Petronilla's eleventh-hour accusation seems an attempt by Pembridge to explain how William came to be arrested and numbers among several additional but probably false details provided by Pembridge that indicate "how quickly rumour can add to and distort truth."[43] Of Petronilla's last acts, the *Narrative* says only that

---

39. Ibid., 32.

40. Ibid., 2; the curse ends "fi: fi: fi: amen," *fi* being an abbreviation for *fiat*, which can be translated as "let it be" or "make it so."

41. Gwynn, "Provincial and Diocesan Decrees," 69–71.

42. *CSM*, 2:363. This may echo the suspicion of the Templar cords.

43. Williams, "Dominican Annals," 163.

she refused the sacrament of penance. The fact that it was offered to her indicates that reconciliation with the church was open to her, but a church that had brutalized her and demanded her death was apparently not one she wanted any part of.

Petronilla's confession, upon which six of the seven charges (1–5, 7) are based, does not claim that Alice or her associates physically harmed their husbands. Yet such an allegation serves as the sixth charge and the source of the trial, brought before the bishop by the children of Alice's four husbands, who claimed that "by her sorcery she had killed some of their fathers, some she had infatuated and driven to such stupidity of sense that they gave all their property to her and her son, to the perpetual impoverishment of their children and heirs," and that her current husband, the knight John le Poer, was quickly approaching his untimely death due to her magical potions as well.[44] The sixth charge continues that, with the help of Alice's maid, John wrested the keys to her chests from her and upon opening them found a sack of abominable ingredients, which he promptly had delivered to Ledrede.[45] Alice's first husband is usually identified as William Outlaw, but his first name is unknown. Her son of the same name clearly did not number among those who brought this charge against Alice, and no other children from the marriage, or indeed from any of Alice's marriages, are known.[46] The children of her second known husband, Adam le Blund, had legitimate reasons for complaint against Alice and her son, as in 1307 Adam quitclaimed all his property to William.[47] Within two years Adam was dead and Alice had remarried, this time to Richard de Valle. By 1316, he too was dead and Alice had to sue her stepson, also named Richard de Valle, for her dower. Sometime between 1316 and 1324 the ageing Alice wed John le Poer, whose exact identity has not been established. Ciarán Parker has suggested that he may have been Arnold's brother; if this is the case, he recovered from his illness of 1324 to live for nearly three more decades.[48]

---

44. Wright, *Contemporary Narrative*, 2.

45. Ledrede later burned this sack in the middle of town, after he had finally succeeded in having Alice condemned in absentia (Wright, *Contemporary Narrative*, 26; Clyn, 16); see chapter 3.

46. In 1302, Rose Outlaw was arrested with Alice and her then husband, Adam le Blund, but Rose's relation to Alice or her former husband is not specified (see below). Since William Outlaw was not one of the accusers and no other children from her first marriage are known, Williams has suggested that Alice may have had more than four husbands ("'She Was Usually Placed with the Great Men,'" 73).

47. *CJR*, 2:335–36.

48. Parker, "Paterfamilias and *Parentela*," 111.

French Influences and English Lack Thereof

Ledrede interpreted Alice's stepchildren's charge of *maleficia* through a lens shaped by French trials for heresy, most notably against Boniface VIII and the Templars, which were largely the product of King Philip's anger and avarice.[49] Boniface was accused of having three demons, keeping a familiar in a ring on his finger, and conjuring demons by sacrificing a cock.[50] Like the Templars, he was said to be an apostate, a murderer, and a sodomite; to further the guilt of both, he was held culpable of favoring the Templars and accepting money from them, a fairly standard practice among popes as well as kings before the order's fall. In another trial masterminded by Philip and his ministers, the Bishop Guichard of Troyes was claimed to have been the offspring of a sterile woman and an incubus.[51] His own demon allegedly helped him kill by means of poisons like the potions in the Kyteler case; his purported victims included the queen, her mother, and a priest who refused to baptize the bishop's bastard by a nun.[52] These trials occurred during the pontificate of Clement V, who largely acquiesced to Philip's will in the trials of the Templars and the bishop in his efforts to evade the king's like claims against his predecessor. Clement's successor, however, would use Philip's tactics against his own opponents.

The first decade of John XXII's pontificate saw several sensational trials against alleged sorcerers.[53] Within a year of becoming pope in 1316, John had Hugues Géraud, the elderly bishop of John's hometown of Cahors, arrested for plotting to use sorcery and poison to murder him. John interviewed Hugues personally seven times and had him tortured. After confessing to an intricate plot involving magical powders, baptized wax figures, poisons, and accomplices among Jews and the papal household, Hugues was sent to the stake.[54] The following year, John ordered Bishop Bartholomew of Fréjus and two other ecclesiastics to hold an inquisition of several clerics in the papal court accused of necromancy, geomancy, and other "demonic arts," which they would use to harm or kill.[55] The papal mission against diabolical sorcery, commonly alleged of John's adversaries, was particularly active in 1320. Matteo and Galeazzo Visconti, leaders of the Ghibellines and the pope's political opponents, were

---

49. See the discussion in chapter 1.

50. Cohn, *Europe's Inner Demons*, 120–23.

51. Rigault, *Le Procès de Guichard*, 116–18, 125–27.

52. Ibid., 74–89, 95–98. Guichard was imprisoned on these charges until 1313, when his main accuser confessed on the gallows that he was innocent (ibid., 219).

53. Kieckhefer, *Magic in the Middle Ages*, 187; Boureau, *Satan the Heretic*.

54. Thorndike, *History of Magic*, 18.

55. Hansen, *Quellen und Untersuchungen*, 2–4.

brought to trial for entering into a pact with the devil and using wax figures
in their attempts to kill the pope, but the case was dismissed.[56] Eight other
Ghibelline leaders of Ancona were cited to appear before an inquisitor for
demon worship, and over the next five years the pope repeatedly wrote to the
bishop and inquisitor of Ancona, describing his opponents there as heretics
and idol worshippers.[57] The cardinal of Santa Sabina instructed the inquisitors
of Toulouse and Carcassonne in John's name to investigate as heretics those
who adore, sacrifice to, or enter into a pact with demons.[58] Soon afterward, in
a "doctrinal revolution," the pope asked ten experts in theology, canon law, and
the repression of heresy to determine doctrinal foundations for expanding the
definition of heresy to include magic and invocation of demons and to determine if actions could suffice as evidence of heresy, which traditionally had been
understood as a matter of belief, not deed.[59] This revolution would be enacted
in the Kyteler case four years later, and similar dynamics recur in John XXII's
decretal *Super illius specula* as well as in Bernard Gui's manual for inquisitors,
which may have been completed in the year the Kyteler case occurred.[60] The
same year as *Super illius specula* (1326), Bertrand d'Audiran, a canon of Agen,
John Dupont, a cleric of Limoux, and Peter d'Auriac, a layman, were charged
with invoking demons to wreak weather magic as well as murder, and Gerald
Barasci, a prior of St. Sulpice, and lay and religious accomplices were tried for
demonic magic.[61] While these cases as well as John's paranoia focused on male
culprits, two cases that surfaced in 1319 involved women: John absolved a
canon of Autun from any suspicion of wrongdoing arising from his proceedings against a woman accused of sorcery and heretical depravity who confessed
only after torture was applied and died while in prison; and he ordered Jacques
Fournier, then bishop of Pamiers who would be one of John's ten experts in
1320 and his successor as pope in 1334, to proceed against two "sons of Belial,"
a priest and a Carmelite, and a woman named Galharda Enquede for fashion-
ing images, performing incantations, consulting demons, and practicing other
forms of *maleficia*.[62]

---

56. Thorndike, *History of Magic*, 24–27; Cohn, *Europe's Inner Demons*, 130.

57. Cohn, *Europe's Inner Demons*, 130–31.

58. Hansen, *Quellen und Untersuchungen*, 4–5.

59. Boureau, *Satan the Heretic*, 8–67, quote at 27.

60. For John XXII's decretal, see Hansen, *Quellen und Untersuchungen*, 5–6; Bailey, "From Sorcery
to Witchcraft," 966–67. For Gui's manual, see Hansen, *Quellen und Untersuchungen*, 47–55. See also
Wakefield and Evans, *Heresies of the High Middle Ages*, 444–45.

61. Vidal, *Bullaire*, document 67, pp. 113–15; document 72, pp. 118–20.

62. Ibid., document 23, pp. 51–53; Boureau, *Satan the Heretic*, 15–16. The first case shares significant similarities with the Kyteler case, but little about it is known. Vidal, *Bullaire*, document 24,
pp. 53–54.

John's appointment of Ledrede resulted from another innovation. Early in his pontificate, he extended Clement IV's bull *Licet ecclesiarum*, which enabled the papacy to fill benefices that fell vacant at or near the curia, to include those that fell vacant through translation; Ledrede's appointment as bishop of Ossory was the first enactment of this new provision.[63] Mauricius Mac Cerbaill, the native Irish archbishop of Cashel, died a few months before John himself took office, and Edward II urged him to fill the see with an Englishman on the grounds that "the fraudulent tricks, and crafty and deceitful collusions of certain Irish prelates" contributed substantially to the current Bruce invasion of Ireland.[64] Edward suggested Geoffrey of Aylsham, an English Franciscan, to occupy the office and asked that no native Irish be promoted to episcopal office "at least as long as the current disturbances there continued."[65] Instead of Geoffrey, John translated William fitz John, currently the chancellor of Ireland, from the see of Ossory to the archdiocese of Cashel, but he granted Edward's request for an English Franciscan with Ledrede, a man with an obscure past.[66] Edward's letter of gratitude to the pope for the two appointments praises William's honest character, proven faithfulness, holy life, intellectual accomplishments, and other various virtues, but Ledrede is described only as an English Franciscan, suggesting that Edward's gratitude for Ledrede derived solely from these two features.[67] Such a tepid endorsement may be explained by Edward's lack of familiarity with Ledrede, but it would be an appointment both the king and his son would regret.

John acceded to Edward's wish for an English Franciscan at a time of intense conflict within the order over the issue of poverty with which John himself was directly involved.[68] John took a harsh stance against those who strove to uphold Francis's original teachings regarding poverty, the majority known as Michaelists with a more zealous and mystical branch known as Spiritual Franciscans, four of whom were executed for their adherence to Francis's views in May 1318. John issued a series of bulls that maintained that the papacy had the right to modify Francis's Testament, listed a number

---

63. Davidson and Ward, *Sorcery Trial*, 7.

64. Rymer, vol. 2, pt. 1, p. 116.

65. Rymer, vol. 2, pt. 1, p. 117.

66. Neary, "Richard de Ledrede," chap. 1, and Neary, "Richard Ledrede," 273–74, provide the most useful overview of Ledrede's prior history.

67. Rymer, vol. 1, pt. 1, p. 133; Neary, "Richard de Ledrede," 11.

68. For the controversy and John's involvement, see Burr, *Spiritual Franciscans*; Leff, *Heresy in the Later Middle Ages*, 1:51–255; Lambert, *Medieval Heresy*, 208–35; and Lawrence, *The Friars*, 60–64. The controversy also affected Ireland, as is attested by remarks in the *Annals of Inisfallen* (*AI*, 410) and by Clyn (11).

of errors advanced by Spirituals and Michaelists, and pronounced it heretical to maintain, as these Franciscans did, that Christ and the apostles held property neither individually nor in common. Ledrede, however, was the kind of Franciscan John could appreciate, as his extreme concern for the financial fruits of his office and the lavish palace he built for himself in Kilkenny reveal him as the antithesis of a Spiritual Franciscan or Michaelist.[69] Moreover, a letter from Edward III to Innocent VI proclaims that, "forgetful of his original mendicancy," Ledrede fabricated heresy charges in order to extort money from the accused.[70] The allegation can be substantiated by William Outlaw's payment to the bishop of £1,000 shortly after being released from prison and perhaps explains his enthusiasm in his prosecution of William's mother, an exceptionally wealthy woman.[71]

John's own letter of appointment hails Ledrede, who would soon become an active participant in his master's mission against diabolical sorcerers, in much the same terms as Edward described William fitz John, but what brought this otherwise obscure Franciscan to the pope's notice is unknown.[72] Ledrede proclaimed himself "cultivated, educated, and promoted under the wings of the most holy apostolic see," which could indicate that he attended the *studium generale* at Avignon and possibly even became a teacher there; perhaps he distinguished himself while the future John XXII was bishop of Avignon (1310–12).[73] He may also have been an associate of Enrico del Carretto, as both were Franciscans residing in Avignon in 1317. Appointed by John XXII in 1318 to serve as an expert in the case against the Spiritual Franciscans, Carretto in 1320 offered the most forceful argument in favor of John's "doctrinal revolution" of expanding heresy to include demonic magic with actions as sufficient evidence, a tactic Ledrede himself would employ in 1324.[74] Given Kilkenny's political importance within the colony, the king's critical concerns about the sensitivity of the current situation, and Ledrede's loyalty to John's deepest concerns about diabolical sorcery, Ledrede was most likely not "selected by the pope as a moderately suitable choice for a relatively remote and unimportant bishopric."[75] A man who distinguished

---

69. Ware, *De Praesulibus Lageniae*, 778. Ledrede also had extremely ornate stained glass made for St. Canice's east window that a visiting Italian cardinal offered to purchase for £700 in 1648; the offer was declined, and the window was destroyed two years later by Cromwell's forces (Buckley, "Ancient Stained Glass," 241–43).

70. Raine, *Historical Papers and Letters*, 404.

71. Tresham, I.i.31, 34; Wright, *Contemporary Narrative*, 48, 58; see chapters 3 and 4.

72. Theiner, 195.

73. Wright, *Contemporary Narrative*, 7, see also 18; Neary, "Richard de Ledrede," 6.

74. Boureau, *Satan the Heretic*, 43–68. See also Iribarren, "From Black Magic to Heresy."

75. Neary, "Richard de Ledrede," 274.

himself so spectacularly within seven years of his appointment may well have given some prior indication of such an inclination.

England would not have provided an adequate training ground for the situation Ledrede discovered—or created—in his episcopal see, as the country had only moderately more exposure to heresy and diabolical sorcery than did Ireland. After the defeat of Pelagianism in the fifth century and prior to the rise of Lollardy toward the end of the fourteenth, few incidents of heresy occurred in England. The first known trial occurred at Oxford in 1165–66 and led to Henry II promulgating the earliest medieval secular law against heretics, which prohibited his subjects from having any kind of relations with these heretics.[76] His law seems to have had some effect, for after being branded, beaten, and driven from the city, the heretics died amid the cold of winter, as no one would help them. William of Newburgh, who identifies these people as foreigners and Publicans, proclaims that heresy had not reared its head in England since Pelagianism and repeatedly states that it found such opposition that it would not return to England again.[77] Isolated incidents sporadically occurred in the century and a half between the trial of these Publicans and that of the Templars, which Ledrede may have witnessed in France rather than England.[78] However, not until the condemnation of Wyclif and the development of his teachings by Lollards did heresy and its persecution find a home in England.

While accusations of *maleficia* were not uncommon in England, its legal system that enabled defendants to sue their accusers for defamation and its reluctance to employ torture and inquisitorial procedure, as demonstrated in the Templar trial, mitigated against the kind of punishments meted out on the Continent in fourteenth-century sorcery trials.[79] Three cases in the first thirty years of the fourteenth century demonstrate the discrepancy between the tactics used in England and those favored in France and by Ledrede. In 1302, John Lovetot accused a man to whom he owed nearly £1,000 of a variety of crimes, including consulting demons. The defendant was an exceptionally powerful man: Walter Langton, the bishop of Coventry and treasurer of England. Although Lovetot had the pope's support, Langton had the king's and was acquitted of the charges.[80] Twenty

---

76. Stubbs, *Select Charters*, 145–46; Wakefield and Evans, *Heresies of the High Middle Ages*, 724n12.

77. Wakefield and Evans, *Heresies of the High Middle Ages*, 245–47; Moore, *War on Heresy*, 180–82.

78. Wakefield and Evans, *Heresies of the High Middle Ages*, 724n12; Stubbs, *Constitutional History*, 3:381n1; Richardson, "Heresy and Lay Power," 1–3.

79. The conflict between common and canon law is discussed in chapter 3.

80. Rymer, vol. 1, pt. 4, pp. 27–28; Hansen, *Quellen und Untersuchungen*, 2; Lea, *History of the Inquisition*, 3:451; Beardwood, "Trial of Walter Langton."

years later and concurrent with the Kilkenny trial, Coventry was involved in another alleged diabolical plot. Twenty-seven men of the town were said to have enlisted the aid of a necromancer to murder the king and other political and religious leaders through image magic. The plan was first tested on another man of Coventry, who went insane with pain and then died. The necromancer's assistant confessed all and met an unknown fate, the necromancer himself died in prison while awaiting trial, and the twenty-seven Coventry men were all acquitted.[81] The third trial involved a Thomas de Ledrede, who may have been kin to the bishop of Ossory and perhaps is the same man whom the bishop appointed as his attorney in 1339 and 1347.[82] The case, laid before the king's court in 1331, claimed that since the Conquest certain people dwelled in London "who meddled in the arts of magic and necromancy and busied themselves against the faith."[83] Upon investigation, the sheriffs found at Southwark two goldsmiths and a necromancer practicing magic that involved copper and wax figurines underneath which were written the names of their enemies, books and formulas "for killing and raising up those they wished," and alchemy. The man whom one of these figurines represented, Robert of Ely, had hired Thomas de Ledrede as his attorney in a suit against one of the goldsmiths, but the defendant maintained that they had been practicing magic in the hopes of winning Robert's friendship, not harming him, a confession supported by his two accomplices. The court remained unconvinced that such kind concerns had been the motive for their magic, but since they had not actually killed anyone, the necromancer and one of the goldsmiths were to remain in prison until further notice, and the third was released.[84] Thus even when the pope was involved (Langton's trial), when a complete confession was given (the Coventry trial), and when the court was convinced that maleficent magic had been used (the Southwark trial), English authorities chose a decidedly different course than the one upon which Richard de Ledrede embarked.

The Kyteler case concurs with the findings of Richard Kieckhefer:

in the majority of cases, the townsmen or villagers who took their neighbors to court did so for essentially practical reasons. . . . The idea

---

81. Wright, *Contemporary Narrative*, xxiii–xxix; *CPR* (1324–27): 44, Kittredge, *Witchcraft in Old and New England*, 77–78.

82. *Reports of the Deputy Keeper of the Public Records of Ireland*, 47:29; *CPR* (1345–48): 262–63; *CFR*, 5:134–35. By the fourteenth century de Ledrede was already a family name (Neary, "Richard de Ledrede," 2–3). A Thomas de Ledrede was in seisin of one messuage of the Hospitallers in Irishtown near Kilkenny in 1348 (Kenny, *Anglo-Irish and Gaelic Women*, 29).

83. Sayles, *Select Cases*, 5:53.

84. Ibid., 53–57.

of diabolism, developed and elaborated on the Continent, was evidently the product of speculation by theologians and jurists, who could make no sense of sorcery except by postulating a diabolical link between the witch and her victim.[85]

The suit made by Alice's stepchildren derived from a fairly mundane and eminently practical dispute. Ledrede, however, transformed this simple property issue into the manifestation of almost every theory devised by the learned elite, and his charges reflect a marked influence of the paranoid perspective of the pope who appointed him bishop. As Kieckhefer has argued,

> In so far as necromancers contributed to the plausibility of claims about witches, they bear indirect responsibility for the rise of the European witch trials in the fifteenth and following centuries. To the extent that these early witch trials focused on female victims, they thus provide a particularly tragic case of women being blamed and punished for the misconduct of men: women who were not invoking demons could more easily be thought to do so at a time when certain men were in fact so doing.[86]

The possibility of necromancers or their influence within the papal court that shaped Ledrede's attitude toward witchcraft or even among Anglo-Irish religious is far greater than that of Alice's demon lover. An exemplum written by an English-born Anglo-Irishman living in France in the 1270s told of another English-born Anglo-Irishman, "Master Peter de Ardene, well-known to all his contemporary clerics of Ireland," who befriended a Spanish necromancer.[87] The Spaniard performed magic for his friend's entertainment, and Peter must have been quite amused; the activities continued for five nights, by which time Peter had taken an active role. Judging from a fourteenth-century manuscript, the Knights Hospitaller of the former Templar house of Kilbarry apparently approved of the use of magic if it kept rats from their corn or helped heal a wound from a lance.[88] A poem entitled "The Ten Commandments," found in a manuscript from roughly the same time and probably composed in Waterford, reviles those who "liuith op goddis throgh wichcraft" and maintains that "Thai ssul al to the deuil gone" but does not specify the gender of those engaging in

---

85. Kieckhefer, *European Witch Trials*, 36.

86. Kieckhefer, *Forbidden Rites*, 12. See also Bailey, "From Sorcery to Witchcraft."

87. Little, *Liber exemplorum*, 22, see also vi–vii.

88. Sinclair, "Anglo-Norman at Waterford," 226. The *Liber Niger* of Holy Trinity, Dublin, also records an incantation to alleviate toothache (Lawlor, "Calendar of the Liber Niger," 67).

such nefarious activities.[89] Another poem from the same manuscript, however, argues that Satan first approached Eve due to man's natural affection for woman that enables women to persuade men to do their bidding, offering a more female-friendly explanation for a claim that would become a familiar refrain among prosecutors of witchcraft in the fifteenth and later centuries, that women are more susceptible to the devil and thus to witchcraft.[90]

Gender and the Colony of Ireland

Gender was becoming an increasing concern in the fourteenth-century colony, particularly regarding gaelicization. In *A View to the Present State of Ireland*, Edmund Spenser presented "Irishness" as an infection spreading among the "Old English," that is, Anglo-Irish colonists who had been in Ireland for generations; according to Spenser, the disease was carried mainly by women, the Gaelic Irish wives, mothers, and nurses of Anglo-Irish men and children.[91] Although medieval authors did not make the connection between gender and gaelicization as explicit as Spenser would in the sixteenth century, many thirteenth- and fourteenth-century colonists were equally disturbed by the tendency among some of their fellow colonists to adopt Irish customs, language, law, hairstyles, and dress, or to marry or foster their children with native Irish. According to the Statute of Kilkenny in 1366:

> Many English of [Ireland], forsaking the English language, fashion, mode of riding, laws and usages, live and govern themselves according to the manners, fashion and language of the Irish enemies, and also have made divers marriages and alliances between themselves and the Irish enemies aforesaid; whereby the said land and the liege people thereof, the English language, the allegiance due to our lord the King, and the English laws there are put in subjection and decayed and the Irish enemies exalted and raised up.[92]

The statute continued that no English were to enter into any alliance with the Irish, including marriage and fosterage, or to adopt Irish names, customs, or dress, and it particularly castigated those who used Irish language and law.

---

89. London, British Library, Harley 913. See Bliss, "Language and Literature"; *NHI*, 2:708–36; Mullally, "Hiberno-Norman Literature"; and Lucas, *Anglo-Irish Poems*. Edited in Lucas, *Anglo-Irish Poems*, 118.

90. Lucas, *Anglo-Irish Poems*, 104.

91. Spenser, *Works*, 638.

92. The remarks regarding the English language are particularly ironic, as the statutes were written in French (Berry, *Early Statutes*, 430–31; *IHD*, 52, Curtis and McDowell's translation).

The colony's decline was only partly the product of increasing gaelicization. Female inheritance rights under English feudal law played a critical role, as many early colonial lords and their descendants had only female heirs and thus their lands were repeatedly divided. Such was the case in the liberty of Kilkenny itself, inherited by Gilbert de Clare's three sisters after he died at Bannockburn in 1314. This situation, found throughout colonial Ireland, was further exacerbated by absenteeism, as few English men and women who inherited lands in Ireland, including Clare and his sisters, resided there.[93] By 1333, about two-thirds of the English colony belonged to absentee lords, and the percentage continued to increase throughout the fourteenth century.[94] As in the case of Richard de Haverings, the absentee archbishop-elect of Dublin discussed in chapter 1, they continued to receive the produce of their property but contributed little or nothing to its maintenance and defense, thereby enabling the Irish to recover some of those lands. Several other factors also contributed to the colony's decline, but "the passing of so much authority all over Ireland into the hands of absentee landlords in [the fourteenth] century, and the fragmentation of lordships by division among co-heiresses, [ultimately brought] about the decline of the colony."[95]

Female inheritance was a significant concern in the thirteenth- and fourteenth-century colony, and in the Kyteler case. In 1299, one family tried to circumvent female inheritance laws with an agreement that, in the absence of male heirs in the main line, the barony of Ikeathy should pass to "the most noble, worthy, strong, and praiseworthy of the pure blood and name of Rochefordeyns . . . so that the inheritance shall never pass to daughters."[96] This approach, an "ingenious attempt to fit English forms to Gaelic realities," reflects a pronounced influence of native Irish law, in which male successors were chosen from and by members of a kin-group.[97] A similar solution may have underlain Richard de Valle's attempt to deprive his stepmother of her widow's dower in 1316, a right not recognized in native Irish

---

93. *NHI*, 2:169, 269.

94. Frame, *English Lordship*, 52–74.

95. Otway-Ruthven, *A History of Medieval Ireland*, 251. Other factors, including the Gaelic Resurgence, feuds between leading Anglo-Irish families, tensions between the Anglo-Irish and the English, perpetual warfare within Ireland and in other areas of the English king's domain (which often called some of the colony's fighting force to action elsewhere), the Bruce invasion of 1315–18, and later the Black Death, are discussed elsewhere.

96. *CJR*, 1:326. For further discussion of women's exclusion from inheritance, see Kenny, *Anglo-Irish and Gaelic Women*, 30–33.

97. Hand, *English Law*, 173.

law.[98] A daughter of a wealthy Flemish merchant family who had settled in Kilkenny, the young Alice may have gone to her first husband with a sizeable dowry and probably inherited some of her father's property. Her first husband, an Outlaw, was likely a man of some position and wealth, particularly since his kinsman Roger Outlaw became one of the lordship's most powerful men. She presumably had received one-third of this husband's property by 1302, when she was married to Adam le Blund of Callan, the son of Henry le Blund, a wealthy burgess of Kilkenny. Adam's arrangement in 1307 to renounce all claim to his property in favor of Alice's preferred and perhaps only child probably included the third that would have been her dower, but by this time she was already independently wealthy through previous inheritances as well as her lucrative profession, moneylending, in which she engaged with her husbands and her son.[99] Her comfortable finances, however, did not prevent her from claiming her own against the son of her third husband, a prosperous knight of Tipperary, when he tried to dispossess her of her dower.

Alice's considerable wealth made her an attractive target for Ledrede's prosecution. As Cohn has remarked, "All the charges, in fact, are designed to serve one and the same purpose: to show that Lady Alice had no right to her wealth, that it had been wrested from its rightful owners by truly diabolic means, that it was tainted at the source."[100] Her stepchildren were not alone in their hopes to claim themselves as the rightful recipients of her property by this trial. The *Narrative* briefly refers to a previous case found by William Outlaw in the Kilkenny archives, which the loyal text deems "false," in which Ledrede was the defendant in a suit brought by a widow concerning his appropriation of her husband's property. According to the *Narrative*, the only surviving source for the suit, the case was dropped because it did not fall under secular jurisdiction, not because Ledrede was justified.[101] Heresy trials entailed the seizure of the convicted's property, to which the bishop of the diocese held a claim. When Ledrede finally succeeded in gaining the justiciar's assistance in Alice's arrest, he declared that as "a sorceress, a magician, a heretic, and one who has relapsed" (though she had not yet been tried, let alone relapsed), she was to be relaxed to the secular arm and her property confiscated.[102] The ultimate fate of her fortune is unknown, but the case

---

98. Resistance to widow's dower was fairly common in England as well, however; see Ward, "The English Noblewoman," 129, and Walker, "Litigation as Personal Quest."
99. E.g., *CJR*, 2:49, 324; 3:122; Tresham, I.i.14.
100. Cohn, *Europe's Inner Demons*, 138.
101. Wright, *Contemporary Narrative*, 10.
102. Ibid., 25.

against her was based on and permeated with tension over a woman's right to inherit property, a right with which Ledrede had already attempted to interfere.[103]

Women regularly inherited from male—and occasionally female—relatives, but their land and property were often confiscated.[104] Margaret le Blund, perhaps a relative of Alice's second husband, similarly had to fight an avaricious archbishop who sought her fortune. She petitioned Edward I in 1300 regarding an inheritance seized by the archbishop of Cashel, who she alleged was responsible for the deaths of nine members of her family; due to the archbishop's machinations, the royal writs awarding her the property were useless, though she had crossed the turbulent Irish Sea five times seeking redress.[105] The thrice-married Agnes de Valence had her suit against the Geraldine John fitz Thomas, kin to her first husband who had seized her land and claimed her dead, thrown out in 1305, since it came out of the English, rather than the Irish, chancery; she repeated the suit with (colonial) Irish writs and eventually won, though she probably never received her property before her death in 1309. To fitz Thomas, she seemed "a dangerous meddling irritant" whose possession of his family lands rendered them vulnerable to the native Irish.[106] Similar resentment regarding female inheritance in the absence of male heirs played a critical role in seventeenth-century witchcraft accusations in New England, which has far more extant documentary evidence than medieval examples. Regardless whether the heiresses ever received their property, these "aberrations in a society with an inheritance system designed to keep property in the hands of men" were cast as Satan's agents who rejected their proper place and sought to destroy the community.[107] Though such sentiments are evident in the fourteenth-century colony, few if any made the connection that Ledrede and later witch hunters would, that female inheritance indicated Satan's hand, with heiresses as his witches. Alice's popular support, evident even in the hostile *Narrative*, provides a potent reminder, however, that at least some people accepted a woman's right to her wealth.[108]

---

103. See also the seventh constitution of his synod of Ossory (Gwynn, "Provincial and Diocesan Decrees," 61).

104. Conlon, "Women in Medieval Dublin"; Kenny, "The Power of Dower," esp. 62–64, 66–70. See also Maurice fitz Thomas's seizure of Margaret Badlesmere's lands, discussed in chapter 4.

105. Killen, *Ecclesiastical History*, 1:257; Leland, *History of Ireland*, 1:234–35; and Connolly, "Irish Material in the Class of Ancient Petitions," 102.

106. Ó Cléirigh, "Absentee Landlady," 117.

107. Karlsen, *Devil in the Shape of a Woman*, 101.

108. For discussion of other fourteenth-century Kilkenny heiresses and female entrepeneurs, see Kenny, *Anglo-Irish and Gaelic Women*, 19.

The vehemence with which Ledrede pursued this exceptional case suggests an origin in his own gender insecurities.[109] Vern Bullough has proposed that "a previously overlooked explanation for the seeming rise of witchcraft at the end of the medieval period was a growing concern over male potency and performance. . . . [W]hen masculinity is equated with potency and any sign of lack of virility is a threat to one's definition of a man, it becomes easy to accept the existence of malevolent feminine forces."[110] Notions of masculinity dependent on sexual prowess with women and procreation could deem celibate clergy like Ledrede inadequate or even emasculine.[111] Accusations of thievery, with which Ledrede contended for much of his episcopate, were, according to Derek Neal, the main way to undercut a man's masculinity.[112] His association with "MacThomas's Rout," which perhaps was perceived as bestial and uncivilized, not unlike the *beani*, or new university students likened to goats, discussed by Ruth Mazo Karras, might have further undermined others' sense of his masculinity.[113] His constant power struggles with prominent secular leaders, especially Arnold le Poer and Edward III, could suggest he was regarded as less than a man by his secular contemporaries.[114] Yet such interpretations do not well fit the evidence. The *Narrative*, our most detailed source for Ledrede's conflicts and others' perceptions of him, may deliberately conceal aspersions upon his masculinity, but neither that account nor other texts suggest it was questioned or threatened, beyond the threat independent, wealthy women posed to patriarchy generally. Edward undoubtedly regarded Ledrede as less of a man than he was, as he likely regarded virtually all of his subjects. Gender is deeply intertwined with power, but power struggles are not inevitably gendered. Ledrede's contemporaries do not seem to have scorned him because of failings in his masculinity but because of problems with his personality and agenda.

Medievalists have explored multiple approaches to masculinity, such as those of warriors, scholars, and workers, and frequently quote Judith Butler: "gender is an identity tenuously constructed in time . . . through a stylised repetition of acts," which is not "a substantial model of identity" but "a constituted social temporality."[115] By the nature of the surviving texts, however, the perspectives of those upholding society's status quo have perhaps

---

109. Much of this material is discussed further in chapters 3 and 4.
110. Bullough, "On Being a Male," 43.
111. See Swanson's theory of a third gender in "Angels Incarnate."
112. Neal, *Masculine Self*, 13–56.
113. Karras, *From Boys to Men*, 67–108; Karras, "Separating the Men from the Goats."
114. Arnold's label of Ledrede as *trutannus* (tramp) arguably has such gender implications.
115. Butler, *Gender Trouble*, 140–41.

been overemphasized.[116] How accurately these notions of gender reflect the
wider population's views cannot be determined. For example, as thieves
have their own sense of honor, they probably have their own conceptions
of gender that vary from the ones held by those who would see them hang.
Moreover, a wide range of powerful, respectable men in the colony, including Ledrede's adversary Alexander de Bicknor, were also accused of theft.[117]
Such accusations certainly complicated their lives, but the evidence does
not indicate that they significantly influenced their status as men. Similarly,
differences between secular and ecclesiastical notions of masculinity apparently played little role in determining allegiances in the *Narrative*. Ledrede
was virtually alone in his attempt to impose canon over civil law, opposed
by religious and secular alike. His greatest male opponents (Arnold le Poer
and William Outlaw) were secular figures, but they were joined by religious
leaders (Roger Outlaw and Alexander de Bicknor, among others).[118] The
homosocial (male-only) worlds of church leadership and secular government combined both in the lordship and in their opposition to Ledrede.
As that opposition increased, as it did in the years following the Kyteler
case, Ledrede lashed out not at "malevolent feminine forces" but at his male
opponents and associates: Arnold le Poer, Roger Outlaw, Robert de Caunton,
and Alexander de Bicknor.

The *Narrative* provides greater evidence regarding Ledrede's conception
of his own masculinity, modelled after Christ himself and the more recent
example of Thomas Becket. On one level both could be viewed as effeminate
failures, helpless before their secular executioners. Yet (according to Christian
belief) both ultimately showed far superior strength, with Christ conquering
sin, death, and at length the world, while Becket's murder forced the king into
at least a semblance of penance as he himself attained heaven. As Colleen
Conway has argued, Christ's example stands at odds with a dominant elite
masculinity equated with the ruling class, demonstrating superior masculinity by freely and willingly dying for others and the sake of righteousness,
proving the ultimate powerlessness of his opponents.[119] Ledrede saw himself
in strikingly similar terms, repeatedly expressing his willingness to die for

---

116. Anthologies often explore a wider range of approaches to masculinity, such as Cohen and
Wheeler's *Becoming Male in the Middle Ages*.

117. Lydon, "The Case against Alexander Bicknor."

118. His crucial, if temporary, allies likewise bridged the secular (John Darcy) and religious
(William de Nottingham and William de Rodyerd) divide. His fellow friars John Clyn and John de
Pembridge gave him limited annalistic support as well.

119. Conway, *Behold the Man*; see also L. Stephanie Cobb's study of gender and early martyrdom,
Dying to Be Men.

the faith and openly courting conflict with secular leaders. His advanced education and relationship with John XXII further strengthened his sense of his own masculine power and status in the colony. Even if regarded as less of a man by his contemporaries, Ledrede could meet their disdain with confidence, as he based his self-image on the one his society revered as the greatest man of all.

Alice Kyteler

Alice's first appearance in the historical record foreshadows her last, with greed for her wealth giving rise to unfounded accusations. In 1302, she and her husband Adam were accused of murder by her own kinsman, William le Kiteler, sheriff of Kilkenny. This accusation arose after William Outlaw charged the sheriff as well as the then seneschal of Kilkenny, Fulk de la Freyne, of stealing £3,000 that Alice and Adam had entrusted to William for safekeeping, as well as £100 of William's own money; these were both exorbitant sums, although Adam and Alice's nest egg thirty times more so, at a time when the combined value of the Templar estates in Ireland was valued at little more than £400, when annual donations to the Holy Cross at Holy Trinity amounted to approximately £40, and when female laborers received 1/2 d., half of what their male equivalents received, for a day's wages.[120] The sheriff, on the seneschal's advice, dug up the money from underneath William Outlaw's house during the night and attempted to claim it as treasure trove, since it came from the ground. When William protested, the sheriff and the seneschal accused Alice and Adam of homicide and other malicious crimes, "although they had committed none," as well as of harboring Rose Outlaw (relation uncertain), who had been detained for but not convicted of theft, then imprisoned all three and threatened to execute them.[121] The accused had several powerful allies who offered to act as their mainpernors, including Eustace le Poer, Arnold le Poer's uncle and the head of his lineage, and John le Poer, who may be the one who later became Alice's fourth husband. But their most powerful ally was the king, who that same year acknowledged a debt to Alice and Adam of £500 to aid the Scottish wars; he commanded the sheriff of Dublin to have the sheriff and seneschal of Kilkenny appear before the justiciar to answer for their trespass against Alice, Adam, and Rose.[122] William Outlaw,

---

120. Perkins, "The Knights Templars in the British Isles," 223; RCB, *Registrum Novum*, 372; and Conlon, "Women in Medieval Dublin," 184.

121. Tresham, I.i.4.

122. Tresham, I.i.6; Tresham, I.i.4; Wright, *Contemporary Narrative*, 47–48.

Adam le Blund, and William le Kiteler may have overcome their differences by 1305, however, when Outlaw was the sovereign (equivalent to the mayor) of Kilkenny and the three were defendants in a suit against them and several others for harassing a Walter de Kenley in Kilkenny.[123]

This incident serves as a disturbing prelude to the events that would later take Petronilla de Midia's life. The similarities with the trial indicate ongoing resentment directed at Alice due to her wealth and family entanglements. It also suggests an alternative fate for Alice and Petronilla if the charge of *maleficia* had been prosecuted under common rather than canon law and if the developing ideology of witchcraft persecution had not been abruptly applied to an unprepared context. Significantly, the previous charge of murder does not surface in her trial, nor is she denounced for her multiple marriages (except for her allegedly active role in her widowhood) or her profession—the areas in which a modern audience might expect her to be most vulnerable.[124] Though Ledrede accused her son of usury amid the thirty-four counts he ultimately brought against him and linked usury with heresy in the seventeenth canon of his synodal constitution, almost certainly added after the Kyteler trial, he did not make such an allegation against Alice, although he probably could have.[125] In ways, Ledrede's silence is more intriguing than his accusations, and in the person of Alice Kyteler, truth—or as close as we can get to truth—is more fascinating than Ledrede's fiction.

Alice plays a marginal role in the case that ostensibly centers around her, and yet from the margins she emerges as a strong, capable, and complex figure. Born into a prominent family, she increased her power and wealth through multiple marriages into some of the most influential families of the time. She used family connections, political intrigues, and legal process to stop or at least stall Ledrede as she kept herself out of his reach. In one of her few acts shown in the *Narrative*, she left Kilkenny before Ledrede's second citation could reach her and went to Dublin, where she sued Ledrede for defamation and maintained that she had been excommunicated without being cited, warned, or convicted.[126] Ledrede countered that he had convicted her of heresy earlier, but she had since abjured and public report as well

---

123. *CJR*, 2:126, 159. The suit was dismissed.

124. While Alice was accused of murdering her husbands in 1324, the allegations of 1302 were not included, unless the victim of the homicide she and Adam were accused of perpetrating was her only known previous husband, the Outlaw.

125. Wright, *Contemporary Narrative*, 25; Gwynn, "Provincial and Diocesan Decrees," 78–79; see chapter 3.

126. Ledrede's initial citation was rejected by Roger Outlaw partly because Alice had not been excommunicated for forty days; after forty days had passed, he cited her again, and also cited her son (Wright, *Contemporary Narrative*, 1, 3, 15); see chapter 3.

as witnesses had compelled him to cite her for relapse of heresy.[127] Nothing in the *Narrative* or elsewhere, however, supports Ledrede's contention that Alice had been previously tried or convicted for heresy, although he would again proclaim her a relapsed heretic once he finally succeeded in having her condemned.[128] While in Dublin, "the oft-mentioned lady, sorceress, heretic, and magician was permitted to mingle freely in the city with faithful companions, solemnly led by William Doucemanne of Dublin City, as well as many other clerics and lay people, and she was ceremoniously set among the first and the greatest in public assemblies."[129] William Doucemanne, or Douce, was currently the mayor of Dublin, and his close alliance with Alice's family is further indicated by his appointment of William Outlaw as his attorney in 1322.[130] Armed with such powerful and popular support, Alice managed to have the case deferred for a time, as the only one sympathetic to Ledrede's perspective was the precentor of St. Patrick's, William de Nottingham, whose father had been mayor immediately prior to Douce and who may have acted in part out of a feud between the two families.[131] Shortly afterward, however, the political climate switched in Ledrede's favor, and Alice escaped from Ireland, the last known deed of her life.[132]

Several scholars have endorsed the plausibility of Alice's guilt, even while allowing that many of the charges stemmed largely from Ledrede's own mind.[133] Her frequent widowhoods and remarriages up the colonial social ladder, the benefits she received from them, her second husband's quitclaim of all his property to her son shortly before his death, and the potions allegedly found by her supposedly moribund husband and burned by Ledrede may seem suspicious, both then and now, but they hardly prove that she was

---

127. Wright, *Contemporary Narrative*, 15–16.

128. Ibid., 25; see above. Ledrede's summary at the seneschal's court also claims that some heretics had relapsed, and William de Rodyerd's agreement to help Ledrede against Alice also claims her to be relapsed (see chapter 3).

129. Wright, *Contemporary Narrative*, 16.

130. Williams, "'She Was Usually Placed with the Great Men,'" 79. Douce served as mayor 1322–24 and 1330–31 (*NHI*, 9:549). For his daughter Joan's will, see Kenny, *Anglo-Irish and Gaelic Women*, 48.

131. Williams, "'She Was Usually Placed with the Great Men,'" 80. Within a few years, William de Nottingham would again surface in a claim of heresy; see chapter 5.

132. According to Pembridge, Alice took Petronilla's daughter with her (*CSM*, 2:362); he does not say if this was an act of charity or hostage taking.

133. E.g., Ewen, *Witchcraft and Demonianism*, 33; Massey, *Prior Roger Outlaw*, 34; Russell, *Witchcraft in the Middle Ages*, 190–91; Seymour, *Irish Witchcraft and Demonology*, 43; Williams, "'She Was Usually Placed with the Great Men,'" 69. Virtually all nineteenth- and early twentieth-century historians of Ireland that I have consulted wholly endorse Ledrede's findings and actions. Killen, *Ecclesiastical History*, provides an important exception, but he too thinks Alice likely qualified as what was defined as a heretic at the time (see below).

guilty of witchcraft or murder, a conclusion colonial leaders only reluctantly accepted after Ledrede's relentless campaigning. Killen offers the most imaginative theory of Alice's guilt, including that she shared not only the slander of Waldensians but also their beliefs.[134] Since Waldensians were driven into Flanders at the end of the twelfth century, he argues, some adherents may have been among the Flemings who relocated to Kilkenny, including Alice.[135] Yet Killen neglects an important fact: no such beliefs are attributed to Alice either in the *Narrative* or in contemporary chronicles. The charges brought against her and her accomplices in 1324 present heresy as a matter of practice rather than belief; only the first charge concerned belief, but even then it is temporary apostasy for purely practical reasons. From the eleventh century on, ecclesiastical authorities interpreted alternative understandings of Christianity advanced by heretical groups as arising from and evidence of their allegiance with Satan. The Kyteler case postulates the demonic allegiance, but without reference to theological heresy, except any implicit in such an allegiance, and their alleged practices are almost entirely derivative of this allegiance as well. While the evidence that Alice could have been guilty of witchcraft or murder is tenuous at best, the evidence that she was guilty of heresy is virtually nonexistent, even within the *Narrative* itself.

Family feuds involving Alice's own kin, her stepchildren, and the larger political context as well as her wealth were the case's primary catalysts, yet the state of early fourteenth-century Anglo-Irish politics would trap many a wight in its web—though, to be sure, very few would have had £3,000 to squirrel away in 1302. An underlying cause of this persecution may be the threat she and women like her—strong, independent heiresses—presented to the colony and its patriarchal values. As with Adducc Dubh O'Toole five years later, perhaps Alice was perceived as representing insidious forces then besetting the colony; Adducc's associated threat was the native Irish, and Alice's could have been female inheritance and its related issue, absentee landlords. If the *Narrative's* claim that allegations that heretical sorceresses infested Kilkenny first arose at Ledrede's visitation is accurate, Alice's name may have been put forward then, perhaps by men such as her stepson Richard de Valle, who were angered by the benefits she received from her multiple marriages and the active role she took in business. Those who desired her wealth, like Fulk de la Freyne and William le Kiteler, may have played on Ledrede's fear

---

134. Guilt may be a somewhat misleading term, as Killen, *Ecclesiastical History*, advances a Protestant perspective that presents medieval heretics such as Waldensians and Lollards as more enlightened Christians than Catholics, whom he often suggests were the true heretics.

135. Killen, *Ecclesiastical History*, 1:280–85.

of women in league with the devil.[136] Perhaps too her marriage into the le Poer family, which since 1290 had followed the distinctly Irish system of kin accountability, made her vulnerable to charges of gaelicization, which within a few years of the Kyteler case would be linked with heresy.[137] Her frequent marriages may have reminded her opponents of native Irish marriage customs, which allowed for divorce and remarriage and outraged colonists and the church; while Alice was repeatedly widowed rather than divorced (although the fate of her first husband is unknown), perhaps that served to convince others besides her stepchildren that she facilitated the demise of her husbands by means of *maleficia*, which included magic as well as poison.[138] Yet the general impression given in the *Narrative* is that popular support remained behind Alice and against Ledrede; moreover, the other heresy trials in fourteenth-century Ireland did not raise the spectre of sorcery, nor did they involve women among the accused, even when instigated by Ledrede.[139] The Kyteler case thus seems an anomaly introduced into Ireland by a man trained in France who interpreted a claim of *maleficia* perpetrated by a woman against her husbands as the feminine face of the subversive society John XXII and his like believed to be pursuing the destruction of Christendom.

The Dawn of the Devil-Worshipping Witch

The Kyteler case marks the first time in European history that people accused of witchcraft were prosecuted as an organized heretical sect and also introduced fornication into the demonic pact. Though sexual excess had long been alleged of heretical meetings, witchcraft was not yet heir to heresy's sins, as the identification of witchcraft with heresy was still being forged in Avignon and elsewhere by the learned elite, centering on clerical necromancy. The trials in France as well as England with which the Kyteler case shares similarities focused primarily on male perpetrators; while some of the

---

136. In 1295, Fulk apparently interfered with another woman's property as well; see Kenny, *Anglo-Irish and Gaelic Women*, 26.

137. Cole, *Documents Illustrative of English History*, 71; see also *CJR*, 2:19.

138. Williams points out that John le Poer's symptoms could have been brought on by arsenic or thallium poisoning ("'She Was Usually Placed with the Great Men,'" 69), but old age seems an equally probable cause; in addition, Ledrede may have presented John's supposed symptoms so that they would seem indicative of poisoning.

139. As Kieckhefer has pointed out, the Templar trial involved diabolism, but not sorcery (*European Witch Trials*, 12); in addition, the charges of diabolism were unanimously rejected by the Templars in their trial in Ireland and did not surface in the allegations of outside witnesses (see chapter 1). Ledrede was accused of slandering the queen's chamber with sorcery allegations, however (Sayles, *Documents*, 131; see chapter 4).

accused, including the Templars, were said to be sexual deviants, the allegation is treated as further evidence of their general depravity rather than an
aspect of demonic worship. Significantly, however, the sexual act between
demon and witch was still separate from the witches' sabbath in the Kyteler
case. Though Petronilla allegedly watched, Alice and Robert are portrayed
as having a monogamous relationship, and their sexual relations were said to
have occurred *de die* (during the day).[140] The description of the witches' nocturnal meetings does not include charges of sexual impropriety, apart from
excommunicating their husbands; Russell adds an orgy to the nightly rites,
but this does not appear in the *Narrative* or in the fourteenth-century annals
that discuss the case.[141] Although several scholars have claimed the Kyteler
case to be the first in which a woman was accused of having acquired the
power of sorcery through sexual intercourse with a demon, such a dynamic
is not explicit in the *Narrative*.[142] Intercourse is presented as part of Alice and
Robert's relationship but not necessarily the means by which she attained
her magical skill.

The Kyteler case marks the dawn of the devil-worshipping witch, but
the ingredients for such a stereotype were well in place by the fourteenth
century. While the association between women and witchcraft as well as
the notion of sexual relations between women and nonhumans both have
biblical precedent, and other elements further shaped such notions within
medieval Christianity, vestigial paganism particularly prevalent in Dianic rites
greatly contributed to the correlation between women and witchcraft as well
as between witchcraft and demon worship, as ecclesiastical authorities identified pagan deities as demons.[143] The tenth-century Canon *Episcopi* rejected
the beliefs of "certain wicked women, previously perverted by Satan and
seduced by phantasms and the delusions of demons," that they rode upon
beasts with Diana and "innumerable throngs of women" to serve the Goddess as pernicious nonsense, but nonsense arising from Satan himself, who
deludes the mind of a *muliercula* (little woman) and subjugates her to him
"through faithlessness and unbelief, then instantly transforms himself into
different people's appearances and likenesses." It did not deny the practice

---

140. Wright, *Contemporary Narrative*, 32.

141. Russell, *Witchcraft in the Middle Ages*, 192; Russell and Alexander, *New History of Witchcraft*, 92.

142. Such claims can be found in Cohn, *Europe's Inner Demons*, 140–41; Davidson and Ward, *Sorcery Trial*, 1; Williams, "'She Was Usually Placed with the Great Men,'" 69.

143. 1 Samuel 28; Genesis 6:1–4. Nahum 3:4 links feminine sexuality with witchcraft. Exodus 22:18 reads in the Vulgate "maleficos non patieris vivere," but the Hebrew specifies a sorceress. See Russell, *Witchcraft in the Middle Ages*, 45–100, and, for the identification of pagan deities with demons, Bieler, *Irish Penitentials*, 104–5.

of witchcraft or sorcery, however, instructing bishops and their ministers to eradicate any such practices and to remove from their dioceses any men or women who engaged in them, equating them with heretics.[144] An alternative form of the canon makes the connection between women and witchcraft or sorcery more explicit, referring solely to women as those who used *maleficia et incantationes* (malicious magic and enchantments) to change love into hatred and vice versa or to steal or harm property, as well as those who claim to take nightly rides on beasts transformed into women's likeness.[145]

While these deluded *mulierculae* were not said to harm children or engage in orgies during their nightly revels, such charges arose very early in Christian history, first as accusations against Christians by outsiders, then in the second century by Christians against other Christians whom they considered heretical.[146] In the eleventh century, the church began responding more harshly to heresy, with the first medieval execution for heresy occurring at Orléans in 1022. According to Adémar of Chabannes, this sect adored the devil, who sometimes took the form of an Ethiopian and brought them great wealth daily, and was led by a man who carried ashes of dead children.[147] Paul of Chartres's account of the same sect added allegations of nightly orgies that followed a demon's arrival "in the likeness of some sort of little beast" and the extinguishing of lights; he claimed also that they engaged in child sacrifice "in the manner of the old pagans," with the victim's ashes being made into a sort of perverse eucharist.[148] Like descriptions of nefarious nightly deeds were attributed to Cathars, Patarenes or Publicans, and Waldensians, among others. In an account that he claims to be hearsay from former heretics, Walter Map apparently was the first to label these nightly meetings a "synagogue" and one of the first to specify the "little beast" as an enormous black cat, which would be kissed by the heretics, "some the feet, more under the tail, most the private parts."[149] In 1159 John of Salisbury expanded upon the Canon *Episcopi*, rejecting not only belief in witchcraft but concomitant belief in nightly orgies with babies sacrificed, cut up, and devoured as "demonic delusion" and ignorant superstition among those who lack faith. But in 1233 Gregory IX set a papal seal of approval upon such allegations

---

144. Hansen, *Quellen und Untersuchungen*, 38–39; see also Russell, *Witchcraft in the Middle Ages*, 292–93.

145. Russell, *Witchcraft in the Middle Ages*, 291.

146. Such accusations had been used before the rise of Christianity; see Cohn, *Europe's Inner Demons*, 1–15.

147. Wakefield and Evans, *Heresies of the High Middle Ages*, 75.

148. Ibid., 78–79.

149. Ibid., 254; Map identifies the heretics who were driven from England in 1165 as members of this sect.

by portraying these demonic orgiastic frenzies as actual occurrences among heretics.[150] These allegations would resurface in the trial of the Templars; though the sexual crimes imputed to them focused on homosexual acts, some Templars confessed to having intercourse with demons in female form at their reception as well.[151] Aquinas gave new life to the old idea of the pact when he argued that by accepting help from a demon a person has entered into a pact with it.[152] The cardinal of Santa Sabina, writing in the name of John XXII, built upon that understanding when he equated the demonic pact with heresy in 1320.[153] Various elements of these two strains, witchcraft beliefs and antiheretical propaganda, coalesced in the Kyteler case.

While French sorcery and witchcraft trials in the first quarter of the fourteenth century listed by Kieckhefer reflect the reverse of the gender ratio of the trials overall from 1300 to 1500, the third that involved women often ended with their death at the stake.[154] Ledrede's innovation was in equating a band of witches with a heretical sect, but such might seem a logical conclusion for a student of John XXII. Though John focused on learned male practitioners of ritual magic, the allegation of *maleficia* had been brought to Ledrede about a much married woman; he thus switched the method of her demonic worship from books of necromancy to sex. Yet even this charge seems a late development, as much as the trial's chronology can be discerned within the *Narrative*. Ledrede apparently acted against Alice on the basis of the stepchildren's charge of *maleficia* alone and extended his allegation to include her son primarily if not entirely because of his vehement defense of his mother; only later would her accomplices come to include seven women and three other men.[155] Ledrede's contributions to the *Red Book of Ossory* indicate the thoroughness with which he approached his office, and it seems likely that he would take a similar approach to prosecution. Perhaps as his proceedings progressed he researched the history of witchcraft, and by the

---

150. John of Salisbury, *Policraticus*, 2.17, pp. 105–6; Moore, *War on Heresy*, 274–76.

151. Barber, *Trial of the Templars*, 207.

152. See Hopkin, "Share of Thomas Aquinas," 81–127, esp. 92–93, 115.

153. Hansen, *Quellen und Untersuchungen*, 4–5.

154. Kieckhefer, *European Witch Trials*, 108–11; see also Bailey, "From Sorcery to Witchcraft," 987. Kieckhefer lists nineteen verified sorcery or witchcraft trials that occurred in France 1303–23, about a third of which involved female defendants; half of those ended with the women's deaths at the stake. Kieckhefer does not include the case of the woman condemned and tortured by the canon of Autun; she died in prison and the fate (and sex) of her alleged accomplices is unknown. Over half of the cases concerned male religious defendants; when clerical necromancy is separated out from the sample, the percentage of female defendants increases considerably.

155. Significantly, Ledrede did not make what would seem another likely conclusion for a disciple of John XXII, that William Outlaw was the offspring of Alice's demon lover.

time he had imprisoned Petronilla he had cultivated a detailed image of witches that he fused with slander against heretics.

The *Narrative*, however, was written with the advantages of hindsight, and from the start it identifies women as the agents of these unholy crimes. The first identification of the culprits reflects a fascinating gender discrepancy, in which a masculine adjective (*hæretici*) modifies a feminine noun (*sortilegæ*).[156] Due to the gender ambiguities of Latin, it is not always clear which sex is intended, as the masculine and feminine forms of nouns and adjectives are often indistinguishable, but the *Narrative* repeatedly uses feminine plurals for the defendants, which included four men and thus would grammatically necessitate the use of the masculine plural.[157] While the details of Alice's accomplices vary as much as the labels Ledrede used against her, the seven charges outlined in the beginning of the text make explicit mention only of women as the perpetrators, as did Petronilla's confession upon which six of the charges were based. Thus, the *Narrative* repeatedly presents a group of women as the explicit target of Ledrede's prosecution, even though one-third of the accused were male and even before, among the text's internal events at least, anyone had been accused of a crime except Alice Kyteler and then her son William. The fourth charge against Alice and her female friends makes the gender dynamics behind the trial explicit: the nocturnal rites involved not only an unholy appropriation of the church's power, but also a subversion of the male dominance of marriage. Their sin was against God because it was against their husbands and the church, an indivisible trinity of dominance in the mind of Ledrede.

The initial charge alone cast Alice as the antithesis of the Blessed Virgin, to whom Ledrede was deeply devoted, and the additional six charges further emphasize their differences.[158] Whereas Mary, "whom," according to Ledrede, "no woman resembles, excels or comes near," was praised for her humility, meekness, virginity, poverty, and sinlessness, Alice was putatively proud, determined, much married, inordinately wealthy, and allegedly guilty

---

156. Wright, *Contemporary Narrative*, 1. I have verified this in the manuscript (*heretici sortilege*, London, British Library, Harley 641, fol. 186v).

157. Immediately after listing the twelve accused Ledrede describes them as "notatas, diffamatas, et vehementer suspectas" (Wright, *Contemporary Narrative*, 23); also see the remarks regarding Petronilla's death (quoted above). The editors of the modern translation have commented upon this discrepancy (Davidson and Ward, *Sorcery Trial*, 46n69), but Ward's translation occasionally misrepresents the Latin, as *personas* (a feminine noun meaning "persons") is often translated as "women" (e.g., 46, 52, 54; see also 52, where *pauperiores*, which could be either masculine or feminine plural, is translated as "poorer ladies").

158. About two-thirds of his sixty songs celebrate either the Virgin or the Nativity; see also William Outlaw's penance, discussed in chapter 3.

of heinous crimes.[159] Massey has commented upon the dichotomy "between the figure of the pure young virgin feeding her child milk (a frequent symbol in Ledrede's poems) and the evil old woman feeding her husband poison," as alleged of Alice in the sixth charge, almost certainly the trial's initial impetus.[160] Moreover, the fifth charge portrayed her and her accomplices as a perversion of the loving mother that Mary represented, alleging that they chopped up dead babies to help make those poisons and potions that they then used against their husbands.[161] Alice's repeated remarriages, particularly the last, which probably occurred when she was in her fifties, further emphasize her divergence from the Virgin.[162] In addition, whereas Mary humbly submitted to the Lord's will and was filled with the Holy Spirit at the Annunciation, celebrated in Ledrede's songs, Alice, according to the *Narrative*, engaged in sexual intercourse with a demon that was so physical it left a mess for Petronilla to clean up. Mary's "partner" was God on high, whereas Alice's demon lover was from the lowest rungs of hell.

Later Accounts of the Kyteler Case

Subsequent accounts of the trial continue and exacerbate Ledrede's negative portrayal of Alice. A record slightly later than the *Narrative*, the *Annales Hiberniae* of his fellow Franciscan John Clyn of Kilkenny, thoroughly upholds Ledrede's and the *Narrative's* verdict and adds its own condemnation of Ireland's heretics:

> Prior to [Petronilla], from the days of yore, it had not been seen nor heard in Ireland that someone should suffer the death penalty for heresy. She was the first [to be so executed] according to the memory and account of all then living; not, I say, because she was the first to sin in such fashion, but because she was the first to suffer the just judgment of death for heresy.[163]

---

159. Ledrede, *Latin Poems*, Poem 54, pp. 134–35 (Colledge's translation). In one of his poems Ledrede hails Mary as free of original sin, clarifying in a subsequent poem that she was sanctified in the womb (ibid., Poem 10, pp. 24–25; Poem 41, pp. 100–101); *pace* Colledge, Ledrede did not advance "the much controverted doctrine of the Immaculate Conception" (ibid., xlv), but Thomistic teaching.

160. Massey, *Prior Roger Outlaw*, 35.

161. While Petronilla confessed to using those potions to alter the appearance of women (Wright, *Contemporary Narrative*, 32), the charges Ledrede brought against Alice and her associates do not specify women as the targets of their harassment, indicating his interests in portraying women as perpetrators rather than victims.

162. The last wedding may have been held in Kilkenny while Ledrede was resident as bishop and may have been a notable social occasion, given the prominence of both parties.

163. Clyn, 16.

A man who freely expressed his opinions of the people whose acts he recorded, Clyn has surprisingly little to say about the bishop who shared his order and ruled his see, mentioning him only in connection with his appointment to office and his prosecution of the Kilkenny heretics. While he evidently supported Ledrede's actions in this matter, he did so without endorsing Ledrede himself. Clyn may have written his annals at Fulk de la Freyne's homonymous son's request and could have been biased against Alice and her son, whose wealth his friend's father tried to steal.[164] John de Pembridge, a Dominican of St. Saviour's in Dublin, also recorded these events at approximately the same time as Clyn. He, however, added a variety of charges that do not surface in the *Narrative* and seem to have been later additions.

Almost as much as the *Narrative* itself, Pembridge's additions portray Alice and her associates in the image of what would become the stereotypical witch. He multiplies by three the cocks admitted by Petronilla, adds her last-minute accusation against William Outlaw of wearing a diabolical belt for a year and a day, and claims Alice would sweep up all the dirt of Kilkenny to the house of her son, "conjuring as she said, may all the good fortune of Kilkenny come to this house."[165] While the *Narrative* describes her magical ingredients in fairly generic terms, according to Pembridge they included a host inscribed with the name of the devil and ointments that she would apply to a beam called a "Cowltre," which she and her followers could then use to fly throughout the world.[166] As Williams has noted, if any of these things had surfaced during the trial or its immediate aftermath, they would have been included in the *Narrative*.[167] In addition, certain statements suggest Pembridge misrepresented or was misinformed about some of the facts of the trial. For example, though both Clyn and the *Narrative* place the trial and Petronilla's execution in 1324, Pembridge dates it to 1325; whereas the *Narrative* specifies that as penance William Outlaw had to re-cover St. Canice's Cathedral with lead, Pembridge identifies St. Mary's as the object of William's reroofing penance; moreover, he claims William became a target of Ledrede's investigation only after Petronilla's execution, which was clearly not the case. Perhaps stories had started to circulate about the spectacular events of 1324 that Pembridge then recorded in his annals, or perhaps as a Dominican personally interested in heresy, as several entries in his annals suggest, he introduced certain elements from other trials of which he was aware.[168] At

164. Williams, "Annals of Friar John Clyn," 72.
165. *CSM*, 2:362.
166. Wright, *Contemporary Narrative*, 2, 26; *CSM*, 2:363.
167. Williams, "Dominican Annals," 163.
168. *CSM, s.a.*, 1287, 1307, 1312, 1328.

the very least, however, his annals indicate that the attitude toward Alice in Dublin had drastically altered in the decade or so since she had freely associated with colonial leaders at public gatherings.

The elaborate and fanciful picture painted by Pembridge remained a favorite among subsequent historians. Another Kilkennian, James Grace, repeats Pembridge's claims in his *Annales Hiberniae* of 1537–39, although he stresses her sexual relations with an incubus, not mentioned by Pembridge, as the smoking gun that convicted her of diabolical sorcery.[169] A few decades later, Raphael Holinshed added nine peacocks' eyes to Pembridge's nine cocks and set Pembridge's description of Alice's nefarious sweeping activities to verse: "To the house of William my sonne, hie all the wealth of Kilkenny towne," which was repeated by Campion in the seventeenth century and echoed by Yeats in his poem *Nineteen Hundred and Nineteen*, which further describes Alice as "lovelorn."[170] Thus, in Irish legend and even among some contemporary scholars, Alice remains largely as Ledrede defined her. Yet a tale of uncertain date recorded in R. B. Cragg's *Legendary Rambles* offers an intriguing twist.[171] Following either Holinshed or Campion, whose accounts are virtually identical, the tale relocates Alice's activities to Clapdale Castle in fifteenth-century England and makes her the foster mother of John de Clapham.

In this account, Alice is described as a witch sworn to the devil, yet she remains a sympathetic figure who has the support of the local people, retains respect for the church, and performs her witchcraft for the benefit of her shiftless foster son. Apart from her allegiance to the devil and her magical acts, the crimes told in the tale are all those of John de Clapham, fighting on the Lancastrian side in the War of the Roses with the help of demon armies conjured by his foster mother. After John kills two prisoners in a church, the demon army deserts him, as Alice had him swear not to profane a house of God, and he is killed shortly thereafter by the Duke of York. Alice is subsequently taken prisoner by Yorkist forces, and under the authority of the bishop of Ossory, then holding a visitation in Lancaster for some unexplained reason, she is tried for and convicted of witchcraft on evidence that first appears in Pembridge, including the eucharist inscribed with the devil's name. Both the bishop and the jury are sympathetic, however, as she acted out of love for her foster son and never hurt anyone through her sorceries.

---

169. Grace, *Annales Hiberniae*, 100.

170. Holinshed, *Chronicles of England, Scotland, and Ireland*, 220; Campion, *Historie of Ireland*, 86; and Yeats, *Selected Poems*, 113.

171. I thank Bernadette Williams for bringing this tale to my notice and providing me with a copy.

Convinced of her genuine repentance, the bishop performs an exorcism that nearly kills her, after which she shouts hallelujah and is restored to sanity. Her penance mirrors that of William Outlaw, repairing the roof of Clapham's church with lead.

While Ledrede and his contemporary and subsequent historians would have gladly sent Alice to the stake, this author gives his tale and her life a different ending: "She lived a few years with the holy sisters at Twistleton, and died in the odour of sanctity, her soul returned to its Maker, and her body lay at rest in holy ground."[172] The primary bases on which Alice originally became suspected of witchcraft, her marriages, sexuality, and wealth, are wholly excised in this retelling; Alice is not identified as a widow, wife, demon lover, or birth mother, and she has no money to pay for the reroofing but does so with a mine of which she alone seems to know. Williams has suggested the source of the tale may be Alice's escape from Ireland with the possible goal of Flanders, but her journey stopped at Clapdale and a legend subsequently developed around her.[173] While such a theory is intriguing, the tale's heavy reliance on other accounts of the Kyteler case, including verbatim passages, mutatis mutandis, suggests that the author may have taken Campion's last words on the subject, that Alice was "conveyed into England, since which time no man wotteth what became of her," as an occasion to write a continuation of her tale.[174] Or perhaps Clapdale had its own legend of a witch about whom little was known, except that people regarded her favorably and she helped her foster son in his efforts against the Yorkists, and the author decided to fill the gaps with details from the Kyteler case.

Captivating as the witchcraft of the Kyteler case has remained for centuries, it tells a fraction of the story, one with more intrigues and complex characters than a Chaucerian tale, as the following chapter further illustrates. A striking standard for something that resists standardization and an alarming anomaly, the case displays tendencies not otherwise prevalent in witchcraft trials until the following century and occurred in an area that hitherto had not witnessed such ecclesiastical machinations and never really would again. Various theories have been advanced as to the overwhelming majority of women

---

172. Cragg, *Legendary Rambles*, 39.

173. Williams, "'She Was Usually Placed with the Great Men,'" 83.

174. Campion, *Historie of Ireland*, 86; also Holinshed, *Chronicles of England, Scotland, and Ireland*. Pembridge first made this claim (*CSM*, 2:363–64). Neither the *Narrative* nor Clyn mentions Alice's refuge after she fled Kilkenny. One example of close conformity to the sources is that, as Alice swept the bridge of Clapham, she said, "Into the house of John, my sonne, // Hie all the wealth of Clapham towne" (Cragg, *Legendary Rambles*, 31, 38).

among the victims of the witch craze, but such theories are based on an epidemic raging for centuries and arising primarily in countries with a long and active history of religious persecution, and none accurately describes Ireland's experience. While various "catastrophes" were currently besetting the colony, Alice and her accomplices were not blamed for them; nor does the evidence suggest they were healers or midwives, although the potions ascribed to them have led one scholar to theorize that Alice may have engaged in such activities.[175] The putative preponderance of women in heretical movements that Russell has theorized greatly contributed to the large number of female defendants in witch trials clearly does not apply to Ireland, as the Kyteler case is the only known medieval heresy trial in Ireland that involved women.[176] Nor does his argument that female alienation may have prompted women to engage in such practices seem applicable, as Alice appears to have been integrated fully within colonial society and the possibility that she or her accomplices actually practiced sorcery seems remote indeed.[177]

Even the standard solution of misogyny as the source of the witch craze is far from compelling in the Kyteler case. Ledrede clearly resented what he interpreted as certain women, and one woman in particular, usurping male prerogatives in the Catholic church and marriage, but that does not prove he hated and feared women as a sex. While Ledrede may well have abhorred women as much as he adored the Virgin Mother, perhaps indicated by his focus on Mary's differences from other women rather than on the similarities she shares with her sisters, his mission against heretics in Ireland that continued for decades otherwise involved only men. Significantly, however, he did not accuse them of witchcraft or sorcery, whereas he is said to have slandered the queen's chamber with such allegations, indicating that to him sorcery was a sex-related, if not sex-specific, crime.[178] The use of gender in the *Narrative* reveals that Ledrede specifically targeted women in his prosecution of the Kyteler case, as does the preponderance of women among the accused, but it is unclear why or when he widened the net from mother and son to include at least ten additional defendants, about whom little to nothing else is known. Nor does the evidence attest to rampant misogyny in the early fourteenth-century colony. The poem on the Fall (cited above) explains Satan's advances to Eve as arising from man's love of woman, not her deviousness, weakness, or any other negative qualities.[179] Gerald fitz Maurice, the son of Arnold le

---

175. Killen, *Ecclesiastical History*, 1:282.

176. Russell, *Witchcraft in the Middle Ages*, 281–82.

177. Ibid., 202, 283–85.

178. Sayles, *Documents*, 131; see chapter 4.

179. In Lucas, *Anglo-Irish Poems*, 104.

Poer's archenemy and Ledrede's occasional ally Maurice fitz Thomas, wrote a spirited defense of women in the second half of the fourteenth century, but what specifically prompted him to rebut "all the blame they have always had" is unknown.[180] Some colonists were concerned about female inheritance rights, but the detrimental effects of female inheritance on the administration of the lordship apparently did not cause them to offer diatribes against women. Alice had been targeted before for her wealth, but not for her sex; while her stepchildren did accuse her of *maleficia*, they presumably did not share Ledrede's understanding of the charge nor anticipate the additional allegations he would make against her. Few could, as the stereotype of the witch was still shadowy before a Franciscan handpicked by John XXII for episcopal office in a land that many Europeans regarded as the most remote corner of the Western world first combined several of the elements that culminated in that stereotype, and in the victimization of those to whom that stereotype was applied.[181]

---

180. Jackson, *Celtic Miscellany*, 101.

181. A Dublin Dominican added other prototypical elements within twenty years of the Kyteler case, still decades before a witchcraft trial that shared in this stereotype to a similar degree is known to have occurred in Europe.

❧ CHAPTER 3

The Churlish Tramp from England

Richard de Ledrede Tries the Alice Kyteler Case

In his prosecution of the Kyteler case, Richard de Ledrede encountered vehement opposition from Arnold le Poer, seneschal of Kilkenny and kin to Alice's current husband, and Roger Outlaw, prior of the Hospitallers at Kilmainham, chancellor of Ireland, and kin to her first husband; the two men not only refused to arrest those Ledrede accused but actively defied the bishop and even had him arrested. Their position may have been motivated by personal loyalties, but the feud hinged on the conflict between common and canon law and anticipates the ethnic tensions of the later trials. Arnold repeatedly scorned Ledrede as an outsider in the colony due to his English birth and papal appointment and attempted to persuade parliament to dismiss his accusations by presenting them as an attack on the "isle of the saints" against which they must all unite. This tactic failed, and the tide turned in Ledrede's favor long enough for Alice's alleged apprentice Petronilla de Midia to suffer two more novelties introduced into Ireland by Ledrede—torture and death at the stake—after Alice herself had fled the country. Previous studies of the Kyteler case have interpreted Ledrede's success as inevitable, a conclusion this chapter challenges; it also situates the case within the larger conflict between civil and ecclesiastical jurisdiction and explores the nascent Irish nationalism that emerges in the case.

Ledrede's Constitutions

Ledrede's predecessor in office was William fitz John, an Englishman elected by his fellow canons of St. Canice's Cathedral in 1302. Fitz John was solidly a "king's man" and served as chancellor of the colony while he was bishop of Ossory (1314 and 1316) and archbishop of Cashel (1317–22), being replaced in 1322 by Roger Outlaw.[1] He was one of the main proponents of a statute passed at the Kilkenny parliament of 1310 that forbade native Irish religious to enter colonial communities.[2] He apparently was a man of personal laxity, if the claims that he fathered fourteen daughters and married them to nobles with substantial dowries have any truth.[3] He also had some trouble with the denizens of his diocese, but he seems to have been more concerned with royal affairs than religious ones, and reform may have been necessary after his episcopate.[4] One key issue during Ledrede's synod was clerical marriage, which had previously been a problem in Ossory, and one on which fitz John may well have turned a blind eye, given his own alleged indiscretions.[5]

Several documents included in the *Red Book of Ossory* reveal the diligence and determination with which Ledrede approached his office, an impression further substantiated by the speed with which he held a synod and the constitutions it enacted.[6] These are copies of statutes and ordinances that predate his appointment to office that are almost without exception concerned with ecclesiastical liberty.[7] They include portions of Magna Carta that protect the freedom and privileges of the church and its confirmation by Edward I in 1297; Statutes of Westminister II concerning ecclesiastical and civil jurisdiction; the statutes *Circumspecte agatis* of 1286 that defined the boundaries between the two jurisdictions, and *Articuli Cleri*, issued thirty years later, that attempted to define said boundaries more clearly.[8] Also found in the *Red Book* is Ledrede's 1319 taxation assessment of Ossory, another alacritous act

---

1. Outlaw served as chancellor 1322–31, 1332–34, 1334–37, and 1338 until his death on February 6, 1341 (*NHI*, 9:502).

2. Berry, *Early Statutes*, 272–73; Otway-Ruthven, *A History of Medieval Ireland*, 138. The statute was repealed shortly after at the request of Walter Jorz, archbishop of Armagh; the Irish Remonstrance, however, blamed Jorz for its enactment (*IHD*, 41; see chapter 5).

3. Gwynn, *Anglo-Irish Church Life*, 9.

4. E.g., *CJR* 2:42–43; Neary, "Richard de Ledrede," 22.

5. *CPL*, 1:190, 197–98, 250. Clerical marriage was more accepted in Gaelic Irish areas, but also occurred frequently among the Anglo-Irish; see Kenny, *Anglo-Irish and Gaelic Women*, 121–26.

6. The *Red Book* is a compilation of texts from the thirteenth to the sixteenth centuries, several of which are from Ledrede's archives; see Gwynn, "Provincial and Diocesan Decrees," 35; Lawlor, "Calendar of the Liber Ruber," 160; Neary, "Richard de Ledrede," 13–25.

7. Neary, "Richard de Ledrede," 17.

8. Lawlor, "Calendar of the Liber Ruber," 183; Neary, "Richard de Ledrede," 17.

fulfilling Edward II's order that such assessments be made in Ireland to evaluate the effects of the Bruce invasion, as well as an assessment of 1306, which a note attributes not to William fitz John, but to Ledrede, who compiled it from the Register of the Curia, the Register of the Clerks near London, and the Register at St. Paul's, London.[9] The *Red Book* also preserves the only extant copies of the constitutions of the synods of Alexander de Bicknor (ca. 1320) and John of St. Paul (1352), archbishops of Dublin, which Ledrede would have attended as their suffragan.[10]

The constitutions of Ledrede's own synod of October 6, 1317, also found in the *Red Book*, aimed at reforming the clergy, ensuring their liberties, and regulating their relations with the laity.[11] Over half of the initial statutes prescribed proper clerical behavior, including demanding that those who kept "concubines" were to separate from them within a month of the publication of the constitutions or suffer suspension from office and a loss of a third of the fruits of their benefices, castigating priests who celebrated clandestine marriages, and demanding that those who had cure of souls be promoted to the priesthood within a year and reside in their parishes.[12] Several of the synod's constitutions repeat the tenets of *Circumspecte agatis*, particularly regarding clerical immunity; those who defame clerics, lay their hands on ecclesiastical property, or violate sanctuary ipso facto became excommunicate.[13] The fourteenth statute almost certainly marks the conclusion of the original constitutions, declaring where (St. Canice's) and by whom (Ledrede, with the consent of most of the clergy of the diocese and "the larger and saner part of the chapter," indicating some resentment and dispute) the preceding synodal statutes had been ordained, and that they were to be recited at an annual synod to be held in St. Canice's on the Tuesday after St. Michael's Day.[14] Yet two more statutes and a general sentence of excommunication against offenders were appended at a later date that differ considerably in tone from the others and show the unmistakable influence of the Kyteler case.

In the fifteenth statute, Ledrede's opponents suffer from comparison with "pagans, gentiles, and Saracens, as even they are accustomed in their sects to

---

9. *CCR* (1318–23): 73 (June 4, 1319); Lawlor, "Calendar of the Liber Ruber," 175.

10. Gwynn, "Provincial and Diocesan Decrees," 71–90.

11. Ibid., 57–71.

12. Clandestine marriage did not involve a public church ceremony, nor was a public announcement (the banns) made in advance, which enabled objections to the union to be raised. They were private exchanges of vows that may or may not have involved others, including a priest. Such marriages were generally recognized by the church; see Kenny, *Anglo-Irish and Gaelic Women*, 52–53, 81–84.

13. Neary, "Richard de Ledrede," 22–23; Powicke and Cheney, *Councils and Synods*, 2:974–75.

14. Gwynn, "Provincial and Diocesan Decrees," 65.

revere and honor their priests and pontiffs before others, as is evident in the Quran and their books."[15] Singularly in world history, "a new and pestiferous people" has arisen in the diocese, filled with a diabolical spirit and separating itself "from the community of all worshippers of God."[16] It attacks God's bishops and priests both in life and in death by destroying and plundering Christ's patrimony in Ossory and thus deserves divine malediction. The culprits harass bishops and their ministers who attempt to enforce ecclesiastical jurisdiction in accordance with canon law including disputing with them in secular courts; for the detriment they do to themselves and others a special remedy must be instituted, to which the chapter and clergy unanimously assent. The statute then echoes Canon 15 of the Second Lateran Council, declaring that anyone who harms a bishop or other man of God, or impedes his jurisdiction, would be excommunicated ipso facto, and if restitution has not been made by the time of their death and an unknowing priest has given them ecclesiastical burial, the body is to be exhumed "and those diabolical members to be thrown beyond sanctuary onto a dung heap."[17] Ledrede's vendetta against Arnold le Poer was undoubtedly the impetus behind this statute, and his corpse endured the kind of fate Ledrede here stipulated.

The sixteenth statute fulminated against those who "defraud" the church by arranging for the dispersal of their goods prior to their deaths, some "so that they might be able to kill others more freely without harm to their goods," some from perhaps less sinister motives but similarly defrauding the church, their creditors, and most cruelly, their own souls.[18] The arrangement made by Alice's husband Adam le Blund to quitclaim all his property to her son William Outlaw may have been at the forefront of Ledrede's mind. The statute orders that any who make such arrangements shall be denied ecclesiastical burial unless the bishop gives special license and that those who receive property from these arrangements shall be denied entrance to the church. It continues that these two statutes are to be read in the vernacular in every parish church on the first Sunday of Advent and Lent every year and then offers a general sentence of excommunication that is to be read verbatim "in the mother tongue" before clergy and laity in each and every church, with bells ringing and candles burning, during masses with the highest attendance. The

---

15. Ibid., 66. Ledrede also cites the reverence shown by the Jews to Melchisedek and Aaron and their sons and successors.

16. Ibid., 67.

17. Ibid., 68. Ledrede slightly altered the Second Lateran phrasing. The council was concerned with the protection of clerics in general, Ledrede with his personal protection, and thus he emphasized episcopal immunity.

18. Ibid., 68.

subjects of the sentence include those who harass or defraud St. Canice's or other Ossory churches, "sacrilegious sorceresses, common heretics, usurers," those who obtain exemption from ecclesiastical jurisdiction in testamentary, matrimonial, or purely spiritual matters, and any and all who assist or support such "children of iniquity."[19]

The curse offered by Ledrede in this general sentence of excommunication outdoes even the most cantankerous of Celtic saints.[20] It begins by invoking the authority of the Trinity, Mary, Michael, the celestial virtues, patriarchs, prophets, John the Baptist, John the Evangelist, Peter, Paul, Stephen and all the martyrs, Canice and Ciarán (the patrons of Ossory), Francis (the founder of Ledrede's order), and all the holy virgins and saints, by which the malefactors are excommunicated. After naming those to whom the excommunication applied, it deftly weaves the Psalms and other biblical references into a chilling curse.[21] The excommunication Ledrede alleged that Alice and her female accomplices issued against their husbands shares a similar closing line and accoutrements but pales in comparison.[22] After describing the conditions under which the curse is to be recited, the constitution continues that any priest or rector who fails to do so should be excommunicated as well, although not ipso facto. The curse's force and thoroughness elucidate Ledrede's character and the vengeance that consumed him following the Kyteler case.

---

19. "[S]acrilegos sortilegas, publicos hereticos, usurarios . . . iniquitatis filiis" (ibid., 70). Again a masculine adjective (*sacrilegos*) modifies a feminine noun (*sortilegas*).

20. See Bitel, "Saints and Angry Neighbors." Note Davies's argument that such curses arose from honor, not anger ("Anger and the Celtic Saint"). Ledrede's curse shares more similarities with English and French curses; see Little, *Benedictine Maledictions*.

21. "Sint a deo et beata Maria virgine omnibus sanctis dei et nobis maledicti: interius et exterius maledicti, in via maledicti, in agro maledicti, in civitate maledicti, in domo et extra domum maledicti, egredientes et regredientes maledicti, manducando bibendo dormiendo et vigilando stando atque sedendo et quicquid operis sive in bello sive in pace faciendo. Deleantur de libro vivencium et cum iustis non scribantur. Fiat habitacio eorum deserta: in habitaculo eorum non sit qui habitet. Obscurentur oculi eorum ne videant, et dorsa eorum curventur. Effunde, domine, super eos iram tuam, et furor ire tue comprehendat eos : appone iniquitatem super iniquitatem eorum, et non intrent in iusticiam tuam: fiat mensa eorum coram ipsis in laqueum, et in retribuciones et scandalum. Scrutetur fenerator omnem substanciam eorum, et diripiant alieni labores eorum. Et quia dilexerunt malediccionem, veniat ad eos: et noluerunt benediccionem, et elongabitur ab eis. Fiant dies eorum pauci, et possessiones eorum accipiant alteri. Fiant filii eorum orphani, et uxores eorum vidue. Deus conterat dentes eorum, et lingue eorum nunquam loquantur sapienciam. Sitque pars et societas eorum cum Datan et Abiron, cum Saphira et Ananias, cum Iuda et Pilato, cum Simone et Nerone. Et sicut extinguuntur iste lucerne, ita claritas lucis visionis dei ipsis extinguatur: et anime eorum qui huiusmodi maleficia fecerint seu faciant in futurum cadant in infernum cum diabolo et ministris eius, nisi a commissis resipiscant et ad emendacionem congruam veniant. Fiat. Fiat" (Gwynn, "Provincial and Diocesan Decrees," 70–71).

22. In its current form the *Narrative* reads "fi: fi: fi: Amen"; *fi* is presumably an abbreviation for *fiat*, i.e., "let it be."

Chronological Overview of the Kyteler Case

Ledrede's Initial Citations and Civil Resistance

Ledrede's frustrations in his prosecution of the Kyteler case that incited such vengeance centered around three men: Alice's son, William Outlaw; his kinsman, Roger Outlaw; and Arnold le Poer, another relative by marriage.[23] After citing the seven charges brought against Alice and her as yet unspecified accomplices, the *Narrative of the Proceedings against Dame Alice Kyteler* states that Ledrede wrote to Roger as chancellor to ask for his assistance in their arrest, "as the custom is."[24] Ledrede could not legally make such an arrest himself but had to depend on the secular arm, which nearly proved the case's undoing. The *Narrative* then alleges that William bribed secular officials, in particular Roger and Arnold, to resist the bishop, a claim repeated by Pembridge.[25] It would have had to have been quite a sum to buy the kind of loyalty Alice and William received from Roger and Arnold; their relations to Alice by marriage, William's blood-relations with Roger, and William's status as Arnold's liveryman seem more plausible motives for their assistance. Roger and Arnold also may have independently and intensely disliked Ledrede and found his claims outrageous and insupportable. Four years prior to the Kyteler case, Ledrede had already antagonized secular authorities sufficiently to result in his arrest, according to a letter from John XXII to the justiciar; the cause is unknown but most likely did not involve allegations of heresy, as the letter attributes the arrest solely to "false accusations" made against Ledrede and contains no reference to heresy, a matter of critical importance to the pope.[26] Perhaps the accusations arose over Ledrede's petition early in his episcopacy against the sheriff of Dublin for extorting money, a petition seconded by the commonalty of the cross-lands of Ossory.[27]

Roger and Arnold responded to Ledrede's request with disapproval and urged Ledrede to desist or at least delay the case indefinitely. The bishop refused, declaring that a *causa fidei* (a case pertaining to the faith) could not be so handled. The chancellor then replied that no warrant could be issued until a public prosecution had been held and the accused excommunicated

---

23. A thorough chronological overview of the case is necessary in order to contextualize its multiple irregularities and contradictions. Summarizing the case obscures Ledrede's misconduct and the diverse strategies and reactions of those around him.

24. Wright, *Contemporary Narrative*, 3.

25. *CSM*, 2:363.

26. *CPL*, 2:206–7. This may be related to the seizure of his temporalities in 1318; see below.

27. Sayles, *Documents*, 88–89.

FIGURE 6.   The Augustinian priory of Kells in Ossory. Photo by the author.

for at least forty days, in accordance with English law.[28] Ledrede implicitly accepted Roger's characterization of the events to date by demanding that heretics be handled differently from other excommunicants, as they will flee, to the scandal and danger of the faith. His reasoning failed to move Roger, and Ledrede acquiesced by issuing a citation of Alice at her son's home, where she was staying at the time.[29] She, however, fled, apparently to Dublin, where she began proceedings of her own against the bishop. On the day she was to appear in court, Roger sent several clerics to defend her who claimed that "in a crime as detestable as is the crime of heresy" she did not need to appear but could use proxies.[30] Ledrede then consulted with his senior clerics to devise a legally sound basis for continuing his prosecution of Alice. "With the order of the law observed in every way," he excommunicated her for the requisite "forty days and more" and also cited her son William for heresy and aiding and supporting heretics.[31]

---

28. See below. Logan, *Excommunication*, 17; Woodcock, *Medieval Ecclesiastical Courts*, 95–96.

29. This could support the possibility that Alice and John's marriage was then under strain (Wright, *Contemporary Narrative*, 3).

30. Ibid., 4. This seems a questionable argument; see below.

31. Ibid. Forty complete days had to elapse between the sentence of excommunication and the request for arrest; *et amplius* was a variable period, from the forty-first day to as much as twenty years (Logan, *Excommunication*, 73–77). Given Ledrede's eagerness, the writ was probably requested as soon as possible.

Ledrede's Arrest

William and Arnold then went to meet with Ledrede at Kells in Ossory, where he was holding a visitation. They argued about the matter "almost until midnight," with neither side yielding.[32] The following day, a Tuesday during Lent, Arnold had Ledrede arrested, a scene the *Narrative* reports in detail, with Ledrede portrayed as the persecuted party who would willingly endure "not only prison but even death" for his righteous cause, one of several indications of Ledrede's martyr, and specifically Becket, complex.[33] He expressed compassion for the bailiff, Stephen le Poer, who by carrying out his master's task brought upon himself a sentence of excommunication that only the pope could absolve, in accordance with *Si quis suadente*, Canon 15 of the Second Lateran Council. To ensure that such a sentence would apply, Ledrede refused to be arrested without Stephen laying hands upon him, although Stephen refused and Ledrede acquiesced after consulting with the members of his entourage that the manner of arrest sufficed "according to the country's customs."[34] First, however, he asked to see the warrant for his arrest, which he kept and would brandish later against Arnold.

En route to the prison, Stephen suggested that Ledrede visit Arnold and ask for sureties and mainpernors so that he could avoid imprisonment, but Ledrede refused, saying, "My son, well you know that from the time of the founding of God's church in Ireland, archbishops and bishops who are under God and our lord the pope have been subject (only) to the king of England in temporal matters."[35] Ledrede thus disregarded the seven centuries that the church had flourished in Ireland prior to the 1172 Synod of Cashel, at which Irish prelates acknowledged Henry II as their temporal overlord, and apparently endorsed the perspective of *Laudabiliter*, which claimed that the Irish had renounced Christianity in some way and needed to be restored to the faith by the English king. Ledrede continued that such religious authorities are not only superior to their secular counterparts in spiritual matters, but their equals in temporal ones. He furthered his importance by reminding his audience that he was "a bishop who was nurtured, educated, and promoted under the wings of the most holy apostolic see," and as such could never allow himself to be dragged into secular courts in such a manner.[36] Whereas before the righteousness of his cause alone gave him the strength to face

---

32. Wright, *Contemporary Narrative*, 4.
33. Ibid., 5.
34. Ibid., 6.
35. Ibid., 7.
36. Ibid.

imprisonment or even death, now it was somewhat secondary, as again he said he would suffer either fate "before [he] would let the church, God's bride, be subject to worldly servitude," particularly since it involved a case of the faith that did not pertain to secular courts in any way.[37]

Ledrede rejoiced in his imprisonment, declaring upon arrival that what he suffered for his faith in Christ would bring him greater honor than anything else in his life, except for performing baptism and consecration. He remained imprisoned in Kilkenny Castle apparently for seventeen days, during which time the date for William's appearance in court to face Ledrede's charges had passed.[38] Ledrede placed Ossory under interdict from prison, which the *Narrative* states was in strict accordance with the decretal *Si quis suadente*. Ledrede arranged for an elaborate procession to bring the sacrament to him in prison, parading before his subjects what he denied them. After receiving it, he publicly entrusted his body to his persecutors, playing again the part of the willing martyr. A sermon was delivered based on the beatitude "Blessed are those who endure persecution" (Matthew 5:10), and according to the *Narrative*, support for the bishop swelled. Seeing the prison treated as a place of pilgrimage, Arnold ordered that Ledrede was to have no more than one companion and two servants. His constable responded that "this is a new and unheard of thing in Ireland, that this bishop has been imprisoned," although this was at least the second time Ledrede had been arrested and the records of colonial Ireland provide ample evidence of such treatment or worse of bishops and other religious by secular authorities, something of which representatives of both Ireland and England vociferously complained at the Council of Vienne.[39] The constable continued that he was not sufficient to guard "such a great prelate," and Arnold relented by allowing those who wished it to have free and easy access to Ledrede.[40]

During Ledrede's imprisonment, Arnold sent criers throughout the area to try to find others with complaints against the bishop. He repeatedly held inquests with the assistance of Roger Outlaw and Walter de Islip, the treasurer of the colony and the custodian of Kilkenny, which led to several severe accusations against Ledrede, though only William Outlaw's attempt to revive the testamentary case is specified; the bishop was not convicted, however, for which the *Narrative* repeatedly thanks God. The *Narrative* also repeatedly maintains that in temporal affairs Ledrede was not subject to any secular

---

37. Ibid.

38. Ibid., 11. Arnold's uncle, Meiler le Poer, the bishop of Leighlin, assisted in Ledrede's release.

39. Ehrle, "Ein Bruchstück," 370–71, 377, 380; Watt, *The Church and the Two Nations*, 134, 144–45; Theiner, 171; *CPL*, 1:611, 613, 2:102, 228; *AI*, 366–67; see also chapter 4.

40. Wright, *Contemporary Narrative*, 9.

authority save the king, an overstatement of his episcopal immunity under English law. It concludes the account of the multiple inquests with the statement that all who participated in them were ipso facto excommunicated and thus he was not bound to answer any of them, an apparent acknowledgement that his episcopal rights were not so extensive as he and the *Narrative* claimed, and adds again that no fear of prison or torture could cause the bishop to allow the church to be subjected to secular servitude.

Ledrede's Proceedings and Resistance to Them Resumed

Once released, Ledrede again cited William and Alice *in causa fidei* (in a case of the faith).[41] Roger Outlaw then cited Ledrede to appear before the justiciar to answer Arnold's accusations on the same day as William and Alice were to appear in court. William de Rodyerd, the dean of St. Patrick's and the archbishop of Dublin's vicar, also became involved, summoning Ledrede before him for the same reason and also to explain why he had placed his diocese under interdict. Ledrede sent a proctor in his stead, explaining that he could not safely travel to Dublin since all roads passed through le Poer lands; his excuse fell on deaf ears and Rodyerd removed the interdict, although the *Narrative* claims that he later explained that he would not have done so if he knew the righteousness of Ledrede's case, as he later would.[42] Ledrede presumably met with the justiciar, though the *Narrative* mentions only that the summons prevented him from prosecuting William and Alice yet again as well as the fine (£1,000) for failing to appear. No meeting between the justiciar and the bishop or his representatives is discussed until the following scene, in which the justiciar plays a passive role.

On April 23, the first date given in the *Narrative*, at the advice of his clergy who were "expert" in such matters, Ledrede sent the Dominican prior and the Franciscan guardian of Kilkenny to Arnold's court to seek the assistance of the secular arm in his case, but Arnold answered that the bishop would come to his court at his own peril. Asserting that faith fears neither threats nor terrors from judges, Ledrede donned his finest episcopal vestments and carried the host before him to the seneschal's court in a candlelight procession composed of equal numbers of Dominicans and Franciscans as well as his own chapter and clergy. Several nobles blocked his entrance, but again the

---

41. Ibid., 12. *Causa fidei* also implies that it is a cause of the faith; the case is taken up for the sake of the faith itself. *Causa* means both case and cause.

42. Ibid., 13. Arnold was seneschal of Carlow and Wexford as well as Kilkenny, and his family had extensive holdings in the southeast of Ireland.

bishop declared that the faith could not be cowed by threats; he continued toward the seneschal with the host elevated, demanding of the seneschal, the justiciar, the sheriff, and the bailiffs that, "out of reverence for and love of Christ, whom he held in his hands," his case should be heard.[43] Abuse and insults were Arnold's response, who showed none of the honor and reverence owed to Christ and attempted to expel Ledrede, to the scandal of the people. Ledrede countered by calling all to witness that the secular courts had denied the church an audience concerning a case of the faith that aimed to eradicate heretics. Arnold then relented somewhat, declaring that "that worthless, churlish tramp (*trutannus*) from England, with that lump of dough (*hordys*) he carries in his hands" be made to stand at the bar with thieves, which prompted Ledrede to lament this to be the worst treatment Christ had received since he stood before Pontius Pilate.[44]

Ledrede repeated his request that Arnold assist him in his prosecution of heretics and their fautors as his office required, but Arnold refused. Ledrede held up a book of decretals, which he offered to read before the people so that ignorance could not be claimed as an excuse for disobedience. Arnold told him to take his decretals to the church and preach there, as he would never agree to help him. Ledrede responded with a summary of the proceedings to date, saying that in his recent visitations he had discovered that some people were known for heresy, some of their followers had relapsed, and others were their fautors. Again he asked the secular arm to assist him in their immediate arrest, repeating his words three times in English and French and reading out the names of the accused: Alice Kyteler and her son William. He cited "common opinion and suspicion" as justification, further evidence that he had not yet procured the evidence that formed the basis of six of the seven charges ultimately brought against Alice and her accomplices and that his investigation at this point concerned only the mother and son, although his summary implies that more than two people numbered among the accused, as do the charges that begin the *Narrative*.[45]

---

43. Ibid., 14.

44. Ibid. The *Narrative* is the only source for these words. *Trutannus* was a term applied to a monk who had quit his monastery or a cleric who had left his parish without leave (Davidson and Ward, *Sorcery Trial*, 45n68); Arnold meant that Ledrede was a swindling tramp who had no legitimate place in Ireland, but belonged in England. I follow Ward's translation of *hordys* (ibid., 45); Wright theorized that *hordys* meant "dirt" (*Contemporary Narrative*, 56). Although the initial insult seems in keeping with Arnold's character, the attack on the eucharist seems suspect. Adding an insult to the eucharist makes the connection Ledrede saw in all disagreements with him—derision of his holy office and contempt for God himself.

45. Wright, *Contemporary Narrative*, 15.

Alice's Countersuit

The next act in the *Narrative* was initiated by Alice, her suit against the bishop for defamation and excommunication without proper process being observed. Again, the bishop sent a proctor, who argued that the *sortilega* (sorceress) had previously been convicted by Ledrede and then abjured, and his office demanded that he prosecute her for a relapse of heresy.[46] Despite the *Narrative*'s overwhelming bias in Ledrede's favor, Alice's countersuit apparently had the greater merit. By the *Narrative*'s own admission, Ledrede attempted to have Alice arrested for heresy, not its relapse, without excommunicating her for forty days or holding a public prosecution. The case was heard in court, but the critical issue seems to have been not Alice's guilt but whether Ledrede had proceeded in accordance with the law, and the court apparently found against him. He thus waited forty days before repeating his request for her arrest, but no mention of another public process is made. His repeated attempts to cite her for heresy do not refer to relapse. The first use of the term (*relapsos*), in his summary of the proceedings at the seneschal's court, is directed against the followers of the heretics, whereas Alice is repeatedly identified as their leader, and the use of the masculine plural attests that it did not specifically or at least singularly apply to Alice. His repeated reliance on *fama publica* (public opinion) indicates that he had not yet obtained a conviction against her, and she never confessed to anything that she could then recant. His change of tactic from prosecuting her for heretical sorcery to a relapse of heresy may have been motivated by an attempt to capitalize on Boniface VIII's decretal *Ut inquisitionis*, which deprived convicted heretics of the right to appeal and of which Ledrede made much use later in the trial. His first outside supporter, William de Nottingham, the precentor of St. Patrick's, echoed *Ut inquisitionis* during this hearing, maintaining that in a crime so detestable as heresy no appeal should be allowed, particularly when it involved relapse. Irrespective of Ledrede's claims and Nottingham's support, neither heresy nor its relapse had yet been proven either according to the chronology of the *Narrative* or according to the standards of the judge, who dismissed (*spretis*) Ledrede's allegations. Though Ledrede clearly favored canon above common law, even by the standards of the former his prosecution was an extreme example of "a perversion of the inquisitorial process caused by overzealous and underscrupulous judges."[47]

---

46. Ibid., 16.
47. Kelly, "Inquisition and the Prosecution of Heresy," 451.

The Dublin Parliament

About the time of Alice's appeal, Roger Outlaw again cited Ledrede to appear before the justiciar, this time at the Dublin parliament that commenced May 13. As prelates would be present, Ledrede believed his case might find a more favorable audience, inspiring him to find a safe route to Dublin, though the *Narrative* claims that an ambush lay in wait for him. Upon arrival, he found both the king's and the archbishop's courts influenced against him, and his repeated demands for the case to be heard were denied. He had a chance meeting with Arnold and William, the latter dressed in Arnold's livery, arriving with a royal letter for matters to be considered in parliament. One concerned the rights of the church as defined by Magna Carta, to which Arnold added,

> If a tramp from England or somewhere has obtained a bull or privilege from the papal curia, we are not bound to obey that bull, unless it has been enjoined on us under the king's seal. We say this because, as you well know, heretics have never been found in Ireland; rather, it is customarily called the isle of the saints. Now, however, some foreigner comes from England and says we are all heretics and excommunicants, claiming for himself some papal constitutions that we have never heard of before now. And since defamation of this land touches every one of us, you all ought to unite against this man.[48]

Arnold thus laid claim to the history of Ireland that predates the Norman invasion, a Christian history that Ledrede earlier rejected, and exhorted his audience to national unity specifically in distinction from England and the papacy, a unity based not on language, blood, or culture, but on Ireland itself.[49] Though he acted as the king's representative and explicitly considered himself subject to him, *trutanni de Anglia* (tramps from England), as Arnold allegedly labelled Ledrede, were another matter entirely.

This nationalist ideology seems little more convincing than the similar propaganda proposed by native Irish leaders in the Remonstrance of 1317, which argued in favor of Edward Bruce's kingship of Ireland partly by emphasizing the cultural connections between Ireland and Scotland due to their shared blood, language, and traditions. The proponents of the Remonstrance could easily find a flaw with Arnold's rationale for nationalism, had they encountered it: the only reason the colonists inhabited the land for

---

48. Wright, *Contemporary Narrative*, 17.
49. Ibid., 7; see above.

which Arnold expressed such loyalty is because they had taken it by force, and they had subsequently lost any claims of overlordship by their relentless persecution of the Irish, of which the Remonstrance provides several examples. Yet his words could express a modern sentiment of Irish nationalism that rejects English or papal authority within Ireland and argues for a unity that transcends religious, cultural, or class differences to find its strength in a loyalty shared by all who inhabit Ireland. They also highlight the tensions between the colonists and the English that would peak in 1341.[50] Moreover, the possibility exists that Arnold le Poer, who was reputed to be an ally of the Leinster Irish, who successfully petitioned in 1316 for two Irishmen to be admitted to English law, whose family practiced the Irish system of kin accountability and, according to Curtis, followed Brehon law, may have genuinely been able to see beyond the ethnic divide to envision a kind of kinship between colonists and natives.[51]

Ledrede countered Arnold's rhetoric with his own, declaring that *una parvula cartula* (one teeny, tiny charter), as Ledrede styled Magna Carta, could not possibly contain all the privileges of the church. He insisted that he had not defamed Ireland and its inhabitants as heretics and excommunicants.[52] Rather, he had singled out evildoers in the midst of good folk, as Judas was discovered to be a traitor in the midst of the apostles. In the diocese of Ossory, one diabolical nest had been discovered that was more foul than any other in the English king's dominion, and when he had attempted to root it out, as his office required, he encountered opposition unheard of in modern times. He informed his audience that Arnold had thrown not only him, but also Jesus himself, out of court and refused to assist him in a case of the faith, thereby incurring excommunication. Yet as a man "nurtured under the wings of the Roman church" and personally selected by the pope, he would not be intimidated in a matter pertaining to the faith; any further obstructions that Arnold might create would be met joyfully.[53] Arnold departed, and Ledrede attempted to find allies in his case, but none would stand with him publicly against Arnold. William de Rodyerd, the dean of St. Patrick's and Bicknor's vicar, then counselled him to make peace with Arnold so that his case could proceed more smoothly, and Ledrede agreed.

---

50. *CSM*, 2:383; see chapter 4.

51. Tresham, I.i.13; Grace, *Annales Hiberniae*, 58–59; Otway-Ruthven, *A History of Medieval Ireland*, 220; Sayles, *Documents*, 81; Curtis, *History of Medieval Ireland*, app. 3.

52. Perhaps this exchange helped plant the seed in William de Rodyerd's mind, to slander the native Irish in such a way; see chapter 5.

53. Wright, *Contemporary Narrative*, 18.

A peace was brokered between the two by Rodyerd and the bishops of Ferns, Kildare, Emly, and Lismore.[54] They understandably sided with Ledrede when he produced Arnold's writ for his arrest, and Arnold was made to apologize to Ledrede before the entire parliament, to which Ledrede replied that he would gladly have suffered ten times worse, provided Arnold no longer gave succor to heretics but allowed the bishop to prosecute them. The two embraced and kissed, though Arnold did not seek absolution, which the *Narrative* condones since only the pope could release him from excommunication. Ledrede then wrote to the chancellor, again asking for the arrest of Alice, without any mention of her accomplices, including her son.[55] Rodyerd seconded Ledrede's request against Alice on account of her heresy and relapse, but Alice left Dublin, apparently returning to Kilkenny.[56] Ledrede also asked the justiciar (John Darcy), the chancellor (Roger Outlaw), the treasurer (Walter de Islip), and other members of the king's council to come to Kilkenny and assist him in his case, and the justiciar, "a Catholic man," assented. Ledrede, remaining in Dublin, arranged for one of his officials and two clerics to conduct an investigation of the heretics in Ossory, but government officials in Ossory ordered these three men arrested, and Arnold le Poer instructed the sheriff (John de Rocheford) and William Outlaw to conduct their own investigation into the bishop's claims.[57]

A Degree of Success for Ledrede

The inquest in Kilkenny divided the citizens into three groups, and in one Alice and "her six accomplice sorcerers" were publicly condemned.[58] Arnold and his men then had the poorer defendants arrested, while Alice openly escaped. The *Narrative* relates that news of the arrest delighted Ledrede, even though secular officials had refused to arrest the culprits at his request. After returning to Kilkenny and examining those arrested, who confessed to the charges and acknowledged Alice as their "mother and mistress," Ledrede wrote to Roger Outlaw on June 6, asking him to continue the investigation and appending a copy of Boniface VIII's *Ut inquisitionis*, which demands that

---

54. The bishop of Kildare was Walter le Calf, the one bishop to send his representative to the Templar trial in Dublin (see chapter 1).

55. Perhaps William Outlaw's exemption was part of the peace agreement between Ledrede and Arnold.

56. Wright, *Contemporary Narrative*, 21.

57. Ibid.

58. The *Narrative* adds "as aforesaid" (ibid., 21), but six associates had not been mentioned previously, and subsequently she was alleged to have eleven associates.

secular rulers obey bishops in matters of the faith.[59] He also wrote to Walter de Islip, asking for his help in arresting Alice and her now eleven named accomplices.[60] Islip, however, was reluctant to help, which the *Narrative* attributes to his friendship with William Outlaw, and so Ledrede sent a similar letter to the justiciar, who, after reading *Ut inquisitionis*, ordered Arnold le Poer to make the arrests. Still the secular officials debated the matter, but Ledrede eventually succeeded in having William appear before him at St. Mary's in Kilkenny, where he accused him of thirty-four separate counts, including heresy, aiding heretics, adultery, usury, and clericide. William was allowed a respite for response until the justiciar came to Kilkenny, but when Darcy arrived, it was not William but Alice who was tried in absentia. She was convicted as "a sorceress, magician, heretic, and one who has relapsed" and ordered to be handed over to the secular arm and her possessions confiscated.[61] Despite this conviction, the *Narrative* complains, Alice "is allowed to wander far too freely even to the present day, to the scandal of the faith and the church."[62] Unable to lay his hands on Alice herself, Ledrede burned a sackful of her reputed magical instruments in the center of Kilkenny.

The following day (July 3) Ledrede returned to the Kilkenny court, this time with a writ with the king's seal ordering the arrests, presumably from the justiciar. Arnold and Walter de Islip then informed the sheriff that he was to execute the writ, but, the *Narrative* laments, "that has not be done even to the present day," since Walter and Arnold told the sheriff privately not to comply with the writ.[63] Learning this, Ledrede went to visit Walter at the Franciscan friary in Kilkenny, where he, the justiciar, and the chancellor were staying, asking again for assistance. Walter replied that they would gladly assist in a matter of faith that did not conflict with royal liberties, but the arrest and detention of these people clearly did so conflict, unless they were allowed bail. Darcy also favored this interpretation of the conflict between common and canon law and reversed his previous position on the case. Roger and Walter then added insult to injury, with the former relocating to William Outlaw's house, to Ledrede's great indignation, and holding banquets there. Ledrede retaliated by again summoning William to appear before him for heresy, and this time, somewhat inexplicably, in proceedings that included reading *Ut inquisitionis* in the vernacular, William at last confessed to aiding and abetting heretics. Neither was he convicted of nor did he confess to

---

59. Ibid., 22. Mistress means leader, as in female master.
60. Ibid., 23; see chapter 2.
61. Wright, *Contemporary Narrative*, 25.
62. Ibid., 26.
63. Ibid.

heresy itself, however, though he had several times been accused of it, and Ledrede here added that William was "also noted for and vehemently suspected of heresy."[64]

William was thus imprisoned, and Walter and Roger went to Ledrede, asking that he be pardoned. After consulting with his more learned clergy, Ledrede set a day to do so, when he set William's penance as hearing three masses per day for a year, feeding paupers, and re-covering St. Canice's roof with lead. The penance, described as less than William deserved, was to serve as a reminder to all never to oppose the church in a matter of the faith nor to aid heretics. At the sentencing, Ledrede once again read *Ut inquisitionis* in the vernacular, to ensure that all would realize that William was still under excommunication; the *Narrative* adds its dismay that he did not seek absolution from the bishop, without maintaining that such absolution could be given only by the pope, as it had in the cases of Arnold and Stephen le Poer, the bailiff who had arrested Ledrede. Walter and Roger then continued to pressure Ledrede to allow William sureties and bail, but Ledrede responded that *Ut inquisitionis* included no such allowances and that special treatment should not be granted to the rich; for some reason not included in the *Narrative*, however, William was granted such sureties and was able to freely move about within Kilkenny. The *Narrative* claims that William's many friends offered Ledrede bribes to go easy on him, but the bishop replied that not for all the gold it would take to fill St. Canice's could he be bought in a matter of the faith.

Ledrede also learned that William was not performing his penance but was sending gifts to suspected heretics in prison and to witnesses hostile to him and also was hiding some whom the writ had ordered arrested on this matter, possibly including his mother, although the *Narrative* does not provide names. Outraged, Ledrede wrote Walter de Islip threatening letters outlining his office's requirements according to canon law, and after consulting with lawyers in Dublin, Walter agreed to assist Ledrede. The secular officials of Ossory swore an oath to do so as well, although Arnold le Poer did not, which, if he were excommunicated, would likely not be valid anyway. William Outlaw was brought before Ledrede again and stood accused of contempt of the keys for failing to perform his penance as well as of relapse. The grounds for the latter are somewhat unclear; perhaps the rumors alleging that he was bestowing gifts on and hiding suspected heretics would suffice, but the *Narrative* does not specify the reasons behind his alleged relapse. Instead,

---

64. Ibid., 28. For a discussion of vehement suspicion, see Lea, *History of the Inquisition*, 1:433, 455–58.

it claims that additional witnesses had brought forth evidence against him, possibly referring to Petronilla de Midia, who was executed the same day and whom Pembridge maintains added allegations against William just before her death. William's lawyers agreed to adjourn the case until January, and William was returned to prison.

That day, November 3, Ledrede received another vindication, the execution of Petronilla de Midia, whose confession either formed the basis of six of the seven charges Ledrede brought against Alice and her accomplices or conformed virtually verbatim to six of the charges Ledrede had already composed against them. No mention is made of her arrest, unless she was one of the *pauperiores* (poorer folk) imprisoned while Alice was allowed to escape.[65] Any trial she may have received is lost in the account, which notes that Ledrede had her whipped six times for sorcery and "finally" (*demum*) she was found to be a heretic.[66] The *Narrative* does not say that she was examined prior to her torture, nor that she confirmed her confession separately from torture, a requirement for the confession to be considered valid.[67] This seems to be the first and perhaps only time torture was applied in medieval Ireland in order to elicit a confession in a religious trial: it is highly unlikely that it was employed in the trial of the Templars; no mention is made of torture in the subsequent heresy trials; and English common law, which governed the colony as well, did not allow for the use of torture, although it was at last applied after much debate toward the end of the trial of the Templars in London. The reason for her execution is unclear, as she is not described as *relapsa*, nor does the *Narrative* say she refused to abjure her heresy, and others with whom she was accused received much lighter sentences, such as having their clothes marked by a cross or being exiled.[68] While the *Narrative* claims her to be the first heretic among many burned in Ireland and also speaks of those among the accused who were publicly burned, no other names are provided; moreover, chronicles written in Kilkenny and Dublin within ten to twenty-five years of the case report only her execution, indicating that hers was a solitary fate among those accused in Kilkenny in 1324.[69]

A week later, Ledrede visited William in prison, at William's request. William prostrated himself half naked in the mud before the bishop as well

---

65. The *Narrative's* internal chronology, however, indicates that her (and Alice's ten other named alleged accomplices') arrest was requested only after the *pauperiores* were arrested.

66. Wright, *Contemporary Narrative*, 31–32.

67. Peters, *Torture*, 57.

68. Wright, *Contemporary Narrative*, 40; see chapter 2.

69. Wright, *Contemporary Narrative*, 33, 40; Clyn, 16; *CSM*, 2:362–64; Flower, "Manuscripts of Irish Interest," 337.

as many clergy and laymen, begging to atone for his offenses against him. Ledrede, however, refused to consider any personal grievances he might have against William until he acknowledged his heinous sins against God. Ledrede castigated him for his wealth, favoring heretics, oppressing the innocent, freeing the guilty, and having the effrontery to ask for mercy, which he had never shown himself, especially by imprisoning clerics. He added that the many laity and clergy present all demanded his total degradation and compared him to Lucifer, but he then offered him the possibility of redemption, by begging God's mercy. William pleaded with him to grant him absolution from excommunication, to which Ledrede replied that no absolution could be had until William performed his penance or offered sufficient guarantee, and William promised that either he or his friends would provide that guarantee shortly.

Ledrede preempted Roger Outlaw's visit to his kinsman to arrange the guarantee by visiting the chancellor himself and warning him against the scandals threatening both secular and ecclesiastical courts should William be dealt with too leniently. He reminded him that, in his presence as well as that of the justiciar and other members of the king's council, Alice had been publicly condemned as a heretic and by the unanimous decision of the clergy declared both a heretic and relapsed; her goods were confiscated "and she was handed over by the church to the secular court to be punished for her faults," another example of Ledrede's overstatement or the text's inaccuracy.[70] Although Roger was personally aware of this and had also received Ledrede's patent letters reporting it so that Alice would meet her proper legal fate, Ledrede continued, he still allowed Alice to wander about, and nothing could be done without him, since he was not only chancellor but also acting justiciar when the justiciar was away. So scandalized was the archbishop's vicar (i.e., Rodyerd) that he was currently undertaking proceedings against those who assist heretics, a thinly veiled threat of Roger's own future trial as a fautor, which was brought not by Rodyerd but Ledrede.[71] Ledrede then continued that though Roger wore the dress of a religious and ought to help him, he refused to assist in the prosecution of the "mother heretic" and her son, described here as suspect in the faith, and though Roger could take his choice of several possible lodgings, he chose to stay "in that heretical home, namely that cave of heretics, the reputed cesspit (latrina) of the church," that is, William Outlaw's house, where he brought additional scandal to the king

---

70. Wright, *Contemporary Narrative*, 35.

71. Rodyerd's explicit interest in heresy has significant implications for the case of Adducc Dubh O'Toole; see chapter 5.

by carrying out his government work there.[72] The bishop also castigated him for repeatedly refusing to take the oath to assist him against heretics, as he was bound to do by canon law, and for the ways in which Roger's clerics and assistants impeded Ledrede's prosecution. Ledrede finished his harangue with a threat that if he continued to interfere with the case he would inform the pope, "who will shake and rattle the keys of Blessed Peter and the holy Roman church over your head, so that the sound will be heard not only throughout England and Ireland but from Ireland to the Greek sea," and with an acknowledgement that, though the chancellor could seize his temporalities, as royal officials frequently did to Ledrede, this would not change the law one bit.[73] To prove the legitimacy of his warnings and reminders, the constitutions and decretal letters were publicly read by a lawyer.[74] According to the *Narrative*, Roger then burst into tears and explained any error he may have committed as arising from ignorance, yet he still refused to take the oath to assist Ledrede without consulting with the royal council.

The matter of the oath was apparently dropped, for later that day Roger visited Ledrede to arrange William's performance of penance. Ledrede sent him to the dean and chapter, but the oath on which Ledrede had earlier so vigorously insisted is not mentioned again. It was agreed that on William's behalf Roger would provide workmen for the reroofing of St. Canice's with lead, to be completed within four years; he apparently laid it on a bit thick, as the roof collapsed in 1332.[75] Roger also offered the churches of Gowran, a former Templar property transferred to Roger's order, the Hospitallers, and Gavilmoy (Galmoy) to the dean and chapter as guarantee; should the reroofing not be completed within four years, the dean and chapter would retain the churches and their revenues for five hundred marks, though the revenues were worth a thousand.[76] Temporarily satisfied, Ledrede went to the prison and absolved William from the sentence of excommunication for aiding

---

72. Wright, *Contemporary Narrative*, 35.

73. Ibid., 36.

74. These constitutions could possibly refer to the recent additions he had made to his own synodal statutes.

75. Alternatively, perhaps this penance was never completed, leaving the roof in a weakened state and thus susceptible to collapse.

76. William le Kiteler was among the witnesses of the surrender of Gowran and its property by the master of the Templars in Ireland on February 3, 1307, and in 1314 it passed into the hands of Nicholas de Balscot (Mac Niocaill, "Documents Relating to the Suppression of the Templars in Ireland," 210–11). In 1317, Roger Outlaw petitioned the pope to ensure that Templar property in Ireland was transferred to the Hospitallers (*CPL*, 2:131–32) and was ultimately quite successful in this mission (Massey, *Prior Roger Outlaw*, 23–24). Whether Roger had the right to offer this property is not clear. Leslie identifies Galmoy with Eirke (*Ossory Clergy and Parishes*, 253, 265).

heretics, though he had to remain incarcerated until his purgation, set for mid-January 1325.[77]

Fearing that William might be able to excuse himself from purgation on the grounds that he could not communicate with friends and counsellors, Ledrede arranged for him to do so, provided that such people faithfully adhered to canon law. Through such counsel, William discovered that he could not be purged, as he did not have enough compurgators and the church had ample evidence against him, although little of that is provided in the *Narrative* and no other source supports such an assertion, apart from Pembridge's claim of Petronilla's last-minute accusation of the diabolical belt. When at last the day of his purgation arrived, William again prostrated himself before the bishop and acknowledged that his rise to wealth and power involved irregularities and negligence that may have alienated his neighbors. He threw himself on the mercy of Ledrede and the church, which must surely have mercy on him and any sinner, and renounced the vows of his neighbors, since he could not trust them. Ledrede was outraged by William's tactics, which could exempt him from the courts of justice, but after consultation with his clergy, he agreed to William's request, though he demanded more time to deliberate about an appropriate solution, during which William was to be released from his chains but kept in prison. The deliberation took a week and, according to the *Narrative*, resulted in the decision that because William was under such grave suspicion and had not performed purgation, he was to be presumed convicted.[78] Accordingly, he swore on the Gospels and wrote a renunciation of heresy and sorcery as well as of their support, which he signed with his own seal. Ledrede displayed William's renunciation for all to see; William swore to obey the church's mandates and at last received total absolution.

William was given additional penances: to make a pilgrimage to the Holy Land at his own expense and if old age or infirmity prevented him from doing so, he or his heirs must give the same sum for pious causes at the discretion of the diocese, dean, and chapter; since Ossory had been placed under interdict for so long because of William, he must pay for a priest to

---

77. The *Narrative* (Wright, *Contemporary Narrative*, 31) states that it was to be the first day the courts would be open after St. Hilary's Day (January 13); Clyn (17) states that it occurred on Thursday, in the octave of St. Hilary (January 17).

78. Exactly what he was presumed convicted of is unclear. He had already confessed to aiding and abetting heretics, but not to the thirty-three other charges brought against him, and the *Narrative* implies that the additional witnesses and evidence implicated him in a much graver sin, possibly heresy itself. A presumptive guilty verdict on the evidence and procedures provided in the *Narrative* would be a travesty of both civil and religious courts; see below.

permanently celebrate mass in St. Mary's before a statue that Ledrede would have made and painted; because of his opposition in a case of the faith and his grievous persecution of a bishop, "which is a cause of martyrdom," he must visit Becket's shrine and there make a public confession; until he had done so, he must abstain from meat on every Tuesday.[79] Finally, William also conceded that should he fail in future obedience to the church, bishop, or other religious, he would pay £1,000 sterling, and then he left a free man. He seems to have paid this fine promptly, as on January 25, Roger Outlaw and several others, including Fulk de la Freyne (most likely the son of the man who had tried to steal over £3,000 from William and his mother in 1302) and a de Valle, acknowledged a debt to Ledrede of £1,000 sterling, and the same day Ledrede acknowledged satisfaction of that debt.[80] The following year, William acknowledged that he owed Roger the same amount.[81] Despite his earlier contention that not for all the gold that would fill St. Canice's could his mercy be bought, Ledrede may have allowed £1,000 of silver to suffice in lieu of the additional penances. The *Narrative*, however, does not mention the payment, though it occurred within days of William's purgation, possibly because the payment would not present Ledrede in a favorable light.

The *Narrative* then ends with a summary of the fates that befell other members of the pestiferous sect of Robin son of Art, which are without secondary confirmation. It praises God's grace and Ledrede's determination that enabled the destruction of "that nastiest nest" (*nidus ille turpissimus*), despite overwhelming opposition from such powerful and skilled lawyers, and maintains that though almost everyone supported the bishop in his prosecution (a claim contrary to the evidence), in all of Ireland none but Ledrede would have dared oppose them. It closes with Ledrede's courting of martyrdom that had so far eluded him, as it would continue to do.[82] Though the circumstances surrounding and date of Ledrede's death are unknown, he lived to a ripe old age—over a hundred, if a letter about him written in the last few years of his life (ca. 1357) can be believed.[83] This letter, from Edward III to Innocent VI, portrays him as anything but a saint, however; it maintains that he hounded colonists on trumped-up charges of heresy and sorcery in an effort to extort money from them, asserts that since his aspirations of becoming inquisitor of Ireland were thwarted he spread slanderous stories at the

---

79. Wright, *Contemporary Narrative*, 39.
80. Tresham, I.i.31; Wright, *Contemporary Narrative*, 58. For the de la Freyne family and its many Fulks, see Brooks, *Knights' Fees*, 184–85.
81. Tresham, I.i.34; Wright, *Contemporary Narrative*, 48.
82. Wright, *Contemporary Narrative*, 40.
83. Raine, *Historical Papers and Letters*, 403–6; see chapter 4.

curia about the state of the faith in Ireland, and requests that he be replaced with William Charnells, a Dominican who was then bishop of Ferns. The *Narrative's* pro-Ledrede propaganda may have found favor at the papacy, but inhabitants of Ireland and England, most prominently the king, remained unconvinced, as this letter and ensuing events attest.

Conflict between Canon and Common Law

The conflict between canon and common law played a critical role in the prosecution of the Kyteler case and in the *Narrative*, which is more concerned with defending the primacy of religious authority in a case of the faith than with providing a coherent account of the trial against Alice and her associates. Ledrede's greatest weapon in his prosecution, apart from the eucharist that he carried before him as both weapon and shield, was the decretal *Ut inquisitionis*. This emphasized the purely ecclesiastical nature of a heresy case and demanded the obedience of secular officials to bishops and inquisitors investigating such a case; if any secular official should not provide assistance, "let him know that he will be struck with the sharp point of excommunication, and, if his pertinacious spirit should have resisted censure for a year, he shall be judged himself a heretic."[84] According to this decretal, then, Arnold le Poer, Roger Outlaw, John Darcy, Walter de Islip, and their ministers were required to offer Ledrede the assistance he repeatedly sought, yet all refused to do so, Darcy being the least intransigent.[85] Ledrede and the *Narrative* attribute their opposition to bribes from and friendship with William Outlaw, but they had solid justification for their resistance in common law and, to a lesser extent, canon law.

According to inquisitorial procedure, *fama publica* (public opinion) indicating the guilt of a person or persons of a given crime formed the basis of initiation of proceedings against them. Alice's stepchildren's accusation of *maleficia* might suffice, but they would be considered suspect witnesses as they clearly had a personal stake in her guilt and the wealth they claimed should be theirs. Ledrede repeatedly referred to *fama publica* claiming Alice was a notorious heretic. Given the abuse she suffered in 1302, as well as her and her son's wealth, which William acknowledged caused hostility against and suspicion of him, Alice and William probably were resented in their community. It is doubtful, however, that anyone, including her stepchildren, would

---

84. Davidson and Ward, *Sorcery Trial*, 72 (Ward's translation).

85. The bind between common and canon law fell doubly hard on Roger (the prior of the Hospitallers) and Walter (a canon of St. Patrick's), who were members of religious orders as well as secular officials.

have equated their behavior with heresy and demon worship, as Ledrede did. Even if Ledrede had a crime, *fama publica*, and trustworthy witnesses to support his proceedings, Alice was then supposed to appear in person before the court, be presented with the charges, and be allowed a defense, but this did not happen.[86] At no point was Alice herself present at her own trial. At the first hearing, her own proctors allegedly claimed that for a crime of heresy she did not have to be present, which Ledrede and the *Narrative* accepted, although this is a misrepresentation of an inquisition's requirements; failure to appear at one's own heresy trial was interpreted as evidence of guilt, and the accused was consequently to be arrested by secular officials.[87] Perhaps this very defense was a misrepresentation of Alice's lawyers' argument, one which Ledrede hoped to use to procure her arrest, particularly since this hearing seems not to have been a matter of Alice's guilt or innocence but of whether Ledrede's proceedings had been legally sound, which they had not.

If Ledrede's proceedings thus far were questionable according to canon law, they violated common law. Prior to 1382, England and its dominions had no explicit procedure for invoking the secular arm against heretics, and bishops largely had to rely on the means by which obdurate excommunicants were brought to justice.[88] A bishop could request secular assistance against an excommunicated party under his jurisdiction only if they had remained obdurate for at least forty days.[89] According to the *Narrative*, however, Ledrede immediately demanded Alice's arrest once he had learned of her guilt from her "accomplices" and unnamed others, although it seems more likely that he initially acted solely on the basis of the stepchildren's allegations.[90] The *Narrative* does not state that Ledrede excommunicated Alice prior to ordering her arrest; presumably he did so, but this very omission as well as his eagerness for her arrest indicates that he was attempting to use excommunication vindictively rather than medicinally, as he had not given her the chance to become contumacious.[91] Roger Outlaw rejected Ledrede's request for her arrest on the grounds that a public process had not yet been held and she had not been excommunicated for the forty days. The first hearing may have served as that public process, as it is the only process mentioned, but if it began as an investigation into Alice's innocence, it ended with the verdict that Ledrede needed to wait forty days before he could order her

---

86. Kelly, "Inquisition and the Prosecution of Heresy," 446.
87. Hamilton, *Medieval Inquisition*, 43.
88. Logan, *Excommunication*, 69.
89. Ibid., 80; Woodcock, *Medieval Ecclesiastical Courts*, 95–96.
90. Wright, *Contemporary Narrative*, 3.
91. Logan, *Excommunication*, 72.

arrest. His citation of William Outlaw for heresy and aiding and abetting heresy seems equally questionable, as no evidence is provided against him at this point. Ledrede equated himself with both Christ and the church, and he interpreted interference with his prosecution as treason against the faith; thus William Outlaw's heresy was assisting his mother and opposing Ledrede, as it would later be for Arnold le Poer and Roger Outlaw.

As Ledrede based many of his accusations of heresy on opposition to him and his office, Arnold le Poer seems to have had a similar motivation for his arrest of Ledrede, which violated the decretal *Si quis suadente* and of which both Ledrede and the *Narrative* made considerable use. While Arnold may have had solid grounds for his arrest, such as the bishop's violation of common law, the *Narrative* makes no mention of them, and in the end Ledrede was released without conviction. The arrest provided Ledrede with more justification in his proceedings than his previous claims had, as his fellow religious, including four bishops, were outraged by this act and forced Arnold to apologize to Ledrede. Some scholars have interpreted this act as rendering Ledrede's success in the Kyteler case "inevitable."[92] But while the arrest ultimately served Ledrede's interests more than Arnold's, such treatment of ecclesiastics was far from *nova et inaudita* (new and unheard of), as the *Narrative* claims, in England or the colony, in Ledrede's personal history as bishop of Ossory, and in the subsequent events of the trial, in which three more ecclesiastics attempting to conduct Ledrede's investigation of heretics were arrested by secular leaders of Ossory, with barely a whimper from either Ledrede or the *Narrative*.

Another factor, wholly absent from the *Narrative*, may have played a pivotal role in garnering support for Ledrede and his cause: ethnic tensions involving his order in Ireland.[93] From the late thirteenth century on, Franciscans and Dominicans had been said to "make much of [the Irish] language" and incite insurrection among the Irish people.[94] The matter became of critical importance during the Bruce invasion and its aftermath. In 1316, Edward II wrote to the Franciscan minister general, demanding action against Irish brothers who supported Bruce and spurred the Irish to rebellion.[95] On April 7, 1324, a commission appointed by John XXII to investigate Edward's charges headed by William de Rodyerd declared that unruly Irish Franciscans

---

92. Williams, "'She Was Usually Placed with the Great Men,'" 80; Lanigan, "Richard de Ledrede," 26.

93. These tensions are discussed further in chapter 5.

94. *CDI*, 3:10, 4: no. 2035; FitzMaurice and Little, *Materials for the History*, 52–53; Cotter, *Friars Minor in Ireland*, 31–41.

95. Rymer, vol. 2, pt. 4, p. 99; see also Theiner, 194.

were to be relocated in primarily Anglo-Irish houses and no native Irish were to be guardians of the friaries that had caused the greatest problems. Apparently an outcry ensued, for during the Dublin parliament at which Arnold le Poer proclaimed Ledrede to be attacking the isle of saints and Ledrede scorned Magna Carta as *una parvula cartula*, Rodyerd offered a clarification of the mandate he claimed had been misinterpreted, allowing two of the eight problem friaries as well as four unnamed other houses to retain Irish guardians, and these six friaries would then constitute a single Irish custody. After this prescription was added, Ledrede was the first to confirm this arrangement, followed by the bishops of Waterford and Connor.[96] As he was probably the highest-ranking Franciscan at the parliament, his support in this matter may have been solicited by Rodyerd, who in turn offered to support him in his prosecution of the Kyteler case.[97] In addition, a primary consideration at this parliament was the policing of leading Anglo-Irish families by the heads of their lineage, as both Arnold le Poer and Maurice fitz Thomas agreed to do; their feuding, in which Ledrede was to play a key part, erupted into open warfare the following year, threatening the tenuous stability of the colony.[98] Arnold's role in this legislation and both his and his family's importance and feuding in the colony may have simultaneously emphasized his power and made him vulnerable to additional antagonists, such as Ledrede.

Ledrede's prosecution may also have struck a chord with Rodyerd and other Anglo-Irish leaders, who for decades had been embroiled in bitter warfare with the native Irish, particularly those who lived in the Wicklow mountains bordering Dublin. Within a few years of Ireland's first execution for heresy, that of Petronilla de Midia, Dublin ecclesiastical leaders sent a native Irishman from the Wicklow mountains to the stake on extremely tenuous charges of heresy. The most detailed account of the case was delivered by William de Nottingham, the precentor of St. Patrick's who advanced Ledrede's cause and that of *Ut inquisitionis* during Alice's countersuit, and the preface to the account notes that it reflects the perspective of the dean of St. Patrick's, that is, William de Rodyerd, who was also the absent archbishop of Dublin's vicar. The account contains possible references to the Kyteler case

---

96. Curtis, *Calendar of Ormond Deeds*, vol. 1, *1172–1350*, 237–42. The manuscript containing the legislation seems to have been composed by or for Ledrede, further evidence of his thoroughness (Ó Clabaigh, *Friars in Ireland*, 38).

97. Ireland had no Franciscan archbishops and only two other Franciscan bishops at this time: Michael Mac Lochlainn, bishop of Derry (whom Phillips has tentatively identified as the author of the Remonstrance and would be unlikely to support Rodyerd's aims; see chapter 5), and Robert Petit, bishop of Clonfert, then at Exeter.

98. Tresham, I.i.30; Berry, *Early Statutes*, 306–9; see chapter 4.

and calls for a crusade against the native Irish and the Anglo-Irish who had been infected with their heresy, thus capitalizing on Ledrede's prosecutions and the colonial fear of gaelicization. Dublin's ecclesiastical leaders, such as Rodyerd and Nottingham, seem likely to have been inspired by Ledrede's mission against heresy to employ similar tactics against the Gaelic Irish who for so long had been thorns in their side, and they possibly facilitated Petronilla's execution so that a precedent had been set.

Even with the support of Rodyerd and Nottingham, however, Ledrede's success was far from assured. While immediately after the parliament, certain *pauperiores* (poorer people) were arrested, the investigation was conducted under secular, rather than ecclesiastical, authority, as the ecclesiastics Ledrede had commissioned to carry out the inquisition were arrested by leading magnates of Ossory; furthermore, one of the secular officials was a primary defendant, William Outlaw. Though Ledrede found some cause for celebration in their arrest, he was still far from satisfied and wrote to the keeper of Kilkenny (Walter de Islip) and the chancellor (Roger Outlaw) to arrest twelve others. His letters, however, fall short of the requirements of the writ for arrest, *Significavit*, as they contain no reference to excommunication but state only that certain named persons of his diocese had been accused and were strongly suspected of heresy.[99] Though Ledrede attached *Ut inquisitionis* to the letters, both Walter and Roger refused to order the warrant, perhaps because of the manifest irregularities of Ledrede's request.[100] The decretal apparently was more compelling to the justiciar, who promptly issued *Significavit*, although the writ as it appears in the *Narrative* contains significant alterations, "the blackest heresy known to the common lawyer."[101] Instead of referring to the forty-day excommunication of the accused necessary to justify their arrest, it states only that they were implicated (*irretiti*) in heretical depravity and asks for their castigation and correction.[102] The *ministri reipublicæ* (government agents) were understandably confused by the writ, maintaining that they were not specifically bound to arrest and imprison the accused, who furthermore could escape through sureties and bail. Ledrede asked for Darcy's personal presence to assist him in this matter, and Darcy agreed, although he does not seem to have arrived until July 2, when before Darcy, Islip, Arnold

---

99. The descriptions vary somewhat in the two letters. In the letter to Roger Outlaw, they are described as "de hæresibus notatæ, diffamatæ, et . . . indictatæ"; to Walter de Islip, "notatas, diffamatas, et vehementer suspectas" (Wright, *Contemporary Narrative*, 22–23).

100. If the request for the writ did not contain the necessary information, it could not be granted (Logan, *Excommunication*, 80, see also 41–42).

101. Peter Walmsley in Davidson and Ward, *Sorcery Trial*, 55n95.

102. Wright, *Contemporary Narrative*, 24.

le Poer, and Roger Outlaw, Alice Kyteler was publicly condemned for heresy in absentia and her belongings burnt.[103]

While the officials seem to have acquiesced to Ledrede's display on July 2, shortly thereafter Walter and Roger argued in Darcy's presence that they could not assist in the arrest because it violated royal liberties by denying the accused bail. *Significavit* did not allow bail until satisfaction had been made to the church, unless fraud had been a factor, but the ambiguity of the writ as issued by Darcy and the possibility that Alice alone had been excommunicated for forty days made the writ irregular and ineffective, to the consternation of the state officials. Ledrede may have obtained a subsequent writ that he was then bringing before Walter, Roger, and Darcy, but this writ or the fraud inherent in the irregular form of *Significavit* necessitated the possibility of bail. According to Peter Walmsley, Ledrede was attempting to pervert *Significavit* into a writ used to compel appearance in court by arrest in a criminal case, but even such a writ would follow only after other legitimate methods had failed.[104] Since Ledrede refused the possibility of bail, the arrest could not be lawful, an argument that convinced Darcy, and the arrest of Alice's alleged accomplices, apart from that of her son, is not mentioned until the dubious concluding summary of the *Narrative*. While William Outlaw was eventually arrested, this occurred only after he had confessed to aiding and abetting heretics.

The case against William provided further tensions between common and canon law. During William's imprisonment and after consultation with lawyers, Walter de Islip was at last compelled to issue letters directing secular officials to swear the oath to assist Ledrede in his investigation. While Ledrede attempted to deny William bail in accordance with *Ut inquisitionis*, arguments from common law were apparently more persuasive, as bail was allowed. By the time of William's second appearance in court, Ledrede claimed to have acquired direct evidence against him, which would preclude the possibility of compurgation according to canon law, yet Ledrede did allow compurgation.[105] It was William, rather than Ledrede, who eventually refused compurgation, allegedly because he could not find sufficient sureties. This claim rings hollow, given his power and influence in the colony and the number of men who along with Roger Outlaw acted as surety for his sizeable debt to Ledrede on January 25, as well as those whom the *Narrative* claims were attempting to bribe the bishop to treat William leniently. As a confessed fautor of heretics

---

103. The date is provided by Clyn, 16.
104. Walmsley in Davidson and Ward, *Sorcery Trial*, 57n101.
105. Davidson and Ward, *Sorcery Trial*, 61n110.

but not a convicted heretic himself, William was entitled to absolution once he demonstrated contrition by accepting penance and offering a guarantee that he would perform it, and this path William chose.[106] Though Ledrede was outraged, the dean and chapter accepted his contrition. The *Narrative* gets one last jibe in by claiming William was presumed convicted because he refused purgation and the church had such a strong case against him; an unfounded claim, not least because little to no evidence against William is provided in the *Narrative* apart from his confession of aiding heretics, which further demonstrates the extent to which Ledrede was willing to twist canon law and disregard common law in his vendettas.[107]

Ledrede among Inquisitors

At the start of her study of medieval inquisitors, Karen Sullivan traces an inquisition's general steps. The inquisitor arrives in town on a mule, goes to the church where the parishioners have gathered, preaches to them about the Catholic faith and the heretics in the region who teach contrary doctrine, and warns them that the pope has authorized him to act against these heretics and that anyone who clings to their false faith will damn their immortal souls. Over the next few weeks, he meets privately with those who voluntarily seek to confess their involvement in heresy, who name their associates, receive a light penance, and are reconciled. After a grace period has elapsed, he summons the accused who have not yet come forward, who are interrogated without their accusers being identified. Lawyers (if present) are expected to help clients confess rather than establish innocence, and torture can be applied if confessions are not forthcoming. After the inquisitor has finished the examinations and made his judgements, he gathers everyone together again for another sermon against heresy, reading confessions and requiring heretics to confirm them. He then assigns them their penances, much like those the *Narrative* assigned to Alice's alleged accomplices, and also names any who refused to recant their heresy and so would be relaxed to the secular arm, to be burned at the stake the following day.[108] Idealistic aspects aside, this portrait accurately sketches how inquisitions often did and were expected to unfold. While the Kyteler case fell wide of the mark, Ledrede most likely held himself to and justified his approach by such a standard.

---

106. Ibid., 65n119; Woodcock, *Medieval Ecclesiastical Courts*, 97.

107. While vehement suspicion sufficed for punishment according to inquisitorial procedure, it did not suffice for conviction; see Lea, *History of the Inquisition*, 1:433–34, 455–56.

108. Sullivan, *Inner Lives of Medieval Inquisitors*, 1–2. See Wright, *Contemporary Narrative*, 40, for the penances of Alice's accomplices.

Inquisitions were designed to elicit confessions, although ideally those would result in reconciliation rather than execution, which represented a soul lost to God and his church.

Some inquisitors embraced their role as vicarious executioners, however. Conrad Tors and his associate John, colleagues of Conrad of Marburg, declared that they would happily burn one hundred innocent people if one guilty person was among them, and their actions suggest the truth of that sentiment.[109] Their example is extreme, but not unique.[110] Ledrede himself seems to have rejoiced in aspects of his vengeance, although perhaps not to the extent the king suggested in 1357.[111] The Kyteler case was his first and really only inquisition, as his subsequent accusations did not reach trial, apart from Roger Outlaw's demand to clear his name. Ledrede apparently sought execution not only for Petronilla, but for others, especially Alice, as well.[112] Shortly before Arnold le Poer died in prison awaiting trial on Ledrede's charges, Ledrede expressed satisfaction that Arnold's family and friends had died horrible deaths and animals had desecrated their corpses.[113] The treatment Arnold's corpse received further suggests Ledrede's intentions while he was still alive. Generally, however, such results were to be avoided; by one estimate executions accounted for only one percent of inquisitorial sentences in the thirteenth and fourteenth centuries.[114] Of the 207 extant sentences of the Dominicans Bernard of Caux's and John of Saint-Pierre's extensive inquisitions in the Lauragais in the mid-thirteenth century, 184 were to wear the yellow cross while 23 were sentenced to life in prison; none was executed.[115] Bernard Gui, a Dominican active in southern France at the same time as Ledrede's prosecutions, reconciled the vast majority of the 636 people he convicted. He relaxed 42, specifying that 3 more should meet the same fate if they could be found.[116] Gui's approach to inquisition shared marked similarities with Ledrede's, making the latter's quest for vengeance all the more evident.

---

109. Sullivan, *Inner Lives of Medieval Inquisitors*, 76.

110. Other examples include Robert le Bougre, Conrad of Marburg, and Heinrich Krämer, who played a pivotal role in the development of the witch craze.

111. Raine, *Historical Papers and Letters*, 403–6.

112. Note the *Narrative's* claim that multiple people were burned (Wright, *Contemporary Narrative*, 40).

113. Sayles, *Documents*, 134.

114. Yves Dossat, cited in Ames, *Righteous Persecution*, 185.

115. Pegg, *Corruption of Angels*, 126.

116. Sullivan, *Inner Lives of Medieval Inquisitors*, 126. James Given lists slightly different numbers: of the 633 sentences he lists, forty-one were burned alive, though three more who were already dead would have been burned if alive (*Inquisition and Medieval Society*, 69; see also Ames, *Righteous Persecution*, 184).

While Gui's statistics indicate a more judicious approach to execution, he assumed that all accused of heresy were guilty. He acknowledged pangs of conscience if those executed had never confessed, but preferred the possibility of killing the innocent to letting an unrepentant and unconfessed heretic escape.[117] He recognized that an inquisitor might not be an objective instrument of justice, but rather than counselling inquisitors who acted out of anger and avarice to overcome their passions or to excuse themselves from a case if they could not do so, he advised them to conceal their wrath or greed so as to avoid accusations of cruelty or covetousness. His primary concern was protecting the inquisitor's reputation and thus his efficacy in the war against heresy.[118] Jacques Fournier, to whose papal court Ledrede would later flee and who was the sole Cistercian included in John XXII's 1320 commission to establish connections between magic and heresy, was "the terror of heretics," yet, unlike Ledrede, he avoided torture, and his 578 interrogations from 1318 to 1325 resulted in 5 deaths at the stake.[119] William of Paris, who died a few years before Ledrede took office, but whose handling of the Templar trial may have inspired him, offers critical perspective on relationships between church and state. His experience as the first concurrent royal confessor and papal inquisitor affirms Christ's observation that "no one can serve two masters."[120] As Sean Field has demonstrated, William's role in merging "a new conceptual link between the spiritual safety of the realm and the personal salvation of the monarch," which included bringing inquisitorial appointments and actions in line with Philip IV's preferences, caused him to fall from papal favor. His more cautious handling of subsequent trials, including avoiding torture, indicates that he had learned from "his overconfident attempt to manipulate inquisitorial proceedings against the Templars for royal benefit. . . . Insincere confessions elicited through force had come back to haunt William with the Templars," in part because they darkened the inquisitor's reputation.[121] Ledrede, however, may have not learned that lesson, but instead adopted William's earlier, more audacious approach. Thus, even in comparison with his fellow inquisitors, Ledrede seems somewhat extreme.[122] While a far cry from Conrad Tors and John, the combination of intense secular opposition and his subsequent exile may have prevented

---

117. Sullivan, *Inner Lives of Medieval Inquisitors*, 136–37.

118. Ibid., 143–45.

119. Mollat, *Popes at Avignon*, 27; Moore, *War on Heresy*, 328; Ladurie, *Montaillou*, xiv.

120. Matthew 6:24, Luke 16:13.

121. Field, *The Beguine, the Angel, and the Inquisitor*, quotations at 72–73, 92, and 94–95.

122. His extremism seems even more pronounced, given that Bernard and William were Dominicans and Ledrede was Franciscan; see Grieco, "Pastoral Care," and Ames, *Righteous Persecution*.

him from exacting such vengeance. By Bernard Gui's standards Ledrede was a failure, as he hid neither his avarice nor his anger, not even in the *Narrative*, which reads as his personal propaganda. The executions that he seems so desperate to obtain further assert his failings; a successful inquisitor enabled the accused's reconciliation with the church, not her death.

In the end, the Kyteler case was a failure for all involved, particularly for Petronilla de Midia, who lost her life, and Alice Kyteler, who lost life as she had known it. Neither canon nor common law wholly prevailed; an uneasy truce was established between Ledrede and Roger Outlaw and Arnold le Poer that would be broken within a few years, resulting in Roger's exoneration for aiding heretics, Arnold's death in prison while awaiting trial for heresy, and Ledrede's exile from Ireland. William Outlaw presumably performed part of his penance, at least acknowledging the £1,000 fine, but he otherwise seems to have continued on much as he had before. The turbulent and tense political situation enabled Ledrede's demonic obsession to materialize into death at the stake, but the responsibility for the affair remains his. He transformed a case of *maleficia* into a manifestation of John XXII's deepest fears, providing a remarkably accurate precursor of the witch hunts of the fifteenth and following centuries. His aspirations to martyrdom that twisted Becket's model and seem specious, his overidentification of himself and his office with Christ and the church, his belief that priests should be revered almost to the point of worship, and his sense of superiority owing to his special relations with the apostolic see and to the education he received there, which would have included familiarity with trials such as the Templars', proved a fatal combination for Petronilla. The thoroughness and diligence with which Ledrede approached office, as demonstrated by the *Red Book of Ossory*, indicate that he could have been a positive force in the colony, which often suffered from neglect by absentee bishops and archbishops or by those who cared more for secular than spiritual concerns, such as his predecessor, William fitz John. Yet his ambitions, arrogance, and vengefulness caused him to equate opposition to him with heresy against the church, leading to his own downfall as well as the demise of Petronilla and eventually Arnold. The Kyteler case essentially ends where the *Narrative* does, but violent aftershocks continued to erupt over the following five years and lingered for the remaining three decades of Ledrede's episcopate. These involved not only the primary characters in the *Narrative*, but the papacy, all four archbishops of Ireland, and the king of England, who described Ledrede as a sort of inquisitor manqué. Ledrede undoubtedly would not have appreciated such an assessment, but its accuracy is unmistakable. The Kyteler case was simultaneously his greatest success and the failure that consumed him; the ensuing years of his episcopate witnessed a string of further failures on the same front.

❦ CHAPTER 4

Moments of Lucidity Dedicated to Malice

Ledrede's Continuing Conflicts in the Colony

The five years following the Kyteler case saw Richard de Ledrede involved in three more heresy proceedings, a bitter dispute with his metropolitan, a conspiracy against the king, and a conflict between king and pope specifically over his claims of heresy in Ireland, claims that led to his absence from his see from 1329 until 1347. Although Ledrede and Arnold le Poer ostensibly reconciled at the Dublin parliament of May 1324, Ledrede could not forgive Arnold's treatment of him and spent the next five years pursuing revenge. To facilitate this end, he allied with Maurice fitz Thomas, the unruly Geraldine lord of Desmond and Arnold's chief secular adversary, and allegedly took part in a plot to make Maurice king of Ireland. After Arnold had died in prison awaiting trial for heresy and Roger Outlaw had been exonerated for charges of aiding heretics, Ledrede turned against his co-conspirators, wielding his most potent weapon against Robert de Caunton, Maurice's right-hand man. In his attempts to try Robert for heresy Ledrede encountered his most formidable opponent, Alexander de Bicknor, the archbishop of Dublin, who had been absent from Ireland during the proceedings against Alice and her alleged accomplices. Robert sought sanctuary with Bicknor, and the archbishop ordered Ledrede to desist in his persecution of Robert; Ledrede refused, and the two entered into a heated conflict that lasted until the end of Bicknor's life, in which each accused the other of aiding heretics and of heresy itself. While the king did not openly

favor Bicknor over Ledrede, as he had his own complaints against the archbishop, he repeatedly wrote to the papacy complaining of Ledrede's behavior,
in particular his empty allegations of heresy against faithful citizens. Three
successive popes, however, stood solidly by Ledrede, especially regarding his
pursuit of heretics in Ireland.

This chapter traces these developments and explores them primarily in
terms of the colony's chaotic politics and the tensions within its ecclesiastical
hierarchy. More so than the others, this chapter is fully entrenched within the
colony, revealing to a greater extent its diverse factions, the infighting among
colonists, and the ways in which heresy was wielded as a weapon within
personal feuds. It traces Ledrede's subsequent career, which contextualizes his
conduct in the Kyteler case and further illuminates his character. It discusses
his involvement in five heresy proceedings: against Arnold le Poer, Roger
Outlaw, Robert de Caunton, and Alexander de Bicknor, and against him by
Bicknor. Only one of those cases, that of Roger Outlaw, reached trial, which
was held outside Ledrede's jurisdiction and exonerated Roger. Arnold died
in prison while awaiting a trial in Dublin initiated by Ledrede, but this also
would have been held outside his jurisdiction and likely would have reached
a verdict similar to Roger's. None of the allegations demonstrates legitimate
concern about the orthodoxy of the defendant's religious beliefs; all conform
to the general nature of heresy allegations in fourteenth-century Ireland: a
means to attack one's opponents rather than to protect the faith.

Several scholars have read the Kyteler case and its aftermath as a "bizarre
manifestation of the Mortimer-Despenser quarrel [of England] in Ireland,"
with Ledrede siding with the pro-Mortimer faction "for reasons known
only to himself."[1] Certain elements seem to support such a theory: Arnold le
Poer served as Hugh Despenser's seneschal of Kilkenny and greatly benefited
while Despenser numbered high among Edward II's favorites; the month
after Despenser's death in December 1326, Roger Mortimer and his lover,
Queen Isabella, deposed Edward II, had him murdered in a particularly brutal fashion after nearly a year's imprisonment, and placed Edward III upon
the throne but kept power firmly in their own hands for the next three
years; during this unrest in England, open warfare erupted in Ireland, led on
opposing sides by Arnold le Poer and Maurice fitz Thomas, often presented
as one of Mortimer's primary supporters in Ireland; and at the pinnacle of
Mortimer's power, Maurice was made earl of Desmond while Arnold was

---

1. Lydon, *Ireland in the Later Middle Ages*, 55 (Lydon later revised his opinion somewhat: *NHI*,
2:299); see also Orpen, *Ireland under the Normans*, 4:223–25; Clarke, *Fourteenth Century Studies*, 25–29;
Curtis, *History of Medieval Ireland*, 202; and Ledrede, *Latin Poems*, xxiv–xxv.

allowed to die in prison.[2] As Frame has pointed out, however, the Mortimer-Despenser interpretation "is misleading in almost every respect."[3] While Arnold did benefit from his association with Despenser, his fortunes were not inextricably tied to his English overlord but derived from multiple factors. In the summer of 1327 he was confirmed as the seneschal of Kilkenny and granted custody of Kilkenny Castle, which apparently had temporarily belonged to Ledrede, possibly to assuage his anger at his imprisonment there.[4] Despite his experience and investment in Ireland, no evidence suggests that Mortimer had any Anglo-Irish allies before 1328, with the possible exception of Thomas fitz John, earl of Kildare.[5] Far from being Mortimer's Irish pet, Maurice fitz Thomas was a maverick whom Mortimer rightly regarded as the primary obstacle to his power in Ireland, and the two were on opposing sides of a lawsuit for most of the Mortimer ascendancy.[6] The case ended in July 1329 with Maurice returning to Margaret Badlesmere lands of which he had deprived her, but the result was far from a loss for Maurice, as Mortimer lavished him with many rewards, including the earldom of Desmond.[7] Yet Maurice's alliance with Mortimer occurred only after Arnold le Poer's death and lasted less than a year, as Mortimer himself fell from grace in 1330.[8]

The primary problem with the Mortimer-Despenser interpretation of the Kyteler case and its aftermath is that it portrays events in Ireland as a pale reflection of events in England, thereby discounting the chief factors: local politics and the personalities behind them. The English quarrel played no role in the Kyteler case and a marginal one in its aftermath, both of which were largely shaped by Ledrede, who especially ill fits the Mortimer-Despenser interpretation; the former was caused by his transformation of a complaint of *maleficia* into a manifestation of French fears and propaganda about heresy and sorcery, and the latter by his vengeance against his opponents in the Kyteler case. In his vendetta against Arnold and Roger, Ledrede

---

2. Walter of Hemingburgh, *Chronicon*, 2:297–98.

3. Frame, *English Lordship*, 176.

4. *CPR* (1327–30): 108; *CFR*, 4:45–46.

5. Frame, *English Lordship*, 176. In 1323, Alexander de Bicknor and Roger Outlaw informed the king that Mortimer's influence was threatening the colony, but their claims may have been exaggerated and whatever influence he may have had in 1323 was ephemeral (ibid., 167–68). Mortimer served as lieutenant of Ireland April 1317 to May 1318 and justiciar of Ireland June 1319 to December 1320 (*NHI*, 9:472). He was the lord of Trim by right of his wife as well as the lord of Leix through his grandmother. He unsuccessfully opposed Edward Bruce at Kells in 1315 (*CSM*, 2:345, 348; for his earlier deeds in Ireland, see 337–38).

6. Frame, *English Lordship*, 187.

7. Rymer, vol. 2, pt. 3, p. 31. For a list of his other rewards, see Frame, *English Lordship*, 188–89.

8. Arnold's death may have played a role in Maurice's amenability to an alliance with Mortimer; see Frame, *English Lordship*, 187.

enlisted the aid of Maurice fitz Thomas, who was openly at war with Arnold and his family by 1325; when that alliance was no longer to his advantage or no longer served Maurice's interests, Ledrede turned on Maurice's closest companion. The primary actors in the drama of 1325 to 1329 kept an eye on the English arena and tried to play it to their advantage, but their interests, motivations, and actions were vested in Ireland, not England, and they were far from puppets pulled by English strings.

The Desmond-le Poer Feud

Maurice's and Arnold's histories first intertwined in 1311, when Maurice was still a minor and Arnold served as one of the pledges for his kinsman Stephen, who had abducted Maurice's mother.[9] Both had close ties with Richard de Burgh, the "Red Earl" of Ulster who in 1290 referred to Arnold's father Robert as his *cosyn* and provided the le Poer family with their most powerful support.[10] Richard's daughter Katherine wed Maurice in 1313, perhaps in an attempt to heal the long-standing rift between the de Burghs and the Geraldines.[11] Both took an active role in resisting another of Richard's sons-in-law, Robert Bruce, and his brother when they invaded Ireland, and it is possible that their enmity began then, as Bruce's "victory by default" at Skerries in January 1316 was attributed by Pembridge to infighting between the colonial defenders.[12] The Bruce brothers attempted to incite the native Irish to join their cause, claiming a cultural affinity between the Scottish and the Irish; though their success on that front was mixed at best, many Irish clans took advantage of the unrest to wage their own wars against the English and Anglo-Irish in Ireland.[13] The most successful of these was the Battle of Dysert O'Dea in 1318, during which Richard de Clare, lord of

9. *CJR*, 3:189–91; see also 1:295, and Kenny, *Anglo-Irish and Gaelic Women*, 105. Maurice was born in 1293 and came into his inheritance in 1314 (Cokayne, *Complete Peerage*, 4:237).

10. Cole, *Documents Illustrative of English History*, 71; Parker, "Paterfamilias and *Parentela*," 103.

11. Clyn, 11; Pembridge dates it to 1312 (*CSM*, 2:341). The wedding of Maurice's kinsman Thomas fitz John to another of the Red Earl's daughters, which took place at about the same time, may have shared a similar purpose.

12. Quotation from Frame, *Ireland and Britain*, 84; claim of feuding from Pembridge (*CSM*, 2:347). Robert did not join his brother in Ireland until January 1317, when the invasion was in dire straits (Frame, *Ireland and Britain*, 77–78). For references to Arnold's and Maurice's involvement in resistance to the Bruce invasion, see Phillips, "Documents on the Early Stages of the Bruce Invasion"; *CCR* (1313–18): 189; Frame, *Ireland and Britain*, 86, 89, 94–96, 108, 121–22.

13. One example is the Irish of Desmond, who rose against Maurice fitz Thomas in the summer of 1315, preventing him from joining the justiciar's campaign against the Scots at that time (Phillips, "Documents on the Early Stages of the Bruce Invasion," 261–62).

Thomond, was killed, leaving a young child, Thomas, as his only heir.[14] John le Poer, Arnold's brother and possibly Alice Kyteler's fourth husband, initially was granted custody of Thomas's Thomond lands, the greatest stronghold of which was Bunratty Castle, but in that same year Maurice fitz Thomas entered Thomond with Brian Bán O'Brien, the main rival of the victor of Dysert O'Dea and de Burgh ally Muirchertach O'Brien for the kingship of Thomond.[15] By 1320, Maurice was declared a custodian of Thomas's lands, and when Thomas died the following year, Maurice refused to renounce custody to Thomas's aunt, Margaret Badlesmere; this prompted a lawsuit that was not resolved until the summer of 1329, after Maurice had been promised the many plums that he promptly received after ceding to Margaret her rightful property.[16] Orpen has suggested that the Decies, where the le Poers held land and Maurice was lord, may have been another point of contention between the two families.[17] Given the two men's personalities, they probably would have conflicted wherever they came into contact, but the precise origins of their hostilities are obscure.

Although the first evidence of their feud does not occur until the summer of 1325, an event related by the *Narrative of the Proceedings against Dame Alice Kyteler* could suggest a start by May 1324. Ledrede avoided an ambush en route to the Dublin parliament, and on his return he learned that those who had lain in wait for him had been killed by their own enemies and their leader, Arnold's kinsman, had been captured and mortally wounded the day before.[18] While the *Narrative* does not name the enemies and Maurice was not Arnold's only opponent, the feud that would openly erupt the following year might have been preceded by skirmishes such as this. Moreover, at this same parliament, a chief consideration was the lawlessness of members of leading Anglo-Irish families, and the heads of the families, including Arnold and Maurice, were made to swear to police their kinsmen and followers.[19] This practice, an adaptation of the native Irish system of kin liability, *cin comfocuis*, which had also been adopted at the parliament of 1310 and was followed by the le Poers as early as 1290, was a recognition by the colonial

14. Simms, "Battle of Dysert O'Dea."

15. *AI, s.a.* 1318. The feud between the de Burghs and the Geraldines was played by the rival O'Briens and vice versa; the de Burghs supported one faction of the O'Briens and the Geraldines the other (Simms, "Battle of Dysert O'Dea," 62). Thus Maurice's support of Brian Bán O'Brien indicates his perpetuation of the feud between his family and that of his wife.

16. See O'Brien, "Territorial Ambitions of Maurice fitz Thomas."

17. Orpen, *Ireland under the Normans*, 4:224.

18. Wright, *Contemporary Narrative*, 16–17 and 22.

19. Tresham, I.i.30, Berry, *Early Statutes*, 306–9.

government of the limitations of royal authority within the colony.[20] Rather than to an absent king and his representatives, members of these large lineages looked to the leaders of their own families, who maintained private armies that they used in their feuds with one another.[21] The legislation of 1310 and 1324 may have been an attempt to remedy a fact of colonial life, but it also fostered the independence of Anglo-Irish magnates and left few checks on rivalries that often erupted into open warfare, as would soon be the case with Arnold and Maurice.

On June 28, 1325, John Darcy warned the two men to desist in their attacks on each other, although what attacks prompted his warning are not known.[22] The justiciar's admonishment may have had some success; perhaps they chose to wage their war in the legal arena, as each wrote letters to the English council that year, but their contents have been lost.[23] Maurice, however, flouted royal authority by storming Bunratty in November 1325, which he apparently lost during the previous year and a half, and allegedly had the castle's constable, Richard de Armeston, blinded and his tongue cut out.[24] Darcy was forced to act against Maurice and set out in February 1326 to retake Bunratty as well as to work a truce between Arnold and Maurice, suggesting that the problems in Thomond were connected to their hostilities.[25] Arnold went to England perhaps in part about the matter and received signs of his favor, as on July 1 he obtained a grant of the first wardship or custody worth £100 to fall vacant.[26] In his absence, Arnold's cousin and co-leader of his lineage, John le Poer, baron of Dunoyl, apparently worked out an agreement with Maurice; on July 14 they were granted four months to sheriff their kin and followers, and actual sheriffs were not to hinder their policing by attempts to arrest them.[27]

One week before this armistice of sorts, Maurice allegedly hosted a conspiratorial meeting with quite an impressive attendance list: Maurice's kinsman Thomas fitz John, the earl of Kildare and justiciar from May 1327

---

20. Hand, "English Law in Ireland," 407–8, 417–18; Cole, *Documents Illustrative of English History*, 71. The policy was repeated for the le Poers in 1305 (*CJR*, 2:19), and in 1308 John le Poer, baron of Dunoyl, was elected sheriff of Waterford because of his ability "to chastise to the full all such malefactors of his race" (*CJR*, 2:118).

21. See Frame, *Ireland and Britain*, 191–220.

22. Tresham, I.i.32.

23. *Rotuli Parliamentorum*, 1:437–38; Frame, *English Lordship*, 172.

24. Sayles, "Legal Proceedings," 8–9.

25. Frame, *English Lordship*, 173.

26. Tresham, I.i.33; *CCR* (1323–27): 639; *CPR* (1324–27): 280, 282. On the following August 18, the king instructed Roger Outlaw to deliver to Arnold a custody worth such an amount (Tresham, I.i.37).

27. Tresham, I.i.33–34.

to April 1328; John de Bermingham, who was made the earl of Louth due to his defeat of Edward Bruce; John's brother William de Bermingham; James le Botiller, soon to be earl of Ormond; James's uncle Thomas le Botiller; Maurice's chief retainers, Maurice fitz Philip, Thomas fitz Gilbert, and Robert de Caunton; Maurice's main Irish ally, Brian Bán O'Brien, and his primary subchief, MacConmara; and Richard de Ledrede, bishop of Ossory.[28] Ledrede's presence at this conspiracy has been a source of some consternation, but his longing for revenge against Arnold le Poer, his subsequent behavior, and his anomalous inclusion in this band of military men, most of whom were clearly allied with Maurice fitz Thomas throughout 1326 to 1329, make his involvement seem probable.[29] Edmund Colledge, in his introduction to Ledrede's poems, proclaims the plot to be "no more than a garbled, Power [i.e., le Poer] version of the famous inter-family war."[30] Yet the conspiracy did not come to light until 1332, three years after Maurice's primary le Poer adversary had died in prison due to charges levelled by Ledrede and three years into Ledrede's nearly twenty-year exile, when few in Ireland except the archbishop of Dublin and the chapter of Ossory were particularly concerned about the absent bishop. While Arnold's brother John was the first juror to witness the indictment against Maurice, he was the only le Poer among the thirty jurors and the next year would serve as one of Maurice's main-pernors.[31] The feud between the le Poers and Maurice fitz Thomas diminished substantially after Arnold's death, and other evidence strongly indicates that the conspiracy did in fact occur, although perhaps not precisely as was reported by the jury at Clonmel in February 1332.

According to the indictment, these twelve men met at Kilkenny on July 7, 1326, where they swore upon the Gospels to support each other in four aims: to rebel against the king of England and assert their own control over Ireland;

---

28. For this conspiracy and Maurice's other like acts, see Sayles, "Rebellious First Earl"; Sayles, "Legal Proceedings"; Richardson and Sayles, *Parliaments and Councils*, 12–17. Thomas fitz John and Maurice fitz Thomas were the heads of the two most powerful and prominent branches of the Geraldines, and William de Bermingham was the husband of the widow of Richard de Clare, who died at the Battle of Dysert O'Dea (see above).

29. Sayles explains Ledrede's presence as further evidence of the bishop's eccentricities and mental disorder ("Rebellious First Earl," 207). If the *Narrative*'s claim of an ambush is accurate (Wright, *Contemporary Narrative*, 16–17, 22) and if Maurice fitz Thomas played a role in overcoming it, perhaps the alliance between Maurice and Ledrede had already been established, or perhaps it arose in 1325, when Maurice and Arnold were openly at war.

30. Ledrede, *Latin Poems*, xxiii–xxiv.

31. Sayles, "Legal Proceedings," 6. A le Blund and two de Valles were jurors as well. If Arnold's brother is to be identified with Alice's fourth and final husband, as Ciarán Parker suggests ("Paterfamilias and *Parentela*," 111; see chapter 2), then one might expect him to feel considerable gratitude for the man who allegedly saved him from Alice's attempted murder.

to elect Maurice king of Ireland and ensure that he was crowned; to share Ireland in proportion to the role they played in winning it from the English king; and to destroy any who attempted to oppose them.[32] Since Arnold le Poer and members of his lineage were loyal to the king, on November 2, 1327, Maurice fitz Thomas led two thousand men, including several of his co-conspirators and four de Valles, to attack and pillage le Poer lands in Tipperary and Waterford, and the unrest there lasted for three and a half years.[33] Ledrede was said to be the instigator of at least one of the murderous raids, at Moytobir.[34] Three aspects seem suspect in these findings: the earl of Kildare's involvement, the earl of Louth's endorsement of Maurice's pretensions to kingship, and le Poer loyalty to the king as the cause of Maurice and Arnold's feud. As Frame has pointed out, all evidence indicates that Thomas fitz John was working diligently on Edward III's behalf at this time, and it seems highly unlikely that he and the earl of Louth would endeavor to place Maurice, who ranked beneath them, upon a nonexistent throne. Frame finds le Poer support of the king as a source of the feud more plausible, though he is careful to note the king in question was Edward III, not Edward II, as proponents of the Mortimer-Despenser interpretation would have it.[35] Yet if loyalty to the king were sufficient justification for attack by Maurice and his allies, they would have had considerably more targets from which to chose than the le Poers and their patrons, the de Burghs, who had lost their patriarch, the Red Earl, in 1326. He was survived by a young grandson, and whatever loyalty Maurice may have felt toward his father-in-law was quickly eclipsed by his ambitions, the long-standing feud between their families, and his hatred for Arnold, and in 1327–28 he attacked both families with equal vengeance.[36]

Frame also rejects "the fanciful charge about Maurice fitz Thomas and the kingship," but such aspirations seem quite likely given his character, although they may not have been part of the meeting in July 1326.[37] A jury held at Limerick in 1331 did not mention this conspiratorial gathering, but it too

---

32. Sayles, "Legal Proceedings," 6. Again, the number of a coven (provided one adds a demon to the twelve) surfaces in accusations of illicit doings. Furthermore, treasonous meetings were called "conventicles"; for example, Maurice fitz Thomas's suspected attempt at holding an alternative parliament at Callan in 1344 was labelled as such (Clyn, 30). See also the 1326 order, discussed below.

33. Sayles, "Legal Proceedings," 6–7.

34. Carrigan, *History and Antiquities*, 53; Neary, "Richard de Ledrede," 55.

35. Frame, *English Lordship*, 180–81.

36. *CSM*, 2:364; Frame, *English Lordship*, 179–86. Maurice's support of Brian Bán O'Brien suggests his relations with his father-in-law had cooled, if they ever could have been described as warm, by 1318. Maurice would also be quite harsh toward the kin of his second wife, Aveline, daughter of Nicholas fitz Maurice of Kerry, starving one of her brothers to death and blinding another; see Kenny, *Anglo-Irish and Gaelic Women*, 89.

37. Frame, *English Lordship*, 181, see also 268–71.

proclaimed that "for five full years Maurice had developed such an inflated sense of pride and greed that he intended to take the whole land of Ireland for himself and have himself crowned a false king."[38] The attempt to place Edward Bruce on an Irish throne may have inspired Maurice "to believe that what a Scot from outside had thought it possible to achieve might well be brought about by a Geraldine from inside," and he may have been further encouraged by the plotting of Isabella and her lover to depose Edward II, as they would soon successfully do.[39] He brought together both Gaelic Irish and Anglo-Irish in his army, known as "MacThomas's Rout," which terrorized his lands in Munster and wherever else he set his sights.[40] His ability to transcend ethnic divisions in his company as well as his personal adoption of many Irish customs and open opposition to royal authority has caused Curtis to hail him as "the first of the 'Patriot leaders' in the long history of Anglo-Ireland," but his loyalty lay solidly with himself, not the land or the people of Ireland, whatever their ethnicity.[41] He exploited and harassed Irish and Anglo-Irish equally, repeatedly attacked royal property, and rebelled against royal authority, yet managed to escape the king's wrath and died holding the king's most powerful and trusted office in Ireland, the justiciarship. Hothead may be too simple a term to describe Maurice fitz Thomas, yet it is no less apt for its simplicity, and it also applies to his adversary, Arnold le Poer.

Arnold's behavior as described by the *Narrative* readily attests to his temper and passion; while some of his insults may have been exacerbated by narrator bias, many of them ring true, and he certainly later rued his rash arrest of the bishop. Pembridge reports that Arnold scorned Maurice as a *Rymoure*, which has been interpreted various ways.[42] According to Orpen, Sayles, and Neary, it painted him with the brush of treason, associating him with wandering Irish bards who used their words to incite indigenous Irish to attack the English at every opportunity; according to Frame, it conveyed Arnold's discomfort with Maurice's gaelicization; and according to Evelyn Mullally, "the point of Arnold's insult was that composing harmless *vers de salon* was all that Maurice was fit for."[43] However Maurice himself interpreted the slur, it

---

38. Sayles, "Legal Proceedings," 8.

39. Sayles, "Rebellious First Earl," 204, 206.

40. Sayles, "Legal Proceedings," 8. For some examples, see ibid., 8–9, 17–18.

41. Curtis, *History of Medieval Ireland*, 224, see also 206, and Sayles's response ("Rebellious First Earl," 226).

42. *CSM*, 2:364.

43. Orpen, *Ireland under the Normans*, 4:223; Sayles, "Rebellious First Earl," 208; Neary, "Richard de Ledrede," 48; Frame, *Ireland and Britain*, 216; Mullally, "Hiberno-Norman Literature," 333. The poetic dimensions of the insult have added significance, since Maurice's son Gerald was known for Irish poetry.

was meant to sting and it clearly did, inciting him further to attack Arnold's lands. Nor were Arnold's feuds with Ledrede and Maurice isolated incidents. His relations with John de Boneville, a prominent man within the colony, changed from friendship and support in 1308 to open hostility by 1309.[44] In January 1310, Arnold was ordered by the king to cease his siege of Boneville, seneschal of Kildare and Carlow, in his castle.[45] Shortly thereafter, Boneville was murdered, and Arnold and his men plundered his manor of Balyethan.[46] Arnold himself stood accused of the murder, which apparently was committed by David de Offyntoun in an attack in which Arnold and many others took part, but he was acquitted at the Kildare parliament of 1310 on the basis of self-defense.[47] This parliament also established a truce between Arnold and Boneville's relatives, not unlike the peace brokered between Arnold and Ledrede almost fifteen years later.[48] As the leader of the le Poer lineage and the seneschal of Kilkenny, Carlow, and Wexford, Arnold engaged in several skirmishes with other families, such as the Roches, but his archenemies were Ledrede and Maurice, who gave worse than they got in their vengeance against him.

The tension between Arnold and Maurice, concurring as it did with the instability within the English crown, made the government uneasy.[49] On December 12, 1326, the sheriffs of Munster were ordered to prevent *conventicula illicita* (illicit gatherings) that were being organized by both Irish and English lords to harm "the king's faithful people," and Arnold and Maurice, two of Maurice's co-conspirators, John and William de Bermingham, as well as John de Barry, a le Poer ally, were warned not to participate in such meetings in any way.[50] It is improbable that these men were planning to play a part in the English civil war and virtually inconceivable that Arnold and Maurice were acting in concert. Maurice may well have had his eye on an imaginary Irish throne by that time, but the simplest interpretation, rather than the paranoid one of those who then held a tenuous grasp on the English throne, is that these magnates were solidifying their positions against

---

44. *CJR*, 3:5, 27–28, 42; McEnery and Refaussé, *Christ Church Deeds*, no. 536, p. 89. For Boneville's history, see Brooks, *Knights' Fees*, 87; Wright, *Contemporary Narrative*, 54, 56.

45. Tresham, I.i.13.

46. *CJR*, 3:163–64, see also 217, 230–31, 247.

47. *CSM*, 2:339. This justification seems somewhat at odds with the events of the attack as it can be pieced together from the justiciary rolls (see preceding note).

48. Clarke, *Fourteenth Century Studies*, 29.

49. Edward II was then fleeing Mortimer and Isabella's invasion and was thought to be heading for Ireland; it was further alleged that Edward had made contact with Robert Bruce (Frame, *English Lordship*, 177).

50. Tresham, I.i.35.

their own enemies in Ireland.[51] On July 16, 1327, Maurice, his allies John de Bermingham, James le Botiller, and Maurice de Rocheford, and Arnold's more level-headed kinsman, John le Poer of Dunoyl, were admonished by Mortimer (in the name of Edward III) for failing to obey the justiciar, the earl of Kildare, in protecting the lordship and fending off its enemies.[52] It seems likely that their own feuding prevented them from rendering Thomas fitz John the assistance he needed, rather than that they deliberately were defying the Dublin government, and the situation soon deteriorated.[53] According to Pembridge, it began with Maurice killing several de Burghs, to whose aid Arnold rushed. "Due to the harsh words Lord Arnold had said," Maurice and William de Bermingham led a large assault against Arnold's lands in Munster and Ossory.[54] Many le Poers were killed, and according to Clyn, nearly all of their lands were burned and destroyed.[55]

Arnold and John le Poer of Dunoyl were forced to flee to Waterford, and the justiciar, Thomas fitz John, attempted to arbitrate between the two factions, setting a day to hear their disputes. Perhaps from fear that the earl of Kildare would favor his Geraldine kinsman, Arnold went to England, and during his absence Maurice's attacks intensified, including a raid in which Peter, the son and heir of the baron of Dunoyl, was killed along with about twelve other le Poers.[56] The king's ministers became alarmed at the relentless warfare and put cities on alert out of concern that MacThomas's Rout would lay siege to them. Maurice and his men took umbrage at what they felt to be misplaced apprehension and commanded (*mandaverunt*) the king's council to come to Kilkenny so they could clear themselves of any suspicion of harming the king, maintaining that their intentions were solely to avenge themselves upon their enemies. The king's counselors, including Roger Outlaw, heard them at the Kilkenny parliament in February but replied cautiously, declaring they would consider the case more fully a month after Easter, and apparently referred the matter to the king.[57] Although the annalists report a virtual slaughter of the le Poers and the wholesale destruction of their lands as well as the peremptory attitude Maurice and his allies adopted toward the king's ministers, the king (more accurately, Mortimer) admonished both sides

51. Frame, *English Lordship*, 177.

52. Rymer, vol. 2, pt. 2, p. 193.

53. Frame, *English Lordship*, 179.

54. *CSM*, 2:364. This is the assault to which the Clonmel jury referred; see above, and also Clyn, 19, and *CSM*, 2:364–65.

55. Clyn, 19.

56. Clyn, 19; Flower, "Manuscripts of Irish Interest," 338.

57. *CSM*, 2:365.

equally, sending letters in June 1328 that instructed Maurice, John de Bermingham, James le Botiller, Arnold, his brother John, and Walter fitz William
de Burgh to cease their attacks and advised them to use royal courts rather
than battlefields to resolve their quarrels.[58] These letters had about as much
effect as the ones issued in the summers of 1325 and 1327. Although Roger
Outlaw led a force into Munster to attempt to arbitrate, Maurice's vengeance
remained unabated, as he continued to gather a large force to destroy the le
Poers and the de Burghs.[59]

Sometime in the summer of 1328, Arnold returned to Ireland, possibly
in the company of William de Burgh, the Red Earl's grandson, and James le
Botiller went to England, where Mortimer made him earl of Ormond. Mortimer was at last winning Anglo-Irish allies to his cause, perhaps aggressively
seeking them because his plans for Ireland would antagonize English lords.[60]
Maurice and his allies continued their attacks on the le Poers, including a raid
by the de Cauntons on September 20, 1328, in which John son of Benedict
le Poer was killed. But the next great act in the feud belonged to the religious
rather than the military realm.

Ledrede's Vendetta against Arnold le Poer

In the years since the Kyteler case, Ledrede apparently had not let the war pass
him by, nor limited himself to instigating an armed attack upon Arnold by
Maurice fitz Thomas (a man who needed little instigation). A dispatch to the
king attests that Ledrede's behavior was a cause of concern for the justiciar,
Thomas fitz John.[61] After complaining that Roger Outlaw, the chancellor,
was too distracted by other matters, in particular the needs of his order, to
provide the justiciar with the counsel and assistance he required, the letter
summarizes an indictment made by the knights, sergeants, and people of
Ossory against Ledrede that accused him of inciting both English and Irish
to rise against the king.[62] It also alleges that the bishop had slandered the
queen's chamber with accusations of sorcery and other evils and had vilified
the king's *foialx et loialx* (faithful and loyal people) with heresy accusations;
hence his temporalities had been taken into the king's hand. Ledrede was
summoned to England in September 1327, possibly to answer these charges,

---

58. Rymer, vol. 2, pt. 3, pp. 13–14.
59. *CSM*, 2:367.
60. Frame, *English Lordship*, 185–86; *CPR* (1327–30): 336.
61. Sayles, *Documents*, 131.
62. It is tempting to connect Roger's distraction with Ledrede, but if the two were related the
justiciar presumably would have said so.

but he did not go.[63] A letter written May 1332 from the dean and chapter of Ossory to the king maintains that Ledrede cleared himself of these charges at the Kilkenny parliament of 1328, the same one at which Maurice and his men offered to purge themselves of any suspicion of harming the king.[64] In addition to the bishops of Cork, Lismore, and Waterford, his compurgators included Maurice fitz Thomas, James and Thomas le Botiller, and John and William de Bermingham, providing further evidence of his connection to the men with whom he stood accused of treason and of plotting to destroy Arnold le Poer, and rendering his proclaimed innocence suspect.[65]

The indictment's claim that Ledrede had accused the queen's chamber of sorcery raises the specter of his allegations against Alice and again suggests that to him sorcery was a sex-related if not sex-specific crime. Hugh Despenser, Arnold le Poer's English overlord and one of Isabella's opponents, had been convinced that magical plots were being hatched against him in 1324, which may have suggested the possibility of Isabella and her chamber's supposed nefarious dealings to Ledrede.[66] Perhaps her role in the overthrow of her husband deeply disturbed his Christian and patriarchal values, causing him to interpret her actions as sorcery akin to his accusations of Alice and her associates, who he likewise claimed rebelled against their rightful lords and masters, their husbands. He also may have planned to use these accusations to aid Maurice fitz Thomas's efforts to become king of Ireland. Then again, the claim could be an attempt by the good people of Ossory to win the English court firmly to their side against Ledrede by having his slander touch not only the king's faithful and loyal subjects but the queen herself. The allegations of heresy are similarly obscure; they may suggest lingering resentment over Ledrede's behavior in 1324, his claims against Robert de Caunton, other heretical proceedings otherwise unknown, or his accusations against Arnold le Poer.[67] According to Pembridge, about November 25, 1328, Ledrede informed the king's council that Arnold had already been convicted in his presence on several counts of heretical depravity.[68] While Ledrede was inclined to make

---

63. *CPR* (1327–30): 164.

64. Richardson and Sayles, *Parliaments and Councils*, 202–4; Neary, "Richard de Ledrede," 61; Frame, *English Lordship*, 181–82n103, see also 212.

65. The bishop of Lismore, John Leynagh, was the same man who had brokered peace between Arnold and Ledrede at the Dublin parliament in 1324.

66. *CPL*, 2:461. John XXII took a surprisingly nonchalant attitude toward Despenser's concerns.

67. Since Ledrede's fellow conspirators helped to purge him of these charges, it is unlikely that he had already made his accusation against Robert de Caunton, however.

68. *CSM*, 2:367–68.

such premature assessments of his proceedings against alleged heretics, the indictment relayed in the justiciar's letter could suggest that Ledrede had at least charged Arnold with heresy before April 5, 1328, and that Arnold still enjoyed enough popularity and influence in Ossory while his lands and people were being ravaged by MacThomas's Rout for his supporters to act in his defense against his adversary and Maurice's ally.[69] The reference to instigations of rebellion by both Irish and English sounds quite similar to complaints made against Maurice and further substantiates the probability of Ledrede's involvement in Maurice's plotting and warfare.

A letter from Ledrede to the king likely written in 1328 lays out his case against Arnold without pretensions of a previous conviction.[70] It repeats his complaints about Arnold's behavior during the Kyteler case and adds new ones that apparently arose in the following four years. It begins with a summary of the allegations against Alice and her associates that are reduced to render them essentially as apostates, maintaining that they despised and rejected the eucharist and denied the articles of faith. Surprisingly, no mention is made of sorcery, which played such a critical role in the Kyteler case, perhaps because Ledrede did not wish to remind the king, Mortimer, or Isabella of his accusations against the queen's chamber. It then relates Arnold's refusal to assist Ledrede in his proceedings against heretics, equating his opposition to the bishop with opposition to the church and describing it as a scandal and shame to the dignity and crown of the king of England.[71] Ledrede then recounts his version of Arnold's treatment of him on April 23, 1324, which makes manifest Ledrede's apotheosis. One would scarcely know that he had been in court, as he substitutes the eucharist he carried for himself. It was not Ledrede whom Arnold attempted to dismiss from his court and ordered to stand at the bar with criminals but *le corps Dieu* (God's body). He also maintains that Arnold reviled the eucharist as *diablerie e hurdys* (devilry and dough), recalling the *Narrative*'s version of the insult, "that worthless, churlish tramp from England, with that lump of dough (*hordys*) he carries in his hands."[72] While it is possible that in his anger at Ledrede Arnold referred to the eucharist as dough, it would be indicative of his temper rather than of his actual regard for the eucharist. His problems were not with the church and

---

69. Thomas fitz John's letter must predate his death on April 5, 1328.

70. Sayles, *Documents*, 132–34.

71. That Arnold's behavior was a scandal, shame, and injury to both the church and the king is a repeated refrain in the letter.

72. Sayles, *Documents*, 133. *Diablerie* is the letter's only possible reference to sorcery; if it is to be taken as such, Ledrede would be accusing le Poer of accusing him of sorcery. Wright, *Contemporary Narrative*, 14.

its sacraments but with the bishop, who emerges as a vicious, petty, arrogant, stubborn man in his own words, in his letters and constitutions, and in the *Narrative*, which may have been written by him and certainly shares his viewpoint.[73] Ledrede identified himself as the church incarnate and the embodied mystery of the eucharist; thus he equated attacks upon him as attacks upon them and consequently as heresy. This perspective found few supporters in 1324, and his "devilry" addition indicates that he knew he needed to exacerbate Arnold's words if he were to gain a sympathetic ear in his proceedings against Arnold. He continues that Arnold's revilement of the eucharist, which he again asserts was the worst abuse inflicted upon Christ since he stood before Pilate, made it clear to the church and the people that he was one of the heretics himself, although the *Narrative* makes no such claim.

Ledrede next offers a summary of his seventeen-day prison stint on Arnold's orders. Here, however, he omits the *Narrative*'s claim, that the arrest of a bishop was *nova et inaudita* (new and unheard of), most likely because the tactic was not uncommonly employed by kings of England, one of whose assistance he was currently beseeching.[74] This letter instead focuses on the manner in which his arrest was deliberately calculated to interfere with his proceedings against heretics, that it caused the entire diocese to be placed under interdict, and that it resulted in Arnold's excommunication, a sentence under which he remained, as he continued to scorn the keys of the church. The letter then catalogs the crimes allegedly committed by Arnold against the church and its champion, Ledrede. Arnold and his rout attacked and stripped several churches, then took the pyxes that held the eucharist and threw them in a ditch. Such deeds, if they occurred, were more likely acts of distraint than pillage, to which Ledrede added accusations of defilement of the eucharist in order to bolster his claims of Arnold's blasphemy.[75] When Ledrede protested these acts against God and the church, the letter continues, Arnold responded by ordering his family and following to rob and destroy the bishop and his clergy as well as to kill the latter, promising them the king's peace if they did so and holding good to his promise. The letter next describes an attack on the priory of St. John of Kilkenny, which Arnold offered as an "example of evildoing to others," and details the property Arnold plundered and its value. Ledrede alleges that others did imitate his example, for his followers stole

---

73. The similarities between the *Narrative* and Ledrede's letter to the king complaining about Arnold serve as one basis for identifying Ledrede as the *Narrative*'s author; see Neary, "Richard de Ledrede," v. Maude Clarke first identified Ledrede as the author of the *Narrative* in 1937 (*Fourteenth Century Studies*, 24).

74. Wright, *Contemporary Narrative*, 9; see chapter 3.

75. Davidson and Ward, *Sorcery Trial*, 90n63.

horses, silver, and clothing from the clergy and their tenants in the cross of Ossory before continuing on to Clonmore; here they not only plundered the food barns of the church but pillaged the village as well, for which they were excommunicated, "and soon thereafter, all died the worst death, and dogs and mastiffs chewed their bones, just as God wished."[76] This probably refers to the deeds of MacThomas's Rout, which persecuted the le Poers relentlessly and which Ledrede evidently identified with God's righteous wrath. Apparently, God did not wish such a fate for Arnold just yet; despite the letter's reference to no less than five separate sentences of excommunication upon him, including one issued by two hundred priests the day after the "attack" on St. John's, Arnold yet lived to be a festering wound in Ledrede's side.

The letter ends with another summary of Arnold's deliberate defiance of Ledrede on April 23 and reminds the king of the critical importance of heresy cases and of the great scandal that ensues if one shirks one's duty.[77] Arnold neglected to play the part his office required and in the process revealed himself to be a heretic; the king must not repeat his mistake, for then the scandal inherent in denying the church in a case of the faith and in tolerating such blatant heretics in the realm would spread to the court of England. Ledrede may have regarded his position as "defence of 'Holy Church' and its liberties," but he seems instead to be attempting to make secular officials his servants in direct violation of English common law.[78] Arnold had solid legal reasons for resisting Ledrede, as did Roger Outlaw and Walter de Islip. The crimes upon churches detailed in Ledrede's letter may have simply been an exercise of his office of seneschal, and the claim that he encouraged his followers to murder clerics and granted them immunity for doing so seems unlikely. Though it was not uncommon for colonists and native Irish to attack churches and clergy, as Ledrede's own behavior attests, no evidence verifies Ledrede's claim that Arnold himself perpetrated these raids.[79] Arnold's diplomacy skills clearly paled in comparison with Roger Outlaw's and Walter de Islip's, but only in Ledrede's view did Arnold's scorn for the bishop constitute heresy, and then apparently as an afterthought as that accusation does not surface in the *Narrative*. While the response to this particular letter is unknown, later letters from the king about Ledrede suggest that he did not receive the king's favor at this time.

---

76. Sayles, *Documents*, 134.
77. Ibid.
78. Quotation from Neary, "Richard de Ledrede," 57.
79. See Rymer, vol. 2, pt. 3, p. 28, and below.

Unfortunately for Arnold, Ledrede had more success in Dublin late in 1328, when Arnold was imprisoned due to the bishop's claim that he had previously been convicted for heresy. Roger Outlaw's appointment as acting justiciar following Thomas fitz John's death may have prompted Ledrede to push his case against Arnold le Poer, but probably the success of his ally Maurice fitz Thomas in his vengeance against Arnold and his family and Arnold's return in the summer of 1328 were the primary impetuses.[80] About Arnold's supposed previous conviction for heresy nothing is known; it probably was another of the bishop's empty claims, or perhaps the conviction had been irregular. Frame asserts that Roger Outlaw, then acting justiciar, had "little option but to arrest him pending the trial of the case," which is repeated nearly verbatim by Davidson and Ward, but such an interpretation presumes the veracity and legality of Ledrede's claim and disregards the agility with which Roger, Arnold, and others avoided arresting those whom Ledrede wished arrested on charges of heresy.[81] Nevertheless, the king's council did order Arnold's arrest, and he was imprisoned in Dublin Castle to await a hearing of his heresy case, appointed for the Dublin parliament in January 1329. Ledrede then repeated the excuse he had employed in 1324, claiming that he could not travel to Dublin because his enemies lay in wait along the way. He did not send a proctor to prosecute the case, as he had for Alice's appeal and Rodyerd's demand that he explain his interdict of Ossory. "Since the king's council did not know how to put an end to this matter," the case was delayed, which likely was Ledrede's intent and proved to be Arnold's demise.[82]

Although Roger Outlaw had been forced to comply with Arnold's arrest, he apparently endeavored to assist him as he had William Outlaw, since Ledrede promptly denounced the acting justiciar as a fautor of Arnold's heresy, although the charge could stem from the bishop's smoldering resentment of Roger's own conduct during the Kyteler case. Roger, however, had had enough and asked the council that he be allowed to purge himself, and the council agreed. For three days criers were sent out to see if any wished to pursue the case against Roger, but no one did.[83] Bishops, abbots, priors, the mayors of Dublin, Cork, Limerick, Waterford, and Drogheda, and many knights and prominent citizens gathered at Dublin, and six men were elected to decide the case. Upon examination, the

80. Neary, "Richard de Ledrede," 57.
81. Frame, *English Lordship*, 186; Davidson and Ward, *Sorcery Trial*, 13.
82. *CSM*, 2:368.
83. *CSM*, 2:368.

six judges—William de Rodyerd, the dean of St. Patrick's who had eventually supported Ledrede in 1324 and who likely was the one to prosecute the recent case against Adducc Dubh O'Toole; Robert de Gloucester, the prior of Holy Trinity; the abbot of St. Thomas; the abbot of St. Mary's; and Masters Elias Lawless and Peter Willeby—unanimously found Roger "honest, faithful, and zealous in his faith" and "prepared to die for the faith."[84] To celebrate his vindication in the face of Ledrede's dangerous defamation, Roger threw a great feast for all who wished to come. Arnold le Poer, however, could not attend, as he languished in prison, still awaiting his own trial, which had been postponed until the next parliament, which would begin April 2.

Although it was unlikely that he was ill treated while in prison and he could have reasonably expected to be cleared of heresy once his case was heard, Arnold died excommunicate in prison on Tuesday, March 14, 1329.[85] Perhaps the tragedies inflicted upon his family in the last few years had already greatly weakened him. His body was subjected to the stipulations of Ledrede's fifteenth statute; it was taken to the Dominican church of St. Saviour's, where it remained for a long time unburied.[86] The fate seems particularly bitter, as Arnold's own uncle, whose heir he was, laid the first foundation stone of the reconstructed Dominican house after it had been destroyed by fire in 1304.[87] Benedict O'Sullivan offers the hope that loyalty to the le Poers enabled the Dominicans to eventually offer his body decent interment, or perhaps Ledrede's disgrace and the wrath of the archbishop of Dublin directed at Ledrede, or petitions by Arnold's diminished but still powerful family or by his friend Roger Outlaw, enabled his body to find a more peaceful resting place, but what ultimately became of his body is unknown.[88] Ledrede had at last achieved some form of victory over Arnold le Poer, but it was not a victory he could long enjoy.

---

84. *CSM*, 2:369. Peter de Willeby, a canon of St. Patrick's, is likely the rector of Ballygriffin who had attended the Templar trial nearly twenty years earlier; see chapter 1. He is described as Alexander de Bicknor's official in a document from 1323 (Archdall, *Monasticon Hibernicum*, 2:137).

85. Clyn, 20.

86. Gwynn, "Provincial and Diocesan Decrees," 68; see chapter 3; *CSM*, 2:369.

87. *CSM*, 2:332. The friary was subsequently deliberately destroyed by Dublin citizens in 1316 for fear of the Bruce invasion and thus had to be rebuilt again (ibid., 353).

88. O'Sullivan, " Dominicans in Medieval Dublin," 90; note that O'Sullivan mistakenly identifies Arnold as Eustace's son, rather than nephew. According to a letter written ca. 1358, some of the bodies of those Ledrede threw into prison to die were buried in unconsecrated ground and others lay still unburied (Raine, *Historical Papers and Letters*, 404–5; see below); as this letter was written about thirty years after Arnold's death, the former fate more likely applied to his corpse.

FIGURE 7. The last remaining medieval tower of Dublin Castle, where Arnold le Poer died and where the Templars and likely Adducc Dubh O'Toole were imprisoned as well. Photo by the author.

The Caunton Case and Ledrede's Quarrel with Bicknor

The events that caused Ledrede's exile, already underway by June 14, are not related by the annalists but can be pieced together from letters by and about the bishop.[89] At some point after the deposition of Edward II, Ledrede wrote to Queen Isabella, a surprising attempted ally considering his alleged sorcery accusations, asking for her help in his desire to come to England to see her and her son and in protecting his diocese during his absence.[90] Sayles and Colledge have dated this letter to 1327, the latter presuming the summons in September 1327 was issued in response to his request, but it seems more probable that the summons was to answer charges of slandering the queen and inciting rebellion.[91] While any date from January 1327 to June 1329 is possible, this letter most likely was a product of Ledrede's fears when the tide began to turn against him in the early months of 1329. He and Maurice were still thick as thieves in February 1328, when Maurice, the le Botillers (Butlers), and the de Berminghams helped to purge him of slander and rebellion charges, but they may have parted ways by November 1328, when Ledrede was pursuing his vengeance against Arnold in his own particular idiom, without any discernible help from Maurice. Then again, his alliance

---

89. *CPR* (1327–30): 400.

90. Sayles, *Documents*, 125.

91. Sayles, *Documents*, 125; Ledrede, *Latin Poems*, xxvii.

with Maurice, the new earl of Ormond, and the earl of Louth may have helped to give his allegations of heresy the force they initially lacked in 1324, explaining the promptness with which Arnold was arrested in late November 1328. Perhaps Roger Outlaw's assistance of Arnold and personal defense included mounting a campaign against Ledrede that was bolstered by Roger's exoneration and made Ledrede an expendable liability for Maurice and his men. Or maybe Maurice decided he no longer had any use for the bishop after Arnold's death in March 1329. Whatever the reason, it seems most likely that the rift between Ledrede and Maurice occurred in the first half of 1329, the probable period when Ledrede accused Maurice's own Robert de Caunton of heresy, which brought him into confrontation with his metropolitan, Alexander de Bicknor. The vulnerability of his position after January 1329 serves as plausible justification for his rather desperate move of seeking the queen's good graces, although he may have felt similarly vulnerable from le Poer retaliation should he go to England to plead his case, whichever case that might be, before the queen in 1327–28 as well.

The evidence for the Caunton case that proved Ledrede's undoing derives solely from papal letters written in 1343 and 1347; these do not date the case, but they make it evident that it occurred prior to and was a primary cause of Ledrede's exile in June 1329.[92] These letters, which parrot Ledrede's perspective, can also be compared with Ledrede's petition to Edward III, which Sayles dates to 1341 and must postdate March 26, 1340, as it includes another letter to the king written on that date.[93] The petition contains no reference to the proceedings against Robert; if they had been legitimate, he would be expected to have mentioned them, particularly since the lengthy petition makes much of Bicknor's citation of Ledrede for heresy and aiding heretics. Perhaps the omission was due to his fears, no doubt justified, that the king's patience was stretched thin when it came to his inquisitions. Nor do the papal letters shed any light on the nature of Robert's alleged heresy. Robert was probably not one of the heretics "Ledrede believed had slipped through the net in 1324."[94] He is not mentioned in the *Narrative*, and he was in league with Ledrede from 1326 to 1328. According to the findings of a Limerick jury in 1331, Robert de Caunton aided and abetted Maurice in all his nefarious doings, and in the various hearings of Maurice's conduct that relate to events that predate Robert's death in 1340, Robert repeatedly appears second only to Maurice; after Robert's death none of his retainers

---

92. *CPL*, 3:136, 231–32; Theiner, 286–87.
93. Sayles, *Documents*, 173–77; also see Neary, "Richard de Ledrede," 63–65.
94. Neary, "Richard de Ledrede," 62.

seems to have occupied such a favored position.[95] Given Ledrede's predisposition to interpret disrespect for him as heresy, and since Robert probably shared the passionate and unrestrained nature of his Geraldine lord, perhaps he belittled the bishop in some fashion during the course of their alliance, which Ledrede later transformed into heretical conduct. Or perhaps Robert was sent by Maurice to inform Ledrede that the Desmond Geraldine could not or did not wish to support him in the face of mounting opposition to the bishop, or that his services were no longer required after Arnold had died, and Ledrede responded by imprisoning him as a heretic. Alternatively, Robert may have been selected as a target by Ledrede due to his closeness with Maurice, whom Ledrede did not dare to attack directly, once their relations had soured. Whatever the cause of the case, the evidence of the papal letters when considered with Ledrede's petition suggests that it began shortly before or after the Dublin parliament of April 1329 and caused a violent conflict between Ledrede and his metropolitan at that time.

Bicknor and Ledrede may have first become acquainted in 1317 at Avignon, where they were made archbishop of Dublin and bishop of Ossory respectively. Evidence of possible tension between the two emerges as early as August 1320, when John XXII wrote to Bicknor and the dean of Dublin not to allow Ledrede's possessions pertaining to his episcopal see to be molested, although the pope could have been requesting that the archbishop act as protector of his suffragan who had recently been arrested rather than reprimanding him for improprieties.[96] During the Kyteler case, Bicknor was absent from Ireland on the king's business, but by May 1325 his feud with Hugh Despenser and other deeds cast him from the king's grace. Edward wrote to the pope, asking that he be removed from office, but the pope refused.[97] Due to his alleged misdeeds while treasurer of Ireland from 1308 to 1314, which included forging his accounts with the help of Walter de Islip, his deputy treasurer and successor, and appropriating some of the property of the Templars and John de Boneville, Bicknor was briefly imprisoned later that year and his property confiscated; soon thereafter he was excommunicated by the pope for failing to pay a debt.[98] Probably due to his hatred of Despenser and Edward II's enmity, Bicknor joined the side of Mortimer

---

95. Sayles, "Legal Proceedings," 5–46.

96. *CPL*, 2:206. Niav Gallagher interprets this letter as proof of early stages of their quarrel ("Alexander Bicknor," 94).

97. Rymer, vol. 2, pt. 2, pp. 136–37.

98. See chapter 1; Mac Niocaill, "Documents Relating to the Suppression of the Templars in Ireland"; Lydon, "The Case against Alexander Bicknor"; Lydon, "Enrolled Account"; Gallagher, "Alexander Bicknor," 62–82; Richardson and Sayles, *Administration of Ireland*, 3, 47.

and Isabella; when they succeeded, he apparently received a pardon and his temporalities were restored.[99] In July 1327 the investigation into his acts as treasurer was reopened, however, and he was not fully pardoned by the king until 1344, although he served as chancellor and acting justiciar of Ireland from February until May 1341.[100] It is not clear if he was ever absolved from his sentence of excommunication, since in 1347 Clement VI described him as having disregarded the sentence for twenty years, and he seems to have remained recalcitrant for the two years left of his life.[101]

Thus Bicknor was in a fairly precarious position himself when he opposed Ledrede in the first half of 1329. According to his petition to the king, Ledrede was summoned along with Bicknor to attend a parliament at Dublin, and both complied.[102] Since the petition identifies John Darcy as the justiciar, this parliament must postdate his reappointment to that office on February 19, 1329, but predate Ledrede's exile in June, and thus must have been the April parliament in 1329.[103] During this parliament, Bicknor invited the bishop to meet with him at St. Patrick's on the pretext of discussing certain matters that arose at the parliament. When he arrived, he learned that Bicknor had arrayed a host at the church to murder him due to the archbishop's anger over a case involving the church and pending in the papal court, presumably the Caunton case. He was badly beaten and his cries could be heard throughout the city, prompting the justiciar, then at the castle, to investigate and put an end to the attack.[104] Shortly afterward, Bicknor cited the bishop to appear before him in Dublin "concerning a case of enabling heresy and of heresy itself," and Ledrede appealed to the papacy.[105]

A letter of Clement VI written nearly twenty years later makes the events immediately preceding the appeal somewhat clearer, although it must be kept in mind that both the petition and the letter tell solely Ledrede's side of the story.[106] It relates how after Ledrede had proceeded according to the

---

99. *Calendar of Memoranda Rolls* (1326–27): 67; Gallagher, "Alexander Bicknor," 68–69, 74.

100. *Calendar of Memoranda Rolls* (1326–27): 282; *CPR* (1343–45): 201–2.

101. Theiner, 287 and 299; see below.

102. Apparently Arnold's death allowed Ledrede a temporary respite from his fears of travelling to Dublin, but Bicknor's opposition would give him new cause for concern.

103. Sayles, *Documents*, 175; Neary, "Richard de Ledrede," 63–65. While Darcy also served as justiciar from February 1, 1324 to May 1, 1327, only one parliament was held at Dublin during that time, the May 1324 parliament described in the *Narrative*, which Bicknor did not attend as he was out of the country, as he was for most if not all of Darcy's first justiciarship. Darcy does not seem to have yet taken office by the April 1329 parliament (see *CSM*, 2:369 and below) and may not even have yet been in Ireland, raising the possibility that the attack was a fabrication by Ledrede.

104. Sayles, *Documents*, 175.

105. Ibid., 175–76.

106. Theiner, 287; *CPL*, 3:231, see also 136.

law against Robert de Caunton as vehemently suspected of heresy and had him imprisoned, Bicknor publicly pledged himself to Robert's defense and attempted to prohibit Ledrede from continuing the case. Ledrede defied the archbishop, and Bicknor ordered the seneschal of Kilkenny to release Robert, which he did. It then summarizes the attack upon Ledrede by the archbishop's men, but the precise chronology of the attack vis-à-vis the Caunton case is shadowy, as it is here invoked to explain Ledrede's refusal to travel to Dublin, "a place notoriously unsafe even for the bishop himself," when Bicknor summoned him there to answer charges of his own assistance of heretical depravity.[107] Bicknor's citation placed Ledrede in a dilemma, since if he did not heed his metropolitan's summons he could be cited for contumacy, which he resolved by appealing to the Holy See against Bicknor, "his mortal enemy."[108] Bicknor, however, disdained the appeal and repeated the summons. According to Ledrede, the archbishop's ulterior motive in summoning him to Dublin was to finish what he had begun at St. Patrick's, and he laid traps for the bishop throughout the city. Ledrede decided to go to Avignon to plead his case before the pope in person, and when Bicknor learned of this he ordered all the ports closed and obtained a warrant for his arrest, which Roger Outlaw, the chancellor, was no doubt only too happy to provide.[109] Ledrede, however, managed to escape and arrive safely in Avignon, where he continued his vendetta against Bicknor and the supposed heretics he claimed infested Ireland.

Fortunately, not all of the sources relate Ledrede's versions of events, as the king wrote to John XXII on June 18, 1329, complaining of his behavior and asking the pope not to put much credence in his claims. The letter does not mention Ledrede's quarrel with Bicknor nor his proceedings against Caunton, nor indeed any of his heresy accusations and trials, but instead focuses on Ledrede's disruptions of the king's peace. It describes the murder and mayhem in Ireland that Ledrede instigated and for which he promised pardon to the perpetrators, although "given the nature of his pastoral office, he ought to have used wholesome exhortations to pacify those souls who were agitated with anger."[110] Ledrede disturbed the king's peace in other ways, which the king chose not to recount in this letter, though he said he would do so elsewhere. This most likely refers to the heresy proceedings that the king and his council wished to treat more cautiously, as they knew Ledrede was on his way to the papacy as well as the fervor with which John XXII

---

107. Theiner, 287.
108. Sayles, *Documents*, 176; Theiner, 287.
109. Theiner, 287; Sayles, *Documents*, 176.
110. Rymer, vol. 2, pt. 3, p. 28.

opposed heresy, which he too defined quite loosely. The letter continues that when the king appointed agents to investigate these events and punish those responsible, "as if conscious of his guilt" Ledrede furtively escaped Ireland and came to England.[111] Yet even though Ledrede had been summoned to appear before the king and explain himself, again he secretly escaped. Since the king understood that the bishop had harassed the good people of Ireland in many ways and planned to go to Avignon to lay lies before the pope, he beseeched the pope not to heed the tall tales that Ledrede was sure to tell about the king, his faithful people, or the current state of Ireland, which he would attempt to masquerade as religious zeal and orthodox piety.[112] The letter ends with the hope that the pope's paternal providence would be able to heal Ledrede's malice, but Ledrede's malice continued to fester for at least as long as Bicknor remained alive.

One figure who may have been critical in Ledrede's downfall is marginal in the records of the events immediately relating to it. Roger Outlaw had been an associate of Bicknor at least since 1323 when they traveled together to England to warn the king of the rising influence of his enemies in Ireland and to ask that he personally come to the colony, and the two remained close throughout Outlaw's career.[113] He was a powerful and influential man in the colony, holding the office of chancellor from 1322 until his death in 1341 with a few brief interruptions, often acting in the justiciar's stead when he was out of the country or the colony was between justiciars, and serving as Walter de Islip's deputy treasurer during the Bruce invasion and again in 1325–26. Ledrede's accusation that he helped Arnold in his heresy, made in late 1328 or early 1329, implies that Roger was working on Arnold's behalf to refute the bishop's charges or otherwise undermine him. His own connections and character exonerated him from Ledrede's allegations, but that may have inspired him all the more to have the bishop discredited and to free his friend, who would soon die in prison. Arnold's death while still excommunicate and uncleared, as well as the demonstration of Roger's own continued influence and respect among colonial leaders, perhaps emboldened his campaign against the bishop; he may have found considerable support at the April parliament, which had planned to hear Arnold's case and quite probably would have cleared him. Roger was the acting justiciar from Thomas fitz John's death in April 1328 until Darcy's arrival, which Ledrede's petition

111. Rymer, vol. 2, pt. 3, p. 28.

112. Perhaps here the king was recalling Ledrede's veiled threat that if he did not assist in the prosecution of Arnold, he too could be labelled a heretic (Sayles, *Documents*, 134); see above.

113. Chaplais, *War of Saint-Sardos*, 178; see above. Massey, *Prior Roger Outlaw*, 22.

places in April, but according to Pembridge, writing sometime between 1332 and 1347, Roger was still serving as such at the April parliament.[114] Here he managed to make peace between the de Burghs and Maurice fitz Thomas, a remarkable achievement no doubt much facilitated by Arnold's death, which was preceded in January by the death of the other great le Poer leader, the baron of Dunoyl. With the end in sight of the feud that raged between the de Burghs, the le Poers, and the Barrys on one side and Maurice fitz Thomas, the le Botillers (Butlers), the Berminghams, and the de Cauntons on the other, Ledrede would understandably feel vulnerable, even without opposition from his metropolitan.

While the sources are fragmentary, biased, and often contradictory, a plausible if imprecise picture emerges of Ledrede's last acts in Ireland in 1329. Since he felt safe enough to travel to the Dublin parliament and visit Bicknor at St. Patrick's, he apparently did not feel seriously threatened by Bicknor, Maurice, or Roger. If he had already imprisoned Robert for heresy, he could expect a confrontation with Maurice, probably Bicknor, and possibly Roger, who might identify with his latest victim, even if he were the enemy of a fallen friend. If Ledrede expected a confrontation, he would almost certainly not have attended, as he repeatedly had refused summons to Dublin with less danger in the past and would do so again in the immediate future. Perhaps, however, he had arrested Robert but did not believe that to have yet come to the attention of those three men, or his desire to gloat over his victory over Arnold caused him to disregard the many signs of his imminent downfall, such as that the man who had recently been cleared of his accusations relating to Arnold's heresy was acting as justiciar at this parliament. Ledrede states that Bicknor attacked him during this parliament; while his portrait of the attack is not entirely credible, particularly since John Darcy may not yet have been in Ireland, clearly some kind of conflict did occur.[115] Certainly the business of the parliament, which Ledrede claims Bicknor used to lure him to St. Patrick's, would not have been in Ledrede's favor, and he may have mistakenly gone to St. Patrick's hoping to find an ally. Perhaps during the parliament Maurice provided a full account, real or imagined, of Ledrede's involvement in the attacks on the le Poers, and Bicknor was attempting to castigate him, or Bicknor supported Roger's campaign against the bishop and revealed his position at this meeting. Ledrede may then have rushed back to

---

114. *CSM*, 2:369; Williams, "Dominican Annals," 155.

115. The exact date of Darcy's return to Ireland is not known, although he had arrived by June, when he furthered the peace between the feuding parties that Roger Outlaw had begun at the April parliament.

Kilkenny and lashed out at Robert de Caunton, but whatever the exact date of Robert's arrest, Bicknor's public support of him almost certainly did not predate the meeting at St. Patrick's. Thus it was over the next two months that Bicknor and Ledrede wrangled over the Caunton case, and the Dublin government prepared to move against Ledrede for inciting rebellion. While Bicknor turned Ledrede's own weapons upon him, citing him to appear before him for assisting heretics and heresy itself, Roger and his associates summoned him to the secular court to answer charges of rebellion, both of which Ledrede failed to heed; the secular and spiritual representatives then conjoined in the writ for his arrest.[116]

It has been suggested that Bicknor would not have made accusations of heresy if Ledrede's innocence had been manifest, but Bicknor's allegations probably mirrored those made by Ledrede.[117] The Kyteler case was one of spite, initially that of Alice's stepchildren, that Ledrede transformed into a diabolical sorcery case in which religious belief was of secondary concern. His proceedings against Arnold and Roger resulted from his ongoing grudge against them and Arnold in particular to which Ledrede applied a veneer of doctrinal impropriety, accusing him of blaspheming the body of Christ. His case against Robert is obscure but again seems a product of personal vengeance rather than actual religious error. What charges Bicknor might have levelled against the bishop are unknown, other than that he aided heretics and was suspected of heresy himself; undoubtedly they arose from his own resentment of and hostility toward Ledrede, who directed the same accusations against him. These mutual recriminations would have seemed perfectly in keeping with Ireland's other examples of heretical proceedings from the prior twenty years as well: the Templar trial, a minor offshoot of an international affair with similarly suspicious origins; the case against Philip de Braybrook, also the result of a long-standing feud between the accused and his accuser; and the execution of Adducc Dubh O'Toole, a man more likely condemned for his ethnicity than for his religious beliefs or lack thereof. "Innocent" is an ambiguous term; clearly powerful people rightly regarded the bishop with distrust, and perhaps he was even suspected of the rather convoluted yet simplistic understanding of heresy that had become common in the colony by 1329, but no evidence indicates that he might have been thought guilty of heresy by a more exacting standard.

---

116. Considering Roger Outlaw's concerns in 1324, it is noteworthy that the required forty-day period is just possible during this time.

117. The suggestion is Neary's ("Richard de Ledrede," 65).

The king seems to have censured his letter of June 18, 1329, and the others that soon followed regarding Ledrede's heresy allegations.[118] His advice to be wary of the bishop seems to have had some success, however; unlike his two successors, John XXII apparently did not instruct Irish ecclesiastics to investigate Ledrede's claims of heresy, though he did pressure the king to restore Ledrede's temporalities.[119] On May 10, 1331, the king agreed to the pope's request, provided Ledrede submit to him for having defied the summons.[120] But, perhaps from pressure from Bicknor, Ledrede's refusal to make submission, or the king's own ambivalence on the matter, the temporalities were not restored until 1339, despite the dean and chapter of Ossory's claim in 1332 that Ledrede had been cleared of the charges for which his temporalities had been seized in 1328 and a repeated royal order for the restoration in 1335.[121] His ongoing feud with his metropolitan and other concerns for his safety prevented him from returning to Ireland until 1347; apart from at least three trips to Avignon, in 1329–31, 1334–35, and 1346–47, and probably another in 1342–43, he spent his exile in England, often performing various "episcopal odd jobs for a living."[122] But the events of 1328–29 were never far from his mind, and he repeatedly complained of Anglo-Irish heretics and the resistance he had encountered in his pursuit of them.

Ledrede's Exile

Ireland witnessed a dizzying series of events during Ledrede's absence, and by the time of his return nearly all of his former conspirators and enemies had died.[123] Within days of Ledrede's furtive flight from Ireland, John de

---

118. June 30, 1329 (Rymer, vol. 2, pt. 3, p. 30), February 22, 1330 (ibid., 38–39), and February 25, 1331 (ibid., 59–60); the last pleads Bicknor's case against Ledrede but does not mention heresy.

119. Although John XXII was deeply concerned about heresy and instructed the archbishops of Ireland as elsewhere to preach against the "heretics" then plaguing Italy in 1326 (*CPL*, 2:473, 478; Theiner, 233–34), he seems to have been fairly unconcerned about the possibility of heresy in Ireland and dismissed other allegations of heresy from Dublin leaders that reached him a few years after Ledrede; see chapter 5. He apparently took a harsher view of those who preached against papal constitutions, however, as on February 22, 1334, he commended the archbishop of Cashel for informing him of such *perversis religiosis* and instructed him and Bicknor to publish the process against them (Theiner, 261–62), but nothing more of the case is known.

120. *CCR* (1330–33): 240.

121. *CFR*, 4:134–35; Neary, "Richard de Ledrede," 69–71; Richardson and Sayles, *Parliaments and Councils*, 202–4; Neary, "Richard de Ledrede," 69.

122. Ledrede, *Latin Poems*, xxviii. For Ledrede's years in exile, see Neary, "Richard de Ledrede," 68–84.

123. Frame, *English Lordship*, 196–294.

Bermingham, the earl of Louth, was killed by a mob.[124] His brother William was hanged by the justiciar in the summer of 1332 for charges relating to his conspiracy with fitz Thomas.[125] The following year, William de Burgh, the "Brown Earl" of Ulster, was murdered by members of his own family.[126] Robert de Caunton was killed in the streets of Kilkenny in April 1340.[127] James le Botiller died in 1338 and Roger Outlaw in 1341, both uneventfully. Of the primary players, only Bicknor and the seemingly indestructable Maurice fitz Thomas remained. The latter was elevated to earl of Desmond within months of Ledrede's departure, and though he remained relatively well behaved for a little over a year, he was imprisoned in 1331 and again in 1332–33, with juries finding him guilty of treasonous and deplorable acts.[128] He was mainperned in May 1333 by the most powerful lords in the land, including his adversaries, the Brown Earl of Ulster (one of the last acts of William's life, as he was killed the following month), Arnold's son Eustace, and Arnold's brother John le Poer. This time Maurice's version of good behavior lasted for ten years, but by 1345 he was openly rebelling against the king and allegedly conspiring once again to make himself king of Ireland.[129] The one who paid the greatest price for Maurice's treason, however, was Eustace le Poer, who joined Maurice's rebellion in the summer of 1345.[130] Although Maurice had many supporters, including de Burghs, de Cauntons, and many Irish, only two of them are known to have been executed as a result of the rebellion, one of them Eustace le Poer.[131] Others of his family were exiled, and leadership of the le Poer lineage became inexorably fractured.[132] This was the final and greatest wound inflicted on Arnold by his old enemy, who managed once again to escape the king's wrath. Though he had been the center and source of this rebellion, Maurice was pardoned in 1349; in his remaining years he received considerable favors and trust from Edward III, who

---

124. Clyn, 20; *CSM*, 2:369–70; Lydon, "Braganstown Massacre."
125. *CSM*, 2:77; Clyn, 24.
126. Clyn, 24–25; *CSM*, 2:378–79; Orpen, *Ireland under the Normans*, 4:245–49.
127. Clyn, 29.
128. Sayles, "Rebellious First Earl," and "Legal Proceedings"; see above.
129. Frame argues against the accusations that Maurice was again attempting to have himself crowned king of Ireland (*English Lordship*, 268–74; for the plot, see Sayles, "Legal Proceedings," 20–22). While the specific means of his attempts may have been misrepresented, it seems plausible that, whetted by his almost absolute independence in Desmond, he yearned to place all of Ireland under his yoke. Such aspirations also help to explain his open revolt against the king and royal authority in 1344–45.
130. Clyn, 31; Parker, "Paterfamilias and *Parentela*," 111–13; Frame, *English Lordship*, 274–75.
131. Sayles, "Legal Proceedings," 24–28; Clyn, 32.
132. Parker, "Paterfamilias and *Parentela*," 113.

appointed him justiciar, his term of office cut short by his death in January 1356.[133]

These events, however, were only remotely related to the bishop, who continued to view Ireland in precisely the terms in which he had left it. He persistently petitioned successive popes about the heretics he maintained still infested Ossory and Dublin. After a fairly short stay in England, Ledrede returned to Avignon in 1334 to plead his case once again, but the matter was briefly delayed, as John XXII died in December and the conclave quickly elected Jacques Fournier, who then became Benedict XII. Perhaps because of his own experience as an inquisitor, he proved an even greater champion of Ledrede than his predecessor had; on November 6, 1335 he wrote two letters to Edward, the first asking again that Ledrede's temporalities be restored, the second advancing his cause against heretics.[134] The latter describes "certain pernicious heretics who wear many faces": some said Jesus was a sinful man whose punishment had been just; others sacrificed to demons and "believed otherwise about the sacrament of the body of Christ than did the Roman Catholic Church."[135] The first group does not surface previously or subsequently in Ledrede's representations of heretics in Ireland and is not mentioned again in the letter; it may be the heresy he alleged of Robert de Caunton, but it was a fairly common belief imputed to heretics, as had been done in the trial of the Templars. The second group is a composite of his complaints during the Kyteler case: they rejected the sacraments, said they were not bound by papal decretals, consulted demons in the manner of pagans, and "by their superstitions drew Christ's faithful after them."[136] After some impassioned words about the dangers of heresy, the pope chides the king for not having inquisitors of heresy in England or Ireland, so that heretics are not commonly discovered and punished there.[137] Thus the church asks the king to act as the protector of the faith by immediately writing to the justiciar and other ministers of Ireland and instructing them to aid Ledrede and other prelates of Ireland in seizing, punishing, and extirpating

---

133. For the last decade of Maurice's life, see Frame, *English Lordship*, 284–97. An addendum to Pembridge's annals offers Maurice great praise and relates how his body was first taken to St. Saviour's, where Arnold's body had remained unburied in 1329, before being translated to his family burial place, the Dominican priory in Tralee (*CSM*, 2:392). William de Bermingham was also buried at St. Saviour's after he was hung by Anthony de Lucy (ibid., 377).

134. Theiner, 269–70.

135. Theiner, 269.

136. Theiner, 269. The second complaint recalls Arnold's supposed retort to Ledrede, "Go to the church with your decretals" (Wright, *Contemporary Narrative*, 15). It may also refer to the concerns John XXII expressed in February 1334 (Theiner, 261–62).

137. Theiner, 269.

the heretics "and other heretical sects newly spawned in those parts," as well as their believers, fautors, receivers, and defenders.[138] Despite the "sacrifice of gratitude owed to eternal majesty" that this service would constitute, Edward declined to fulfill the papal request on this matter, although he did act anew to have Ledrede's temporalities restored.[139]

Conspicuously absent from this letter is any reference to Bicknor, whose feud with the bishop continued to rage during the latter's exile. The same day as the two letters to Edward, Benedict instructed the bishops of Ferns and Lismore and the dean of Waterford to assist Ledrede against ecclesiastics and nobles who illegitimately possessed his property and if necessary to invoke the secular arm.[140] Bicknor, either as one of the usurpers or as one who should be expected to protect his suffragan, is again apparently deliberately unnamed, as is heresy. While Bicknor's relations with the king were becoming more harmonious, and Edward had disregarded Benedict's request to assist Ledrede in his mission against heretics, the king was becoming more favorable to the bishop, and not just on matters relating to his temporalities.[141] On June 3, 1339, Edward instructed the acting justiciar to annul the warrant for Ledrede's arrest issued at the instigation of Bicknor, "the venerable father."[142] The letter allows for Ledrede's version of events (that he had appealed against Bicknor to the papacy before the writ had been issued), describes the writ as surreptitiously and erroneously issued, and maintains that it was illicit for a prelate to be arrested. Two years later, Ledrede again complained to the king about Bicknor, rehearsing the events that led to his exile but also adding allegations about a more recent event.

According to Ledrede's petition, Bicknor came to Kilkenny at the head of a large armed force and proceeded to plunder church lands near the cathedral and steal cattle and other animals for their own sustenance. The archbishop's men also attacked the bishop's manors in Kilkenny and Agthour (Aghoure), destroying and burning his property.[143] Ledrede's complaints can

---

138. Theiner, 269. To what the "newly spawned heretics" referred is not known; as with Ledrede's own complaints, perhaps the Counter-Remonstrance found a more credible audience in Benedict XII (see chapter 5).

139. Theiner, 269.

140. *CPL*, 2:521–22.

141. In December 1337 Edward received an indult from Benedict XII that allowed him to associate with Bicknor and receive his advice on secular matters, despite Bicknor's being excommunicated (*CPL*, 2:536).

142. Rymer, vol. 2, pt. 4, p. 47. However, the letter included in Ledrede's petition indicates that the order for Ledrede's arrest to answer Bicknor's complaints was reissued on March 26, 1340 (Sayles, *Documents*, 176).

143. Sayles, *Documents*, 174–75. For the history of Aghoure, see Leslie, *Ossory Clergy and Parishes*, 122–29, 192–93.

be somewhat substantiated. Clyn reports that Bicknor held a visitation of Ossory in 1335, which had not been done by an archbishop of Dublin in forty years; perhaps he lashed out at the absent bishop's property or simply made use of it while staying there.[144] Benedict's letters to the bishops of Ferns and Lismore on November 6, 1335, may have been related to these or similar acts.[145] In 1347 Clement VI repeated Ledrede's complaints that Bicknor had all of Ledrede's property ruined and occupied his manors, and also alleged that Bicknor extorted double the procurations in his yearly visitation in Ossory.[146] While Ledrede's complaints should be treated with caution, Bicknor was not above abusing his position, particularly over a man whom he loathed who was not present to defend himself or his diocese.

Despite Ledrede's grievances against Bicknor, the archbishop does not figure in surviving papal letters relating to Ledrede until the pontificate of Clement VI. Probably after yet another visit by Ledrede to Avignon, in 1343 Clement instructed the archbishops of Armagh and Cashel (both native Irishmen) and the archdeacon of Kildare to cite Bicknor for opposing Ledrede's proceedings against and defending Robert de Caunton and for hindering his appeal to the pope.[147] Whether the archbishops and archdeacon complied is unknown, but even if they did, it is unlikely that Bicknor heeded the summons. Still unsatisfied and perhaps desperate to return to his diocese, Ledrede journeyed once more to Avignon in 1346 to press his case, and in April 1347 he at last achieved the success for which he had worked for so long. A series of letters, issued on April 9–10, show the development of Clement's own anger against Bicknor, no doubt exacerbated by Ledrede's increasingly graphic tales of woe. The first letter briefly recounts the attack at St. Patrick's and the events leading up to it before granting Ledrede absolution from the sentence of excommunication issued by Bicknor.[148] This apparently did not satisfy Ledrede, and the following day Clement exempted him, his diocese, and all its denizens both lay and religious from his metropolitan's jurisdiction for as long as Ledrede presided over Ossory and the persecution continued, and he declared any sentence that may be issued to the contrary invalid.[149] The letter of exemption compresses Ledrede's last five years in Ireland, so that Ledrede's appeal from Bicknor to the pope, which occurred in 1329,

---

144. Clyn, 27. Thomas de Chaddesworth also used visitation as a means to antagonize his opponents, although his was considerably more irregular than Bicknor's; see chapter 1.

145. *CPL*, 2:521–22; see above.

146. Theiner, 287.

147. *CPL*, 3:136.

148. Theiner, 286.

149. *CPL*, 3:232; see also Wadding, *Annales Minorum*, 8:20.

immediately follows his seventeen-day stint in prison, which occurred in 1324, and identifies the jailors as the heretics themselves. While it could intend that by the very act of arresting a bishop they had become heretics, a stronger and more precise definition is implied, and it most likely refers to Arnold le Poer, who was not denounced by Ledrede for heresy until about 1328. It also makes much of Ledrede's pitiful plight as an exile, greatly exacerbated by his concern for his diocese and his clergy and laity who had assisted the bishop in opposing the heretics and were abused by Bicknor in his absence.[150]

Other letters were issued about the matter on April 10 to the archbishop of Cashel, Ralph O'Kelly, and the archbishop-elect of Armagh, the famous Richard fitz Ralph, instructing them to investigate Ledrede's complaints about heretics who had escaped from Ossory into Dublin, where they had been fostered by Bicknor, and to ask the aid of the secular arm if necessary.[151] The portrait of Bicknor as lord over a den of heresy presumably refers to Robert de Caunton's flight to Dublin after being released from prison and indicates the change in Clement's tone toward the archbishop that concurs with his radical solution of releasing Ledrede from his jurisdiction. O'Kelly and fitz Ralph, who had recently been in Avignon, may have been consulted about the case prior to this letter, but as they both had considerable experience and understanding of Ireland and its inhabitants, one a native Irishman and the other an Anglo-Irishman born and raised in Ireland, they probably would have seen through Ledrede's vitriol.[152] O'Kelly showed himself intolerant of actions taken against supposed heretics by a Franciscan in his archdiocese six years later, and fitz Ralph demonstrated considerable skill and sensitivity in navigating the ethnic tensions and accusations each group hurled at the other during his archiepiscopacy.[153] While he took a less objective attitude toward the friars, some of his concerns over their behavior arose from the possibility that those of his archdiocese might use unfounded allegations of heresy against their secular rivals, an idea perhaps first planted

---

150. The grant describes the exile as lasting for nine years, but this does not accord with the evidence for Ledrede's activities at the time. I am inclined to follow Neary's suggestion that "decem" has been omitted before the "novem annos" in the letter ("Richard de Ledrede," 72n32).

151. Theiner, 286–87; *CPL*, 3:227, 231.

152. Walsh, *Richard FitzRalph*, 262. O'Kelly is sometimes described as being "of mixed race," i.e., both native Irish and Anglo-Irish, (e.g., ibid., 248) or even English (Ware, *Whole Works*, 479), but both his parents seem to have been Irish, even if Bale's claim that he was the product of an adulterous affair between William O'Kelly's wife and David O'Buge, the Carmelite theologian, is accurate; see B. H. Blacker's revised version of Philomena Connolly's entry on Ralph O'Kelly (Ó Ceallaigh) in Matthew and Harrison, *Oxford Dictionary of National Biography*, 41:414–15.

153. For O'Kelly, see chapter 5. Walsh, *Richard FitzRalph*, 318–48.

in his mind by Ledrede's behavior.[154] Thus it seems unlikely that they would have counseled the pope to endorse Ledrede's perspective unilaterally had they been consulted about the matter while in Avignon. They may have complied with Clement's mandate, as a letter to Bicknor's successor suggests, and fitz Ralph may have been happy to do so given his feud with Bicknor over primacy in Ireland, but no evidence directly relating to their investigation is extant.[155]

Another letter issued April 10, also to O'Kelly and fitz Ralph, provides the most detailed extant account of the Caunton case and intensifies the rhetoric against Bicknor. It maintains that for fifteen years Bicknor had been suspected as an aider and defender of heretics and as a heretic himself, and that for twenty years he had disregarded the sentences of excommunication, suspension, and interdict that had been placed upon him.[156] The same might be said of Clement VI himself as well as his predecessors, however, since they continued to entrust religious matters to the archbishop and few papal letters written to or about him during this period give any indication that he was excommunicated or suspended from office.[157] The letter of absolution issued only the day before mentions the claim that Bicknor aided heretics, but also refers to him as "our venerable brother."[158] Moreover, if Bicknor were already excommunicated, Ledrede's excommunication arguably could be considered invalid and he would not need papal absolution; a similar argument could apply to the grant of exemption. Considering Clement's unusual solution of removing Ledrede and his diocese from his metropolitan's jurisdiction, this increased vehemence is not surprising, but given his and his predecessors' previous treatment of the archbishop it seems somewhat suspect and can probably best be explained by Ledrede's powers of persuasion rather than the pontiff's personal regard for Bicknor, at least before April 10, 1347.

---

154. Walsh, *Richard FitzRalph*, 373. Interestingly, fitz Ralph influenced John Wyclif and came to be regarded as "the godparent of Lollardy" (ibid., 453); this reverence among heretics did not prevent his canonization by Catholics in 1545, however.

155. Theiner, 299; see below; Walsh, *Richard FitzRalph*, 257–68.

156. Theiner, 287. The specification of fifteen years in reference to Bicknor's own alleged heresy suggests that Ledrede made these accusations during one of his trips to Avignon in 1329–ca. 1331 or 1334–35.

157. In March 1333 John XXII described Bicknor as excommunicated (*CPL*, 2:326), and in December 1337 Benedict XII allowed Edward III to communicate with him and receive his secular advice despite his excommunication (ibid., 536). Multiple papal missives were written to or about him during this twenty-year period, most of which give no indication that Bicknor was regarded as excommunicated at this time (e.g., ibid., 2:513, 3:125; Theiner, 261–62).

158. Theiner, 286.

Ledrede's Last Years in Ireland

Thus the stage was set for Ledrede's victorious return to Ireland, and he received further encouragement a week later when Edward III ordered his temporalities restored for as long as he remained bishop.[159] He returned to his diocese by September, and the following December he was pardoned by the king "for all homicides, felonies, robberies, larcenies, conspiracies, seditions, oppressions, firing of houses and trespasses whatsoever and for breaking of prison as well in England as in Ireland."[160] The earl of Desmond's recent rebellion might have reminded the king of Ledrede's own misbehavior during the Desmond-le Poer war, but the comprehensive pardon was in keeping with the clemency he would soon extend to the earl. Significantly, like William Outlaw in 1325, Ledrede chose the path of forgiveness rather than purgation; thus by the reasoning he had applied to William he admitted his guilt. While he may have taken this course due to his wariness of secular courts in Ireland, the testimony about him from 1327 to 1332 makes his involvement in such acts almost certain, or at least exceedingly difficult for him to be exonerated.[161] Despite this blank slate, Ledrede apparently had not learned from the error of his ways or the kindness of the king, as his remaining thirteen years demonstrate.

Bicknor and Ledrede apparently avoided each other from the latter's return to the former's death in the summer of 1349; at least no evidence relating to their continued quarrel survives.[162] Yet the death of his most formidable adversary does not seem to have improved Ledrede's position, particularly once the pope revoked his exemption from his new metropolitan, John of St. Paul, on June 22, 1351.[163] Shortly thereafter, Clement asked that John quickly wrap up the process against heretics in Dublin that the archbishops of Cashel and Armagh were said to have begun, if they had not been

---

159. *CPR* (1345–48): 402; Neary, "Richard de Ledrede," 79. In July, Clement urged Edward to order his ministers in Ireland to ensure that Ledrede received the property taken from him while he had gone to the curia to discuss heretics in Ireland (*CPL*, 3:253), portraying a near twenty-year exile as one journey. In August, Edward ordered the justiciar to restore the temporalities (*CCR* [1346–49]: 318).

160. *CPR* (1345–48): 408 and 441.

161. Sayles, *Documents*, 131; Rymer, vol. 2, pt. 3, p. 28; Sayles, "Legal Proceedings," 6. His later acts also make his guilt seem probable.

162. For Bicknor's death, see Ware, *Whole Works*, 331, and for his probable tomb and monument in St. Patrick's, see Lawlor, "Monuments of the Pre-Reformation Archbishops of Dublin." Despite his burial as befit an archbishop, it is not clear if he ever was absolved from excommunication; Clement's letter to Bicknor's successor seems to imply that little had changed since 1347, as he repeats the claim that Bicknor favored heretics, etc., yet also refers to Bicknor as being of "good memory" (Theiner, 299).

163. Theiner, 298–99; *CPL*, 3:461.

concluded already.[164] Whether John did continue the process or if O'Kelly and fitz Ralph had in fact begun one is not known; like all papal missives pertaining to Ledrede's claims of heresy, it was a dead letter, at least as far as evidence is concerned. Though Clement continued to endorse Ledrede's perspective about heresy in Ireland, without Bicknor's persecution of the bishop he had no reason to allow the unusual arrangement he had devised in 1347 to continue.

While his position with the papacy remained favorable at this time, Ledrede's behavior soon caused secular officials to act against him. In 1350, he was summoned before the justiciar, Thomas de Rokeby, regarding his resistance to and excommunication of William Bromley, who was attempting to collect the king's subsidy.[165] This subsidy, which was to be levied on ecclesiastical as well as lay property and used for defense against the native Irish, had been granted by a council at Kilkenny in 1346, but several prelates, led by Ralph O'Kelly and three of his suffragans, vehemently opposed it.[166] Making the first clear declaration that taxation could not be levied without consent, they used their most powerful weapons against it, excommunicating those who attempted to collect the subsidy and setting severe punishments for those who contributed: beneficed clergy would be ipso facto deprived of their benefices, lay tenants ipso facto excommunicated.[167] While Ledrede and O'Kelly were here on the same side, it is not known if they were united or if Ledrede was simply taking advantage of his fellow prelates' rigorous opposition; even without it, Ledrede may have refused to contribute, as he was ever resentful of any act by secular powers that encroached upon his ecclesiastical rights and revenues. The justiciar found him guilty, and his temporalities were recommended to be seized once again, which they soon were.[168]

Ledrede's situation was about to become even worse. In March 1351, the king revoked the pardon of 1347 due to an investigation into Ledrede's conduct that had found him guilty of multiple counts of sedition; if the king had known of the extent of his guilt, he said, he would never have pardoned

164. Theiner, 299; see also Bliss, *Calendar of Entries: Petitions to the Pope*, 216.

165. Dublin, National Library of Ireland, NLI 1–4, *Collectanea de rebus Hibernicis*, comp. Harris, 2:230; McNeill, "Harris," 350.

166. Richardson and Sayles, *Irish Parliament*, 112. One of those who opposed it was John Leynagh, the bishop of Lismore who had helped to establish peace between Arnold le Poer and Ledrede at the Dublin parliament of 1324 (see chapter 3) and to purge Ledrede in 1328 (see above).

167. Watt, *The Church and the Two Nations*, 202; Dublin, National Library of Ireland, NLI 1–4, *Collectanea de rebus Hibernicis*, comp. Harris, 2:208; McNeill, "Harris," 348–49.

168. Dublin, National Library of Ireland, NLI 1–4, *Collectanea de rebus Hibernicis*, comp. Harris, 2:230; McNeill, "Harris," 350.

him.[169] The justiciar was ordered to take his temporalities into the king's hand and continue the investigation of Ledrede's behavior.[170] Ledrede was required to submit to the king for his many offenses, and in July 1355 his temporalities were restored.[171] Yet a letter written only a week later attests to Ledrede's contempt for the king's peace and greed and cruelty toward his fellow religious. The letter, from Innocent VI to the bishops of Waterford and Ferns and the abbot of Voto (in Ferns), tells how eleven named laymen of Ossory with their accomplices attacked Inistioge priory, wounded the prior, Stephen de Kerkyom, brutally killed one of the canons, and ripped out the eyes and tongue of another.[172] With the help of these laymen, Ledrede then forced Stephen to resign the priory into his hands. Stephen appealed to the papacy, and Innocent responded by instructing the bishops and abbot to excommunicate the malefactors, though it is not clear if Ledrede is to be included in the sentence, with absolution possible only from the pope.[173] This evidence of a vicious assault independent of the Desmond-le Poer politics supports his earlier opponents' accusations that he instigated attacks to indulge his own anger and avarice; one can imagine the damage he inflicted upon a man he yearned to destroy with MacThomas's Rout at his disposal, considering what he achieved with a rag-tag bunch of Ossory laymen in a raid on a hapless priory.

Stephen de Kerkyom received the king's protection against these malefactors for two years in October 1355, and presumably because of the atrocity Ledrede's temporalities were once again seized and their keeper was instructed to ensure that he submitted himself to the king for his many transgressions.[174] Whether he did so is not known, and only one further record of his life is extant. About 1357, Edward III wrote to Innocent VI about the bishop, offering an overview of his forty-year episcopacy.[175] Its portrait is far from flattering. The Franciscan bishop, "forgetful of his former mendicancy," trumped-up charges of heresy and sorcery against good and faithful

169. *CPR* (1350–54): 55.

170. *CFR*, 6:292.

171. *CCR* (1354–60): 152.

172. The mutilation of the canon recalls Maurice's mutilation of Richard de Armeston; see Sayles, "Legal Proceedings," 8–9, and above. The bishop of Waterford was Roger Cradock, who prosecuted the MacConmaras for heresy. The bishop of Ferns was William Charnells, whom Edward III desired to replace Ledrede.

173. Theiner, 309; *CPL*, 3:574.

174. *CPR* (1354–58): 281; Tresham, I.i.64.

175. Raine, *Historical Papers and Letters*, 403–6. The letter cannot be precisely dated but must have been written after Innocent became pope on December 30, 1352; it also says Ledrede had been bishop for forty years, which indicates a date of ca. 1357. Raine ascribes it to ca. 1358 but does not provide any reason for doing so.

people in order to extort money from them; other victims were thrown in prison to die and their bodies left to rot unburied. After his request of John XXII to appoint him inquisitor of England was denied, he contented himself with spreading slander about the state of the faith in Ireland. He has committed multiple crimes of various natures, including murder and arson, for which he has escaped punishment. He continues to oppress his clergy, and his churches are falling into ruin. Due to his advanced age, which the letter claims to be one hundred, he is afflicted with various infirmities, including "having become so deaf that he cannot hear the confessions of the faithful without them shouting, and suffering from dementia almost constantly, although sometimes he enjoys moments of lucidity, which he dedicates to malice."[176] Thus, on behalf of the clergy and people of Ireland, the king asks that Ledrede be removed from office and replaced with William Charnells, the bishop of Ferns whom Innocent had asked to handle the aftermath of the attack on Inistioge.

Although the vast majority of sources relating Ledrede's trials and tribulations are told from his perspective, his opponents got the last word. The versions told by the two sides agree in the particulars but vastly diverge on the reading, creating a fascinating contrast. Virtually all of the letter's claims can be corroborated. The elaborate palace he built for himself in Kilkenny, made from the remains of three churches, and his zealous concern for the wealth of his diocese suggest that Lady Poverty had little place in his interpretation of the Franciscan life. The charges of heresy and sorcery brought against Alice and her associates were tenuous indeed and were motivated at least partly by greed for Alice's considerable wealth; furthermore, Ledrede received £1,000 from William Outlaw because of his accusations of heresy.[177] Arnold le Poer was left to die in prison and his body left unburied.[178] Whether Ledrede ever requested that John XXII make him inquisitor of England is not known but not unlikely, and Benedict XII's letter to Edward III, which admonishes him for not having inquisitors in Ireland or England, suggests that Ledrede may indeed have been striving for such an appointment.[179] Ledrede's slander of the state of the faith in Ireland prompted Arnold le Poer to beseech colonial leaders to defend the "isle of the saints" at the Dublin parliament in May 1324, but Arnold's words went unheeded and Ledrede continued to calumniate the country and its inhabitants for over twenty years. Various sources attest to his multiple crimes and to

---

176. Raine, *Historical Papers and Letters*, 405.

177. Tresham, I.i.31, 34; Wright, *Contemporary Narrative*, 48, 58; see chapter 3.

178. The allegation also recalls Ledrede's glee that dogs gnawed the bones of Arnold's fallen family and followers (Sayles, *Documents*, 134).

179. Theiner, 269–70; see above.

his escape from punishment due to his pardon and submission.[180] The attack on Inistioge constituted rather severe oppression of his clergy, and he may have similarly mistreated others during the Desmond-le Poer wars.

While it is unlikely that the bishop was approaching one hundred, he must have been at least eighty by the time this letter was written and he may well have suffered from encroaching senility and deafness.[181] The remark about confessions has a realistic ring to it, as does the specific claim that Ledrede suffered from a disease known as *mala mors* (bad death) in his shin. Certain documents in the *Red Book of Ossory* detail treatments that may have been used by the bishop to alleviate his health problems toward the end of his life.[182] Neary suggests that his lifelong devotion to the church, and the extreme opposition he encountered in his efforts to defend it, might have caused him to become mentally imbalanced in his final years.[183] The fact that the bishop of a neighboring diocese who had been asked to investigate Ledrede's attack on Inistioge is named as his desired replacement raises the possibility of Charnells's complicity in the letter, and he may have provided Edward or his agents with an account of the bishop's sorry state in the last years of his life. Clearly the bishop was not long for this world, as he died in 1360 or 1361, further supporting the letter's claims about his infirmities.[184]

This letter provides a fitting conclusion to Ledrede's life, representative of his deeds as well as the opposition he encountered. Perhaps the bishop believed that all his words and deeds "had one ultimate goal: the protection and glorification of 'Holy Church,'" but his actions contradict that claim.[185] During the earlier years of his episcopacy, when he wrote poems praising the Virgin and her Son, when he approached his office with diligence and relative equanimity, and when he had not yet been consumed with vengeance, such a portrait could be plausible, but the attack on Inistioge priory, for example, is diametrically opposed to the protection and glorification of the church.[186]

---

180. E.g., Sayles, *Documents*, 131; Rymer, vol. 2, pt. 3, p. 28; *CPR* (1345–48): 441.

181. Ledrede was probably born between 1260 and 1275 (Neary, "Richard de Ledrede," 1).

182. Neary, "Richard de Ledrede," 16, 18.

183. Ibid., 87.

184. Ledrede's death is surprisingly not recorded (Neary, "Richard de Ledrede," 1). The treasurer of St. Canice's, Milo Sweteman, was next elected bishop of Ossory, but was rejected, and John de Tatenhall was provided to the see on November 8, 1361; Sweteman had little cause to grumble, as he was made archbishop of Armagh (*CSM*, 2:284).

185. Neary claims that as Ledrede's goal ("Richard de Ledrede," 84).

186. Although it is not known when Ledrede composed his poetic works, Theo Stemmler has argued that the probable period was 1317–24 (Ledrede, *Latin Hymns*, xxi–xxii), a rare time of relative peace for the bishop (apart from his arrest before August 1320).

It may have been in his personal interests, and Ledrede ever equated his own interests—and himself—with the church, but the two were not the same, as Stephen de Kerkyom and his canons could readily attest.

Fourteenth-century Ireland may indeed have harbored actual heretics, but if so neither Ledrede nor anyone else found them. While he did not initiate the Kyteler case, he transformed it into a sophisticated yet superficial sorcery case, and his subsequent accusations—against Arnold, Roger, Robert, and Bicknor—arose from his quest for personal revenge, not concern for purity of the faith. Despite his tendency toward apotheosis, his accusations against Arnold concerning the eucharist suggest that he was quite aware that the object of Arnold's scorn was not the body of Christ but himself. That to him was heresy, and it had little to do with defense of the church, except in Ledrede's own mind. To pursue his vengeance against Arnold, he turned to the ruthless Maurice fitz Thomas and his rout and almost certainly instigated atrocities upon his enemy and his kin; by his own admission he reveled in their deaths and their corpses' desecration. While three successive popes endorsed his claims about heresy, they had limited knowledge of and no experience in Ireland, and they based their support solely on one side of the story. That side dominates the historical records pertaining to Ledrede's actions, but his opponents were powerful men, including the king and his ministers, and thus their voices can also be heard. The truth may lie somewhere in between their competing claims, but Ledrede's own words and deeds demonstrate that he was not the church's constant defender and glorifier, however much he may have tried to convince himself otherwise.

CHAPTER 5

The Heresy of Being Irish

Adducc Dubh O'Toole and Two MacConmaras

While Ledrede was pursuing Anglo-Irish heretics in Dublin and Ossory, ecclesiastical leaders in Dublin held an inquest against a native Irishman for denying the Trinity, the Incarnation, the resurrection, Mary's virginity, the truth of the Bible, and papal authority—in short, for being a non-Christian. Adducc Dubh O'Toole was not alleged to have held alternative beliefs, to have questioned the priesthood, the cult of the saints, or sacraments, as Continental and English heretics often did, or to have committed any particular crimes, even against the colonists with whom his kin were at war. His trial and execution serve as the single specific example in a colonial portrait of the native Irish as a lawless race rife with heresy in a request for a crusade against them and those Anglo-Irish who had been infected with their heresy. John XXII's response may be inferred from his instructions to Edward III in 1331 that Ireland's reformation should be left to impartial parties with balanced participation by Ireland's inhabitants, "pure Irish, and those of a mixed race."[1] His position was perhaps influenced by the virtually identical indictment of colonists he had heard fourteen years earlier from Irish chiefs led by Dónal O'Neill of Ulster, whose long list of complaints included "the heresy that it is no more a sin to kill an Irish person

---

1. *CPL*, 2:500.

than to kill a dog or any other brute beast," a belief and practice common among lay and religious alike.[2]

Attempts to discern the origins of Adducc's heresy from either doctrinal or political grounds, why he specifically and singularly was named as the representative of the heresy colonists claimed to be endemic to the Irish, or why they executed him for heresy when they simply could have killed him, as they did "many of the Irish" in their war against the O'Tooles, have been limited.[3] The colonists' letter requesting a crusade has received relatively little attention, and the Remonstrance's accusations of heresy have been eclipsed by its primary objective: to argue against English rule in Ireland and in favor of Edward Bruce's kingship. This chapter explores the case of Adducc Dubh and the two letters with particular attention to issues of ethnicity in the colony, before turning to the case of the MacConmaras, also native Irishmen executed as heretics by colonists after being beaten in battle. The MacConmaras' prosecutor's native Irish metropolitan retaliated against him, allegedly attacking him with an army, a response reminiscent of Bicknor's reaction to Ledrede's prosecutions. Adducc Dubh was an ethnic sacrifice on a trumped-up charge of heresy within the heart of the colony, the MacConmaras on an increasingly isolated outpost where the native Irish were better able to fight back. The allegations against them were part of a larger portrait of the Irish as deviants in need of correction and control; to better understand these developments and their broader historical context, the chapter begins by tracing the history of heresy in relation to Ireland and the Irish prior to the twelfth-century reform and invasion.

The History of the Heresy of Being Irish

The origins of Christianity in Ireland remain shrouded in mystery, with St. Patrick's *Confession* and *Letter to the Soldiers of Coroticus* offering a rare glimpse into its presumably fifth-century context.[4] His letter indicates that British neighbors perceived the Irish as false Christians from the start. Lamenting the enslavement of recently converted Irish Christians by Christian Britons, he declares, "We have been transformed into strangers. Perhaps they do not believe that we have been given the same baptism, or that we have the same

---

2. Bower, *Scotichronichon*, 394–96; see below.

3. *CSM*, 2:366. Williams's 2013 article makes some steps in this direction, but primarily by insisting that "racial tension was not a factor" ("Heresy in Ireland," 351; see also 347 and 349), without proving the point.

4. Binchy, "Patrick and His Biographers."

God. For them it is shameful that we are Irish."[5] The parallels with the twelfth and subsequent centuries render Patrick's remarks a surprising omission from the 1317 Remonstrance, which similarly condemned the brutal oppression of the Irish by the English under the pretext of false Christianity and assumed ethnic superiority, as discussed below. Patrick himself was a Briton enslaved in Ireland who eventually escaped only to return to help bring the gospel to the island. His writings reveal his humility, courage, and commitment, but offer only fragments of his life in Ireland. They do not mention heresy, but the notes on Fiacc's Old Irish hymn "Genair Patraic," from sometime between the ninth and eleventh centuries, involve him in a heresy conflict. Significantly, the confrontation occurs not in Ireland, but in Gaul: he accompanies Germanus of Auxerre, who actually did come from Gaul to Britain to rid it of Pelagianism; amid his efforts, Germanus learns Pelagianism has overtaken his own city, so he and Patrick travel to Auxerre; as they have no success in lessening its influence, Patrick advises that they should fast against the city for three days and nights, then let God's judgment be upon it; at the end of the fast, the city remains mired in heresy, so the earth swallows it whole, a verdict that Johannes Teutonicus might appreciate.[6] Even in such fantastic tales, however, heresy remained outside of Ireland; those in Britain and Gaul were the heretics, not the Irish.

Patrick's arrival in Ireland is often associated with efforts to eradicate heresy in Britain. Prosper of Aquitaine recorded Pope Celestine sending Palladius as the first bishop "to the Irish believers in Christ" in the year 431, two years after Palladius himself had convinced Celestine to send Germanus to battle Pelagians in Britain.[7] Prosper also praised Celestine for making "the barbarian island [i.e., Ireland] Christian while taking care to keep the Roman island [i.e., Britain] Catholic."[8] Some have theorized that Palladius was thus sent to protect the Irish church from Pelagianism as well, though little evidence beyond Prosper's vague entries supports such a view. Nor is anything known about the identity of these Irish Christians, about whom Prosper cannot be assumed to be well informed. Palladius himself disappears from the record, eclipsed by Patrick's propagandists, who date Patrick's

---

5. "St Patrick's Letter against the Soldiers of Coroticus," in de Paor, *Saint Patrick's World*, 112 (all quotations from *Saint Patrick's World* use de Paor's translation). Patrick's identification with Ireland's inhabitants foreshadows Arnold le Poer's fourteenth-century example.

6. Bede, *Ecclesiastical History*, 65–71; see also Rees, *Pelagius*, 108–14; Bernard and Atkinson, *Irish Liber Hymnorum*, 1:98n10. For Johannes Teutonicus, see the introduction.

7. "The Chronicle of Prosper of Aquitaine," *s.a.* 429 and 431, in de Paor, *Saint Patrick's World*, 79.

8. Chapter 21 of Prosper's *Contra Collatorem* (in de Paor, *Saint Patrick's World*, 71). Prosper strongly supported Augustine and opposed Pelagianism.

return to 432 and portray Palladius as a failure.[9] While Patrick too could have been sent to help bolster the faith against heretical views, he demonstrates no such concerns and his writings ill fit such a purpose.[10] Michael Herren suggests that Patrick's writings are inherently and intentionally anti–Pelagian, due to Patrick's gratitude for God's grace and awareness of his sins.[11] By the same token, however, one could argue that Patrick was Pelagian, emphasizing instead his celebrations of virtuous acts resulting from free will working in concert with divine grace.

Scholars have debated the role of Pelagius and Pelagianism in Ireland for centuries. Jerome declared him to be Irish, a people whom he held in contempt; thus Jerome may have intended Irish as an insult, much as some might use Philistine.[12] Greater evidence associates him and support for as well as opposition to him with Britain, yet Ireland too had its Pelagian influences. Moreover, "Pelagius' 'Pelagian' ideas originated not in Britain but in Rome. Ironically the heresy of the Briton had to be imported to his homeland."[13] These ideas developed in opposition to St. Augustine's later views on original sin and free will. According to Augustine, God gave Adam free will so he could give it back to God and freely choose absolute obedience; because Adam disobeyed the one commandment God had placed upon him, humanity fell into sin, our free will so corrupted that it essentially remains beyond our use; this original sin continues to be transmitted via semen, so from our very conception we are sinners to our core, completely dependent on God's grace both for our salvation and for any good that we might do. Augustine's views disturbed Pelagius, then living in Rome. He instead maintained that, thanks to God's grace, humans retain free will and can choose sin or virtue; thus, each Christian is called to a life of perfect virtue.[14] His critics saw this as denial of the centrality of Christ's sacrifice and God's grace in salvation. Amid a vituperative debate between the two and their supporters, Augustine had Pelagius declared a heretic and exiled in 418, though his teachings continued to circulate.

The Irish are often seen as key to Pelagianism's perpetuation. For example, Michael Herren and Shirley Ann Brown contend that Pelagianism "defined

---

9. E.g., Muirchú and Tírechán in Bieler, *Patrician Texts in the Book of Armagh*, 72–73, 164–67. Patrick's hagiographers also portray Patrick quite differently than he portrays himself.

10. Thompson, *Who Was Saint Patrick?*, 54, 57.

11. Herren and Brown, *Christ in Celtic Christianity*, 82–85.

12. Walsh and Bradley, *History of the Irish Church*, 6; Kenney, *Sources for the Early History of Ireland*, 161–62; see also Kelly, "Pelagius," 100. For Jerome's remarks, see *In Hieremiam prophetam*, 2, 120.

13. Kelly, "Pelagius," 101.

14. I have greatly simplified Augustine's and Pelagius's complex arguments. Elaine Pagels's *Adam, Eve, and the Serpent* offers a particularly accessible study of their debate (see 98–150).

the common Celtic Church" and continued to influence its theology and practice for centuries, which may overstate the evidence, not least because of the hypothetical nature of a "common Celtic Church."[15] Furthermore, the debate between Augustine and Pelagius was far from the last word within the church on the role of free will in salvation. Yet at least some Irish continued to openly draw not just on Pelagius's ideas, but on his writings. For example, the eighth-century Old Irish Würzburg glosses on the Pauline epistles cite Pelagius over ten times more frequently than any other authority.[16] Pelagius remained one of the preferred authorities in early medieval Irish exegesis, along with Jerome, Gregory the Great, and Isidore.[17] Irish scholars did not remain entirely uncritical, however. In the Würzburg glosses one added that Romans 5:15 refutes heretics, perhaps intending Pelagianism but possibly intensifying Pelagius's own critique; significantly, however, heretical associations did not prompt him to reject Pelagius as an authority.[18]

The Paschal controversy proved the most pervasive element in the early medieval portrait of the Irish as heretics. This controversy was not confined to the Irish; for the first several centuries, Christians repeatedly devised different computations for dating Easter, attempting to integrate solar and lunar calendars. A primary computation among the Irish was the eighty-four-year cycle established by the Council of Arles in 314, which may have been brought by an early missionary, perhaps Palladius himself. Rome, however, favored the nineteen-year cycle of Victorius of Aquitaine, which was not published until 457 nor adopted in Gaul until 541 and needed regular corrections from Rome.[19] The controversy involved the essentials of constructing Christian time (as Easter determines other Christian periods and dates), the uniformity of the faith, and the distinction between Christianity and Judaism. Easter is tied to Passover, which some Jews observed starting on fourteen Nisan, yet since the Council of Nicaea the church insisted that it

---

15. Herren and Brown, *Christ in Celtic Christianity*, 278, although they recognize the inadequacies of the term "Celtic Church" (ibid., 3–9). Cf. Márkus's argument that Herren and Brown's "Pelagianism" instead continues "pre-Pelagian/pre-Augustinian" church orthodoxy (Márkus, "Pelagianism and the 'Common Celtic Church'").

16. Pelagius is cited 1,311 times; the next highest is Jerome, with 116 attributions (though four are actually from Pelagius). The total for authorities other than Pelagius—Origen (another condemned heretic), Hilary, Jerome, Augustine, Gregory, and Isidore—is 233, though fourteen of those are actually from Pelagius (Kenney, *Sources for the Early History of Ireland*, 635–36; see also Zimmer, *Pelagius in Irland*, 40–112).

17. Michael Herren, in Duffy, *Medieval Ireland*, 66.

18. Stokes and Strachan, *Thesaurus Paleohibernicus*, 1:509. See Kelly, "Pelagius," 115, and Ó Cróinín, "'New Heresy for Old,'" 505n3. Consider Pelagius's own words and de Bruyn's commentary (*Pelagius's Commentary*, 18–24, 41–46, 94).

19. Ó Cróinín, "'New Heresy for Old,'" 511.

be distinct from Passover. The Irish were often accused of quartodecimanism ("fourteenthism"), which was condemned at the end of the second century. Quartodecimans, such as St. Polycarp, a revered martyr of the second century, observed Easter on fourteen Nisan, no matter the day, so that Easter was the same day as Passover.[20] The Irish celebrated Easter solely on Sunday, but if Passover fell on a Sunday, it could coincide with the Irish Easter (though few if any Jews were present in early medieval Ireland to make the coincidence apparent). As Dáibhí Ó Cróinín has demonstrated, even when the Irish tried to conform to Rome and follow Victorius's table in the mid-seventh century, they still were accused of quartodecimanism, given the errors in his computation and the lag time between Rome issuing corrections and the Irish receiving them.[21] This also entailed an accusation that the Irish were trying to revive Pelagianism, on the assumption that Easter concurring with Passover denied the need for the saving grace of Christ's Resurrection.[22] As Irish influence spread through *peregrini* (pilgrims) such as Saints Colum Cille (d. 597) and Columbanus (d. 615), who left Ireland and established monastic communities throughout Britain and the Continent, as well as through foreign students who returned home after training in Irish schools, Irish differences in calculating Easter became increasingly regarded as dangerously divisive. This prompted allegations of Irish heresy throughout the sixth and seventh centuries by church leaders such as Gildas, Aldhelm, and Theodore of Canterbury.[23] Cummian's *De controversia Paschali* offers intriguing Irish perspective on this debate; after much reflection upon various authorities, ultimately Cummian chose conformity with Rome over continuity with Irish practices from the past.[24]

Columbanus, on the other hand, chose a spirited defense of not just himself but the Irish generally when he faced false accusations of quartodecimanism after he moved to Francia (Gaul) around 591.[25] Columbanus's letters reveal his erudition, integrity, and strength of character and devotion,

---

20. Polycarp attributed the practice to the apostle John; see Irenaeus's letter to Pope Victor, which recalls Polycarp and Pope Anicetus's agreement to disagree peaceably on the matter, quoted in Eusebius's *Church History* (Schaff and Wace, *Nicene and Post-Nicene Fathers*, 243–44). Columbanus cited Polycarp and Anicetus's example in his defense of his practices and request for tolerance (Columbanus, *Opera*, 24–25).

21. Ó Cróinín, "'New Heresy for Old,'" 511–15.

22. Ibid., 516.

23. Cullen, "A Question of Time," 202.

24. Walsh and Ó Cróinín, *Cummian's Letter*. Cummian's decision was part of a larger decision among the southern Irish to adopt the Roman Easter in 632. Most Irish conformed by the early eighth century.

25. As Clare Stancliffe notes, Judaizing may have been the primary charge and quartodecimanism secondary ("Columbanus and the Gallic Bishops," 205–7).

but also at times a lack of tact; thus it was perhaps not surprising when he was exiled from Burgundy in 610. A few years later, after relocating to Italy, Columbanus waded into the Three Chapters controversy with another forceful letter, this one intimating that heresy had corrupted the curia itself. The controversy refers to debate in Italy regarding lingering Nestorianism, which Columbanus's new patrons, Theudelinda and Agilulf of Lombardy, felt Boniface IV favored. Urging the pope to hold a council to expunge any error within the curia and to prove the integrity of his faith, Columbanus also reproves the pope for not condemning and excommunicating heretics, meaning Nestorians and others who deny Christ's two natures, human and divine.[26] Yet he demonstrates a lack of familiarity with these heresies, repeatedly attributing his knowledge on the matter to information from others. He contrasts the allegations against Boniface with the purity of Irish faith, which inspires him to speak so boldly to the pope:

> For all we Irish, inhabitants of the world's edge, are disciples of Saints Peter and Paul and of all the disciples who wrote the sacred canon by the Holy [Spirit], and we accept nothing outside the evangelical and apostolic teaching; none has been a heretic, none a Judaizer, none a schismatic; but the Catholic faith, as it was delivered by you first, who are the successors of the holy apostles, is maintained unbroken. Strengthened and almost goaded by this confidence, I have dared to arouse you against those who revile you and call you the partisans of heretics and describe you as schismatics.[27]

Ironically, given Jerome's estimation of the Irish and Columbanus's fierce native pride, one of Columbanus's proofs of the purity of Irish faith is their loyalty to Jerome; as he wrote to Gregory the Great in his vigorous defense of Irish methods for calculating Easter, "anyone impugning the authority of St. Jerome will be a heretic or reprobate in the eyes of the Western Churches, whoever that [person] may be" (*quicumque ille fuerit*).[28] Thus, by extension, anyone with a favorable view of the Irish could be a heretic, but Columbanus does not address Jerome's anti-Irish prejudice. He argues that no one, not even the pope (nor presumably Jerome!), "can possess a monopoly in the interpretation of the Faith . . . 'by all men everywhere freedom should be given to the truth.'"[29] He perceives the Bible itself as the ultimate judge

---

26. Herren and Brown, *Christ in Celtic Christianity*, 52–54.
27. Columbanus, *Opera*, 39 (all quotations from Columbanus follow Walker's translation).
28. Ibid., 9.
29. Ibid., lxxii, 51.

of heresy and orthodoxy, if necessary as interpreted by erudite ecclesiastical leaders working in concert. His "corporate rather than hierarchical" understanding of the church differs from the approach that regards heresy as primarily an issue of obedience, which is further emphasized by his confidence in chastizing the leader of the western church.[30] "Columbanus reflects an older view of the church in different areas linked through horizontal bonds of charity, rather than as a single hierarchy which stretches up vertically."[31] While his is among the most active early medieval Irish voices regarding heresy, again it remains foreign to Ireland and the Irish; it is something he associates with the pope and the Continent, not his people or his country.

Columbanus's reference to "Judaizers" probably relates to criticisms of the Irish for continuing Old Testament practices, which lie at the heart of St. Boniface's allegations against an eighth-century *peregrinus* on the Continent (Austrasia) for his "Irish peculiarities."[32] Clemens was accused of rejecting church statutes and synods, "imposing Judaism upon Christians," advocating levirate marriage, and teaching that when Christ harrowed hell he rescued all its inhabitants.[33] Sven Meeder's thoughtful analysis of this case explores evidence for the primacy of the Bible in Irish thought; common practices among both the Irish and the Israelites, such as polygamy; a potential tendency among missionaries to offer hope that Christ would save pagan ancestors, which the Irish may have favored, given their preservation of their pre-Christian past; and the possibility that Clemens espoused Pelagianism. As he notes, however, it cannot be determined how accurately Boniface represented Clemens, who was condemned in large part due to Boniface by the Council of Rome in 745 and left no records of his own. Boniface, the Anglo-Saxon "Apostle of Germany," probably portrayed "Clemens as the Irish sinner expected by a Continental audience," conditioned as they were by anti-Irish sentiments in the works of Jerome, Bede, and the like.[34] Moreover, Boniface did not just convert pagans in his missionary work; he strove to undo what he saw as insidious Irish influences among those who had adopted Christianity because of *peregrini* and their monasteries, establishing his own approach and communities as preferred alternatives. Encountering

---

30. Ibid., lxxii.

31. Stancliffe, "Columbanus and the Gallic Bishops," 213. As Stancliffe notes, part of the bishops' frustration was Columbanus's refusal to submit to their authority, likely due to his Irish context (ibid., 210–11, 214).

32. Meeder, "Boniface and the Irish Heresy of Clemens," 251 and 279. Celebrating Easter on Passover would be a primary example of alleged "Judaizing" practice.

33. Quoted (in English) in Meeder, "Boniface and the Irish Heresy of Clemens," 258.

34. Ibid., 279.

and resenting Irish differences on the Continent, Boniface presented them as dangerously wrong, even to the point of heresy.

In 747, Pope Zacharias echoed Boniface's appraisal of Clemens and referred his fate to Boniface. The following year, Zacharias replied to Boniface's complaints about another potential Irish heretic, Virgil (Fergal) of Salzburg, for "his perverse and abominable teaching."[35] Whereas Clemens disappeared from the record after Zacharias's letter, Virgil went on to become bishop of Salzburg less than twenty years later and was canonized in 1233. Another highly respected *peregrinus*, John Scottus Eriugena (i.e., John the Irishman from Ireland), also had to contend with allegations of heresy the following century. He too exchanged Ireland for Francia, becoming a celebrated scholar in the court of Charlemagne's grandson, Charles the Bald. In 850 he wrote *De divina predestinatione* at Archbishop Hincmar's request in response to the double predestination theory advanced by Gottschalk of Orbais. Drawing heavily on early Augustine, Eriugena emphasized free will, as proof of our creation in God's image and as necessary condition for a judgment day that holds any meaning, and rejected claims of predestination of sin or evil as heretical.[36] While also vehemently opposing Gottschalk's theory, Hincmar regarded Eriugena's reply as smacking of Pelagianism; indeed, the Council of Valence's description of Eriugena's work as *pultes scottorum* repeats Jerome's portrait of Pelagius as "stuffed with Irish porridge."[37] His teachings on predestination were similarly denounced at the Council of Langres four years later (859), but Eriugena remained a powerful and respected scholar in Charles's court.[38] In 860, the papal librarian Anastasius wrote to Charles praising John for his learning and holiness, all the more remarkable in a "barbarian."[39]

Eriugena's works remained influential for centuries, and according to Henry of Susa, his *Periphyseon* helped shape the pantheism of Amaury of Bene, with whom it was condemned in 1225.[40] Thomas Duddy suggests that his teachings influenced the heresy of the Free Spirit, a tenuous link, in part because no such sect existed, as discussed in the Introduction.[41] Moreover, the connection is based on pantheism leading to self-deification, which

---

35. Quoted (in English) in Carey, "Ireland and the Antipodes," 1.

36. As Dermot Moran notes, however, Eriugena often modifies Augustine (*Philosophy of John Scottus Eriugena*, 115).

37. Council of Valence, quoted (in English) in ibid., 29n7, see also 33.

38. Ibid., 35.

39. Quoted (in English) in Kenney, *Sources for the Early History of Ireland*, 582.

40. Moran, *Philosophy of John Scottus Eriugena*, 87.

41. Duddy, *History of Irish Thought*, 40–42.

misrepresents the thought of figures most associated with this heresy, such as Marguerite Porete and Meister Eckhart.[42] Furthermore, Eriugena was not pantheist.[43] Eriugena seems susceptible to charges of apocatastasis and universal salvation, given his Neoplatonic understanding that everything ultimately returns perfected to God; this could be seen as an "Irish" attitude toward hell, considering the allegations against Clemens. Yet Eriugena does not seem to have been condemned for this, and heresy does not exist in the abstract. While aspects of his teaching were condemned in his lifetime, and his *Periphyseon* centuries later, his remains one of the most respected early medieval minds. Significantly, the condemnations occurred on the Continent, and his problematic influence was allegedly upon Continental heretics, not Irish.

To return to Ireland, no evidence of trials surfaces until Bernard of Clairvaux's dubious twelfth-century claim about the cleric of Lismore, but penitentials attest to concerns about heresy.[44] Yet none offers a clear definition, beyond an ascriptural belief, with one qualified exception. The Penitential of Columbanus specifies the followers of Bonosus, a bishop of Naïssus (in what is now southern Serbia), who rejected Mary's perpetual virginity, as heretics; the entire section on heresy, however, was likely a later addition made in Burgundy.[45] Cummian's *De controversia Paschali* (ca. 633), a letter to Ségéne, abbot of Iona, defending his decision to follow Roman observance, reveals procedure adopted to avoid heresy. It follows a process prescribed by Innocent I: examining scripture to illuminate the matter, then turning to patristic pronouncements, before considering statements of synods and councils, then gathering a group of ecclesiastical leaders for discussion, and ultimately referring it "to the chief of the cities" (i.e., Rome).[46] In the end, Cummian and his companions decided that unity with Rome took precedence over fidelity to Irish practices. In contrast, Columbanus passionately argued for the superiority of Irish computations, also due to the Bible, patristic pronouncements, and conciliar statements. He further invoked a right guaranteed by Canon 2 of the First Council of Constantinople (381), that "churches of God among barbarian peoples must be administered in accordance with the custom in

---

42. Eriugena did directly influence Eckhart, however; see Moran, *Philosophy of John Scottus Eriugena.*

43. Moran, *Philosophy of John Scottus Eriugena,* 84–89.

44. Bieler, *Irish Penitentials,* 104–5, 122–23, 160–61, 186–87, and 236–39.

45. Ibid., 5, 245n7; see also Columbanus, *Opera,* 179n1.

46. Ó Cróinín, *Early Medieval Ireland,* 152–53, quotation (in English) 153.

force at the time of the fathers."[47] He insisted upon the right of the Irish to continue their customs, including the dating of Easter, even if they lived in Frankish lands. He argued that their practices harmed no one (*nulli molesti*), and that all Christians should be "joint members of one body, whether Franks or Britons or Irish or whatever our race be"; they might disagree with each other, but they ought to be able to live together in peace.[48] The use of Pelagius further illustrates Irish approaches to doctrinal difference, being "more tolerant of diversity in ecclesiastical matters. Although relying primarily on orthodox Fathers for the exegesis, they also used 'heretics,' the biblical apocrypha, and, at times, their imagination."[49]

Thus the heresy of being Irish long predates the fourteenth century. Patrick offers relevant remarks from the fifth century, and the prototype was further developed by associations with Pelagius and the Paschal controversy. By the early seventh century, the Irish had gained a reputation for being heretics, Judaizers, and schismatics, prompting Columbanus's fierce rejection of such slander. Yet, while heresy was repeatedly a concern of those outside Ireland, it was rarely so for those within it. The *Romani*, who advocated greater conformity with Rome, might be at odds with *Hibernenses*, or those who preferred to continue Irish customs, but their disagreements apparently did not devolve into heresy accusations.[50] Cummian's letter could suggest otherwise, however. He asks Ségéne, a *Hibernensis*, to "direct me to some better understanding by your words or with more valid writings and more certain proofs—if you have any—and I will gratefully accept it, as I have accepted this [i.e., conformity with Rome]. If, however, you do not have any, be silent and do not call us heretics."[51] Walsh and Ó Cróinín argue that this "clearly implies that one of the Iona charges [against Cummian] was heresy."[52] The lack of evidence of such allegations leaves the matter uncertain, however, especially since the heresy would be conformity with Rome and other evidence attests to Irish acceptance of diversity, including regarding Easter. Cummian could be returning the allegation when he writes, "It is proper to heretics not to correct their opinion; to prefer a perverse opinion rather than abandon one they had defended."[53] Yet his words must be read in the context of his overall

---

47. Tanner, *Decrees of the Ecumenical Councils*, 1:32 (Tanner's translation). For Columbanus's words, see Columbanus, *Opera*, 24–25.

48. Columbanus, *Opera*, 23–24.

49. Kelly, "Pelagius," 116.

50. Ó Néill, "*Romani* Influences."

51. Walsh and Ó Cróinín, *Cummian's Letter*, 75 (all translations from Cummian's letter follow Walsh and Ó Cróinín's translation).

52. Ibid., 16.

53. Ibid., 95.

defense of his decision, which he does not use to attack others. For example, as he says to Ségéne,

> Approve these things if you wish; if not, disclaim them with catholic testimonies; if you wish to do neither of these, we shall say this: *We must all appear before the judgement seat of Christ, so that each one may answer for his own body.* Also, We should not judge *before the time* when *He shall come Who shall bring light to things now hidden in darkness and shall disclose the purpose of hearts.* And *Judge not that you be not judged. For with the judgement you pronounce you shall be judged.* And *Who are you to pass judgement on the servant of another? It is before his own master that he stands or falls.* The burden of what I say is on you, as I see it, and the burden of what you say is on me, unless you demonstrate it with the words of Holy Scripture.[54]

Cummian demonstrates considerable thoughtfulness in his choice of conformity with Rome over continuity with Irish customs, but he does not resort to allegations of heresy if others choose differently. Instead, in accordance with scripture he defers judgment to God. Similarly, while Columbanus has scathing words about Victorius's competence, he does not cast aspersions upon the integrity of his faith or the faith of those who follow his computation. Difference of practice clearly does not bother him, although theological error, such as that espoused by Nestorians and perhaps, Columbanus fears, Boniface IV, he denounces. In his view, reproving theological error is the right of all, so that an exiled Irishman castigates the head of the church. Significantly, however, both he and Eriugena entered these debates only at the request of their Continental associates, Theudelinda and Agilulf for Columbanus and Hincmar for Eriugena; consultations with Rome influenced Cummian's perspective as well.

While Irishmen such as Columbanus, Clemens, and Eriugena repeatedly faced allegations of heresy, and Pelagianism and the Paschal controversy contributed to a sense of the Irish generally as heretics, these concerns consistently arose on the Continent, not Ireland. Whether it be Patrick battling Auxerre's Pelagians, the Three Chapters controversy, or later Amaury of Bene, these heretical elements occurred outside Ireland. Perhaps due to their freedom from Roman rule, a lack of centralization, and their location at the edge of the known western world, the Irish were more accepting of diversity in ecclesiastical organization, ways of practicing the faith, and including

---

54. Ibid., 91. Throughout the work, Cummian emphasizes that he is defending himself, not attacking Ségéne.

"heretical" voices like Pelagius in their theology and exegesis.[55] Moreover, the Bible broadly interpreted remained their ultimate authority, and the Bible reflects a range of perspectives. Conformity in itself was no virtue, nor did unity depend upon it. Columbanus's plea applies to the wider world: should not Christians be able to share the earth, even if they have differences, if one day they will share heaven?[56] Yet others distrusted such diversity, influencing the image of the Irish as heretics in the early Middle Ages, apostates in the twelfth century (justifying the island's invasion), and then heretics again in the fourteenth. Prejudice underlies this portrait. As Jerome's racist rants, Anastasius's surprise that a "barbarian" could be as brilliant and holy as Eriugena (a full four centuries after Patrick and Palladius), and countless other comments indicate, the Irish and even Ireland itself were regarded as not just different but inferior. Alexander III's letter to Henry II in 1172 echoes this view, condemning the Irish not only for renouncing Christian faith and virtue, but also for fighting "over a kingdom which the Roman emperors, the conquerors of the world, left untouched in their time."[57] His words imply that Ireland was beneath Roman contempt, its inadequacies intensified by Roman neglect, and the Irish failed further by fighting to keep it. In the fourteenth century, the O'Tooles led the Irish in continuing this fight; consequently, one was sacrificed at the stake, cast as the incarnation of this anti-Irish rhetoric.

The O'Tooles

In the twelfth century, the O'Tooles exchanged the plains of Kildare for the mountains of Wicklow as their primary homeland, at least partly because of the wars waged by Diarmaid MacMurrough and his allies from England. Like their most celebrated son St. Lorcán (Laurence), they initially seem to have adjusted reasonably well to the new political realities in Wicklow, where they were surrounded by settlers.[58] In the third quarter of the thirteenth century Archbishop Fulk de Saundford gave Glenmalure and its environs to Murtough O'Toole, perhaps in an effort to use him to police other native Irish.[59] If such were the plan, however, it backfired drastically. Almost immediately after Fulk's death in 1271, Thomas de Chaddesworth, who had witnessed the grant as Fulk's official, took hostages from the O'Tooles and their neighbors

55. Sharpe, "Some Problems Concerning the Organization of the Church"; e.g., Bieler, *Patrician Texts in the Book of Armagh*, 186–87.

56. Columbanus, *Opera*, 16–17.

57. *IHD*, 21 (Curtis and McDowell's translation).

58. Orpen, *Ireland under the Normans*, 4:11–15; *NHI*, 2:256; Lydon, "Medieval Wicklow," 156–59.

59. McNeill, *Calendar of Archbishop Alen's Register*, 136; Lydon, "Medieval Wicklow," 157.

FIGURE 8. Glenmalure, stronghold of the O'Tooles. Photo by the author.

the O'Byrnes, marking the beginning of renewed hostilities between colonists and the leading Irish clans of the Wicklow mountains.[60] Fortunately for the O'Tooles, Glenmalure was excellently appointed for defense and would become "the graveyard of many an army sent out from Dublin" for centuries, starting with those who fought under the prior of the Hospitallers in 1274.[61] The O'Tooles and O'Byrnes were soon joined by the MacMurroughs, their occasional overlords, in their frequently victorious efforts against the colonists, and though temporary peace was often attempted between the various factions, by the fourteenth century the O'Tooles in particular had become the scourge of the Dublin colonists, whose lands and stock they frequently attacked. So feared was their war cry, "fionnachta abú," that in 1312 a band of Anglo-Irish robbers used it to terrorize the residents of Haughstown in Co. Kildare so that they would flee their homes.[62]

The O'Tooles had a range of relations with colonists.[63] Like other native Irish, they took advantage of the unrest caused by the Bruce invasion to increase their own efforts against the colony. With the help of the O'Byrnes as well as the hibernicized Harolds and Archbolds, they devastated a considerable

60. *CDI*, 2:313.

61. *NHI*, 2:257; *CSM*, 2:318; Clyn, 9.

62. *CJR*, 3:244.

63. For a detailed overview of Leinster in which the O'Tooles figure prominently, see O'Byrne, *War, Politics and the Irish of Leinster*, especially 5–35 and 58–91.

amount of colonial holdings in Wicklow.[64] They also suffered serious losses during this time, including a defeat in 1316 in which four hundred of their army was killed and their heads sent to hang from Dublin walls; the story did not end there, however, for, Pembridge relates, the dead miraculously came back to life, fought together, and shouted "fionnachta abú."[65] Despite constant tensions between the clan and colonists, some O'Tooles integrated with the Anglo-Irish. For example, Archbishop Alexander de Bicknor built a castle at Tallaght in the 1320s primarily to guard against the attacks of the O'Tooles, but its castellan was a member of that same family, Malmorth O'Toole.[66] Murcadh son of Nicholas O'Toole was a valued member of the royal army, and both Clyn and Pembridge took note of his murder in Dublin 1333 during parliament, which he may have been attending.[67] At least some O'Tooles were supposed to be protected by English law and thus could not be discriminated against as "mere Irish." In 1299 Walter O'Toole, who may have been Adducc's father, brandished in court a ninety-year-old charter from William Marshal granting his great-grandfather and his heirs the right to use English laws.[68] He also testified that he, his father, and his father before him had all served in juries and assizes as well as in courts of the king, which he offered to prove; his evidence as to the jury participation and the like was not included in this case, but several O'Tooles are known to have served on juries, including perhaps that same Walter in 1299, and Elias and Simon O'Toole in a case around 1260.[69]

The threat the Leinster Irish posed to the colony briefly took on a more menacing dimension in early 1328, when they overcame their divisions to unite behind a king, Dónal mac Airt MacMurrough. After his inauguration, Dónal ordered that his standard be placed a mere two miles from Dublin "and afterwards carried throughout all the lands of Ireland."[70] These acts of this new king of Leinster, who led the most feared clans of Wicklow and

---

64. Gilbert, *Historic and Municipal Documents of Ireland*, 457; *CSM*, 2:348–49, 356.

65. *CSM*, 2:96, 350–51.

66. Frame, *Ireland and Britain*, 228–29.

67. Ibid., 269; Clyn, 25; *CSM*, 2:379.

68. *CJR*, 1:271. Walter produced this charter in order to prove the illegality of the appropriation of his land by two colonists, who had claimed that since he was Irish they did not have to respond to his charges (a common defense colonists used against Irish they had wronged). O'Byrne states that Adducc Dubh was "probably" this Walter's son (*War, Politics and the Irish of Leinster*, 26), without citing supporting evidence.

69. *CJR*, 1:270; McNeill, *Calendar of Archbishop Alen's Register*, 110–12. Elias is further described as "serjeant of the country" in Archbishop Luke's time (1230–55; McNeill, *Calendar of Archbishop Alen's Register*, 111).

70. *CSM*, 2:365–66. This occurred before Quadragesima of Pembridge's 1327, so February 21, 1328.

claimed sovereignty over an area that abutted Dublin itself, probably caused many colonists to suspect with alarm that his ultimate goal was kingship of Ireland.[71] To paraphrase Sayles's remarks about Maurice fitz Thomas, what a Bruce from Scotland had attempted might seem far more feasible for a native Irish ruler, particularly if he could unite Irish clans who frequently battled the colonists but for various reasons, especially their own infighting, could not overcome them.[72] Dónal's threat, however, proved short-lived, as he was quickly captured and imprisoned in Dublin Castle. According to Pembridge, "after his capture many misfortunes befell the Leinster Irish . . . and many Irish were killed."[73] One of those misfortunes was the capture and execution of David O'Toole, who may have been the chief of the O'Tooles for nearly seventy years.[74] Another was the arrest and execution of Adducc Dubh O'Toole for heresy.

The "Heresy" of Adducc Dubh O'Toole

Adducc Dubh O'Toole's heresy has often been noted but rarely understood. The majority of those who discuss his case repeat the findings against him and accept them at face value, the nineteenth-century historian P. L. O'Toole being a notable exception.[75] He remarked, "O'Toole and heresy! Attuned in any chord, pitched in any key, there is a dissonance in the sound that fails to harmonize upon the ear. Burn an O'Toole for heresy in the fourteenth century, and burn, ravage, and destroy them, for their stubbornly refusing to be made heretics of, in the sixteenth, seventeenth, and eighteenth centuries."[76] His partisan perspective does not entirely miss the mark. He characterizes Adducc's crime as treason rather than heresy, theorizing that he fought during the Bruce unrest, but more likely his involvement in the upheaval of 1327–28 led to his arrest and execution.[77] Even this, however, is conjecture.

---

71. Lydon, "Medieval Wicklow," 172.

72. Sayles, "Rebellious First Earl," 204; see chapter 4.

73. *CSM*, 2:366.

74. O'Toole, *History of the Clan O'Toole*, 149, 153–54, 167–68.

75. Those who accept the findings include Lydon, "Medieval Wicklow," 173; Williams, "Dominican Annals," 163, " Heretic's Tale," and "Heresy in Ireland," 346–48; Neary, "Richard de Ledrede," iv, 32n34; FitzMaurice and Little, *Materials for the History*, 119; Leland, *History of Ireland*, 1:287; Sinnott, "Adam Duff O'Toole"; O'Byrne, "O'Toole (Ó Tuathail), Adam"; Dwyer, *Witches, Spies and Stockholm Syndrome*, 135–43. In addition to O'Toole, Orpen (*Ireland under the Normans*, 4:219n3), Ronan ("Anglo-Norman Dublin and Diocese," 46:585), and Clarke ("Street Life in Medieval Dublin," 152) also serve as exceptions.

76. O'Toole, *History of the Clan O'Toole*, 165.

77. Ibid., 166. O'Toole mistakenly dates Adam's arrest and execution to 1326 (ibid., 165), hence his focus on the activities of the previous decade.

What brought Adducc to the authorities' notice or in fact any aspect of his history prior to his trial has escaped the records. His father was apparently a Walter or Balthor Dubh O'Toole, and he may have been a priest or a monk, but his only definite appearance in the records relates to his supposed heresy and execution.[78]

According to Pembridge, Adducc Dubh O'Toole was convicted on the grounds that "contrary to the Catholic faith he denied the Incarnation of Jesus Christ, said that there could not be three Persons and one God, declared that the Most Blessed Mary, Mother of the Lord, was a whore, denied the resurrection of the dead, declared that the Holy Scriptures were nothing more than fables, and rejected the authority of the sacred Apostolic See."[79] This alleged heresy constitutes a denial of the very basics of Catholicism and, if true, would technically render him an apostate, not a heretic.[80] Who precisely found him guilty of heresy is unclear; Pembridge says simply that it was done "by decree of the church," but the archbishop, Alexander de Bicknor, was then in England, dealing yet again with his misdeeds as treasurer from 1308 to 1314.[81] His vicar, William de Rodyerd, most likely was a leading figure in Adducc's trial, particularly considering his support of Ledrede's prosecutions in Kilkenny, as well as the affiliation between St. Patrick's, of which Rodyerd was dean, and the so-called Counter-Remonstrance of ca. 1331. However, in the sixteenth century James Grace attributed Adducc's fate to "a secular decree," which could be a mistake or could point to an irregularity in Adducc's trial and execution.[82] Yet, due to Thomas fitz John's death on April 5, Roger Outlaw was acting justiciar at the time, and he seems unlikely to play a leading role in the burning of an alleged heretic, especially on such dubious grounds.

---

78. *CSM*, 2:366; O'Hart, *Irish Pedigrees*, 1:764. Presumably both father and son were brunettes or had swarthy complexions, hence the epithet "dubh," i.e., "black" or "dark." Conor son of Balthor O'Toole numbered among the king's O'Toole hostages in 1325–26 (Frame, *Ireland and Britain*, 261). Sinnott suggests he was a priest ("Adam Duff O'Toole," 414), due to a 1302 reference to an Adam O'Toole (*CSM*, 2:lxxxvi). This does not identify Adam as a priest, however, but implies that he is a monk of Dunbrody Abbey; moreover, there may have been many Adam O'Tooles. Adducc is an Irish diminutive form of Adam.

79. *CSM*, 2:366; emended by Gilbert. Pembridge dates the trial to 1327, but the new year started March 25 and Adducc's fate is recorded immediately following the uprising of the Leinster Irish and Dónal mac Airt MacMurrough's inauguration, which Pembridge dates to before Quadragesima 1327 (i.e., February 21, 1328). Thus Adducc was likely tried and convicted in March 1328; his execution Pembridge states occurred on the Monday after the octave of Easter in 1328, i.e., April 11, 1328. At times scholars erroneously date Adducc's trial and execution to 1327, due to this confusion.

80. Such technicalities were not necessarily recognized at this time, however. See above.

81. *CSM*, 2:366.

82. Grace, *Annales Hiberniae*, 108.

On April 11, 1328, Adducc was burned at the stake in Dublin at Hoggen Green, the site of Viking burial mounds that were quite close to All Hallows', the priory at which Philip de Braybrook was to perform his penance. That same year, his kinsman David was executed in an equally brutal fashion. Though the Dublin council allowed Dónal MacMurrough to languish in Dublin Castle until he escaped in 1330, David O'Toole, who was captured about the same time, was taken from Dublin Castle to the Tholsel, where Nicholas Fastoll and Elias Asshebourne, justices of the Bench, sentenced him to be dragged by horses' tails through the city to the gallows, where he was hanged.[83] These executions seem different facets of the same colonial policy toward the O'Tooles. If Adducc was a priest or monk, perhaps that is why colonial authorities decided to prosecute him for a religious crime, whereas David, a military and political leader, was tried on secular grounds. Or perhaps Adducc outraged colonial authorities in some other way or was randomly selected among O'Toole prisoners, and Rodyerd and his ilk decided to sacrifice him to their newly devised scheme inspired by Ledrede's prosecutions and revitalized interest in *Laudabiliter*, to use him as the incarnation of their claim that all the Irish were heretics or non-Christians against whom the pope should call a crusade so that they could be vanquished once and for all.[84] And then again, maybe Adducc Dubh O'Toole did vociferously deny the basic tenets of Catholicism, which eventually brought him to the notice of colonial authorities, either civil or ecclesiastical, who were coincidentally at war with his family but who sentenced him to death entirely on the basis of his religious beliefs, or lack thereof, after he persisted in maintaining them despite authoritative attempts at correction.

As implausible as this last scenario seems, it has dominated discussions of Adducc's case, which FitzMaurice and Little declare a "case of genuine heresy."[85] Neary proclaims his case as well as that of the MacConmaras twenty-five years later to be "clear-cut cases of apostasy such as might have occurred at any time in the Middle Ages," and thus any connection made between them and Ledrede's prosecutions to be "unjustified."[86] Williams accepts the findings against Adducc as accurate, and also labels his kinsman

---

83. For Dónal, see *CSM*, 2:366, 372. Five years later, Dónal was serving Edward III in Scotland as a paid banneret (Frame, "Military Service in the Lordship of Ireland," 122). O'Toole says Dónal and David were taken in the same battle (*History of the Clan O'Toole*, 167). For David, see *CSM*, 2:366–67. An identical fate to David's was inflicted upon William MacBaltor, possibly an O'Toole, by Justiciar Wogan on July 21, 1308, following Wogan's defeat in Glenmalure (*CSM*, 2:336–37).

84. Note Ledrede's 1328 letter describing his alleged heretics as apostates, discussed above (Sayles, *Documents*, 133).

85. FitzMaurice and Little, *Materials for the History*, 119.

86. Neary, "Richard de Ledrede," iv, see also 32n34.

Figure 9. Trinity College Dublin stands on the eastern edge of what used to be Hoggen Green, where Adducc Dubh O'Toole was executed for heresy in 1328. Photo by the author.

David a heretic.[87] Dwyer likewise accepts them, arguing that Adducc's atheism was a response to the church's role in English oppression of the Irish.[88] Sinnott offers an unusual twist by proclaiming him "the patron 'saint' of Irish Humanism," a martyr for freethought who, had he survived, might have been able to transform the religious landscape of Ireland.[89] Olden refers to him as a "reputed heretic," but also claims his teachings foreshadow Wyclif's followers.[90] Neither Wycliffites nor Lollards, however, rejected the Trinity, the Incarnation, or the resurrection of the dead, nor did they proclaim Mary a whore and the Bible merely fables; while they did challenge papal authority, that was not an uncommon reaction among groups effectively outlawed and persecuted even unto death by papal pronouncements against them. This somewhat simplistic attitude toward Adducc's alleged heresy and heresy in general exhibited by otherwise exacting historians of Ireland points to their lack of familiarity with heresy itself. The same could be said of Adducc's prosecutors, who had the Templar trial and Ledrede's convoluted charges against Alice and her alleged accomplices as their primary guides. Apparently rejecting the latter model as too far-fetched and the more sensational aspects of the former as too unsavoury, they adapted the Templars' alleged apostasy to fit their case against the native Irishman and his people. If Adducc Dubh O'Toole was a martyr for any cause, it was "for being Irish at the wrong place and at the wrong time."[91]

A Call for Crusade

Among annalists only Pembridge records his fate, but Adducc plays a critical role in a letter from the justiciar and council of Ireland to John XXII. Apart from the Holy Spirit, Christ, his mother, the king, the pope, and one of the pope's predecessors, Adducc is the only person the letter names, although a preface notes that it reflects the perspective of the dean and chapter of Dublin and was delivered by William de Nottingham, the precentor of St. Patrick's.[92] As it refers to Adducc's execution and was

---

87. Williams attributes the identification to Pembridge ("Dominican Annals," 163), but he does not include "heretic" among his many negative terms for David (*CSM*, 2:366–67). Her 2013 article, "Heresy in Ireland," offers a more nuanced understanding of Adducc's case, but repeats her earlier assessments.

88. Dwyer, *Witches, Spies and Stockholm Syndrome*, 135–43.

89. Sinnott, "Adam Duff O'Toole," 414.

90. In Stephen and Lee, *Dictionary of National Biography*, 42:337.

91. MacGowan, "Birmingham Six."

92. In Watt, "Negotiations between Edward II and John XXII," 19. William held this office until at least 1357 (Lawlor, *Fasti of St. Patrick's*, 55); William de Rodyerd, Thomas de Chaddesworth's successor, served as dean until 1338 (ibid., 14–15).

addressed to John XXII, the letter can be dated between April 11, 1328 and December 1334. According to Watt, Nottingham delivered the letter to the justiciar, who forwarded it on to Andrew Sapiti, a Florentine lawyer, who presented it to the pope on behalf of the justiciar and king's council.[93] Two justiciars exercised office during this period—John Darcy (ca. May 1329–February 12, 1331; February 13–September 29, 1333; January 19, 1334–March 14, 1335) and Anthony de Lucy (June 3, 1331–December 3, 1332)—and two other men served during the interims, including Roger Outlaw, who was acting justiciar as well as chancellor when Adducc was burned (April 6, 1328–May 1329).[94] Roger was unlikely to support such an endeavour, and Lucy was more concerned with bringing rebellious Anglo-Irish colonists under control than calling for a crusade against the native Irish, to whom he worked to extend English law.[95] Thus the justiciar was likely John Darcy, who offered Ledrede intermittent support in his prosecutions, and his stint as justiciar from 1329 to 1331 seems the most likely period during which it was issued, perhaps in an attempt to capitalize on Ledrede's flight to Avignon to complain about heretics in Ireland.

The letter begins by paraphrasing *Laudabiliter*, reminding John that Ireland was given to the king of England by Pope Adrian to extend the boundaries of Christendom. In that vein, as well as in the vein taken by Ledrede in 1324, the letter erases Ireland's long Christian history prior to the arrival of Henry II, reducing it to some ambiguous period during Edward's predecessors' reign when faith, peace, and charity flourished in Ireland. During the reigns of Edward II and III, however, "in that same land of Ireland, heresy and dissension have arisen and are spreading among the Irish, a sacrilegious and ungovernable race, hostile to God and humanity."[96] The Irish had burned 340 churches in the province of Dublin alone, disrespected priests who held the eucharist in their hands (recalling Ledrede's ongoing complaints against Arnold le Poer), murdered many Christians, scorned God's mandates, "blasphemed against the Holy Spirit and the Blessed Virgin Mary, Mother of Christ, and explicitly denied the resurrection of the dead."[97] Moreover, they maintained that the king of England obtained lordship over Ireland by means of "false suggestion and false bulls," proclaimed that it is not a sin to kill or rob an Englishman even if he is a good and faithful Christian, terrorized

---

93. Watt, *Church in Medieval Ireland*, 145, and "Negotiations between Edward II and John XXII."
94. *NHI*, 9:472–73, 502.
95. See Curtis, *History of Medieval Ireland*, 205–9, and chapters 2 through 4.
96. In Watt, "Negotiations between Edward II and John XXII," 19.
97. Ibid; my translation changes the tenses of blaspheming and denying.

the clergy, and practiced incest and adultery.[98] After this catalog of crimes, "Aduk Duff Octohyl" is named as a kind of heresiarch who endangers not only native Irish but also Anglo-Irish by his perverse teachings.

According to the letter, Adducc was legitimately convicted not only of heresy and blasphemy before his spiritual judge, but also of relapse, "and because of this he was handed over to secular care to suffer his punishment." Before his arrest, however, he led many Irish souls into damnation, and unless the papacy were to lend immediate aid, many more would meet a similar fate, since neither ecclesiastical nor secular authorities dared to combat "such bad believers, founders, enablers, shelterers, and defenders" of heresy, for fear of death. Nor were the "mass of burdensome Irish" alone in their criminal conduct, for they were aided by "the very sons of iniquity, certain English born in Ireland." Thus the letter ardently entreats the pope, "may your glorious clemency deign to call a crusade (*crucesignationem*) for the well-being of your soul and the souls of countless others who are fighting a just war against those evildoers."[99] It continues that those in the colony who were fighting the malefactors with their own resources were impotent without papal help, and ends with the request that the papacy allow penitent malefactors to return to the bosom of the church.

The letter sheds considerable light on the agenda of the justiciar and council of Ireland, as well as of the dean and chapter of St. Patrick's who were for the most part royal servants themselves, but it offers little new regarding the nature of Adducc's supposed heresy, except that here it was claimed he was convicted not just of heresy but also its relapse—another trick most likely learned from Ledrede, or perhaps from the example of the prosecution of Philip de Braybrook by another dean of St. Patrick's, Thomas de Chaddesworth. The beliefs attributed to Adducc in Pembridge's summary, that he blasphemed the Virgin Mary and denied the resurrection of the dead, here figure among the catalog of crimes for which the Irish generally are condemned. The letter also alleges that he led many of his fellow Irish into his error, but no evidence substantiates this claim that the Irish rejected the resurrection, Mary's virginity, and so on. While an analogous accusation regarding

---

98. These accusations, with the exception of the last, stem from the "Remonstrance of Irish Princes," either as accusations the Irish levelled against the colonists or as a misrepresentation of the Remonstrance's argument; see below. The last claim had been levelled against the Irish by authorities in England since the eleventh century and was repeated by Alexander III in his letter to Henry II praising his invasion of Ireland and blessing his claim to its lordship; see Lanfranc, *Letters*, Letters 9–10, pp. 69–71; *IHD*, 21; and Introduction.

99. In Watt, "Negotiations between Edward II and John XXII," 20. Requesting that the pope call a crusade against one's opponents was not uncommon in the fourteenth century; see Tyerman, *Invention of the Crusades*, 47.

Mary would be levelled against two MacConmaras twenty-five years later, the similarities can be laid at the feet of their prosecutors. Rather than some shared cult against the Virgin secretly propagated by the Irish regardless of region, surfacing twice only amid colonial prosecutions after clashes between the Irish and the colonists, and eluding contemporary native Irish sources, whether religious or secular, it seems far more probable that colonial authorities wielded accusations of heresy as a weapon against their Irish opponents in the hopes that they could enlist the papacy's aid so that outside forces, weapons, and money might at last enable them to complete the conquest begun in the twelfth century. The letter's rather clumsy identification of Irish attacks on colonial areas with heresy supports this probability, as does the fact that nearly a century later the Irish parliament asked Henry V to request the pope to call a crusade against the native Irish. This time, however, allegations of heresy were notably absent; instead the parliament justified such a request on the basis of native Irish rebellion against the king, though they had sworn allegiance to his predecessor, Richard II.[100]

The idea of using accusations of heresy against the native Irish was likely planted by Ledrede's prosecutions, with which the two men identified in the preface, the dean and the precentor of St. Patrick's, were involved, as was John Darcy, the justiciar under whom the letter was probably issued.[101] William de Nottingham became Ledrede's first supporter during Alice's defamation suit, when Ledrede changed his tactic from prosecuting her for heretical sorcery to a relapse of heresy, a tactic Nottingham may have ensured colonial authorities adopted in their case against Adducc Dubh O'Toole.[102] William de Rodyerd initially disapproved of Ledrede's actions, but before long he became the bishop's most consistent and valuable supporter.[103] At the Dublin parliament of 1324, when Ledrede helped Rodyerd resolve the Franciscan situation, Rodyerd brokered a peace between Ledrede and Arnold le Poer and soon after seconded Ledrede's case against Alice.[104] Toward the end of the *Narrative*, after Petronilla de Midia had been executed and William Outlaw imprisoned, Ledrede informed Roger Outlaw that Rodyerd was currently

---

100. Berry, *Early Statutes*, 564–67; Leland, *History of Ireland*, 2:14. The Remonstrance is careful to exculpate the Irish on similar grounds; see below.

101. Significantly, the letter does not reference Alexander de Bicknor, the archbishop of Dublin who vehemently opposed Ledrede's heresy proceedings since at least 1329 and who was absent from Ireland during Adducc's trial and execution in 1328.

102. Wright, *Contemporary Narrative*, 16.

103. Ibid., 13.

104. Curtis, *Calendar of Ormond Deeds*, 1:237–42; see chapter 3. Wright, *Contemporary Narrative*, 20–21.

undertaking proceedings of his own against heretics and their fautors.[105] This comment increases in significance given that Rodyerd was the highest rank-ing ecclesiastic in Dublin during Adducc's trial and execution, and thus most likely was his prosecutor and judge. Ledrede clearly took a favorable view of the justiciar, but Darcy's support of Ledrede's actions was mixed, depending on whose position he found most persuasive at the time.[106] These three men are the only ones the *Narrative* names as Ledrede's supporters, and as two of them are the only ones identified in connection with the letter calling for a crusade, albeit one by his office (dean) rather than his name, and the third is most likely the justiciar under whom it was issued, a connection between the letter and Ledrede's prosecution seems almost certain.

For decades colonial authorities had battled the Irish of the Wicklow mountains and particularly the O'Tooles, and they had experienced a greater scare in early 1328, when the Leinster Irish had united behind a native king. To make matters worse, various Anglo-Irish joined Irish attacks on colo-nial forces and property. Moreover, many ostensibly loyal Anglo-Irish had adopted native customs and even the Irish language, a "degeneration" against which colonial authorities had legislated since 1297.[107] The justiciar's letter suggests that Irishness itself is heresy, proclaiming the entire Irish race as a sac-rilegious people against whom a crusade must be called. The characterization of Adducc's heresy as apostasy calls to mind the charges levelled against the Irish in *Laudabiliter*, that they had fallen away from Christianity and needed to be restored to the faith by the English, a portrayal the letter specifically invoked.[108] As the colonial hold on Ireland became increasingly tenuous, Dublin leaders tried to persuade the papacy to help them complete the con-quest that it had endorsed almost two centuries earlier, claiming themselves impotent in the face of their enemies without this outside support. Those Anglo-Irish who had joined with the native Irish and became infected with their heresy, that is, became gaelicized, were equally to be the targets of this crusade, although it was presumably with them in mind that the letter ends with a request for clemency should any of the malefactors repent the error of their ways.[109]

---

105. Wright, *Contemporary Narrative*, 35.

106. Ibid., 21.

107. Berry, *Early Statutes*, 210–11; Duffy, "Problem of Degeneracy."

108. It also calls to mind Ledrede's 1328 letter describing his alleged heretics as apostates, dis-cussed above (Sayles, *Documents*, 133).

109. This concluding clemency recalls Haverings's similar final remarks regarding Philip de Braybrook; see chapter 1.

The crusade was never called (at least not while England remained a Catholic country), and the attacks of which the letter complained continued, such as an O'Toole raid on Bicknor's castle in Tallaght in 1331 where according to Clyn the dead colonists included "a Templar of the Geraldines."[110] Yet the letter seems to have aroused some sympathy, as in 1332 the pope sent a bull to Bicknor that excommunicated the Leinster Irish and put their lands under interdict.[111] The decree was delivered by a Brother Richard McCormegan, who had recently attempted to negotiate with them on behalf of the colonial authorities on two separate occasions, and earlier had attempted to do the same with the Connacht Irish.[112] The Irish, however, disregarded the sentence and continued their attacks. Yet John also exhibited considerable equanimity when he advised Edward on July 1, 1331, that, since Ireland has "two sorts of people, pure Irish, and those of a mixed race, care should be taken to have governors and officers of the same respectively" if the country were to be properly reformed.[113] Such a response sharply diverges from the one sought by the justiciar's letter, but that letter was not the only representation he had heard of ethnic relations in Ireland. Early in his pontificate, he had received a far more detailed and sophisticated account of Anglo-Irish abuses of the native Irish known as the "Remonstrance of Irish Princes," on which the justiciar's letter is clearly modeled and hence is called the Counter-Remonstrance.

The Irish Remonstrance

In 1317 the Ulster Irish led by Dónal O'Neill wrote a scathing critique of English and especially Anglo-Irish conduct since (and even before) their arrival in Ireland. Recognizing that the papacy had a much closer relationship with English rulers and thus had been subjected to the "snarling and viperous slanders of the English and their unfair and false charges" against the Irish, the native Irish sought to plead their own case to the curia.[114] They reminded John of Ireland's long and glorious history as a beacon of the faith and its humble obedience to Rome prior to 1170. They acknowledged that Adrian IV, "English not as much in his origin as in his feeling and nature," had donated Ireland to Henry II, but said he had done so "at the false and utterly wicked suggestion" of Henry, a man under whom and

---

110. Clyn, 22; see chapter 1.
111. *CSM*, 2:376–77.
112. Frame, *Ireland and Britain*, 264.
113. *CPL*, 2:500.
114. Bower, *Scotichronicon*, 384–85 (Martin Smith's translation).

perhaps even by whom a saint was murdered while attempting to defend the church.[115] Rather than being rewarded with lordship over another land, the letter argues, Henry should have had his own kingdom taken away for Becket's murder; the path chosen by Adrian, "tragically blinded by his affection for the English," had caused justice to be abandoned and the Irish to be handed over for slavery.[116] The letter then details how Henry, his successors, and their ministers had more than failed to uphold their promise to protect the Irish church, to root out vice, and to promote the moral development of Ireland.[117] It describes how "the middle nation" practiced the vilest tyranny over the Irish, denying them access to law and murdering them at will, be they clerics or lay, in church or at home, and even on Trinity Sunday; nor were such acts considered crimes, the letter states, but were praised and rewarded. For each accusation, the letter supplies specific examples, virtually all of which can be independently verified: Peter de Bermingham's massacre of the O'Connors as the final course of a feast to which he had invited them at his home;[118] Thomas de Clare's decapitation of Brian Ruad O'Briain, *suum compatrinum* (his co-godfather), after dragging him by horses' tails following a banquet at his home, Bunratty Castle;[119] Geoffrey de Pencoyt's murder of the MacMurrough brothers as they slept in his home;[120] and so on.

---

115. Ibid., 386–87 (Martin Smith's translation).

116. Ibid., 386, see also 388. As Phillips notes, this compresses time so that Adrian's decree in about 1155, Henry's arrival in 1171, and the murder of Becket in 1170 are treated as if they all occurred in the same year (ibid., 470).

117. According to a 1347 jury, Maurice fitz Thomas made a similar indictment of Edward III to the pope, that Edward was not complying with the terms of *Laudabiliter* and thus should be deprived of lordship of Ireland (Sayles, "Legal Proceedings," 20, 44).

118. This occurred in 1305. For payment given to Bermingham for his murder of the O'Connors and their heads, see *CJR*, 2:82; for the poem praising (or condemning, according to Lucas) Bermingham for this deed, see Lucas, *Anglo-Irish Poems*, 153–55, 209. See also Clyn, 11, and *CSM*, 2:332.

119. This occurred in 1277. See *CT*, 2:10; *AC*, 166–67; *ACl*, 271; *NHI*, 2:253, and Nic Ghiollamhaith, "Dynastic Warfare," 83–85. Perhaps Donnchad, Brian Ruad's grandson, reminded O'Neill of the murder when he went to join him in 1315; see below. Martin Smith translates *compatrinum* as "godfather" (Bower, *Scotichronicon*, 395), but the prefex *com-* has been added to *patrinum* ("godfather"), and multiple godparents could be given to a child. The meaning seems to be that Brian (who was roughly twenty years Thomas's senior) was Thomas's godfather but not his only godfather; it could also indicate that Brian and Thomas together stood as godfather to another child. Such connections were considered as binding as blood by the medieval church, and thus Thomas committed a form of patricide or fratricide.

120. This was in 1282; one of the murdered MacMurroughs was Art, the father of the Dónal who revolted in 1328. See Clyn, 9; *NHI*, 2:259–60; Frame, "The Justiciar and the Murder of the MacMurroughs." These three examples are provided in Bower, *Scotichronicon*, 394. Phillips suggests that a dossier of colonial abuses of the Irish may have been prepared for years prior to the Remonstrance's composition, possibly with the intent of voicing them at the Council of Vienne ("The Remonstrance Revisited," 20); for similar complaints made by anonymous ecclesiastics of Ireland at the Council of Vienne, see Ehrle, "Ein Bruchstück," 370–71, and chapter 1.

Much of the Remonstrance focuses on religious injustices committed by the English against the Irish, beginning with their using a pretense of religion to mask their intentions of the medieval equivalent of ethnic cleansing.[121] Fleeing English persecution, the Irish have become like hunted animals, their wild and impoverished condition endangering not only their bodies but also their souls. The English, who purported to exemplify virtuous and righteous living, have instead trained the Irish so that "their holy and dovish simplicity has been miraculously changed into snakish cunning due to their cohabitation with and the reprobate example of" the English.[122] The letter closely summarizes a statute passed at the 1310 Kilkenny parliament that forbade native Irish from joining religious houses "in the land of peace among the English," a policy that, the letter asserts, had already been common practice among the English, even though many of the houses from which the Irish were excluded had in fact been founded by the Irish themselves.[123] Moreover, the letter maintains,

> Not only their laity and secular clergy but also some of their religious preach the heresy that it is no more a sin to kill an Irish person than to kill a dog or any other brute beast. And in the assertion of this heretical argument, some of their monastics fearlessly declare that if they should happen to kill an Irish person (as often does happen), they would not abstain from celebrating mass for even a single day on account of the murder.[124]

As with crimes committed by secular colonists, the letter provides examples of religious who practiced what they preached: the Cistercians of Granard (Abbeylara) in Ardagh and of Inch in Down, as well as a Franciscan, Simon le Mercer of Drogheda, brother of the bishop of Connor, who made such heretical assertions before Edward Bruce. It then continues that both secular and regular fall from this heresy into the error that they can commit armed robbery against the Irish with impunity and that any who condemned this error were consequently declared an enemy of the king, outlawed and liable to the death penalty.

---

121. Bower, *Scotichronicon*, 388.
122. Ibid., 390.
123. Ibid., 392.
124. Ibid., 394–96; for a related heresy accusation by the French against Boniface VIII, see Tierney, *Crisis of Church and State*, 190. The view persisted in colonial Ireland; later in the century Richard fitz Ralph, the archbishop of Armagh, had to remind the Anglo-Irish "that killing native Irish people might not be a felony in English law, but was nevertheless a sin in the eyes of God" (Frame, "Exporting State and Nation," 151).

The specific condemnation of Cistercians and a Franciscan holds particular significance, as these two orders experienced the most severe ethnic tensions of the religious orders in Ireland. Beginning in the mid-twelfth century with the first Irish Cistercians' complaint to St. Malachy, "We are Gaels, not Gauls," to protest his penchant for French architecture in the building of Mellifont and also the quick departure of most if not all of the French Cistercians who had accompanied Malachy from Clairvaux to help him establish the order in Ireland, a land they considered barbaric, ethnic tensions had existed in the Cistercian order in Ireland.[125] They reached a murderous pitch in the first half of the thirteenth century, when in 1216 visitors appointed by the abbot of Clairvaux to investigate abuses and laxity in the houses in Ireland had been prevented from entering Mellifont (the mother house in Ireland) and Jerpoint (close to Kilkenny) by violence and riots, a resistance openly supported by the abbots of four other Cistercian houses in Ireland.[126] Ten years later, when the general chapter attempted to replace native Irish abbots with English Cistercians, the Irish brothers opposed the replacements, even to the point of murder and maiming.[127] Tensions remained a century later, as the Remonstrance indicates, although the attacks it alleges by the monks of Granard and Inch have not yet been identified. We do hear complaints from the other side, however; for example, four years after the Remonstrance was issued, Edward II complained to the general chapter about Irish Cistercians forbidding Englishmen from entering their houses, discrimination done "in contempt of the king, in opprobrium of all his nation [*lingua*] and in subversion of his lordship."[128]

According to English Benedictine accounts, ethnic tensions incited Irish and Anglo-Irish Franciscans to attack each other so violently that sixteen brothers were killed and many others wounded at a provincial chapter meeting in 1291 in Cork, although this riot may be a product of anti-mendicant propaganda.[129] While such a murderous meeting might be an overstatement, clearly tensions between the "two nations" ran high. Toward the end of the thirteenth century, Nicholas Cusack, the Anglo-Irish Franciscan bishop of Kildare, warned Edward I that "certain insolent religious of the Irish tongue"

125. Bernard of Clairvaux, *Opera*, 365; translation by F. X. Martin in *NHI*, 2:155. See also Meersseman, "Two Unknown Confraternity Letters."

126. O'Dwyer, *Conspiracy of Mellifont*, 16.

127. Ibid., 19–21. See also the letters of Stephen of Lexington, who attempted to resolve the situation (*Letters from Ireland*), and Watt, *The Church and the Two Nations*, 85–107.

128. Quoted (in English) in Watt, *The Church and the Two Nations*, 189; see also *CCR* (1318–23): 404; *CJR*, 2:350–51.

129. Cotter, *Friars Minor in Ireland*, 33–40. Ó Clabaigh seconds Cotter's findings (*Friars in Ireland*, 33–34).

were secretly meeting with Irish kings and inciting them to rebellion.[130] In another letter he fulminated specifically against Franciscans "who in the Irish language spread the seeds of rebellion."[131] The matter took on even greater importance during the Bruce invasion, the time period of the Remonstrance. In 1316, Edward II wrote to the Franciscan minister general, demanding action against Irish brothers who supported Bruce and spurred the Irish to rebellion, or else he would have to apply a "heavy hand" to restrain their evil, and the following year he beseeched the pope for an English Franciscan as archbishop of Cashel to help combat the rebellious Irish.[132] Phillips has proposed that the Franciscan named by the Remonstrance, Simon le Mercer of Drogheda, may have been acting in an official or semiofficial capacity for the English and colonial government when he visited Edward Bruce and made his "heretical" assertions about the Irish.[133] Moreover, he has tentatively identified the author of the Remonstrance as a Franciscan from Armagh, Michael Mac Lochlainn, which would further indicate ethnic tensions within the order.[134] Francis Cotter has suggested that the massacre of the guardian and twenty-two friars in Dundalk by Bruce's army when they took the town in 1315 as well as the destruction of the friary in Castledermot in 1317 may have been retribution for Simon's remark.[135] The remark became widely known, being repeated, mutatis mutandis, by colonists in the Counter-Remonstrance and attested to and condemned, along with other perspectives attributed to the Anglo-Irish in the Remonstrance, by Richard fitz Ralph, the archbishop of Armagh, nearly fifty years later.[136]

The Remonstrance admits that the Irish are not entirely blameless in the current troubles besetting their country, acknowledging that fifty thousand people "of each nation" have been killed in warfare since the time of *Laudabiliter*, a situation that it says will continue unless a solution is enacted.[137]

---

130. FitzMaurice and Little, *Materials for the History*, 52–53 (their translation).

131. *CDI*, 4:2035.

132. Rymer, vol. 2, pt. 1, p. 99; see also Theiner, 194, and chapters 2 and 3.

133. Phillips, "The Remonstrance Revisited," 18; see also Bower, *Scotichronichon*, 476. Simon was acting for the king in 1317 (FitzMaurice and Little, *Materials for the History*, 101–2).

134. Phillips, "The Remonstrance Revisited," 18–20; see above.

135. Cotter, *Friars Minor in Ireland*, 43; see below.

136. Walsh, *Richard FitzRalph*, 285, 325, 342; Frame, "Exporting State and Nation," 151; see also *NHI*, 2:242.

137. Bower, *Scotichronicon*, 388. Another letter reputed to be from Dónal O'Neill, this time to a Desmond king, also acknowledges the culpability of the Irish for their suffering particularly because of their infighting; the letter further declares that the English pope Adrian "deserved to be called antichrist rather than pope" (Wood, "Letter from Domnal O'Neill," 142). The letter is most likely an eighteenth-century forgery, however (Ó Murchadha, "Is the O'Neill-MacCarthy Letter of 1317 a Forgery?"; cf. *NHI*, 2:245n4).

It mentions two possibilities that the Irish had already proposed to Edward: that they hold their land directly from him in accordance with the terms of *Laudabiliter* (a copy of which being appended), or that he divide the land with some semblance of fairness between the native Irish and the Anglo-Irish "in order to avoid profuse bloodshed."[138] As they have received no reply from Edward or his council, the letter adds a remarkable third: Dónal O'Neill, whom the Remonstrance names "king of Ulster," renounced his own rights to the high kingship of Ireland in favor of Edward Bruce, who had already been inaugurated as *ard rí* (high king) through O'Neill's support two years previously.[139] The letter emphasizes the fundamental cultural connections between Ireland (Major Scotia) and Scotland (Minor Scotia) through language, custom, and blood, whereas the Irish and the English, who could not be more dissimilar, "have a natural enmity for each other" arising from centuries of mutual slaughter.[140] The authors apparently found it politically expedient to overlook the fact that the Bruces were half Norman themselves and undoubtedly were more comfortable with French than Gaelic.[141]

Although the Remonstrance takes a variety of attitudes toward Edward II and his predecessors, ultimately it argues in favor of war against him and especially against the Anglo-Irish, whom the letter twice refers to as the "middle nation."[142] The letter claims that the Irish have attempted to be loyal subjects of the king of England in accordance with *Laudabiliter*, but the Anglo-Irish have caused too great a division between the native Irish and the English king, to the detriment of his kingdom.[143] Moreover, Edward's own negligence of Ireland and the Irish compels them to attack the king and their enemies in Ireland. The letter carefully defends this right and exculpates the Irish princes according to the canonical understanding of a just war, maintaining somewhat speciously that neither they nor their fathers have paid homage to Edward or his fathers, nor have they sworn any oath of fealty to the English.[144] Yet the letter skirts an issue of great importance to the recipient: it

---

138. Bower, *Scotichronicon*, 398.

139. Ibid., 400.

140. Ibid., 398, 402.

141. Significantly, the Declaration of Arbroath, written a few years after the Remonstrance, with which it shares many similarities, often hailed as the birth cry of Scottish nationalism, deliberately omits reference to Ireland in its romantic reconstruction of the Scottish past (Fergusson, *Declaration of Arbroath*, 6–7).

142. Bower, *Scotichronicon*, 392 (which claims that the Anglo-Irish call themselves the middle nation) and 400.

143. Ibid., 398 and 396.

144. Ibid., 398, 478–79; Muldoon, "The Remonstrance of Irish Princes." Most Irish kings submitted to Henry II in 1171–72, although the northern kings of the Cenél nEógain and the Cenél Conaill were notable exceptions; see Introduction.

was arguing in favor of the kingship of a man excommunicated, along with his brother Robert Bruce and their supporters generally, for their own efforts against the English king in Minor Scotia. No early fourteenth-century pope was going to favor Irish rulers over an English king, least of all for a Bruce, yet the Remonstrance seems to have had some effect on John XXII.

On May 30, 1318, John forwarded to Edward the letter he had received from the Irish detailing their sufferings at the hands of Henry II and his successors and urged him to redress the situation. He reminded Edward of God's particular compassion and love for innocent victims and that the fortunes of the mighty can swiftly fall due to their unrighteousness.[145] While the potential threat seems all the more menacing since the king held his dominions as the pope's vassal, John had no intention of removing his recognition of Edward's right to the lordship of Ireland. The pope's position was serious enough that it could not be ignored, but Edward simply replied that any injustices in Ireland were committed without his knowledge and against his will.[146] He promised to investigate, however, and claimed that he would henceforth ensure that the Irish were treated fairly.[147] Perhaps Edward even intended to make good on his promise, but a reform of Ireland that suited Edward's interests and those of his ministers would hardly be to the benefit of the native Irish.

The Remonstrance struck a chord elsewhere, as the Counter-Remonstrance makes evident. The Anglo-Irish understandably felt attacked, for they bore the brunt of the Remonstrance's blame. And while many of their complaints against the native Irish were well founded, as even the Remonstrance acknowledges violent resistance to the colonists and the annals are strewn with such examples, the overall impression of the Counter-Remonstrance is that of empty echoed recriminations, misrepresentations, and myopic bias. Its inversion of the Remonstrance's claim that Anglo-Irish were preaching (and practicing) the heresy that it was no sin to kill or rob their enemy rings fairly hollow, particularly since it is not supported by evidence, as it is in the Remonstrance. Its allegation that the Irish maintained that English dominion over Ireland was due to "false suggestion and false bulls" distorts the perspective of the Remonstrance. While it clearly condemns Henry II for his "false suggestion" to Adrian that convinced him to issue *Laudabiliter*, the entire thrust of the Remonstrance rests on its acceptance of the bull

---

145. Theiner, 201; see also *CPL*, 2:440.

146. John also instructed two papal legates, the original recipients of the Remonstrance, to "assist" Edward in his handling of this matter (Theiner, 201–2; *CPL*, 2:440).

147. Rymer, vol. 2, pt. 1, p. 158.

as legitimate, although misguided and unjust. This accusation echoes the claim made against Adducc Dubh O'Toole, that he proclaimed the sanctity of the papacy to be "false," and points to the colonial authorities' agenda in accusing him as the representative of his entire ethnicity's apostasy from Christianity, which they presented as heresy. This confused conception of heresy also surfaces in a petition to Edward about the same time as the Remonstrance, in which the Anglo-Irish described the pre-Christian Irish as "eretiks."[148] This petition also appended a copy of *Laudabiliter*, and while, unlike the Counter-Remonstrance or Ledrede's remarks in 1324, it acknowledged Ireland's Christian past prior to the arrival of the English, it too repeated the claim of *Laudabiliter* that the Irish needed to be restored to the faith by the English. Unlike his predecessor, however, John did not endorse that view, although he fully accepted English dominion of Ireland. While he would not exert himself to ensure that the injustices against the Irish were ended, let alone redressed, neither would he second the obviously self-serving call for a crusade by the colonists, particularly since he had recently heard a scathing account about the colonists themselves from another source, Richard de Ledrede.

The MacConmaras: Blasphemy as Heresy on the Irish Frontier

Issues of Irish identity, colonial insecurity, and heretical depravity combined again in the trial of the MacConmaras at Bunratty Castle twenty-five years after Adducc's execution. Their trial followed a MacConmara and O'Brien defeat by colonists and was conducted by Roger Cradock, bishop of Waterford, who was well outside his diocese. The only charge recorded against them was an insult against Mary, for which Cradock convicted them of heresy and apparently released them to the justiciar, Thomas de Rokeby, or his representatives; less than thirty years after Petronilla de Midia became Ireland's first known executed heretic, these two men became the last. The bishop of Killaloe was curiously uninvolved, but the archbishop of Cashel, his metropolitan and a fellow Irishman, is said to have marched an army to Waterford and attacked Cradock in his private quarters, a more extreme but less prolonged response than Bicknor's; the latter reveals the disruptive impact of heresy on ecclesiastical hierarchy within the colony's confines, the former on its frontier. Rokeby's Irish policies, the battle over Bunratty, and the histories of the two bishops and their metropolitan help clarify the dynamics involved in the MacConmaras' case, but it remains obscure.

---

148. Sayles, *Documents*, 99–100. This petition was issued sometime between 1317 and 1319.

Bunratty Castle and Control of Thomond

Located less than ten miles to the northwest of Limerick on what was then an island, Bunratty was critical for control of Thomond (north Munster), particularly since in clear weather nothing could move upon the Shannon between Limerick and the ocean without being seen from its walls. A castle was first built there in the mid-thirteenth century by Robert de Muscegros; by 1287 it was home to 226 burgages.[149] In 1270 Brian Ruad O'Brien, king of Thomond, increased attacks on Bunratty and other settlements, costing the colonial government dearly not only in lives and property but also in the expense of four military expeditions against him in five years.[150] In an effort to establish a more permanent and secure colonial presence in the area, Edward I granted Bunratty along with the rest of Thomond to Thomas de Clare in January 1276.[151] Thomas exchanged Muscegros's wooden castle for one of stone and otherwise greatly enhanced Bunratty's defenses.[152] He also allied with Brian Ruad, who had been ousted from his kingdom by his nephew, Tairdelbach. This alliance proved short-lived, as the following year Thomas murdered Brian, which the Irish Remonstrance cited as an example of the unprovoked and unfathomable evil of the Anglo-Irish.[153] Shortly thereafter, however, Brian's sons made peace with Thomas, and from then until 1315 Clann Briain Ruaid was consistently allied with Thomas de Clare and his son, Richard.[154]

Clann Briain Ruaid was not the only O'Brien faction, however. Tairdelbach O'Brien and his offspring and supporters, known as Clann Taidc (after Tairdelbach's father), opposed the de Clares as vehemently as they opposed their rival kin. In an arrangement typical of the Irish frontier, Clann Taidc allied with the de Burghs, the earls of Ulster, who opposed the de Clares due to their alliance with the Geraldines, and together Clann Taidc and the de Burghs waged war on the de Clares and their stronghold of Bunratty.[155] Clann Taidc also had the support of the MacConmaras and the O'Deas, two of the primary subclans of the O'Briens, as well as various other native Irish families. The battles between the two O'Brien factions and their allies until

---

149. Orpen, *Ireland under the Normans*, 4:76, 104; Share, *Bunratty*, 13, 22.
150. *AC*, 156–57; *AI*, 370–71; *CDI*, 2:211; Nic Ghiollamhaith, "Dynastic Warfare," 74–75.
151. *CDI*, 2:217; Orpen, *Ireland under the Normans*, 4:66–67.
152. Share, *Bunratty*, 22–23.
153. *CT*, 2:9–10; *AC*, 166–67; *ACl*, 271; *AI*, 372–73; Bower, *Scotichronicon*, 394; see above.
154. *CT*, 2:10; Nic Ghiollamhaith, "Dynastic Warfare," 84.
155. Nic Ghiollamhaith, "Dynastic Warfare," 75; see also chapter 4. For discussion of the various marital as well as military alliances between the de Burghs and Clann Taidc, see Orpen, *Ireland under the Normans*, 4:83–84.

1318 are described in a remarkable text, *Caithréim Thoirdhealbhaigh* ("The Triumphs of Tairdelbach"), "the most vivid picture that has come down to us of the life of medieval Ireland at war," told from the perspective of the native Irish, in particular Clann Taidc and their MacConmara support-ers.[156] In 1312, Richard de Burgh and Richard de Clare made peace with each other and arranged a partition of Thomond between the O'Briens, but the MacConmaras continued the feud against other native Irish, and before the year was out the rival O'Briens had resumed their war as well.[157] In 1314 another attempt at partition and peace was made, but this proved even more ephemeral than the one two years before, and the following year saw a tremendous shift in the various alliances, both among the native Irish and between the Irish and the Anglo-Irish.

The turning point in 1315 was the arrival of Bruce and his Scottish forces, which ended the association between Clann Briain Ruaid and the de Clares. Donnchad, Brian Ruad's grandson and chief of his clan, chose to take advantage of their arrival to attack the English, including "that cantan-kerous restless-roving grasping quibbler de Clare," and consequently went north to Bruce and O'Neill to enlist their aid for his plans for his own kingdom.[158] Meanwhile, Clare allied not only with the de Burghs, but also with Muirchertach O'Brien, Tairdelbach's son and successor. Enticed by Donnchad's description of Thomond, the Scots went with him into Munster and were confronted by Muirchertach's men at Castleconnell in April 1317. After about a week of skirmishes, the Scots learned that Roger Mortimer had landed at Youghal with a sizeable army and promptly retreated to Ulster. Left somewhat stranded by the departure of the Scots, Donnchad neverthe-less proceeded to force Clann Taidc from Quin to Bunratty, at which point Richard de Clare arranged an armistice between the clans.[159] Clare then went to Dublin to attend parliament, which Clann Taidc and *Caithréim Thoird-healbhaigh* regarded as an attempt to sell out Clann Taidc in favor of Clann Briain Ruaid; so, with protection from Burgh, Muirchertach followed him to parliament to plead his own case, to remind the colonial administrators of his loyalty to the king, and to accuse Clare of double-dealing with the Scots

---

156. Robin Flower, in the introduction to *CT*, xvi. The *Annals of Inisfallen* also documents the feud, particularly from 1311 to 1318 (*AI*, 406–29). For the authorship and perspective of *Caithréim Thoirdhealbhaigh*, see Nic Ghiollamhaith, "Dynastic Warfare," 76, 82–83, and Nic Ghiollamhaith, "Kings and Vassals."

157. *CT*, 2:53–54; Orpen, *Ireland under the Normans*, 4:84–85.

158. *CT*, 2:76, 83; Nic Ghiollamhaith, "Dynastic Warfare," 84.

159. *CT*, 2:85–86; Orpen, *Ireland under the Normans*, 4:89; Nic Ghiollamhaith, "Dynastic Warfare," 85.

and Clann Briain Ruaid.[160] Muirchertach had little success, but his failure in parliament was soon eclipsed by resounding successes on the battlefield.

In August 1317, while Muirchertach was in Dublin, his brother Diarmait fought Donnchad and Clann Briain Ruaid near Corcumroe Abbey. According to *Caithréim Thoirdhealbhaigh*, the battle was preceded by omens that combine Christian and pagan elements, including a hideous hag who prophesied doom to Clann Briain Ruaid, one of several such women who appear in the text, their appearances shaped by the nature of their news.[161] Donnchad lamented the battle before it began, bemoaning that kin have come to mutual destruction of each other "merely to give the pale English charter and conveyance of all countries of the Gael."[162] The destruction, however, was not mutual; it was a near annihilation of Clann Briain Ruaid, whose hopes survived in the escape of Donnchad's brother Brian Bán.[163] The following May Clann Taidc had an even greater victory at Dysert O'Dea, again presaged by a supernatural female. Prior to his attack, Richard de Clare saw a woman washing out bloody armor in a stream, a familiar harbinger from Irish secular tales; he had his Irish allies, who spoke her language, ask her identity and purpose, to which she replied that she came from hell and was tending the armor of Clare's men, nearly all of whom would be slain in battle and would come to share her home. Clare tried to comfort his men by declaring that her words would do them no harm "because a witch cannot be truthful," a rare reference to witchcraft beliefs in Ireland around the time of the Kyteler case.[164] She, however, was not a witch but a spirit, and her words proved true, as Clare was killed along with many of his men in a decisive defeat by the O'Deas and their late arriving allies, including Muirchertach O'Brien.[165] According to *Caithréim Thoirdhealbhaigh*, the Irish victors hounded their enemies to Bunratty, which they found burning by the hand of Clare's wife Johanna in response to the news of her husband's death. The text claims that from then until the time of composition, roughly 1345, "never a one of their breed has come back to look after it."[166] Colonial forces remained at the castle for thirty-eight days after Clare's death on May 10, 1318, however, and not until 1332 was the castle captured and destroyed by

---

160. *CT*, 2:86, 117.

161. *CT*, 2:93–94; see also 29, 124–25, 133. The women represent both supernatural soothsayers and the sovereignty Goddess (i.e., incarnation of the sovereignty of Ireland).

162. *CT*, 2:90.

163. I.e., "Brian the White," as his grandfather was "Brian the Red."

164. *CT*, 2:125.

165. Simms, "Battle of Dysert O'Dea," 64–65.

166. *CT*, 2:130. For the date of composition, see Nic Ghiollamhaith, "Kings and Vassals," 212.

FIGURE 10.   Bunratty Castle, rebuilt in the fifteenth century, site of the MacConmaras' execution in 1353. Photo by the author.

the O'Briens and MacConmaras.[167] Richard de Clare's death at Dysert O'Dea left a minor who died three years later as his heir; the division of the de Clare inheritance among heiresses combined with the Irish victory in 1332 "finally extinguished all hope of establishing Anglo-Norman rule in Thomond, and for upwards of two centuries the influence there of the English Crown was negligible."[168]

Even with the removal of the de Clares, Bunratty and Thomond remained a hotbed of contention. Motivated by his hatred of the de Burghs, his desire to bring as much of Ireland as possible under his control, and his alliance with Brian Bán O'Brien, Maurice fitz Thomas attempted to appropriate it for himself, including an attack on Bunratty in 1325 in which the constable's eyes and tongue were cut out.[169] With fitz Thomas's help, Brian Bán continued his clan's opposition to Clann Taidc and their allies, including defeating an army led by Muirchertach, William de Burgh (earl of Ulster), and Tairdelbach O'Connor, the king of Connacht, in 1328. At some point the chief of the MacConmaras apparently switched sides from Clann Taidc

---

167. Simms, "Battle of Dysert O'Dea," 65; Clyn, 24.

168. Orpen, *Ireland under the Normans*, 4:94; see also Otway-Ruthven, *A History of Medieval Ireland*, 237.

169. Sayles, "Legal Proceedings," 8–9; see chapter 4.

to Clann Briain Ruaid as he was said to have joined Brian in Kilkenny on July 7, 1326, in the conspiracy to make fitz Thomas king.[170] According to a jury held at Limerick in 1331, fitz Thomas incited colonists to attack the king's forces and capture the castle that very year.[171] Presumably he would have participated in the O'Brien and MacConmara attack that razed the castle the following year had he not been imprisoned in Dublin Castle for his various misdeeds against the colonial government. Part of his "parole" included leading an expedition against his near twenty-year ally, Brian Bán, in 1335.[172] Consequently, Brian came to terms with Muirchertach, and the rivalry experienced relative peace until 1343, when Muirchertach died and was succeeded by his brother Diarmait as king of Thomond.[173]

Brian Bán protested the succession, possibly because a term of the peace between himself and Muirchertach in 1336 stipulated that Brian would succeed Muirchertach; with the help of MacConmara and others, Brian ousted Diarmait, but soon thereafter MacConmara reversed his position and reinstated Diarmait. Thus twice in the same year MacConmara acted as kingmaker in Thomond, a role *Caithréim Thoirdhealbhaigh* portrays the family as playing since 1242.[174] Whether or not the MacConmaras actually had such power in thirteenth-century Thomond is unclear, but *Caithréim Thoirdhealbhaigh*'s emphasis on their importance indicates how invaluable they had become by the mid-fourteenth century. Diarmait O'Brien remained king until he was deposed in 1360, no doubt "heavily aware of his dependence on MacConmara for his kingship."[175] In 1345, about when *Caithréim Thoirdhealbhaigh* was written and eight years before two MacConmaras were executed for heresy, MacConmara seems to have been more powerful in Thomond than Diarmait O'Brien, judging by the forces they brought with them into the justiciar's army against their former ally fitz Thomas: MacConmara had a man-at-arms, 77 hobelars, and 164 footmen; O'Brien 50 hobelars and 80 footmen.[176] Less than a decade later, when the justiciar's army was arrayed against them, MacConmara was identified as the king of Thomond, not Diarmait O'Brien.[177] After winning the battle, the colonial forces promptly restored Bunratty, where they executed two of MacConmara's men for "heresy."

---

170. Sayles, "Legal Proceedings," 12; Nic Ghiollamhaith, "Kings and Vassals," 211; see chapter 4.
171. Sayles, "Legal Proceedings," 10.
172. Clyn, 27; see chapter 4. Turnabout was fairplay, though; see below.
173. Nic Ghiollamhaith, "Kings and Vassals," 211.
174. *CT*, 2:6, 10, 32, 47–48; Nic Ghiollamhaith, "Kings and Vassals," 209; see also 211–12.
175. Nic Ghiollamhaith, "Kings and Vassals," 212.
176. RC 8/23, 511–12; Nic Ghiollamhaith, "Kings and Vassals," 212n25.
177. London, British Library, Cotton Vespasian B XI, fols 127v, 133r.

Justiciar Rokeby

For over fifteen years before Thomas de Rokeby's appointment, Ireland's colonial administration was in a state of near constant flux. "Justiciars and their deputies were being continually changed, and a tenure period of a year or more was exceptional."[178] During this time, relations between colonists and the English reached a low point; according to Pembridge's entry for 1341, "before this time there had never been such remarkable and palpable hostility between the English of England and the English of Ireland."[179] The conflict was sparked by Edward III's intended restructuring of the colonial administration, including an order to replace all officials with a vested interest in Ireland with Englishmen whose lands, family, and loyalty lay entirely in England.[180] His plans outraged colonists, who responded with their own grievances against English ministers in Ireland, particularly justiciars who had no notion of warfare and its nature in Ireland and officials who came to exploit Ireland for personal gain, unhindered by any concern for the colony.[181] Largely due to such governance, the colonists claimed, one-third of what had been conquered by the English under Edward's predecessors, specifically including Bunratty, had since been lost to the native Irish.[182] The king responded favorably to the colonists' complaints and cancelled his plan, but it was not until Rokeby's appointment that Ireland received a shrewd and successful administrator as well as a skilled military leader as justiciar.[183]

Rokeby had extensive experience in Scottish wars and the administration of the English borders when he arrived as justiciar in December 1349. He quickly dealt with problematic royal ministers, brought the Leinster Irish and their hibernicized allies temporarily into the king's peace, led campaigns against Irish and English rebels in Ossory and Uriel as well, and worked to reform the civil administration.[184] In 1351, he held councils in Dublin and Kilkenny that produced a series of ordinances consisting of twenty-five clauses, nineteen of which would be repeated almost verbatim in the Statute of Kilkenny fifteen years later.[185] In response to "grievous complaints of

---

178. *NHI*, 2:380.

179. *CSM*, 2:383. For a thorough discussion of the conflict, see Frame, "English Policies and Anglo-Irish Attitudes"; and Frame, *English Lordship*, 242–61.

180. *CCR* (1341–43): 184–85.

181. *CCR* (1341–43): 509–16; Berry, *Early Statutes*, 332–63.

182. Berry, *Early Statutes*, 334–37.

183. *NHI*, 2:381; Watt notes that Ralph d'Ufford deserves honorable mention (in *NHI*, 2:380–81). For an overview of Rokeby's career in Ireland, see Otway-Ruthven, "Ireland in the 1350s."

184. *CCR* (1349–54): 163, 205; Curtis, "The Clan System," 116–17; Otway-Ruthven, "Ireland in the 1350s," 48–49.

185. Berry, *Early Statutes*, 374–97.

common folk," the ordinances attempted to eradicate various Anglo-Irish abuses, such as the keeping of private armies in lands of peace, making or breaking truces with the native Irish independent of the official position of the justiciar, and absenteeism. The Anglo-Irish were ordered to follow English law alone, rather than Brehon (i.e., native Irish) law; the ordinances echo Edward I's description of Brehon law as "detestable to God and so contrary to all law that they ought not to be called laws."[186] Furthermore, the Anglo-Irish were forbidden to marry, foster their children, or in any other manner enter into alliances with Anglo-Irish or native Irish enemies of the king, a position that would become more extreme and anti-Irish in the Statute of Kilkenny.[187]

The Execution of the MacConmaras and its Aftermath

Little is known about the campaign that precipitated the deaths of the two MacConmaras. Rokeby began preparing an extensive campaign against the Munster Irish in September 1352.[188] His primary target was Diarmait MacCarthy, lord of Muskerry and son of the king of Desmond, whom he defeated by January.[189] As part of Rokeby's force travelled from Limerick to Askeaton via the Shannon, his campaign against MacConmara apparently coincided with the one against MacCarthy; at any rate, it must have preceded his campaign against the Leinster Irish in September 1353.[190] The late entry in Chronicle A of the "Kilkenny Chronicle" provides a solitary record of the campaign in Thomond and the fate of two MacConmaras that followed it.

Chronicle A records the entry twice in the same ink and hand on folios 127v and 133r; it is likely that the scribe started to write the entry on 133r but, after realizing he did not have sufficient space, began again on 127v.[191] Bernadette Williams has identified multiple chronicles within the "Kilkenny Chronicle," so labelled by Robin Flower in his 1931 edition of the annals.[192] Chronicle A (fols. 126–34) covers the years 1264 to 1322, with the 1353

186. Prynne, 3:1218–19; Otway-Ruthven, "Request of the Irish," 262; Berry, *Early Statutes*, 388–89.

187. Berry, *Early Statutes*, 386–87.

188. For an overview of this campaign, see Otway-Ruthven, "Ireland in the 1350s," 50–51.

189. As with MacConmara and Thomond, London, British Library, Cotton Vespasian B XI, fols. 127v, 133r, inaccurately identifies "McDermound" as king of Munster.

190. Otway-Ruthven, "Ireland in the 1350s," 50.

191. Williams, "The Kilkenny Chronicle," 78. Both have been printed by FitzMaurice and Little, *Materials for the History*, 144. Flower printed only the version on 133r ("Manuscripts of Irish Interest," 336).

192. Flower, "Manuscripts of Irish Interest."

entry being a later addition; the chronicler who composed the entries for the years up to 1316 was likely an Anglo-Irish Franciscan from Castleder-mot friary who started writing after 1310.[193] After the Bruce destruction of Castledermot friary, the chronicle seems to have remained with Franciscans but moved nearer to Dublin, with various hands contributing to it, but the entries suggest that by 1321 it had returned to the Castledermot area.[194] The 1353 entry continues these trends, as Rokeby died in 1357 at Kilkea Castle, close to Castledermot, and the original chronicler was particularly interested in the O'Briens of Thomond.[195]

The entry on 133r is considerably shorter than the version on 127v, stating only that in 1353 Justiciar Rokeby subdued MacConmara and MacCarthy, "and in the same year two heretics were burned who committed contumacy against the Blessed Virgin." The identity of these two heretics is not recorded, nor is that of their judge, nor their place of execution, nor any connection with Rokeby's campaigns. Fortunately, the scribe decided to elaborate on 127v. Here the men are described as "two Irishmen of the clan Kollanes," another name for the MacConmaras, possibly to differentiate them from "the MacConmara," that is, their chief.[196] This entry also specifies the recently restored Bunratty as the site where they were convicted of and executed for heresy, "videlicet de contumelia in beatam virginem Mariam per modum humani coytus commissa." The Latin literally states that the insult (*contumelia*) against Mary was committed by human intercourse; presumably the scribe intended that the MacConmaras claimed either that Mary commit-ted human intercourse or that she was begotten by human intercourse. The former would require reworking of the Latin, but could constitute heresy, as Mary's perpetual virginity had been part of Catholic doctrine since 649, and would be even more incriminating if the intention was that Mary conceived Jesus himself in such a fashion. Possibly, however, the scribe has omitted a final "m" from *commissa* and meant that the MacConmaras were accused of saying Mary was conceived by human intercourse. Yet it would be heresy in Catholicism to suggest otherwise, since Christ alone resulted from a virgin birth. Franciscans were generally enthusiastic proponents of the immaculate conception, which did not become Catholic doctrine until 1854, but that tenet simply removes original sin from Joachim's semen; it does not claim that Mary was not the product of sexual intercourse, an honor reserved solely

---

193. Williams, "The Kilkenny Chronicle," 80–81.

194. Williams, "The Kilkenny Chronicle," 82–85. For the Bruce destruction of Castledermot friary, see FitzMaurice and Little, *Materials for the History*, 101, and above.

195. *CSM*, 2:393; Williams, "The Kilkenny Chronicle," 81.

196. See *CT*, 2:56.

for her Son. Thus, the only record (albeit in duplicate form) of the case against the MacConmaras reveals not only extremely suspicious surrounding circumstances but considerable confusion about the supposed heresy itself, which strengthens the probability that it was a trumped-up charge.

The confusion can also be explained by the scribe's secondary interest in the MacConmaras' case, as he was more concerned with its aftermath and particularly the fate of Roger Cradock, the Franciscan bishop of Waterford, whom he names as their judge. He does not specify that they were relaxed to and then executed by Rokeby but cites Cradock alone, raising the possibility that their punishment was carried out by the spiritual rather than the secular arm. Even without such an illegal act, the trial itself was extremely irregular, as Cradock was the bishop of Waterford, about a hundred miles from Bunratty and separated by several dioceses. It seems likely, given the nature of the entry and the circumstances it depicts, that Cradock was accompanying Rokeby's army when he conducted this trial and decided the sentence, which was then carried out if not by Rokeby then by his representatives, but too little is known about the incident and its surrounding circumstances to presume anything about the precise chain of events. Regardless of Rokeby's or his representatives' involvement, however, Cradock alone was held responsible for his irregular inquisition by his metropolitan, Ralph O'Kelly, the Carmelite archbishop of Cashel.

Chronicle A continues that great conflict arose between Cradock and O'Kelly over the MacConmaras' execution, prompting O'Kelly to attack Cradock shortly before midnight on October 10, 1353. According to the pro-Cradock chronicler, a fellow Franciscan, O'Kelly secretly stole into Waterford cemetery "with a great number of armed men and committed an offense against the said bishop of Waterford in his residence"; he and his army gravely wounded the bishop and many others and plundered his goods at the advice of Walter Reve, who styled himself dean of Waterford, and William Sendall, the mayor. This hostility to Reve, kin to the man who would ultimately succeed where Cradock failed in becoming bishop of the united sees of Lismore and Waterford, and his support as well as the support of the mayor for O'Kelly against Cradock indicate that the incident at Bunratty was not the sole source of contention between them, but clearly it was a significant one, motivated in part by the ethnic tensions that were probably the primary reason for which these two unnamed MacConmaras were executed.

Ralph O'Kelly was a native Irishman who had studied canon law at Rome and Avignon and had served as procurator general of the Carmelites from 1327 to 1333 and again from 1339 until 1344, his six-year hiatus caused by his disagreement with John XXII on the beatific vision. The bishop of Killaloe, in which Bunratty is located, was also a native Irishman, Tomás O'Hogan; his diocese was one of the greatest native Irish strongholds, having had only one non-Irish bishop in five centuries, and that one illegitimately held office and was denounced by Honorius III as an intruder.[197] O'Hogan was almost certainly not consulted in this aberrant trial, nor would he have had much authority while Bunratty was being held by colonial forces, brief though their success may have been. A canon of Killaloe before becoming its bishop in 1343, O'Hogan died the year after the MacConmaras' execution and the year before Bunratty was once and for all lost to the medieval colony; his position on the case is not recorded.

That the MacConmaras were executed by colonial forces, whether strictly ecclesiastical or both ecclesiastical and civil, following a defeat of their kin by those same forces, that their alleged heresy is too convoluted to comprehend, and that it seems extremely dubious that they would make any such statement to colonial forces, who had no official religious jurisdiction over Bunratty, recalls Adducc Dubh O'Toole's trial and execution twenty-five years earlier. As unlikely as the legitimacy of Adducc's case seems, however, it was more solid than the one against the MacConmaras: where Adducc stood accused of multiple counts of blasphemy and apostasy, the MacConmaras apparently allegedly challenged only Mary's virginity or her own virgin birth; while he presumably was tried by representatives of his archbishop, they were tried by a man who had no jurisdiction in the matter and executed at a castle that had been a focal point of tensions between the native Irish, in particular their own kin, and the Anglo-Irish for generations, a castle that had been rubble and ashes for over two decades before their trial, had been hastily rebuilt by colonial forces after the extremely recent victory over their kin, and within two years would once again be reduced to rubble. Why these two men were singled out for such treatment remains even more mysterious than Adducc's scapegoating, particularly since no call for a crusade ensued, but perhaps the colonial forces at Bunratty were trying to resurrect Rodyerd's and Nottingham's scheme to help them win over a part of Ireland they had lost decades before and soon would lose for centuries. Inauguration rites, in which the MacConmaras played a central role in Thomond, retained some pre-Christian influence, but the allegations against them do not suggest that lingering paganism was part of their supposed heresy.[198] If this facet of their

---

197. For a list of the bishops of Killaloe from the eleventh to the sixteenth century, see *NHI*, 9:300–301. For Travers's intrusion, see Theiner, 5–6, 11–12, 25–26, and Watt, *Church in Medieval Ireland*, 103.

198. See Simms, *From Kings to Warlords*, 21–40, and Introduction.

family played any role in their trial and execution, it was the power and prestige it brought them that would make the MacConmaras more likely to be singled out as examples.

Other aspects of the case may have prompted O'Kelly's supposed severe reaction. The feud that ensued between his suffragan and himself was not their only involvement. In 1349, O'Kelly confirmed Robert Elyot, a canon of Waterford, as bishop of Waterford, as his fellow canons had so elected him; the pope, however, provided Cradock to that position in March 1350, and in June 1351 resolved the situation by appointing Elyot bishop of Killala in the province of Tuam.[199] A month later, Clement commanded John of St. Paul, newly archbishop of Dublin, to complete the process against heretics in Dublin that the pope believed O'Kelly and Richard fitz Ralph, archbishop of Armagh, had begun.[200] O'Kelly and fitz Ralph had been enlisted by the papacy to assist in investigating Ledrede's allegations since at least 1347, although it is not known if they complied with the papal requests. Fitz Ralph and O'Kelly may have been on close terms since 1342, when they were both in Avignon and fitz Ralph gave his famed sermon on the immaculate conception to Carmelites, possibly after an introduction from O'Kelly.[201] Moreover, by 1350 fitz Ralph had begun his attack on mendicants, in particular the Franciscans, the order to which both Ledrede and Cradock belonged. Conditions peculiar to Anglo-Irish society and abuses therein by mendicants may have been the primary source of fitz Ralph's general contempt for them.[202] One of his concerns was that friars might trump up charges of heresy against opponents, a concern that would be quite justified in the case of Cradock and Ledrede.[203] While O'Kelly is not known to have shared fitz Ralph's position on the friars, his reaction to Cradock's proceedings indicates that the two men had equal patience when it came to unfounded allegations of heresy made by mendicants and suggests that despite the papal requests the two archbishops did not further Ledrede's cause against supposed heretics in Ireland.

An interesting echo of this case occurred some twenty-odd years later, when the then archbishop of Cashel, an English Franciscan like Ledrede and Cradock, invoked the secular arm against Thomas le Reve, bishop of

---

199. *CPL*, 3:430; *NHI*, 9:309, 329.

200. Theiner, 299; see chapter 4.

201. Walsh, *Richard FitzRalph*, 248. In this sermon, fitz Ralph revealed that he had recently adopted a favorable view of the immaculate conception, but he cautiously maintained that such a belief was a personal one, as he was quite aware of opposition to it, particularly among Dominicans (ibid., 209). His words take on added significance in light of the convoluted claims against the MacConmaras.

202. Walsh, *Richard FitzRalph*, 360.

203. Ibid., 373.

the recently united dioceses of Lismore and Waterford.[204] While in 1356 Cradock received the king's support in his ambitions to be bishop of the joint diocese, a union proposed by English kings and their agents since the early thirteenth century, the pope preferred Thomas, a canon of Lismore whom he appointed bishop of Lismore in 1358; following Cradock's translation to Llandalf in Wales, Urban V united the dioceses with Thomas as bishop in 1363.[205] Thomas did quite well for himself, serving as chancellor in 1367–68 and as one of the main signatories to the Statute of Kilkenny, vowing to invoke all the censures of Holy Church should anyone transgress against them.[206] But by 1374 he and his metropolitan came to blows, quite literally, according to the archbishop, Philip Torrington. Torrington maintained that during his attempted visitation of Waterford, Thomas physically assaulted him, then watched with approval as the archbishop's archdeacon was grievously wounded, then forcefully prevented him from conducting the visitation; for these misdeeds Torrington publicly excommunicated him in 1374. Three years later, however, Thomas remained contumacious, and thus Torrington requested that the secular arm be used against him.[207] Torrington told a nearly identical story about the bishop of Limerick, Peter Curragh, and likewise requested his arrest.[208] When Torrington brought his case to the pope, he claimed Curragh was also guilty of heresy, although no evidence is provided concerning such an offense, apart from his alleged violent treatment of his metropolitan.[209] Apparently, Torrington defined heresy in the same terms Richard de Ledrede had fifty years earlier, and as with Ledrede's complaints, the papacy ordered an investigation into the allegations of which nothing seems to have come to pass. Curragh remained bishop of Limerick for over twenty more years, while Torrington died in 1381, having left Ireland shortly after Curragh's alleged assault in 1375, apparently never to return.[210]

Few facts can be gleaned from the case of Adducc Dubh O'Toole: he was convicted in early 1328 for denying the basics of Christianity, which was presented as heresy; he was executed in April 1328 for this heresy; and his

204. Robson, "Franciscan Bishops of Irish Dioceses," 7.

205. *NHI*, 9:304.

206. Sayles, *Documents*, 224–27; Berry, *Early Statutes*, 466–68.

207. Sayles, *Documents*, 237; Logan, "Visitation of the Archbishop of Cashel," 52–53.

208. Sayles, *Documents*, 236; Logan, "Visitation of the Archbishop of Cashel," 54.

209. Wadding, *Annales Minorum*, 8:592–95; Ware, *Whole Works*, 508–09.

210. Torrington's death is often dated to 1380 (e.g., Ware, *Whole Works*, 479–80; *NHI*, 9:291; Cotter, *Friars Minor in Ireland*, app. 6), but another allegation of heresy made by his vicar-general attests that he lived until 1381 (Curtis, *Calendar of Ormond Deeds*, 2:168–82); see also Logan, "Visitation of the Archbishop of Cashel," 50.

case was used as the single specific example in a letter from colonial authorities, both civil and ecclesiastic, that portrays the entire Irish race as apostates and heretics and pleads with the pope to call a crusade against the native Irish and their Anglo-Irish allies. Most who have discussed Adducc's case have accepted the charges against him essentially at face value, but it seems highly improbable that Adducc preached such a negation of Christianity (apparently without positing anything in its absence), allowed this preaching to come to the attention of colonial authorities, recanted, and then relapsed back into apostasy.[211] As unlikely as the charges against him are on their own, they beggar belief when considered in the context of the ongoing warfare between Adducc's kin and the colonists that was particularly pronounced in the year of his trial, and the manner in which his alleged heresy so closely conforms to the agenda advanced by the Counter-Remonstrance, building upon *Laudabiliter*, that the Irish were deviant Christians or non-Christians against whom a crusade must be called so that the colonists can at last triumph over them. This portrait itself was shaped by centuries of anti-Irish sentiment, such as that endured by Columbanus and Clemens. Why Adducc specifically was chosen as scapegoat in this scheme shaped by Rodyerd and Nottingham after learning from Ledrede remains a mystery, but fortunately John XXII was too well versed in the nature of heresy, too suspicious of the colonists after hearing Ledrede's tales of woe and Dónal O'Neill's Remonstrance, and too opposed to the annihilation of the Irish to support the colonists' call for a crusade, and thus Adducc's was a solitary sacrifice—at least for the next twenty-five years.

Even fewer facts can be discerned about the case of the MacConmaras than that of Adducc Dubh, primarily because their trial and execution occurred on a colonial outpost that had been repeatedly lost to the Irish and would soon fall to them again. If an anonymous Franciscan had not considered the event and its aftermath significant enough to add to an older annal, their deaths, like the rest of their lives as well as their first names, might have been lost to history forever. Yet in ways this last known heresy trial provides a fitting conclusion. It involves direct clerical violence, so frequently alleged by various sides, but this time as the result rather than as the occasion of heresy. The similarities between Adducc Dubh and the MacConmaras are obvious, but in the latter case the colonists seem to have had even less regard for due

---

211. While some medieval Europeans may have rejected the basics of Christianity, the accusations against Adducc seem more likely an invention by colonial authorities in their efforts to defeat the Irish. For discussion of medieval doubt and unbelief, see Arnold, *Belief and Unbelief in Medieval Europe*, and Reynolds, "Social Mentalities."

process, trying it under Cradock without consulting O'Hogan and defining their heresy as an obscure insult against Mary. Rokeby has been assumed to be the instigator behind this trial, but this is far from certain.[212] More likely, men whom he had left behind to hold Bunratty served as the executioners, working in tandem with or at the command of Cradock. What precisely Cradock, a recent arrival in the colony, hoped to gain from this trial and execution is unclear; possibly he had discussed matters of heresy with his fellow English Franciscan Ledrede, whose diocese adjoined his, or possibly Rokeby had familiarized himself with the Counter-Remonstrance and discussed it with Cradock or his men, who then decided to try the tactic again. Yet it seems to have been a solitary event during Rokeby's justiciarship, which saw campaigns against native Irish in several parts of Ireland; if it had been a strategy of Rokeby or his men, one would expect them to have repeated it in the years that followed, when his campaigns, particularly against the Leinster Irish who had already been accused of heresy, met with disaster instead of success, causing the king to replace him in 1355 with Maurice fitz Thomas.[213]

While little can be said with certainty about the case of the MacConmaras, it likely was primarily an ecclesiastical event, as Ireland's previous heresy trials had been, so far as can be determined, and as heresy trials ought to be. Though the instigator of and primary advocate behind the trial of the Templars was the king of France, Edward II ordered their arrest in his domains only after the pope commanded him to do so. Ireland's archbishops and bishops do not seem to have been directly involved, despite being so ordered by both their secular and spiritual overlords, but nearly all of the witnesses against the Templars, as well as those who observed their interrogations and of course their inquisitors, were religious. The concurrent trial of Philip de Braybrook was apparently entirely ecclesiastical, brought by the absent archbishop-elect of Dublin's vicar and the primary inquisitor in the Templar trial, Thomas de Chaddesworth. Ledrede's proceedings reveal a fascinating interplay between religious and secular jurisdiction, but any secular assistance he received was reluctantly given. It is not entirely clear who tried Adducc Dubh O'Toole, but the evidence points to William de Rodyerd and his canons of St. Patrick's, who then characterized Adducc as the embodiment of native Irish evils in their request to the papacy for a crusade against them; here the secular and religious colonial leaders worked together, but the Counter-Remonstrance derived primarily from the dean and chapter of St. Patrick's, as the preface indicates. Rokeby seems to have been a fair-minded

---

212. Gleeson, "A Fourteenth-Century Clare Heresy Trial."
213. Otway-Ruthven, "Ireland in the 1350s," 51–53.

man who genuinely tried to address the underlying causes of Anglo-Irish rebellion and native Irish resistance, and his policies lack the anti-Irish vitriol of the Counter-Remonstrance, the Statute of Kilkenny, and other colonial documents. It seems unlikely, therefore, that he would have devised these charges against the MacConmaras and coerced Cradock to carry out his plan. Possibly men among his forces who had long fought against the O'Briens and MacConmaras in Thomond as well as the O'Tooles in Leinster and who knew of the Counter-Remonstrance were the instigators; possibly it was Cradock himself. Cradock was so regarded by O'Kelly, though it seems unlikely that the archbishop vented his displeasure with his suffragan by leading an army against him in the middle of the night. O'Kelly's opinion of the trial and execution is fairly evident, however, and that sentiment stands six and a half centuries later. Even if they were guilty of casting aspersions on Mary's virginity, that does not suffice for heresy, nor execution. Like Adducc Dubh O'Toole, they were most likely killed for their ethnicity, not their religious beliefs; why a religious slant was added to their execution, however, remains even more mysterious than in the case of Adducc Dubh.

Conclusion

After Ledrede's death in 1360, both colonial and papal interest in heresy in Ireland greatly dissipated, though the church was deeply concerned with heresy and witchcraft elsewhere and tensions between the Irish and Anglo-Irish intensified as the colony continued to shrink. The English and Anglo-Irish persisted in portraying the Irish in much the same terms as the Counter-Remonstrance, but without allegations of heresy or proposing a crusade to complete the conquest. Such accusations did surface, but they were almost exclusively directed against colonists by other colonists, often in fairly petty quarrels: the bishop of Emly's citation of William Lyn, a former Vicar of Aney, and David Browery for heretical depravity in 1375, apparently for abuse of clerics and attacks on churches but possibly because of the bishop's greed for their wealth; Philip Torrington's claims against his suffragan Peter Curragh the following year; and a case brought five years later by Torrington's vicar against the bishop of Cloyne for his incorporation of political remarks and personal animosity into his services.[1] One allegation is based on what would have been a genuinely heretical teaching: the Dominican William Andrew, bishop of Meath from 1380 to 1385, accused the Cistercian Henry Crumpe of teaching that the eucharist was but a mirror

---

1. Seymour, *Diocese of Emly*, 110–11; Wadding, *Annales Minorum*, 8:592–95; Ware, *Whole Works*, 1:508–09; Curtis, *Calendar of Ormond Deeds*, 2:168–82. For Torrington, see chapter 5.

of the body of Christ in heaven; considering Crumpe's diatribes against mendicants, however, this accusation also may have arisen more from the accuser's animosity than from actual doctrinal discrepancy, and nothing is known to have come from Andrew's claims.[2] The one instance initiated by a native Irishman occurred in Raphoe in 1410, where a century and a half earlier the bishop had accused his subjects of idol worship, incest, and aggression toward ecclesiastics.[3] Once again the claims of impropriety originated with the bishop, who complained to his metropolitan about unnamed secular lords appropriating ecclesiastical lands. Yet it was not he but his Anglo-Irish metropolitan, a former canon of St. Patrick's, who identified these lay lords as heretics.[4] None of these cases, however, is known to have reached trial, nor do the accusations seem to have had lasting detrimental effects on the accused.[5] Moreover, with the exception of Andrew's claims against Crumpe, none suggests the presence of actual heretical beliefs in medieval Ireland; they are pale reflections of the trials from 1310 to 1353, which themselves attest to ignorance about heresy and its apparent absence on the island.[6] Not until the "heresy" intended was Protestantism or Catholicism, depending on the side speaking, did such accusations become common.

Similarly, witchcraft trials did not recur in Ireland until Anglicanism was the enforced religion in England and its domains. The next reference to the practice in the records, issued by parliament in 1447, denied that it ever existed in Ireland and protested the use of such accusations as slander against individuals and Ireland itself, thereby demonstrating a patriotism similar to

---

2. Ware, *De Scriptoribus Hiberniæ*, 73. Interestingly, Crumpe may have been the first to use the derogatory term "Lollards," which he levelled against academics in Oxford in 1382; see Lambert, *Medieval Heresy*, 245n12.

3. See Introduction.

4. Burrows, "Fifteenth-Century Irish Provincial Legislation," 63.

5. An interesting case that did reach trial was that of John Martin in Mexico. Martin's case was also permeated by ethnic and national tensions, but between Spanish Catholics and English Protestants. Martin's defense rested on the fact that he was an Irish Catholic who hated the English and their religion, but his judges convicted him because he had "lived among the English and held and believed their false doctrine"; consequently he was garrotted and burned after being tortured on March 6, 1575 (Hair, "An Irishman before the Mexican Inquisition," 315). Also in the New World, Widow Glover's 1688 trial and execution for witchcraft in Boston likely arose in part because she was an Irish Catholic among English Puritans (Karlsen, *Devil in the Shape of a Woman*, 34).

6. In 1391, Richard II granted the archbishops of Dublin and Cashel as well as the bishop of Connor the right to arrest any preachers of heresies or errors condemned by the church, a grant explicitly similar to one made two years earlier to the archbishop of Canterbury, which named John Wyclif, Nicholas Hereford, John Aston, and John Purvey as the erring teachers (*CPR* [1388–92]: 172, 462). Apparently because of this grant, Ronan claims a Wycliffite presence in Dublin ("Anglo-Norman Dublin and Diocese," 47:148), but the basis of the grant is unclear. I have not found other evidence of Wycliffites or Lollards in Ireland, nor has Shannon McSheffrey, an expert on Lollardy (personal correspondence, 1998).

that evinced by Arnold le Poer when he too protested witchcraft allegations.[7] Unfortunately for the thirty-six people executed in Kilkenny in 1578, the next known witchcraft trial resulted in a different conclusion.[8] As the Kyteler case was purely a colonial affair, so were those that followed; all of the accusations appear to have been brought by Protestants against other Protestants.[9] As Elwyn Lapoint has noted in his study of witchcraft in early modern Ireland, "Irish witchcraft [trials are] not Irish at all," but are "thoroughly and prototypically English." Lapoint has explained the absence of such trials among the Irish as "an expression of Irish passive resistance to English authorities—a protest against the ruling order and the judicial system on which it depended."[10] Yet some native Irish did participate in colonial courts, and their own systems could have tried such cases as well. The questions remain for both heresy and witchcraft trials in medieval Ireland: Why were they not brought by the native Irish, to either Irish or Anglo-Irish authorities? And why did the fourteenth century witness all of Ireland's reliably recorded medieval heresy trials?

It is easier to explain why a phenomenon did occur than why it did not, but a few tentative suggestions may be proposed. The diversity of devotion and practice that first flourished in the early Irish church may have fostered an attitude of tolerance for the variety of expressions of Catholic faith. The degree of syncretism with the earlier culture and faith of Ireland, evident also in collections of saints' *Lives* from the fourteenth and fifteenth centuries, indicates a fairly flexible and fluid approach to "proper" Christian belief and conduct.[11] Clearly it demonstrates greater acceptance than some modern scholars have shown, who deem Irish hagiography "a dismal swamp of

---

7. Berry, *Statute Rolls*, 100–101.

8. For this case and the cases and accusations that followed, see Seymour, *Irish Witchcraft and Demonology*; Lapoint's "Irish Immunity to Witch-Hunting" should also be consulted.

9. The case of Bridget Cleary, a Catholic killed by her husband at the end of the nineteenth century, is occasionally identified as a witchcraft case, but it was more accurately the product of faerie and changeling beliefs; see Bourke, *Burning of Bridget Cleary*.

10. Lapoint, "Irish Immunity to Witch-Hunting," 87, 92. Consider also Andrew Sneddon's theory that the native Irish did not perceive witches to be significant threats and had their own "religious, magical or ritualistic means" to ward them off so did not need to resort to trials; in addition, Irish faerie beliefs "made it unnecessary to use the witch figure to explain otherwise mysterious misfortune." In contrast, Anglo-Irish Protestants "did fear malefic witchcraft," but "by the time there were enough Protestants willing to accuse each other of witchcraft in the second half of the seventeenth century, the judiciary seemed unwilling to convict people on the evidence brought before them" (*Possessed by the Devil*, 84).

11. The compilations of Ireland's saints' *Lives* attest to a degree of cooperation between the ethnicities as well as Anglo-Irish interest in Ireland's pre-Norman past. For the primary collections, see Plummer, *Vitae Sanctorum Hiberniae*, and Heist, *Vitae Sanctorum Hiberniae*.

superstition and perverted Christianity."[12] Cummian's example in *De controversia Paschali* and Columbanus's defense on the Continent further attest to an openness to diversity, a reluctance to claim God's role as judge, and a communal rather than hierarchical view of the church. The late adoption of the diocesan system and the political fragmentation that increased the church's decentralization in Ireland may have lessened the likelihood of the exercise of the kind of authority necessary to try someone for heresy. Consider Gerald of Wales's estimation of Irish clergy: though he criticized the Irish mercilessly, he regarded their clergy as exemplary with regard to their personal religious practice; it was primarily as regulators of the laity that they failed.[13] *Contra* Gerald, the Irish clergy did often fulminate and legislate against various abuses, but they did not identify such abuses as heresy, though Anglo-Irish clergy did.[14] Moreover, as Maurice Sheehy has argued, the English brought with them a different concept of the church, that of "a monolithic human corporation [that was] quite foreign to the native people" and that was used to justify not only the English presence in Ireland, but the entire crusading ideology, for which the Irish showed little enthusiasm.[15] The idea of forced conversion or conformity seems at odds with medieval Irish understandings of religion; the *peregrini* who left Ireland in such numbers throughout the Middle Ages undertook pilgrimage primarily as a form of devotion and asceticism rather than to proselytize pagans. The lack of a university also contributed to the relative absence of heresy in medieval Ireland, but male Irish religious regularly traveled to England and the Continent to continue their education, like the young Irishmen severely wounded during a riot on St. Scholastica's Day in Oxford, 1355.[16] Learned disputations resulting in serious differences of opinion on theological issues probably regularly occurred in various monastic and secular schools, religious houses, and the like, without involving allegations of heresy, so far as is known, apart from Malachy's confrontation with the cleric of Lismore. Yet this trial should be held suspect, though believable given Malachy's reforming zeal

---

12. Ó Cróinín, *Early Medieval Ireland*, 211. According to David Binchy, "the plethora of pre-Christian and sub-Christian *motifs*, the survival of animism, heathen mythology, folklore, druidism, primitive magic and secular saga all combine to give the Irish *légendes hagiographiques* an unenviable notoriety" ("Patrick and His Biographers," 57). Such examples could easily be multiplied. Consider as well the scathing assessment of an apparently English eleventh- or twelfth-century satirist (Plummer, *Vitae Sanctorum Hiberniae*, 2:293–94).

13. Giraldus Cambrensis, *History and Topography of Ireland*, 112–16.

14. Here the example of Raphoe in 1410 is particularly illuminating; see above.

15. Sheehy, *When the Normans Came to Ireland*, 51.

16. Burrows, "Fifteenth-Century Irish Provincial Legislation," 63; Haren, "Richard FitzRalph of Dundalk," 97.

and French associations, as it was filtered through Bernard of Clairvaux's eyes and assumptions and may have been invented by him. Then again, it could just be the sources: perhaps the Irish did prosecute alleged heretics, but for whatever reason it has escaped the records. After all, if a later scribe had not thought to add the MacConmara case to the "Kilkenny Chronicle," or if Henry la Warr had not copied Archbishop-elect Richard de Haverings's letter to Thomas de Chaddesworth about Philip de Braybrook, the handful of known heresy trials in medieval Ireland would be reduced still further.

Heresy became a serious factor in Ireland only in the fourteenth century, when the colony was plunged into uncertainty, primarily because of the Gaelic Resurgence. Only two of the trials could be considered direct results of colonial insecurity, however, and none suggests that the accused actually espoused heretical beliefs or were guilty of the allegations against them. The first trial, of the Templars, resulted from international proceedings in which the colonists were compelled to participate, but it also reveals considerable enmity between Anglo-Irish religious, or at least of various religious against the Templars, whom the actions of Philip the Fair had reduced to a scapegoat. It indicates the viciousness with which colonists could turn on each other, with little prompting and for flimsy reasons; the only thing weaker than the grounds on which the witnesses declared the Templars guilty was the understanding of heresy demonstrated by their testimony. The case of Philip de Braybrook followed closely on its heels and, while it contains a veneer of doctrinal impropriety, it also resulted primarily from personal disputes between the heretic and his accuser, who simultaneously served as inquisitor in the Templar trial and almost certainly abused his position as the archbishop's vicar in Philip's case, as he had ten years earlier in his dispute with Philip's chapter. Though Philip was found guilty of a relapse of heresy, he probably never served his extremely light sentence and soon returned to a position of power and respect within his community, indicating others' opinion of the merits of the case against him.

In his letter to the king about Arnold le Poer, Ledrede claims to have discovered "heretics who despised the body of God itself and the sacrament of the altar in his person and otherwise totally denied the articles of the faith," which refers to the Kyteler case without mention of sorcery.[17] Conversely, the only reference to these elements in the charges against the Kilkenny witches is their denial of the faith and their refusal to take part in its rites "for a month or a year, depending on whether they needed more or less from their

17. Sayles, *Documents*, 132.

sorcery."[18] Thus their rejection of Christianity is presented more as a practical and temporary move than as a deeply held conviction, and the other six charges against them also arose from behavior rather than belief. Whatever doctrines the *hæretici sortilegæ* (heretical sorceresses) might have held were not mentioned in the *Narrative*, except for those implicit in sorcery. Arnold's heresy was the disrespect he had shown for Christ and his church in the person of Ledrede, arresting him and later throwing him out of his court while he had the eucharist with him, purportedly as he mocked him as "that worthless, churlish tramp from England, with that lump of dough he carries in his hands."[19] Ledrede's tendency to transform personal affronts against him into heresy against the church most likely was at the root of his accusation against Robert de Caunton; whatever the specific nature of the accusation, when Ledrede's metropolitan ordered him to retract it not only did he refuse to do so, he accused the archbishop of being a fautor of heretics and a heretic himself. Whether or not Ledrede was a *trutannus* (tramp), he was certainly *alienigena* (foreign), and he represented neither the king nor the colonists but himself; his actions in Ireland reveal a complex web of competing factions and shifting alliances within the colony in which only one group was not directly involved, the native Irish.

The Irish were at the burning end of the other two heresy trials, which resulted from the long-held view that the Irish were non-Christians who needed to be restored to the faith first by the English king and then by the colonists. Adducc Dubh's alleged apostasy was combined with a portrayal of the Irish as a heretical race to propose a crusade against the Irish to complete the conquest, which the colonists could not do on their own. It is not clear why he specifically and singularly was named as the representative of this heresy, or why the colonists bothered to try and execute him for heresy when they simply could have killed him, as they did "a great many Irish" in their war against the O'Tooles. The same questions arise for the MacConmaras, whose alleged heresy is even more tenuous. Although these men may have been guilty of heresy, the circumstances surrounding the cases render it extremely unlikely, and the strength of the faith among the Irish throughout the centuries should also be a consideration. Irish Christianity may have differed from a dominant Continental norm, it may have had prominent pagan influences, and it may have been secularized, but it did not deny the Trinity, the Incarnation, or the resurrection, and it especially revered the Virgin.[20]

---

18. Wright, *Contemporary Narrative*, 1.
19. Ibid., 14.
20. For an overview of Irish Marian devotion, see O'Dwyer, *Mary*.

It seems most likely that Adducc's case was brought by men inspired by Ledrede's proceedings who attempted to revitalize outside, and specifically papal, interest in the conquest of Ireland, to bring about a return to the perspective advanced by *Laudabiliter* and its like, and that the execution of the MacConmaras resulted from similar motives. Fortunately for the native Irish, John XXII and his successors took a more equanimous view of the situation between the "pure Irish, and those of a mixed race."[21]

The unity of colonists in Ireland fractured almost immediately upon their arrival and divisions increased among them, especially after the lordship of John. As the Irish started winning back their land; as some Anglo-Irish merged with the Irish through intermarriage, mutual fosterage, and adopting their customs, law, dress, and language; and as the king and titular lords of colonial lands became more removed from events in Ireland, the colonists' identity became increasingly threatened. Although only the Counter-Remonstrance characterized Irishness as a heresy that was starting to spread to the Anglo-Irish population, a similar sentiment is found throughout colonial policies regulating relationships between the colonists and the natives, as well as the relationships between the colonists themselves, most infamously in the Statute of Kilkenny of 1366. Yet, while a similar attitude toward the native Irish persisted among the Anglo-Irish into the modern era, Ireland's last known medieval heresy trial was already more than a decade in the past by the time of the statute. Just as significantly, the colonists' occasional claims of heresy against each other did not proceed to trial after Ledrede's prosecution of Roger Outlaw and Arnold le Poer. Perhaps the vehemence with which Bicknor opposed Ledrede, later matched by O'Kelly's response to Cradock's execution of the MacConmaras, made such prosecutions less attractive to colonists seeking to smear their enemies. Moreover, the papacy entrusted the investigation into heretics infesting Ireland, per Ledrede's repeated complaints, to O'Kelly and fitz Ralph, two men who were likely to be skeptical toward and rigorous in their examinations of such claims; this likely discouraged others from pursuing similar allegations, especially if they were based on politics and ethnicity as opposed to genuine doctrinal deviations. Bicknor (archbishop of Dublin from 1317 to 1349), fitz Ralph (archbishop of Armagh from 1346 to 1360), and O'Kelly (archbishop of Cashel from 1346 to 1361) ruled three of Ireland's four archdioceses, and the fourth, the province of Tuam, was primarily native Irish, both in its constituency and in its archbishops. This outright hostility to or disinterest in heretical prosecutions among

---

21. *CPL*, 2:500.

Ireland's archbishops may have helped diminish the likelihood that others would wield it as a weapon against opponents.

The ability to enforce a "right" and "wrong" way of thinking, especially about something as complex and mysterious as the divine, is arguably inherently political, yet it is an integral aspect of many religions, including Christianity. After much argument, debate, and sometimes bloodshed, creeds develop and adherents affirm allegiance to common core beliefs, often regarded as the one eternal Truth. Heresy consists of persistent deviation from some of those core beliefs, while maintaining others. Intertwined with this concept are the twin enforcers of obedience and authority. The religion's leaders determine its tenets, which develop past the creeds, and require obedience to authority and conformity in at least the central aspects of belief. In heresy, deviant belief also entails disobedience, and at times the latter obscures the former, especially in the later Middle Ages. Modern scholars of heresy recognize a difference between "real," doctrinal heresies and "artificial" heresies, trumped-up charges against adversaries.[22] Real heresies could be as subtle as the Waldensians or as radical as the Guglielmites, who believed that Christ had come again but this time he was a she, a woman named Guglielma of Milan whose followers believed her to be the Holy Spirit incarnate, as Jesus was the incarnation of the Son.[23] Ireland's heresies are of the artificial variety, with the Templars ironically providing the most rigorous example of a proper trial. While the weapon was wielded in the religious realm, it was primarily political and confined to colonists, either against other colonists or against native Irish in their efforts to further colonize the land. The history of heresy in Ireland, particularly between 1310 and 1353, reflects the conflicting interests and shifting identities of the "isle of the saints" in the high and late Middle Ages. Ledrede stands as an influential maverick in this history, but to treat the other trials as a footnote to the Kyteler case, as has been previously done, is to greatly simplify and misrepresent the many different issues involved.

---

22. Lambert, *Medieval Heresy*, 8–9.

23. Newman, *From Virile Woman to WomanChrist*, 182–223. As Newman demonstrates, however, the Guglielmites were radical primarily in their feminist and inclusive aspects; in many ways their practices and beliefs represent "common piety intensified to the point of deviance" (191).

❧ Appendix A

The Articles against the
Templars in Ireland[1]

1. In their reception or sometime after or as soon as they were able to find the opportunity, they denied Christ or Jesus or the crucified or sometimes God and sometimes the Blessed Virgin Mary, and sometimes all the saints of God, led or advised by those who received them.
2. That the brothers as a whole did this.
3. That the majority of them did.
4. That they sometimes did this after their reception.
5. That the receptors said and taught those whom they were receiving that Christ or sometimes Jesus or sometimes Christ crucified is not the true God.
6. That they told those they received that he was a false prophet.
7. That they said that he had not suffered nor was he crucified for the redemption of the human race but on account of his own sins.
8. That neither the receptors nor those being received had hope of having salvation through him, and they said this, or the equivalent, to those whom they received.

---

1. A complete list of the articles is not provided in Oxford, Bodleian Library, Bodley 454. I have compiled this list from the various interrogations, and further compared them with the articles as listed in Wilkins, *Concilia*, Michelet, *Le Procès des Templiers*, and Nicholson, *Proceedings Against the Templars*.

9. That they made those whom they received spit on the cross, or on a representation or sculpture of the cross and an image of Christ, although sometimes those who were being received spat next to it.
10. That they ordered this cross to be trampled underfoot.
11. That brothers sometimes trampled on the cross.
12. That sometimes they urinated and caused others to urinate on the cross, and several times they did this on Holy Friday.
13. That some of them on that same day or on another day in Holy Week were accustomed to assemble for the aforesaid trampling and urination.
14. That they adored a certain cat that appeared to them in their assembly.
15. That they did this in contempt of Christ and the orthodox faith.
16. That they did not believe in the sacrament of the altar.
17. That some of them (did not believe).
18. That the majority of them (did not believe).
19. That they did not believe in other sacraments of the church.
20. That the priests of the order did not speak the words by which the body of Christ is consecrated in the canon of the mass.
21. That some of them (did not do so).
22. That the majority of them (did not do so).
23. That the receptors enjoined this upon them.
24. That they believed and thus it was told to them that the grand master could absolve them from their sins.
25. That the visitor could (do so).
26. That the preceptors, of whom many were laymen, could (do so).
27. That they did this de facto.
28. That some of them (did).
29. That the grand master confessed this in the presence of important people even before he was arrested.
30. That in the reception of the brothers of the said order or about that time, sometimes the receptor and sometimes the one being received were kissed on the mouth, on the navel or on the bare stomach, on the anus or the base of the spine.
31. That sometimes on the navel (this was done).
32. That sometimes on the base of the spine (this was done).
33. That sometimes on the penis (this was done).
34. That in the reception they made those whom they were receiving swear that they would not leave the order.
35. That they regarded them immediately as professed brethren.
36. That they held the receptions of these brothers secretly.
37. That there was no one present except the brothers of the said order.

38. That on account of this vehement suspicion had for a long time worked against the order.
39. That it was generally held (that the order was suspect).
40. That they told brothers whom they received that they could have carnal relations together.
41. That it was licit for them to do this.
42. That they ought to do this and submit to it mutually.
43. That it was not a sin for them to do this.
44. That they did this or many of them did.
45. That some of them (did).
46. That in each province the brothers had idols, namely heads, of which some had three faces and some one, and others had a human skull.
47. That they adored these idols or that idol and especially in their great chapters and assemblies.
48. That they venerated them.
49. That they venerated them as God.
50. That they venerated them as their Savior.
51. That some of them (did so).
52. That most of them (did so).
53. That they said the head could save them.
54. That it could make riches.
55. That it gave them all the riches of the order.
56. That it made the land germinate.
57. That it made trees flower.
58. That they surrounded or touched each head of the said idols with small cords, which they wore around themselves next to the shirt or skin.
59. That in his reception the aforesaid cords or some lengths were given to each of the brothers.
60. That they did this in veneration of an idol.
61. That it was enjoined on them that they should wear the small cords around themselves, as is set out, and wear them continually.
62. That the brothers of this order were generally received in the aforesaid manner.
63. That they did this also at night.
64. That they did this everywhere.
65. That (they did this) for the most part.
66. That those who were not willing to do the aforesaid at their reception or afterward were killed or imprisoned.
67. That some of them (were).
68. That most of them (were).

69. That they enjoined them on oath not to reveal the aforesaid.

70. That this was done under punishment of death or of imprisonment.

71. That nor should they reveal the manner of reception.

72. That neither should they dare to speak about the aforesaid among themselves.

73. That if any were found to have revealed these things, they were punished by death or imprisonment.

74. That they were enjoined not to confess to anyone except a brother of the order.

75. That the brothers of the order, knowing the said errors, neglected to correct them.

76. That they neglected to inform Holy Mother Church.[2]

77. That they did not cease the observance of these errors and the community of the aforesaid brothers, although they had the opportunity for doing so.

78. That the brothers swore to obtain increase and profit to the order in whatever way they could, by licit or illicit means.

79. That they did not think this a sin.

80. That all and each of the aforesaid have been known and manifest among the brothers of the said order.

81. That concerning these things there is public talk and report among the brothers of the said order and outside.

82. That the said brothers in great numbers have confessed the aforesaid, both in judicial inquiry and outside, both before appointed persons and also in many places, also in public places.

83. That many brothers of the said order, knights as well as priests, and also others, in the presence of our lord pope and of the lords cardinal, have confessed the aforesaid or most of the aforesaid errors.

84. That under oaths that they had taken (they had so confessed).

85. That in full consistory (they had so confessed).

86. Ask each brother about his reception, its location, the time, those present, and the manner.

87. Also, if he knew or had heard when and by whom the aforesaid errors began and from where they had arisen, from what cause and circumstances, and all matters pertaining to the aforesaid points, so far as seems appropriate.

88. Ask the said brothers if they know where the heads or idols or any of them are, and how they were transported and guarded and by whom.

---

2. This article does not appear as a separate article in the initial articles asked of the Templars in Britain; see Wilkins, *Concilia*, 2:331–32.

APPENDIX B

The Charges against Alice Kyteler and Associates

1. That in order to obtain their goals through their nefarious sorcery, they wholly denied faith in Christ and the church for a month or a year, depending on if what they needed to obtain through their sorcery was greater or lesser, so that during that time they would not at all believe what the church believed, and they would not revere the body of Christ in any way, nor enter a church, nor hear the mass, nor take the blessed bread nor blessed water.
2. That they sacrificed live animals to demons, then divided their body parts and offered them, having distributed them at crossroads, to a certain demon who called himself Son of (the?)[1] Art from the dregs (*pauperioribus*) of hell.
3. That they sought aid and answers from demons through their sorcery.
4. That in their nightly conventicles, they usurped the jurisdiction and keys of the church, when with waxen candles burning they fulminated sentences of excommunication even against their own husbands, naming one by one every part of their body from the soles of their feet to the top of their head, and in the end they extinguished the candles as they said, "fiat, fiat, fiat, amen."

---

1. Art is a personal name but could also refer to the art of magic or witchcraft.

5. That over an oaken fire they boiled the intestines and interior organs of cocks sacrificed to demons, as aforesaid, mixed with certain horrifying worms, various herbs, and also nails of the dead, buttock hairs, and frequently[2] clothes of children who died without baptism, as well as many other abominable ingredients, in a pot made from the head of a certain decapitated thief, cooking up various powders, ointments, and potions, and also candles from greasy fat left in the said pot, as they said various incantations, to arouse love or hatred, to kill and also to afflict the bodies of faithful Christians, and for innumerable other purposes.

6. That the sons and daughters of four of the said lady's husbands were pursuing public complaints before the bishop, seeking remedy and assistance against her, alleging before a public crowd that she had killed some of their fathers through such sorceries, and had infatuated others and had led their senses into such stupor that they had given all their goods to her and her son, to the perpetual impoverishment of their sons and heirs, wherefor also her husband, the knight, Lord John le Poer (Power), is now brought to such a state through such powders and potions as well as sorceries that he is totally emaciated, his nails removed, the hair gone from all his body, but he was warned by a certain maid of the same lady, and having wrested the keys of the chests from the very hands of the said lady and opening the chests, the said knight discovered a bag full of such horrifying and detestable things in them, which he handed over with his discoveries to the aforeseaid bishop via two religious priests.

7. That the said lady had a certain demon incubus, whom she allows to know her carnally, who calls himself Son of (the?) Art, and sometimes Robin son of Art; who also sometimes appears to her in the form of a cat, sometimes in the form of a black and hairy dog, other times in the form of an Ethiopian with two companions bigger and taller than himself, any one of whom carries an iron rod in his hands; to whom she commits all her property and even herself; from whom she admits that she has received all her wealth and all that she possesses.

---

2. *Crebro* (repeatedly, frequently) is likely a mistake for *cerebro* (brain). Petronilla's confession claims she mixed the ingredients "cum cerebro et pannis pueri decedentis sine baptismo" (with the brain and clothes of a boy who died without baptism); the charges allege Alice and her accomplice did so "crebro et pannis puerorum decendentium sine baptismo" (Wright, *Contemporary Narrative*, 32, 2). This difference may indicate Ledrede's or his scribe's sloppiness in copying the charges from Petronilla's confession. I thank Christine Donnelly for helping me confirm that *crebro* is in the manuscript.

❧ BIBLIOGRAPHY

Primary Sources

Manuscripts

Churchtown, Co. Dublin, Representative Church Body Library
Liber Albus
Liber Niger
Registrum Novum

Dublin, National Library of Ireland
Microfilm 2456 (Justiciar's Letter of ca. 1331)
NLI 1–4, *Collectanea de rebus Hibernicis*, comp. Walter Harris, vols. 1–4

Dublin, Public Record Office of Ireland
Record Commission 7/11, 8/4, 8/5, 8/6, 8/10, 8/11, 8/23

London, British Library
Additional Manuscript 6165
Cotton Vespasian B XI
Harley 641
Harley 913

Oxford, Bodleian Library
Bodley 454

Printed

Beardwood, Alice. "The Trial of Walter Langton, Bishop of Lichfield, 1307–1312." *Transactions of the Americal Philosophical Society* 54 (1964): 1–45.
Bede. *Ecclesiastical History of the English People.* Translated by Leo Sherley-Price. 1955. Reprint, London: Penguin, 1990.
Bernard of Clairvaux. *The Life and Death of Saint Malachy the Irishman.* Edited and translated by Robert T. Meyer. Kalamazoo: Cistercian Publications, 1978.
———. *Sancti Bernardi Opera.* Vol. 3. Edited by J. Leclercq and H. M. Rochais. Rome: Editiones Cistercienses, 1963.
Bernard, J. H., and R. Atkinson, eds. *The Irish Liber Hymnorum.* 2 vols. Henry Bradshaw Society 13–14. London: Harrison and Sons, 1898.
Berry, H. F., ed. "Ancient Charters in the Liber Albus Ossoriensis." *Proceedings of the Royal Irish Academy* 27C (1908–9): 115–25.

——, ed. *Statute Rolls of the Parliament of Ireland, Reign of Henry VI.* Dublin: Alexander Thom, 1910.

——, ed. *Statutes and Ordinances and Acts of the Parliament of Ireland: King John to Henry V.* Dublin: Alexander Thom, 1907.

Bettenson, Henry, ed. *Documents of the Christian Church.* 1943. Reprint, London: Oxford University Press, 1963.

Bieler, Ludwig, ed. *The Irish Penitentials.* 1963. Reprint, Dublin: Dublin Institute for Advanced Studies, 1975.

——, ed. and trans. *The Patrician Texts in the Book of Armagh.* 1979. Reprint, Dublin: Dublin Institute for Advanced Studies, 2000.

Bliss, W. H., ed. *Calendar of Entries in the Papal Registers Relating to Great Britain and Ireland: Papal Letters.* Vols. 1–2, *1198–1342.* London: His Majesty's Stationery Office, 1893–95.

——, ed. *Calendar of Entries in the Papal Registers Relating to Great Britain and Ireland: Petitions to the Pope.* Vol. 1, *1342–1419.* London: Eyre and Spottiswoode, 1896.

Bliss, W. H., and C. Johnson, eds. *Calendar of Entries in the Papal Registers Relating to Great Britain and Ireland: Papal Letters.* Vol. 3, *1342–1362.* London: His Majesty's Stationery Office, 1897.

Bower, Walter. *Scotichronicon.* Vol. 6. Edited by D. E. R. Watt. Aberdeen: Aberdeen University Press, 1991.

Brewer, J. S., and W. Bullen, eds. *Calendar of Carew Manuscripts.* London: Longmans, 1873.

Brown, R. Allen, ed. *The Norman Conquest.* London: Constable, 1984.

——, ed. *Registrum Prioratus Omnium Sanctorum Juxta Dublin.* Dublin: Irish Archaeological Society, 1845.

Calendar of the Close Rolls Preserved in the Public Record Office . . . 1272–1509. 61 vols. 1892–1963. Reprint, Nendeln: Kraus, 1970–80.

Calendar of the Fine Rolls Preserved in the Public Record Office. 22 vols. London: His Majesty's Stationery Office, 1911–62.

Calendar of Memoranda Rolls Preserved in the Public Record Office, Michaelmas 1326–Michaelmas 1327. London: His Majesty's Stationery Office, 1968.

Calendar of the Patent Rolls Preserved in the Public Record Office . . . 1232–1509. 53 vols. 1891–1971. Reprint, Nendeln: Kraus, 1971–72.

Callan, Maeve B. "Dublin's First Heretic? Archbishop-Elect Richard de Haverings' Letter to Thomas de Chaddesworth Regarding Philip de Braybrook, 4 September, 1310." *Analecta Hibernica* 44 (2013): 1–12.

Campion, Edmund. *The Historie of Ireland.* Dublin, 1633.

Chaplais, Pierre, ed. *The War of Saint-Sardos.* London: Offices of the Royal Historical Society, 1954.

Chaucer, Geoffrey. *The Canterbury Tales: Fifteen Tales and the General Prologue.* Edited by V. A. Kolve and Glending Olson. 1989. Reprint, New York: W. W. Norton, 2005.

Clyn, John. *The Annals of Ireland by Friar John Clyn and Thady Dowling, Together with the Annals of Ross.* Edited by Richard Butler. Dublin: Irish Archaeological Society, 1849.

Cole, Henry, ed. *Documents Illustrative of English History*. London: Eyre and Spottiswoode, 1844.

Columbanus. *Sancti Columbani Opera*. Edited by G.S.M. Walker. Dublin: Dublin Institute for Advanced Studies, 1957.

Connolly, Philomena, ed. *Irish Exchequer Payments, 1270–1446*. 2 vols. Dublin: Dundalgan for the Irish Manuscripts Commission, 1998.

——. "Irish Material in the Class of Ancient Petitions (SC8) in the P.R.O, London." *Analecta Hibernica* 34 (1987) 3–106.

——. "Irish Material in the Class of Chancery Warrants Series I (C 81) in the P.R.O., London." *Analecta Hibernica* 36 (1995): 135–61.

——. "List of Irish Entries on the Memoranda Rolls of the English Exchequer, 1307–27." *Analecta Hibernica* 36 (1995): 163–218.

Crosthwaite, John Clarke. *The Book of Obits and Martyrology of the Cathedral Church of the Holy Trinity, Commonly Called Christ Church, Dublin*. Dublin: University Press, 1844.

Curtis, Edmund, ed. *Calendar of Ormond Deeds*. 6 vols. Dublin: Stationery Office, 1932.

Curtis, Edmund, and R.B. McDowell, eds. *Irish Historical Documents, 1172–1922*. 1943. Reprint, London: Methuen, 1968.

Davidson, L.S., and J.O. Ward, eds. *The Sorcery Trial of Alice Kyteler*. Translated by Gail Ward. Binghamton, NY: Pegasus Press, 1993.

De Bruyn, Theodore, trans. and ed. *Pelagius's Commentary on St Paul's Epistle to the Romans*. Oxford: Clarendon Press, 1993.

Dubois, Pierre. *The Recovery of the Holy Land*. Translated by Walther I. Brandt. New York: Columbia University Press, 1956.

Ehrle, Franz. "Ein Bruchstück der Acten des Concils von Vienne." In *Archive für Literatur- und Kirchengeschichte des Mittelalters*, edited by P. Heinrich Denifle and Franz Ehrle, 361–470. 1888. Reprint, Graz: Akademische Druck- und Verlagsanstalt, 1956.

Eriugena, John Scottus. *Treatise on Divine Predestination*. Edited and translated by Mary Brennan. Notre Dame Texts in Medieval Culture 5. Notre Dame: University of Notre Dame Press, 1998.

Finke, H. *Papsttum und Untergang des Templerordens*. 2 vols. Münster: Verlag der Aschendorffenschen buchh., 1907.

Fitzmaurice, E.B., and A.G. Little, eds. *Materials for the History of the Franciscan Province of Ireland, 1230–1450*. Manchester: Manchester University Press, 1920.

Flower, Robin, ed. "Manuscripts of Irish Interest in the British Museum." *Analecta Hibernica* 2 (1931): 292–340.

Frame, Robin. "The Justiciar and the Murder of the MacMurroughs in 1282." *Irish Historical Studies* 18 (1972/73): 223–30.

Freeman, A. Martin, ed. *Annála Connacht: The Annals of Connacht (A.D. 1224–1544)*. 1944. Reprint, Dublin: Dublin Institute for Advanced Studies, 1996.

Froissart, Jean. *Chronicles*. Edited and translated by John Joliffe. London: Harvill Press, 1967.

Gervase of Canterbury. *Opera Historica*. Vol. 1. Edited by W. Stubbs. Rolls Series 73. London, 1879.

Gilbert, J. T., ed. *Calendar of Ancient Records of Dublin.* Vol. 1, *Liber Albus.* Dublin: Joseph Dollard, 1889.

——, ed. *Chartularies of St. Mary's Abbey, Dublin.* 2 vols. Rolls Series 80. London: Longman, 1884.

——, ed. *Crede Mihi: The Most Ancient Register Book of the Archbishops of Dublin before the Reformation.* Dublin: Joseph Dollard, 1897.

——, ed. *Historic and Municipal Documents of Ireland, 1172–1320.* Rolls Series 53. London: Longmans, Green, 1870.

Gilmour-Bryson, Anne, ed. and trans. *The Trial of the Templars in Cyprus.* Boston: Brill, 1998.

Giraldus Cambrensis. *The Autobiography of Gerald of Wales.* Edited and translated by H. E. Butler. 1937. Reprint, Woodbridge: Boydell Press, 2005.

——. *Expugnatio Hibernica.* Edited and translated by A. B. Scott and F. X. Martin. Dublin: Royal Irish Academy, 1978.

——. *The History and Topography of Ireland.* Edited and translated by John J. O'Meara. 1951. Reprint, Mountrath, Portlaoise: Dolmen Press, 1982.

——. *Opera.* Edited by J. S. Brewer, James F. Dimock, and George F. Warner. 8 vols. Rolls Series 21. London, 1861–91.

Grace, Jacobus. *Annales Hiberniae.* Edited and translated by Richard Butler. Dublin: Irish Archaeological Society, 1842.

Greene, R. L. *The Lyrics of the Red Book of Ossory.* Oxford: Basil Blackwell, 1974.

Gwynn, Aubrey, ed. "Provincial and Diocesan Decrees of the Diocese of Dublin During the Anglo-Norman Period." *Archivium Hibernicum* 11 (1944): 31–117.

——, ed. "Some Unpublished Texts from the Black Book of Christ Church." *Analecta Hibernica* 16 (1946): 283–337.

Hansen, Joseph. *Quellen und Untersuchungen zur Geschichte des Hexenwahns und der Hexenverfolgung im Mittelalter.* 1901. Reprint, Hildesheim: G. Olms, 1963.

Heist, W. W., ed. *Vitae Sanctorum Hiberniae.* Subsidia Hagiographica 28. Brussels: Société des Bollandistes, 1965.

Hennessy, W. M., ed. *Annala Uladh: Annals of Ulster . . . a Chronicle of Irish Affairs . . . 431 to 1541.* 4 vols. Dublin: Alexander Thom, 1887–1901.

——, ed. *The Annals of Loch Cé.* 2 vols. Rolls Series 54. London: Longman, 1871.

Ignatius of Loyola. *The Spiritual Exercises.* Translated by Elder Mullan, S. J. New York: P. J. Kennedy and Sons, 1914.

Jackson, K. H., ed. and trans. *A Celtic Miscellany.* 1951. Reprint, Hardmondsworth: Penguin, 1971.

Jerome. *In Hieremiam prophetam libri sex.* Edited by Sigofredus Reiter. Corpus Christianorum Series Latina 74. Turnhout: Brepols, 1960.

John of Salisbury. *Policraticus.* Edited by K. S. B. Keats-Rohan. Turnhout: Brepols, 1993.

Lanfranc. *The Letters of Lanfranc, Archbishop of Canterbury.* Edited and translated by Helen Clover and Margaret Gibson. Oxford: Oxford University Press, 1979.

Lawlor, H. J., ed. "A Calendar of the Liber Niger and Liber Albus of Christ Church, Dublin." *Proceedings of the Royal Irish Academy* 27C (1908–9): 1–93.

——, ed. "Calendar of the Liber Ruber of the Diocese of Ossory." *Proceedings of the Royal Irish Academy* 27C (1908–9): 159–208.

Ledrede, Richard. *The Latin Hymns of Richard Ledrede.* Edited by Theo Stemmler. Mannheim: University of Mannheim Press, 1975.

———. *The Latin Poems of Richard Ledrede, OFM.* Edited by Edmund Colledge. Toronto: Pontifical Institute of Mediaeval Studies, 1974.

Little, A. G. ed. *Liber exemplorum.* 1908. Reprint, Farnborough: Gregg Press, 1966.

Logan, F. Donald, ed. "The Visitation of the Archbishop of Cashel to Waterford and Limerick, 1374–5." *Archivium Hibernicum* 34 (1976–77): 50–54.

Luard, H. R., ed. *Chronica Majora.* Vol. 3. Rolls Series 57. London, 1876.

Lucas, Angela M., ed. *Anglo-Irish Poems of the Middle Ages.* Dublin: Columbia Press, 1995.

Lydon, James, ed. "The Enrolled Account of Alexander Bicknor, Treasurer of Ireland, 1308–14." *Analecta Hibernica* 30 (1982): 9–46.

Mac Airt, Seán, ed. *Annals of Inisfallen.* 1944. Reprint, Dublin: Dublin Institute for Advanced Studies, 1988.

Mac Craith, Sean MacRuaidhrí. *Caithréim Thoirdhealbhaigh.* Edited and translated by Standish Hayes O'Grady. 2 vols. Irish Texts Society 26–27. London: Irish Texts Society, 1929.

MacInerny, M. H. *A History of the Irish Dominicans from Original Sources and Unpublished Records.* Vol. 1, *Irish Dominican Bishops (1224–1307).* Dublin: Browne and Nolan, 1916.

Mac Niocaill, Gearóid. "Documents Relating to the Suppression of the Templars in Ireland." *Annalecta Hibernica* 24 (1967): 181–226.

Mageoghan, Conell, trans. [1627], and Denis Murphy, ed. *The Annals of Clonmacnoise, Being the Annals of Ireland from the Earliest Period to A.D. 1408.* 1896. Reprint, Felinfach: Llanerch, 1993.

Maxwell Lyte, H. C., ed. *Calendar of Chancery Warrants.* Vol. 1, *1244–1326.* London: His Majesty's Stationery Office, 1927.

McEnery, M. J., ed. "Calendar to Christ Church Deeds." In *Twentieth Report of the Deputy Keeper of the Public Records in Ireland,* 36–122. Dublin: Alexander Thom, 1888.

McEnery, M. J., and Raymond Refaussé, eds. *Christ Church Deeds.* Dublin: Four Courts Press, 2001.

McNeill, Charles, ed. *Calendar of Archbishop Alen's Register, c. 1172–1534.* Dublin: J. Falconer, 1950.

———, ed. *Liber Primus Kilkenniensis.* Dublin, 1931.

Meersseman, G. C. "Two Unknown Confraternity Letters of St. Bernard." *Cîteaux in de Nederlanden* 6 (1955): 173–78.

Michelet, Jules. *Le Procès des Templiers.* 2 vols. Paris: Les Editions du C.T.H.S., 1987.

Mills, James, ed. *Calendar of the Justiciary Rolls or Proceedings in the Court of the Justiciar of Ireland, Preserved in the Public Record Office of Ireland.* Vols. 1–2, *1295–1307.* Dublin: Alexander Thom, 1905–14.

Müller, P. Ewald. *Das Konzil von Vienne 1311–12: seine quellen und seine geschichte.* Münster: Aschendorff, 1933.

Nicholls, K. W., ed. "Late Medieval Irish Annals: Two Fragments." *Peritia* 2 (1983): 87–102.

Nicholson, Helen, ed. and trans. *The Proceedings Against the Templars in the British Isles.* 2 vols. Burlington: Ashgate Publishing, 2011.

O' Donovan, John, ed. *Annala rioghachta Eireann: Annals of the Kingdom of Ireland by the Four Masters, from the Earliest Period to the Year 1616.* 7 vols. 1851. Reprint, New York: AMS Press, 1966.

Orpen, Goddard Henry, ed. and trans. *The Song of Dermot and the Earl.* Oxford: Clarendon Press, 1892.

Otway-Ruthven, A. J. "The Request of the Irish for English Law, 1277–80." *Irish Historical Studies* 6 (1948/49): 261–70.

Paris, Matthew. *Chronica Majora.* Edited by H. R. Luard. Rolls Series 57. London: Longman, 1876.

Phillips, J. R. S. "Documents on the Early Stages of the Bruce Invasion of Ireland, 1315–1316." *Proceedings of the Royal Irish Academy* 79C (1979): 247–70.

Plummer, Charles, ed. and trans. *Bethada Náem nErenn.* 2 Vols. 1922. Reprint, Oxford: Clarendon Press, 1968.

———, ed. *Vitae Sanctorum Hiberniae.* 2 vols. Oxford: Clarendon Press, 1910.

Powicke, F. M., and C. R. Cheney, eds. *Councils and Synods.* 2 vols. Oxford: Clarendon Press, 1964.

Prynne, William. *An Exact Chronological Vindication and Historical Demonstration of Our British, Roman, Saxon, Danish, Norman, English Kings' Supream Ecclesistical Jurisdiction over all Prelates, Persons, Causes, within Their Kingdomes and Dominions.* 3 vols. London, 1665–68.

Raine, James, ed. *Historical Papers and Letters.* London: Longman, 1873.

Regestum Clementis Papae V. Rome: Typographia Vaticana, 1885–92.

Reports of the Deputy Keeper of the Public Records of Ireland. Dublin, 1869–.

Richardson, H. G., and G. O. Sayles, eds. *Parliaments and Councils of Medieval Ireland.* Vol. 1. Dublin: Stationery Office, 1947.

Rigault, Abel, ed. *Le Procès de Guichard, Évêque de Troyes.* Paris: A. Picard et fils, 1896.

Robertson, James Craigie, ed. *Materials for the History of Thomas Becket, Archbishop of Canterbury.* 7 vols. London: Longman, 1875–85.

Rothwell, Harry, ed. *English Historical Documents, 1189–1327.* London: Eyre and Spottiswoode, 1975.

Rotuli Parliamentorum, ut et Petitiones, et Placita in Parliamento. 7 Vols. London, 1783–1832.

Rymer, Thomas, ed. *Foedera, conventiones, litterae, et cujuscunque generis acta publica, inter reges Angliae et alios quosvis imperatores, reges, pontifices, principes, vel communitates, ab ineunte saeculo duodecimo.* 10 vols. 3rd ed. 1745. Reprint, Farnborough: Gregg Press, 1967.

Sayles, G. O., ed. *Documents of the Affairs of Ireland before the King's Council.* Dublin: Stationery Office, 1979.

———. "The Legal Proceedings against the First Earl of Desmond." *Analecta Hibernica* 23 (1966): 3–47.

———, ed. *Select Cases in the Court of the King's Bench under Edward III.* 7 vols. London: B. Quaritch, 1958.

Schaff, Philip, and Henry Wace, eds. *Nicene and Post-Nicene Fathers.* Second Series. Vol. 1. 1890. Reprint, Peabody, MA: Henrickson Publishers, 2004.

Schottmüller, Konrad. *Der Untergang des Templer-Ordens.* 2 vols. Berlin: Ernst Siegfried Mittler und Sohn, 1887.

Sheehy, M. P., ed. *Pontificia Hibernica: Medieval Papal Chancery Documents Concerning Ireland.* 2 vols. Dublin: M. H. Gill, 1962–65.

———. "The Registrum Novum: A Manuscript of Holy Trinity Cathedral; The Mediaeval Charters." *Reportorium Novum* 3 (1964): 249–81; 4 (1965–71): 101–33.

Spenser, Edmund. *The Works of Edmund Spenser.* Edited by R. Morris. London: Macmillan, 1895.

Stephen of Lexington. *Letters from Ireland, 1228–29.* Edited and translated by Barry W. O'Dwyer. Kalamazoo: Cistercian Publications, 1982.

Stokes, Whitley, and John Strachan, eds. *Thesaurus Paleohibernicus: A Collection of Old Irish Glosses, Scholia Prose and Verse.* 2 vols. Cambridge: Cambridge University Press, 1901.

Stubbs, W., ed. *Annales Londonienses.* In *Chronicles of the Reigns of Edward I and Edward II,* 1:1–252. London: Longman, 1882.

———, ed. *Select Charters and Other Illustrations of English Constitutional History, from the Earliest Times to the Reign of Edward the First.* 9th ed. Rev. H. W. C. Davis. Oxford: Clarendon Press, 1913.

Sweetman, H. S., and G. F. Handcock, eds. *Calendar of Documents Relating to Ireland . . . , 1171–1307.* 5 vols. 1875–86. Reprint, Nendeln: Kraus, 1974.

Tanner, Norman P., ed. *Decrees of the Ecumenical Councils.* 2 vols. London: Sheed and Ward, 1990.

Tasso, Torquato. *Jerusalem Delivered.* Edited and translated by Anthony Esolen. Baltimore: Johns Hopkins University Press, 2000.

Theiner, Augustinus, ed. *Vetera Monumenta Hibernorum et Scotorum.* Rome: Typis Vaticania, 1864.

Thomas Aquinas. *Summa Theologiae.* Vol. 31, *Faith (2a2ae. 1–7).* Edited and translated by T. C. O'Brien. 1974. Reprint, Cambridge: Cambridge University Press, 2006.

Tresham, Edward, ed. *Rotulorum Patentium et Clausorum Cancellarie Hibernie Calendarium.* Vol. 1, part 1, *Hen. II – Hen. VII.* Dublin, 1828.

Upton-Ward, J. M., ed. and trans. *The Catalan Rule of the Templars: A Critical Edition and English Translation from Barcelona, Archivo de la Corona de Aragón, Cartas Realas, MS 3344.* Woodbridge: Boydell Press, 2003.

———, ed. and trans. *The Rule of the Templars.* Woodbridge: Boydell Press, 1992.

Vidal, J. M., ed. *Bullaire de l'inquisition française au XIVe siécle.* Paris: Librairie Letouzey et Ané, 1913.

Wadding, Luke. *Annales Minorum seu trium a Sancto Francisco institutorum.* 3rd ed. 25 vols. Florentia: Ad Claras Aquas (Quaracchi), 1931–34.

Wakefield, Walter L., and Austin P. Evans, eds. and trans. *Heresies of the High Middle Ages.* 1969. Reprint, New York: Columbia University Press, 1991.

Walsh, Maura, and Dáibhí Ó Cróinín, eds. *Cummian's Letter De Controversia Paschali.* Toronto: Pontifical Institute of Mediaeval Studies, 1988.

Walsingham, Thomas. *Historia Anglicana.* In *Chronica monasterii sancti Albani.* Edited by Henry T. Riley. 2 vols. Rolls Series 28. London: Longman, 1863.

Walter of Guisborough. *The Chronicle of Walter of Guisborough Previously Edited as the Chronicle of Walter of Hemingford or Hemingburgh.* Edited by Harry Rothwell. Camdem Series 89. London: Offices of the Society, 1957.

Walter of Hemingburgh. *Chronicon Domini Walteri de Hemingburgh, De Gestis Regum Angliae.* 2 vols. Edited by H. C. Hamilton. London, 1848–49.

White, Newport B., ed. *The "Dignitas Decani" of St. Patrick's Cathedral Dublin.* Dublin: Stationery Office, 1957.

Wilkins, D. *Concilia Magnae Britanniae et Hiberniae.* Vol. 2. London, 1737.

Williams, Bernadette, ed. and trans. *The Annals of Ireland by Friar John Clyn.* Dublin: Four Courts Press, 2007.

Wood, Herbert. "Letter from Domnal O'Neill to Fineen MacCarthy, 1317." *Proceedings of the Royal Irish Academy* 37C (1926): 141–48.

Wood, Herbert, and Albert E. Langman, eds. *Calendar of the Justiciary Rolls or Proceedings in the Court of the Justiciar of Ireland, Preserved in the Public Record Office of Ireland.* Vol. 3, *1308–14.* Revised by Margaret C. Griffith. Dublin: Alexander Thom, 1952.

Wright, Thomas, ed. *A Contemporary Narrative of the Proceedings against Dame Alice Kyteler, Prosecuted for Sorcery in 1324, by Richard de Ledrede, Bishop of Ossory.* 1843. Reprint, New York: AMS Press, 1843.

——. "The Municipal Archives of Exeter." *Journal of the British Archaelogical Association* 18 (1862): 307.

Secondary Works

Ames, Christine Caldwell. *Righteous Persecution: Inquisition, Dominicans, and Christianity in the Middle Ages.* Philadelphia: University of Pennsylvania Press, 2009.

Archdall, Mervyn. *Monasticon Hibernicum: Or, A History of the Abbeys, Priories, and Other Religious Houses of Ireland.* 3 vols. Dublin, 1876.

Arnold, John. *Belief and Unbelief in Medieval Europe.* London: Hodder Arnold, 2005.

——. *Inquisition and Power: Catharism and the Confessing Subject in Medieval Languedoc.* Philadelphia: University of Pennsylvania Press, 2001.

Bailey, Michael. "From Sorcery to Witchcraft: Clerical Conceptions of Magic in the Later Middle Ages." *Speculum* 76 (2001): 960–90.

——. *Magic and Superstition in Europe: A Concise History from Antiquity to the Present.* Lanham, MD: Rowan & Littlefield Publishers, 2007.

Ball, F. Erlington. *The Judges in Ireland, 1221–1921.* New York: E. P. Dutton, 1927.

Barber, Malcolm. *The New Knighthood.* 1994. Reprint, Cambridge: Cambridge University Press, 2000.

——. *The Trial of the Templars.* 1st ed. 1978. Reprint, Cambridge: Cambridge University Press, 1993.

——. *The Trial of the Templars.* 2nd ed. Cambridge: Cambridge University Press, 2006.

Barry, T. B., Robin Frame, and Katharine Simms, eds. *Colony and Frontier in Medieval Ireland: Essays Presented to J.F. Lydon.* London: Hambledon Press, 1995.

Bartlett, John, and Stuart Kinsella. *Two Thousand Years of Christianity and Ireland: Lectures Delivered in Christ Church Cathedral, 2001–2002.* Blackrock: Columba Press, 2006.

Bartlett, Robert. *Gerald of Wales, 1146–1223.* Oxford: Clarendon Press, 1982.

——. *The Making of Europe: Conquest, Colonization and Cultural Change, 950–1350.* Princeton: Princeton University Press, 1993.

Bethell, Denis. "English Monks and Irish Reform in the Eleventh and Twelfth Centuries." In *Historical Studies 8: Papers Read before the Irish Conference of Historians, Dublin, 27–20 May, 1969,* edited by T. D. Williams, 111–35. Dublin: Gill and Macmillan, 1971.

Binchy, D. A. "Patrick and His Biographers." *Studia Hibernica* 2 (1962): 7–173.

Bitel, Lisa. *Isle of the Saints: Monastic Settlement and Christian Community in Early Ireland*. Ithaca: Cornell University Press, 1990.

———. "Saints and Angry Neighbors: The Politics of Cursing in Irish Hagiography." In *Monks and Nuns, Saints and Outcasts: Religion in Medieval Society; Essays in Honor of Lester K. Little*, edited by Sharon Farmer and Barbara Rosenwein, 123–50. Ithaca: Cornell University Press, 2000.

Bliss, Alan. "Language and Literature." In Lydon, *The English in Medieval Ireland*, 27–45.

Bolton, Brenda, and Anne Duggan, eds. *Adrian IV, the English Pope (1154–59): Studies and Texts*. Aldershot: Ashgate, 2003.

Bolton, Brenda, and Christine Meek, eds. *Aspects of Power and Authority in the Middle Ages*. Turnhout: Brepols, 2007.

Borsje, Jacqueline. "Love Magic in Medieval Irish Penitentials, Law and Literature: A Dynamic Perspective." *Studia Neophilogica* 84 (2012): 1–18.

Borst, Arno. *Medieval Worlds: Barbarians, Heretics and Artists in the Middle Ages*. Translated by Eric Hansen. Chicago: University of Chicago Press, 1992.

Boureau, Alain. *Satan the Heretic: The Birth of Demonology in the Medieval West*. Translated by Teresa Lavendar Fagan. Chicago: University of Chicago Press, 2006.

Bourke, Angela. *The Burning of Bridget Cleary: A True Story*. London: Pimlico, 1999.

Boyce, D. George. *Nationalism in Ireland*. Baltimore: Johns Hopkins University Press, 1982.

Bradley, John, ed. *Settlement and Society in Medieval Ireland: Studies Presented to F.X. Martin*. Kilkenny: Boethius Press, 1988.

Bradshaw, Brendan. "Nationalism and Historical Scholarship in Modern Ireland." *Irish Historical Studies* 26 (1989): 329–51.

Bradshaw, Brendan, Andrew Hadfield, and Willy Maley, eds. *Representing Ireland: Literature and the Origins of Conflict, 1534–1660*. Cambridge: Cambridge University Press, 1993.

Bradshaw, Brendan, and Dáire Keogh, eds. *Christianity in Ireland: Revisiting the Story*. Blackrock: Columba Press, 2002.

Brennan, James. "Richard Ledrede, Bishop of Ossory—Towards a New Assessment." *Old Kilkenny Review* 50 (1998): 10–19.

Briggs, Robin. *Witches and Neighbors: The Social and Cultural Context of European Witchcraft*. New York: Viking, 1998.

Brooks, Eric St. John. "Archbishop Henry of London and His Irish Connections." *Journal of the Royal Society of the Antiquaries of Ireland* 60 (1930): 1–22.

———. *Knights' Fees in Counties Wexford, Carlow and Kilkenny (13th–15th Century)*. Dublin: Stationery Office, 1950.

Brown, R. Allen. *The Normans and the Norman Conquest*. 1969. Reprint, Dover, N.H.: Boydell Press, 1985.

Buckley, M. J. C. "The Ancient Stained Glass of St Canice's Cathedral, Kilkenny." *Journal of the Royal Society of the Antiquaries of Ireland* 26 (1896): 240–44.

Bullough, Vern L. "Heresy, Witchcraft and Sexuality." *Journal of Homosexuality* 1 (1974): 183–201.

———. "On Being a Male in the Middle Ages." In *Medieval Masculinities: Regarding Men in the Middle Ages*, edited by Clare A. Lees, 31–45. Minneapolis: University of Minnesota Press, 1994.

Burgtorf, Jochen. "The Trial Inventories of the Templars' Houses in France: Select Aspects." In Burgtorf, Crawford, and Nicholson, *Debate on the Trial of the Templars*, 105–15.

Burgtorf, Jochen, Paul F. Crawford, and Helen J. Nicholson, eds. *The Debate on the Trial of the Templars (1307–1314)*. Farnham: Ashgate, 2010.

Burr, David. *The Spiritual Franciscans: From Protest to Persecution in the Century after Saint Francis*. University Park: Pennsylvania State Press University, 2001.

Burrows, Michael A. J. "Fifteenth-Century Irish Provincial Legislation and Pastoral Care." In Sheils and Wood, *The Churches, Ireland, and the Irish*, 55–67.

Butler, Judith. *Gender Trouble: Feminism and the Subversion of Identity*. New York: Routledge, 1990.

Byrne, Francis John. *Irish Kings and High-Kings*. London: Batsford Press, 1973.

Callan, Maeve. "The Case of the 'Incorrigible' Canon: Dublin's First Conviction for Heresy in an Ongoing Rivalry between its Cathedral Chapters." *Proceedings of the Royal Irish Academy* 113C (2013): 163–91.

Cameron, Euan. *Waldenses: Rejections of Holy Church in Medieval Europe*. Oxford: Blackwell, 2000.

Carey, John. "Ireland and the Antipodes: The Heterodoxy of Virgil of Salzburg." *Speculum* 64 (1989): 1–10.

Carrigan, William. *The History and Antiquities of the Diocese of Ossory*. 4 Vols. Dublin: Sealy, Bryers, and Walker, 1905.

Charles-Edwards, T. M. *Early Christian Ireland*. Cambridge: Cambridge University Press, 2000.

Cheney, C. R. *Episcopal Visitation of Monasteries in the Thirteenth Century*. 1931. Reprint, Manchester: Manchester University Press, 1983.

Clarke, Howard B., ed. *Medieval Dublin*. 2 vols. Blackrock: Irish Academic Press, 1990.

———. "Street Life in Medieval Dublin." In Clarke and Phillips, *Ireland, England and the Continent in the Middle Ages and Beyond*, 145–63.

Clarke, Howard B., and J. R. S. Phillips, eds. *Ireland, England and the Continent in the Middle Ages and Beyond: Essays in Memory of a Turbulent Friar, F.X. Martin, O.S.A.* Dublin: University College Dublin Press, 2006.

Clarke, Maude. *Fourteenth Century Studies*. Edited by L. S. Sutherland and M. McKisack. 1937. Reprint, Oxford: Clarendon Press, 1968.

Cobb, L. Stephanie. *Dying to Be Men: Gender and Language in Early Christian Martyr Texts*. New York: Columbia University Press, 2008.

Cohen, Jeffrey Jerome, and Bonnie Wheeler, eds. *Becoming Male in the Middle Ages*. New York: Garland, 1997.

Cohn, Norman. *Europe's Inner Demons: An Enquiry Inspired by the Great Witch Hunt*. 1975. Reprint, Chicago: University of Chicago Press, 2000.

Cokayne, George. *Complete Peerage of England, Scotland, Ireland, Great Britain and the United Kingdom, Extant, Extinct, or Dormant*. Edited by V. Gibbs. 13 vols. London: St. Catherine Press, 1910–59.

Conlon, Lynda. "Women in Medieval Dublin: Their Legal Rights and Economic Power." In *Medieval Dublin IV: Proceedings of the Friends of Medieval Dublin Symposium 2002*, edited by Seán Duffy, 172–92. Dublin: Four Courts Press, 2003.

Conway, Colleen. *Behold the Man: Jesus and Greco-Roman Masculinity*. Oxford: Oxford University Press, 2008.

Cosgrove, Art. "Hiberniores Ipsis Hibernis." In *Studies in Irish History Presented to R. Dudley Edwards*, edited by Art Cosgrove and Donal McCartney, 1–14. Dublin: University College Dublin Press, 1979.

——. "Irish Episcopal Temporalities in the Thirteenth Century." *Archivium Hibernicum* 32 (1974): 63–71.

——. *Marriage in Ireland*. Dublin: College Press, 1985.

——, ed. *A New History of Ireland*. Vol. 2, *Medieval Ireland, 1169–1534*. 1987. Reprint, Oxford: Clarendon Press, 2001.

——. "The Writing of Irish Medieval History." *Irish Historical Studies* 27 (1990): 97–111.

Cotter, Francis J. *The Friars Minor in Ireland from Their Arrival to 1400*. St. Bonaventure, NY: Franciscan Institute Publications, 1994.

Cragg, R. B. *Legendary Rambles*. Bingley: Harrison and Sons, 1898.

Crawford, Jane. "Evidences for Witchcraft in Anglo-Saxon England." *Medium Ævum* 32 (1963): 99–116.

Crawford, John, and Raymond Gillespie, eds. *St Patrick's Cathedral, Dublin: A History*. Dublin: Four Courts Press, 2009.

Cullen, Olive M. "A Question of Time or a Question of Theology: A Study of the Easter Controversy in the Insular Church." PhD diss., Pontifical University, St Patrick's College, Maynooth, 2007. http://eprints.nuim.ie/1331/.

Curtis, Edmund. "The Clan System among English Settlers in Ireland." *English Historical Review* 25 (1910): 116–20.

——. *A History of Medieval Ireland from 1086 to 1513*. 1923. Reprint, London: Methuen, 1938.

Davies, R. R., ed. *The British Isles, 1100–1500: Comparisons, Contrasts, and Connections*. Edinburgh: J. Donald Publishers, 1988.

——. "Lordship or Colony?" In Lydon, *The English in Medieval Ireland*, 142–60.

Davies, Wendy. "Anger and the Celtic Saint." In *Anger's Past: The Social Uses of an Emotion in the Middle Ages*, edited by Barbara H. Rosenwein, 191–202. Ithaca: Cornell University Press, 1998.

Deane, Jennifer Kolpacoff. *A History of Medieval Heresy and Inquisition*. Lanham, MD: Rowan & Littlefield, 2011.

De Paor, Liam. *Saint Patrick's World: The Christian Culture of Ireland's Apostolic Age*. Notre Dame: University of Notre Dame Press, 1993.

Duddy, Thomas. *A History of Irish Thought*. London: Routledge, 2002.

Duffy, Seán, ed. *Medieval Dublin II: Proceedings of the Friends of Medieval Dublin Symposium 2000*. Dublin: Four Courts Press, 2001.

——, ed. *Medieval Dublin IV: Proceedings of the Friends of Medieval Dublin Symposium 2002*. Dublin: Four Courts Press, 2003.

——, ed. *Medieval Ireland: An Encylopedia*. New York: Routledge, 2005.

——. "The Problem of Degeneracy." In *Law and Disorder in Thirteenth-Century Ireland: The Dublin Parliament of 1297*, edited by James Lydon, 87–106. Dublin: Four Courts Press, 1997.

Duggan, Anne. "The Power of Documents: The Curious Case of *Laudabiliter*." In Bolton and Meek, *Aspects of Power and Authority in the Middle Ages*, 251–75.

——. "*Totius christianitatis caput*: The Pope and the Princes." In Bolton and Duggan, *Adrian IV, the English Pope*, 138–55.

Dunning, P. J. "The Arroasian Order in Medieval Ireland." *Irish Historical Studies* 4 (1945): 297–315.

——. "Irish Representatives and Irish Ecclesiastical Affairs at the Fourth Lateran Council." In Watt, Morall, and Martin, *Medieval Studies Presented to Aubrey Gwynn*, 90–113.

——. "Pope Innocent III and the Irish Kings." *Journal of Ecclesiastical History* 8 (1957): 17–32.

Dwyer, Finbar. *Witches, Spies and Stockhom Syndrome: Life in Medieval Ireland.* Dublin: New Island, 2013.

Edwards, Robert R., and Vickie Ziegler, eds. *Matrons and Marginal Women in Medieval Society.* Woodbridge: Boydell Press, 1995.

Elliott, A. L. "The Abbey of St. Thomas the Martyr, near Dublin." In Clarke, *Medieval Dublin*, 1:62–76.

Empey, C. A. "The Anglo-Norman Community in Tipperary and Kilkenny in the Middle Ages: Change and Continuity." In Mac Niocaill and Wallace, *Keimelia*, 449–67.

——. "The Sacred and the Secular: The Augustinian Priory of Kells in Ossory, 1193–1541." *Irish Historical Studies* 24 (1984): 131–51.

Ewen, C. L'Estrange. *Witchcraft and Demonianism.* London: Heath, Cranton, 1933.

Ferguson J. F. "The 'Mere English' and 'Mere Irish.'" *Transactions of the Kilkenny Archeological Society* 1 (1850–51): 508–12.

Fergusson, James, ed. *The Declaration of Arbroath.* Edinburgh: Edinburgh University Press, 1970.

Field, Sean L. *The Beguine, the Angel, and the Inquisitor: The Trials of Marguerite Porete and Guiard of Cressonessart.* Notre Dame: University of Notre Dame Press, 2012.

Finan, Thomas. "Prophecies of the Expected Deliverer in Irish Bardic Poetry." *New Hibernia Review* 6 (2002): 113–24.

Flanagan, Marie Thérèse. "Hiberno-papal Relations in the Late Twelfth Century." *Archivium Hibernicum* 34 (1976–77): 55–70.

——. "The Reformation of the Irish Church in the Twelfth Century." In *Two Thousand Years of Christianity and Ireland*, edited by John Bartlett and Stuart Kinsella, 65–84. Blackrock: Columba Press, 2006.

——. "St. Mary's Abbey, Louth, and the Introduction of the Arrouaisian Observance into Ireland." *Clogher Record* 10 (1980): 223–34.

Flanagan, U. G. "Papal Provisions in Ireland, 1305–78." *Historical Studies* 3 (1961): 92–103.

Flint, Valerie. *The Rise of Magic in Early Medieval Europe.* Princeton: Princeton University Press, 1991.

Flower, Robin. *The Irish Tradition.* 1947. Reprint, Dublin: Clarendon Press, 1994.

Forey, Alan. "Could Alleged Templar Malpractices Have Remained Undetected for Decades?" In Burgtorf, Crawford, and Nicholson, *Debate on the Trial of the Templars*, 11–19.

——. *Military Orders and Crusades.* Brookfield, VT: Variorum, 1994.

——. *The Military Orders from the Twelfth to the Early Fourteenth Centuries.* Toronto: University of Toronto Press, 1992.

Frame, Robin. "The Bruces in Ireland, 1315–18." *Irish Historical Studies* 19 (1974): 3–37.

——. *Colonial Ireland, 1169–1369.* Dublin: Helicon, 1981.

——. "'Les Engleys Nées en Irlande': The English Political Identity in Medieval Ireland." *Transactions of the Royal Historical Society*, 6th ser., 3 (1993): 83–103.

——. *English Lordship in Ireland, 1318–1361*. Oxford: Clarendon Press, 1982.

——. "English Officials and Irish Chiefs in the Fourteenth Century." *English Historical Review* 90 (1975): 748–77.

——. "English Policies and Anglo-Irish Attitudes in the Crisis of 1341–42." In Lydon, *England and Ireland in the Later Middle Ages*, 86–103.

——. "Exporting State and Nation: Being English in Medieval Ireland." In *Power and the Nation in European History*, edited by Len Scales and Oliver Zimmer, 143–65. Cambridge: Cambridge University Press, 2005.

——. *Ireland and Britain, 1170–1450*. London: Hambledon Press, 1998.

——. "Military Service in the Lordship of Ireland 1290–1360: Institutions and Society on the Anglo-Gaelic Frontier." In *Medieval Frontier Societies*, edited by Robert Bartlett and Angus MacKay, 101–26. Oxford: Clarendon Press, 1989.

——. "Power and Society in the Lordship of Ireland, 1272–1377." *Past and Present* 76 (1977): 3–33.

Gallagher, Niav. "Alexander Bicknor, Archbishop of Dublin, 1317–49." Master's thesis, National University of Ireland, University College Dublin, 1997.

Gilbert, J. T. *A History of the City of Dublin*. 3 vols. Dublin, 1854–59. Reprint, Shannon: Irish University Press, 1972.

Gillingham, John. "The Beginnings of English Imperialism." *Journal of Historical Sociology* 5 (1992): 392–409.

——. "The English Invasion of Ireland." In Bradshaw, Hadfield, and Maley, *Representing Ireland*, 24–42.

Gilmour-Bryson, Anne. "Priests of the Order of the Temple: What Can They Tell Us?" In Burgtorf, Crawford, and Nicholson, *Debate on the Trial of the Templars*, 327–38.

Ginzburg, Carlo. *Ecstasies: Deciphering the Witches' Sabbath*. Translated by Raymond Rosenthal. New York: Pantheon Books, 1991.

Given, James. *Inquisition and Medieval Society: Power, Discipline, and Resistance in Languedoc*. Ithaca: Cornell University Press, 1998.

Gleeson, Dermot F. "A Fourteenth-Century Clare Heresy Trial." *Irish Ecclesiastical Record* 89 (1958): 36–42.

Gougaud, Louis. "The Isle of the Saints." *Studies* 13 (1924): 363–80.

Graves, James, and J. G. A. Prim. *The History, Architecture and Antiquities of the Cathedral Church of St Canice, Kilkenny*. Dublin: Hodges, Smith, 1857.

Grieco, Holly J. "Pastoral Care, Inquisition, and Mendicancy in the Medieval Franciscan Order." In *The Origin, Development, and Refinement of Medieval Religious Mendicancies*, edited by Donald S. Prudlo, 117–55. Leiden: Brill, 2011.

Grundmann, Herbert. *Religious Movements in the Middle Ages*. Translated by Steven Rowan. Notre Dame: University of Notre Dame Press, 1995.

Gwynn, Aubrey. *Anglo-Irish Church Life: Fourteenth and Fifteenth Centuries*. Vol 2.4 of *A History of Irish Catholicism*. Dublin: Gill and Son, 1968.

——. "The Black Death in Ireland." *Studies* 24 (1935): 25–42.

——. "Ireland and the Continent in the Eleventh Century." *Irish Historical Studies* 8 (1953): 192–216.

——. "Ireland and Rome in the Eleventh Century." *Irish Ecclesiastical Record* 57 (1941): 213–32.

——. *The Irish Church in the Eleventh and Twelfth Centuries.* Edited by Gerard O'Brien. Dublin: Four Courts Press, 1992.

——. "Pope Gregory VII and the Irish Church." *Irish Ecclesiastical Record* 58 (1941): 97–109.

——. *The Twelfth Century Reform.* Dublin: Gill and Son, 1968.

Gwynn, Aubrey, and R. Neville Hadcock. *Medieval Religious Houses: Ireland.* London: Harlow, Longmans, 1970.

Hadley, D. M., ed. *Masculinity in Medieval Europe.* London: Longman, 1999.

Hair, P. E. H. "An Irishman before the Mexican Inquisition, 1574–5." *Irish Historical Studies* 17 (1971): 297–319.

Hamilton, Bernard. *The Medieval Inquisition.* New York: Holmes and Meier, 1981.

Hand, G. J. "The Church and English Law in Medieval Ireland." *Proceedings of the Irish Catholic Historical Committee,* 1959, 10–18.

——. *The Church in the English Lordship, 1216–1307.* Vol. 2.3 of *A History of Irish Catholicism.* Dublin: Gill and Son, 1968.

——. "The Common Law in Ireland in the Thirteenth and Fourteenth Centuries: Two Cases Involving Christ Church, Dublin." *Journal of the Royal Society of the Antiquaries of Ireland* 97 (1967): 97–111.

——. "English Law in Ireland, 1172–1351." *Northern Ireland Legal Quarterly* 23 (1972): 393–422.

——. *English Law in Ireland, 1290–1324.* Cambridge: Cambridge University Press, 1967.

——. "The Mediaeval Chapter of St. Patrick's Cathedral, Dublin I: The Early Period (*c.* 1219 – *c.* 1270)." *Reportorium Novum* 3 (1964): 229–48.

——. "The Rivalry of the Cathedral Chapters in Medieval Dublin." *Journal of the Royal Society of the Antiquaries of Ireland* 92 (1962): 193–206.

——. "The Two Cathedrals of Dublin: Internal Organisation and Mutual Relations, to the Middle of the Fourteenth Century." Master's thesis, University College Dublin, 1954.

Haren, Michael. "Richard FitzRalph of Dundalk, Oxford and Armagh: Scholar, Prelate and Controversialist." In *The Irish Contribution to European Scholastic Thought,* edited by James McEvoy and Michael Dunne, 88–110. Dublin: Four Courts Press, 2009.

Heath, James. *Torture and English Law: An Administrative and Legal History from the Plantagenets to the Stuarts.* Westport, CT: Greenwood Press, 1982.

Hennig, John. "Medieval Ireland in Cistercian Records." *Irish Ecclesiastical Record* 73 (1950): 226–42.

Herren, Michael, and Shirley Ann Brown. *Christ in Celtic Christianity: Britain and Ireland from the Fifth to the Tenth Century.* Woodbridge: Boydell Press, 2002.

Holinshed, Raphael. *Chronicles of England, Scotland, and Ireland.* Vol. 6, *Ireland.* London: J. Johnson, 1808.

Hopkin, Charles Edward. "The Share of Thomas Aquinas in the Growth of the Witchcraft Delusion." PhD diss., University of Pennsylvania, 1940.

Housley, Norman. "Crusades against Christians: Their Origins and Early Developments, *c.* 1000–1216." In *Crusade and Settlement: Papers Read at the First Conference of the Society for the Study of Crusades and the Latin East and Presented to R. C. Smail,* edited by Peter W. Edbury, 17–36. Cardiff: University College Cardiff Press, 1985.

Hughes, Kathleen. *The Church in Early Irish Society.* Ithaca: Cornell University Press, 1966.

———. *Early Christian Ireland: Introduction to the Sources.* Ithaca: Cornell University Press, 1972.

Iribarren, Isabel. "From Black Magic to Heresy: A Doctrinal Leap in the Pontificate of John XXII." *Church History* 76 (2007): 32–60.

Jones, W. R. "The Image of the Barbarian in Medieval Europe." *Comparative Studies in Society and History* 13 (1971): 376–407.

Karlsen, Carol. *The Devil in the Shape of a Woman: Witchcraft in Colonial New England.* 1987. Reprint, New York: Vintage Books, 1989.

Karras, Ruth Mazo. *From Boys to Men: Formations of Masculinity in Late Medieval Europe.* Philadelphia: University of Pennylvania Press, 2003.

———. "Separating the Men from the Goats: Masculinity, Civilization and Identity Formation in the Medieval University." In Hadley, *Masculinity in Medieval Europe*, 189–213.

Kelly, Henry Ansgar. "Inquisition and the Prosecution of Heresy: Misconceptions and Abuses." *Church History* 58 (1989): 439–51.

Kelly, James, and Dáire Keogh, eds. *History of the Catholic Diocese of Dublin.* Dublin: Four Courts Press, 2000.

. Kelly, Joseph. "Pelagius, Pelagianism and the Early Christian Irish." *Mediaevalia* 4 (1978): 99–124.

Kenney, James F. *The Sources for the Early History of Ireland: Ecclesiastical; An Introduction and Guide.* 1929. Reprint, Dublin: Four Courts Press, 1997.

Kenny, Gillian. *Anglo-Irish and Gaelic Women in Ireland, c. 1170–1540.* Dublin: Four Courts Press, 2007.

———. "The Power of Dower: The Importance of Dower in the Lives of Medieval Women in Ireland." In Meek and Lawless, *Pawns or Players?*, 59–74.

Kieckhefer, Richard. *European Witch Trials: Their Foundations in Popular and Learned Culture, 1300–1500.* Berkeley: University of California Press, 1976.

———. *Forbidden Rites: A Necromancer's Manual of the Fifteenth Century.* Stroud: Sutton Publishing, 1997.

———. *Magic in the Middle Ages.* 1989. Reprint, Cambridge: Cambridge University Press, 1995.

Killen, W. D. *The Ecclesiastical History of Ireland.* 2 vols. London: Macmillan, 1875.

King, Robert. *A Primer of the History of the Holy Catholic Church in Ireland.* 3 vols. Dublin: W. Curry, 1845–51.

Kittredge, George. *Witchcraft in Old and New England.* 1929. Reprint, New York: Atheneum, 1972.

Ladurie, Emmanuel LeRoy. *Montaillou: The Promised Land of Error.* New York: Random House, 1979.

Lambert, Malcolm. *Medieval Heresy: Popular Movements from the Gregorian Reform to the Reformation.* 1977. 2nd ed., Oxford: Blackwell, 1992.

Lambert, Malcolm. *Medieval Heresy: Popular Movements from the Gregorian Reform to the Reformation.* 1977. 3rd ed., Oxford: Blackwell, 2002.

Lanigan, K. "Richard de Ledrede, Bishop of Ossory." *Old Kilkenny Review* 15 (1963): 23–29.

Lapoint, Elwyn. "Irish Immunity to Witch-Hunting, 1534–1711." *Éire-Ireland* 27 (1992): 76–92.

Lawless, Warren. "Gaelic Ireland and the Crusades, 1095–1230." http://homepage. eircom.net/~wlawless/History/Crusade.html.

Lawlor, H. J. *The Fasti of St. Patrick's, Dublin.* Dundalk: W. Tempest, 1930.

———. "The Monuments of the Pre-Reformation Archbishops of Dublin." In Clarke, *Medieval Dublin,* 1:227–51.

Lawrence, C. H. *The Friars: The Impact of the Early Mendicant Movement on Western Society.* London: Longman, 1994.

Lea, Henry Charles. *A History of the Inquisition of the Middle Ages.* 3 vols. New York: Harbor Press, 1906.

———. *Minor Historical Writings and Other Essays.* Edited by Arthur C. Howland. Philadelphia: University of Pennsylvania Press, 1942.

Leerssen, Joep. *Mere Irish and Fíor-Ghael: Studies in the Idea of Irish Nationality, its Development and Literary Expression Prior to the Nineteenth Century.* Notre Dame: University of Notre Dame Press, 1997.

Leff, Gordon. *Heresy in the Later Middle Ages.* 2 vols. Manchester: Manchester University Press, 1967.

Leland, Thomas. *The History of Ireland from the Invasion of Henry II.* 3 vols. London: J. Nourse, 1773.

Lerner, Robert E. *The Heresy of the Free Spirit in the Later Middle Ages.* 1972. Reprint, Notre Dame: University of Notre Dame Press, 2007.

Leslie, James B. *Ossory Clergy and Parishes: Being an Account of the Clergy of the Church of Ireland in the Diocese of Ossory, from the Earliest Period, with Historical Notices of the Several Parishes, Churches, &c.* Enniskillen: R. H. Ritchie, 1933.

Levack, Brian P., ed. *Witchcraft, Women and Society.* Vol. 10 of *Articles on Witchcraft, Magic and Demonology.* New York: Garland, 1992.

———. *The Witch-Hunt in Early Modern Europe.* London: Longman, 1987.

Little, Lester K. *Benedictine Maledictions: Liturgical Cursing in Romanesque France.* Ithaca: Cornell University Press, 1993.

Logan, F. D. *Excommunication and the Secular Arm in Medieval England.* Toronto: Pontifical Institute of Mediaeval Studies, 1968.

Lord, Evelyn. *The Knights Templar in Britain.* Edinburgh: Harlow, Longman, 2002.

Lydon, James. "The Braganstown Massacre, 1329." *Louth Archaelogical Society Journal* 19 (1977): 5–16.

———. "The Case against Alexander Bicknor, Archbishop and Peculator." In Smith, *Ireland and the English World in the Late Middle Ages,* 103–11.

———, ed. *England and Ireland in the Later Middle Ages: Essays in Honour of Jocelyn Otway-Ruthven.* Blackrock: Irish Academic Press, 1981.

———, ed. *The English in Medieval Ireland: Proceedings of the First Joint Meeting of the Royal Irish Academy and the British Academy, Dublin, 1982.* Dublin: Royal Irish Academy, 1984.

———. *Ireland in the Later Middle Ages.* Dublin: Gill and Macmillan, 1973.

———. *The Lordship of Ireland in the Middle Ages.* Dublin: Gill and Macmillan, 1972.

———. "Medieval Wicklow: 'A Land of War.'" In *Wicklow: History and Society,* edited by Ken Hannigan and William Nolan, 151–89. Dublin: Geography Publications, 1994.

———. "Nation and Race in Medieval Ireland." In *Concepts of National Identity in the Middle Ages,* edited by Simon Forde, Lesley Johnson, and Alan V. Murray, 103–29. Leeds: University of Leeds Press, 1995.

———. "The Problem of the Frontier in Medieval Ireland." *Topic* 13 (1967): 5–22.

Mac Curtain, Margaret, and Donncha Ó Corráin, eds. *Women in Irish Society: The Historical Dimension*. Dublin: Arlen House, 1978.

MacGowan, Shane/Stiff Music Ltd. "Birmingham Six." *If I Should Fall From Grace With God*. Pogue Mahone Records, 1988.

MacInerny, M. H. "The Templars in Ireland." *Irish Ecclesiastical Record* 2 (1913): 225–45.

Mac Ivor, Dermot. "The Knights Templars in County Louth." *Seanchas Ardmhacha* 4 (1960–62): 72–91.

MacNeill, Eoin. *Phases of Irish History*. 1919. Reprint, Dublin: Gill and Son, 1968.

Mac Niocaill, Gearóid, and Patrick F. Wallace, eds. *Keimelia: Studies in Medieval Archaeology and History in Memory of Tom Delaney*. Galway: Galway University Press, 1988.

Manning, Conleth, ed. *Dublin and Beyond the Pale*. Bray: Wordwell, 1998.

Márkus, Gilbert. "Pelagianism and the 'Common Celtic Church.'" *Innes Review* 56 (2005): 165–213.

Martin, F. X. "Ireland in the Time of St. Bernard, St. Malachy, St. Laurence O'Toole." *Seanchas Ardmhacha* 15 (1992–93): 1–35.

———. "Murder in a Dublin Monastery, 1379." In Mac Niocaill and Wallace, *Keimelia*, 468–98.

Mason, William Monck. *The History and Antiquities of the Collegiate and Cathedral Church of St. Patrick, near Dublin, from Its Foundation in 1190, to the Year 1819*. Dublin, 1820.

Massey, Eithne. *Prior Roger Outlaw of Kilmainham*. Dublin: Irish Academic Press, 2000.

Matthew, H. C. G., and Brian Harrison, eds. *Oxford Dictionary of National Biography*. 61 vols. Oxford: Oxford University Press, 2004.

McDermot, Gerard. "The Burning of Adam Duff O'Toole." *Freethinker* 83 (1963): 250.

McGrath, Fergal. *Education in Ancient and Medieval Ireland*. Dublin: Studies Special Publications, 1979.

McGuire, James, and James Quinn, eds. *Dictionary of Irish Biography*. Cambridge: Cambridge University Press, 2009.

McNeill, Charles. "Harris: *Collectanea de rebus Hibernicis*." *Analecta Hibernica* 6 (1934).

Meeder, Sven. "Boniface and the Irish Heresy of Clemens." *Church History* 80 (2011): 251–80.

Meek, Christine, ed. *Women in Renaissance and Early Modern Europe*. Dublin: Four Courts Press, 2000.

Meek, Christine, and Catherine Lawless, eds. *Pawns or Players? Studies on Medieval and Early Modern Women*. Dublin: Four Courts Press, 2003.

Meek, Christine, and Katharine Simms, eds. *'The Fragility of Her Sex'? Medieval Irishwomen in Their European Context*. Dublin: Four Courts Press, 1996.

Menache, Sophia. *Clement V*. Cambridge: Cambridge University Press, 1998.

———. "Contemporary Attitudes Concerning the Templars' Affair: Propaganda's Fiasco?" *Journal of Medieval History* 8 (1982): 135–47.

Mollat, G. *The Popes at Avignon, 1305–1378*. Translated by Janet Love. London: Harper and Row, 1963.

Moody, T. W., ed. *Nationality and the Pursuit of National Independence*. Belfast: Appletree Press, 1978.

Moody, T. W., F. X. Martin, and F. J. Byrne, eds. *A New History of Ireland.* Vol. 9, *Maps, Genealogies, Lists.* 1984. Reprint, Oxford: Clarendon Press, 2002.

Mooney, Canice, OFM. *The Church in Gaelic Ireland: Thirteenth to Fifteenth Centuries.* Dublin: Gill and Macmillan, 1969.

Moore, R. I. *The Birth of Popular Heresy.* 1975. Reprint, Toronto: University of Toronto Press, 1995.

——. *The War on Heresy.* Cambridge: Belknap Press of Harvard University Press, 2012.

Moran, Dermot. *The Philosophy of John Scottus Eriugena: A Study of Idealism in the Middle Ages.* Cambridge: Cambridge University Press, 1989.

Morrin, James. "The Kilkenny Witchcraft Case." In *Transactions of the Ossory Archaeological Society,* vol. 1, *1874–79,* 213–39. Kilkenny: Printed at the Journal Office, 1879.

Muldoon, James. "The Remonstrance of Irish Princes and the Canon Law Theory of the Just War." *American Journal of Legal History* 22 (1978): 309–25.

Mullally, Evelyn. "Hiberno-Norman Literature and Its Public." In Bradley, *Settlement and Society in Medieval Ireland,* 327–43.

Murphy, Bryan. "The Status of the Native Irish after 1331." *Irish Jurist* 2 (1967): 116–38.

Murphy, Gerard. "Eleventh or Twelfth Century Irish Doctrine Concerning the Real Presence." In Watt, Morrall, and Martin, *Medieval Studies Presented to Aubrey Gwynn,* 19–28.

Neal, Derek G. *The Masculine Self in Late Medieval England.* Chicago: University of Chicago Press, 2008.

Neary, Anne. "The Origins and Character of the Kilkenny Witchcraft Case of 1324." *Proceedings of the Royal Irish Academy* 83C (1983): 333–50.

——. "Richard de Ledrede, English Franciscan and Bishop of Ossory." Bachelor's thesis, Trinity College Dublin, 1978.

——. "Richard Ledrede: English Franciscan and Bishop of Ossory, 1317–c.1360." *Journal of the Butler Society* 2, no. 3 (1984): 273–82.

Neely, W. G. *Kilkenny: An Urban History, 1391–1843.* Belfast: Institute of Irish Studies, 1989.

Newman, Barbara. *From Virile Woman to WomanChrist: Studies in Medieval Religion and Literature.* Philadelphia: University of Pennsylvania Press, 1993.

Nic Ghiollamhaith, Aoife. "Dynastic Warfare and Historical Writing in North Munster, 1276–1350." *Cambridge Medieval Celtic Studies* 2 (1981): 73–89.

——. "Kings and Vassals in Later Medieval Ireland: The Uí Bhriain and the Mic-Conmara in the Fourteenth Century." In Barry, Frame, and Simms, *Colony and Frontier in Medieval Ireland,* 201–16.

——. "The Ui Briain and the King of England, 1248–1276." *Dal gCais* 7 (1984): 94–99.

Nicholls, K. *Gaelic and Gaelicised Ireland in the Middle Ages.* Dublin: Gill and MacMillan, 1972.

Nicholson, Helen. "The Hospitallers' and Templars' Involvement in Warfare on the Frontiers of the British Isles in the Late Thirteenth and Early Fourteenth Centuries." *Ordines Militares, Colloquia Torunensia Historica: Yearbook for the Study of the Military Orders* 17 (2012): 105–19.

————. *The Knights Templar: A New History*. Stroud: Sutton, 2001.

————. *The Knights Templar on Trial: The Trial of the Templars in the British Isles, 1308–1311*. Stroud: History Press, 2009.

————. "The Testimony of Brother Henry Danet and the Trial of the Templars in Ireland." In *In Laudem Hierosolymitani: Studies in Crusades and Medieval Culture in Honour of Benjamin Z. Kedar*, edited by Iris Shagrir, Ronnie Ellenblum, and Jonathan Riley-Smith, 411–23. Aldershot: Ashgate, 2007.

————. "The Trial of the Templars in Ireland." In *The Debate on the Trial of the Templars*, edited by Jochen Burgtorf, Paul F. Crawford, and Helen J. Nicholson, 225-35. Farnham: Ashgate, 2010.

Nolan, William, and Kevin Whelan, eds. *Kilkenny: History and Society*. Dublin: Geography Publications, 1990.

O'Brien, A. F. "The Territorial Ambitions of Maurice fitz Thomas, First Earl of Desmond." *Proceedings of the Royal Irish Academy* 82C (1982): 59–88.

Ó Buachalla, Breandán. "Aodh Eanghach and the Irish King-Hero." In *Sages, Saints and Storytellers: Celtic Studies in Honour of Professor James Carney*, edited by Donnchadh Ó Corráin, Liam Breatnach, and Kim McCone, 200–32. Maynooth: An Sagart, 1989.

O'Byrne, Emmett. "O'Toole (Ó Tuathail), Adam." In McGuire and Quinn, *Dictionary of Irish Biography*. Cambridge: Cambridge University Press, 2009.

————. *War, Politics and the Irish of Leinster, 1156–1606*. Dublin: Four Courts Press, 2003.

Ó Clabaigh, Colmán. *The Friars in Ireland, 1224–1540*. Dublin: Four Courts Press, 2012.

Ó Cléirigh, Cormac. "The Absentee Landlady and the Sturdy Robbers: Agnes de Valence." In Meek and Simms, *'The Fragility of Her Sex'?*, 101–18.

Ó Corráin, Donnchadh. "Nationality and Kingship in Pre-Norman Ireland." In Moody, *Nationality and the Pursuit of National Independence*, 1–35.

Ó Cróinín, Dáibhí. *Early Medieval Ireland, 400–1200*. London: Longman Group, 1995.

————. "'New Heresy for Old': Pelagianism in Ireland and the Papal Letter of 640." *Speculum* 60 (1985): 505–16.

Ó Cuív, Brian, ed. *Seven Centuries of Irish Learning, 1000–1700*. Dublin: Stationery Office, 1961.

O'Doherty, J. F. "Rome and the Anglo-Norman Invasion of Ireland." *Irish Ecclesiastical Record* 42 (1933): 131–45.

O'Dwyer, B. W. *The Conspiracy of Mellifont, 1216–1231*. Dublin: Dublin Historical Association, 1970.

————. "The Crisis in the Cistercian Monasteries in Ireland in the Early 13th Century." *Analecta Cisterciensia* 31, no. 2 (1976): 267–304; 32, nos. 1–2 (1977): 3–112.

————. "Gaelic Monasticism and the Irish Cistercians, c.1228." *Irish Ecclesiastical Record* 108 (1967): 19–28.

————. "The Impact of the Native Irish on the Cistercians in the Thirteenth Century." *Journal of Religious History* 4 (1967): 287–301.

O'Dwyer, Peter. *Mary: A History of Devotion in Ireland*. Dublin: Four Courts Press, 1988.

O'Hart, John. *Irish Pedigrees: Or, The Origin and Stem of the Irish Nation*. 2 vols. Dublin: J. Duffy, 1892.

Ó Murchadha, Diarmuid. "The Battle of Callann, A.D. 1261." *Cork Historical Society Journal* 66 (1961): 105–15.

——. "Is the O'Neill-MacCarthy Letter of 1317 a Forgery?" *Irish Historical Studies* 23 (1982) 61–67.

Ó Néill, Pádraig. "*Romani* Influences on Seventh-Century Hiberno-Latin Literature." In *Irland und Europa: Die Kirche im Frühmittelalter,* edited by Próinséas Ní Chatháin and Michael Richter, 280–90. Stuttgart: Klett-Cotta, 1984.

Orpen, G. H. *Ireland under the Normans, 1169–1333.* 4 vols. 1911–20. Reprint, Oxford: Clarendon Press, 1968.

O'Sullivan, Benedict. "The Dominicans in Medieval Dublin," In Clarke, *Medieval Dublin*, 1:83–99.

O'Sullivan, M. D. *Italian Merchant Bankers in Ireland in the Thirteenth Century.* Dublin: Allen Figgis, 1962.

O'Toole, P. L. *A History of the Clan O'Toole and Other Leinster Septs.* Dublin: M. H. Gill and Son, 1890.

Otway-Ruthven, A. J. "Anglo-Irish Shire Government in the Thirteenth Century." *Irish Historical Studies* 5 (1946): 1–28.

——. *A History of Medieval Ireland.* New York: Barnes and Noble, 1968.

——. "Ireland in the 1350s: Sir Thomas de Rokeby and His Successors." *Journal of the Royal Society of the Antiquaries of Ireland* 97 (1967): 47–59.

Pagels, Elaine. *Adam, Eve, and the Serpent: Sex and Politics in Early Christianity.* New York: Random House, 1988.

Parker, Ciarán. "Paterfamilias and *Parentela*: The Le Poer Lineage in Fourteenth-Century Waterford." *Proceedings of the Royal Irish Academy* 95C (1995): 93–117.

Parker, Thomas W. *The Knights Templars in England.* Tucson: University of Arizona Press, 1963.

Partner, Peter. *The Murdered Magicians: The Templars and Their Myth.* Oxford: Oxford University Press, 1982.

Patschovsky, Alexander. "Heresy and Society: On the Political Function of Heresy in the Medieval World." In *York Studies in Medieval Theology IV: Texts and the Repression of Medieval Heresy*, edited by Caterina Bruschi and Peter Biller, 23–41. Woodbridge: York Medieval Press, 2003.

Pegg, Mark Gregory. *The Corruption of Angels: The Great Inquisition of 1245–1246.* Princeton: Princeton University Press, 2001.

——. *A Most Holy War: The Albigensian Crusade and the Battle for Christendom.* Oxford: Oxford University Press, 2008.

Perkins, Clarence. "The History of the Knights Templar in England." PhD diss., Harvard University, 1908.

——. "The Knights Templars in the British Isles." *English Historical Review* 25 (1910): 209–30.

——. "The Trial of the Knights Templars in England." *English Historical Review* 24 (1909): 432–47.

——. "The Wealth of the Knights Templars in England and the Disposition of It after Their Dissolution." *American Historical Review* 15 (1909–10): 252–63.

Peters, Edward. *The Magician, the Witch, and the Law.* Philadelphia: University of Pennsylvania Press, 1978.

——. *Torture.* Oxford: Basil Blackwell, 1985.

Phillips, J. R. S. "The Irish Remonstrance of 1317: An International Perspective." *Irish Historical Studies* 27 (1990): 112–29.

———. "The Remonstrance Revisited." In *Men, Women and War: Papers Read before the Twentieth Irish Conference of Historians,* edited by T. G. Fraser, Keith Jeffrey, and Thomas Bartlett, Historical Studies 8, 13–27. Dublin: Lilliput Press, 1993.

Prawer, J. "Military Orders and Crusader Politics in the Second Half of the 13th Century." In *Die geistlichen Ritterorden Europas,* edited by J. Fleckenstein and J. Hellmann, 217–29. Sigmaringen: Thorbecke, 1980.

Quiggin, E. C. "O'Conor's House at Cloonfree." In *Essays and Studies Presented to William Ridgeway,* edited by E. C. Quiggin, 333–52. Cambridge: Cambridge University Press, 1913.

Rees, B. R. *Pelagius: A Reluctant Heretic.* Woodbridge: Boydell Press, 1988.

Reynolds, Susan. "Social Mentalities and the Case of Medieval Scepticism." *Transactions of the Royal Historical Society,* 6th ser., 1 (1991): 21–41.

Richardson, H. G. "Heresy and Lay Power under Richard II," *English Historical Review* 51 (1936): 1–28.

Richardson, H. G., and G. O. Sayles. *The Administration of Ireland, 1172–1377.* Dublin: Stationery Office, 1963.

———. *The Irish Parliament in the Middle Ages.* Philadelphia: University of Pennsylvania Press, 1952.

Richter, Michael. *Medieval Ireland: The Enduring Tradition.* New York: St Martin's Press, 1988.

Riddell, William Renwick. "The First Execution for Witchcraft in Ireland." *Journal of Criminal Law and Criminolgy and Police Science* 7 (1917): 828–37.

Rider, Catherine. *Magic and Religion in Medieval England.* London: Reaktion Books, 2012.

Riley-Smith, Jonathan. "Were the Templars Guilty?" In *The Medieval Crusade,* edited by Susan J. Ridyard, 107–24. Woodbridge: Boydell Press, 2004.

Robbins, Rossell Hope. *The Encyclopedia of Witchcraft and Demonology.* New York: Crown Publishers, 1959.

Robson, Michael. "Franciscan Bishops of Irish Dioceses Active in Medieval England: A Guide to the Materials in English Libraries and Archives." *Collectanea Hibernica* 38 (1996): 7–39.

Rolston, Bill. *Drawing Support 2: Murals of War and Peace.* Belfast: Beyond the Pale Publications, 1995.

Ronan, Myles V. "Anglo-Norman Dublin and Diocese." *Irish Ecclesiastical Record* 45 (1935): 148–64, 274–91, 485–504, 576–95; 46 (1935): 11–30, 154–71, 257–75, 377–93, 490–510, 577–96; 47 (1936): 28–44, 144–63, 459–68; 48 (1936): 170–93, 378–96; 49 (1937): 155–64.

Rose, Elliot. *A Razor for a Goat: A Discussion of Certain Problems in the History of Witchcraft and Diabolism.* 1962. Reprint, Toronto: University of Toronto Press, 1989.

Russell, Jeffrey Burton. *Witchcraft in the Middle Ages.* Ithaca: Cornell University Press, 1972.

Russell, Jeffrey Burton, and Brooks Alexander. *A New History of Witchcraft: Sorcerers, Heretics and Pagans.* 2nd ed. London: Thames and Hudson, 2007.

Ryan, John. "The Historical Background." In *Seven Centuries of Irish Learning, 1000–1700,* edited by Brian Ó Cuív, 11–26. Dublin: Stationery Office, 1961.

Ryan, Michael A. *A Kingdom of Stargazers: Astrology and Astronomy in the Late Medieval Crown of Aragon.* Ithaca: Cornell University Press, 2011.

Sayles, G. O. "The Rebellious First Earl of Desmond." In Watt, Morrall, and Martin, *Medieval Studies Presented to Aubrey Gwynn,* 203–29.

Seymour, St. John. *The Diocese of Emly.* Dublin: Church of Ireland Printing and Publishing, 1913.

———. *Irish Witchcraft and Demonology.* 1913. Reprint, New York: Dorset Press, 1992.

Share, Bernard. *Bunratty: Rebirth of a Castle.* Dingle: Brandon Book Publishers, 1995.

Sharpe, Richard. *Medieval Irish Saints' Lives: An Introduction to Vitae Sanctorum Hiberniae.* Oxford: Clarendon Press, 1991.

———. "Some Problems Concerning the Organization of the Church in Early Medieval Ireland." *Peritia* 3 (1984): 230–70.

Sheehy, M. P. "The Bull *Laudabiliter.* A Problem in Medieval Diplomatique and History." *Journal of the Galway Archaeological and Historical Society* 29 (1960–61): 45–70.

———. *When the Normans Came to Ireland.* 1975. Reprint, Cork: Mercier Press, 1998.

Sheils, W. J. and Diana Wood, eds. *The Churches, Ireland, and the Irish.* Oxford: Basil Blackwell, 1989.

Simms, Katharine. "The Battle of Dysart O'Dea and the Gaelic Resurgence in Thomond." *Dal gCais* 5 (1979): 59–66.

———. *From Kings to Warlords: The Changing Political Structure of Gaelic Ireland in the Later Middle Ages.* Woodbridge: Boydell Press, 1987.

———. "Frontiers in the Irish Church—Regional and Cultural." In Barry, Frame, and Simms, *Colony and Frontier in Medieval Ireland,* 177–200.

———. "The Legal Position of Irishwomen in the Late Middle Ages." *Irish Jurist* 10 (1975): 96–111.

———. "Literacy and the Irish Bards." In *Literacy in Medieval Celtic Societies,* edited by Huw Pryce, 238–58. Cambridge: Cambridge University Press, 1998.

———. "Women in Norman Ireland." In Mac Curtain and Ó Corráin, *Women in Irish Society,* 14–25.

Sinclair, K. V. "Anglo-Norman at Waterford." In *Medieval French Textual Studies in Memory of T. B. W. Reid,* edited by Ian Short, 219–38. London: Anglo-Norman Text Society, 1984.

Sinnott, Nigel H. "Adam Duff O'Toole: An Early Irish Heretic." *Freethinker* 89 (1969): 413–14.

Smith, Brendan, ed. *Britain and Ireland, 900–1300.* Cambridge: Cambridge University Press, 1999.

———. *Colonisation and Conquest in Medieval Ireland: The English in Louth, 1171–1330.* Cambridge: Cambridge University Press, 1999.

———, ed. *Ireland and the English World in the Late Middle Ages: Essays in Honour of Robin Frame.* New York: Palgrave Macmillan, 2009.

Sneddon, Andrew. *Possessed by the Devil: The Real History of the Islandmagee Witches and Ireland's Only Mass Witchcraft Trial.* Dublin: History Press Ireland, 2013.

Stancliffe, Clare. "Columbanus and the Gallic Bishops." In *Auctoritas: Mélanges offerts à Olivier Guillot,* edited by Giles Constable and Michel Rouche, 205–15. Paris: Presses de l'Université Paris-Sorbonne, 2006.

Stemmler, Theo. "The Vernacular Snatches in the Red Book of Ossory: A Textual Case-History." *Anglia* 95 (1977): 122–29.

Stenton, F. M. *Anglo-Saxon England.* 3rd ed. 1943. Reprint, Oxford: Clarendon Press, 1971.

Stephen, James. *A History of the Common Law in England.* 3 vols. London: MacMillan, 1883.

Stephen, Leslie, and Sidney Lee, eds. *The Dictionary of National Biography.* 63 vols. London: Smith, Elder, 1885–1900.

Stokes, G. T. *Ireland and the Anglo-Norman Church.* London: Hodder and Stoughton, 1889.

Strayer, Joseph. *The Reign of Philip the Fair.* Princeton: Princeton University Press, 1980.

Stubbs, William. *Constitutional History of England.* Vol. 3. Oxford: Clarendon Press, 1880.

Sullivan, Karen. *The Inner Lives of Medieval Inquisitors.* Chicago: University of Chicago Press, 2011.

Swanson, Robert. "Angels Incarnate: Clergy and Masculinity from Gregorian Reform to Reformation." In Hadley, *Masculinity in Medieval Europe,* 160–77.

Thomas, Keith. *Religion and the Decline of Magic: Studies in Popular Beliefs in Sixteenth- and Seventeenth-Century England.* New York: Charles Scribner's Sons, 1971.

Thompson, E. A. *Who Was Saint Patrick?* Woodbridge: Boydell Press, 1985.

Thorndike, Lynn. *A History of Magic and Experimental Science.* New York: Macmillan, 1934.

Throop, Palmer. *Criticism of the Crusade: A Study of Public Opinion and Crusade Propaganda.* Amsterdam: N. V. Swets and Zeitlinger, 1940.

Tierney, Brian. *The Crisis of Church and State, 1050–1300.* 1988. Reprint, Toronto: University of Toronto Press, 1996.

Tyerman, Christopher. *God's War: A New History of the Crusades.* Cambridge, MA: Harvard University Press, 2006.

———. *The Invention of the Crusades.* Toronto: University of Toronto Press, 1998.

Vogel, Christian. "Templar Runaways and Renegades before, during and after the Trial." In Burgtorf, Crawford, and Nicholson, *Debate on the Trial of the Templars,* 317–26.

Walker, Sue Sheridan. "Litigation as Personal Quest: Suing for Dower in the Royal Courts, circa 1272–1350." In Walker, *Wife and Widow in Medieval England,* 81–108.

———, ed. *Wife and Widow in Medieval England.* Ann Arbot: University of Michigan Press, 1993.

Walsh, John R., and Thomas Bradley. *A History of the Irish Church, 400–700 AD.* 1991; revised ed., Dublin: Columba Press, 1993.

Walsh, Katherine. "Archbishop FitzRalph and the Friars at the Papal Court in Avignon, 1357–60." *Traditio* 31 (1975): 223–45.

———. *Richard FitzRalph in Oxford, Avignon and Armagh: A Fourteenth-Century Scholar and Primate.* Oxford: Clarendon Press, 1981.

Ward, Jennifer. "The English Noblewoman and Her Family in the Later Middle Ages." In Meek and Simms, *'The Fragility of Her Sex'?,* 119–35.

Wardell, John. "The History and Antiquities of St Catherine's Old Abbey, County Limerick." *Journal of the Royal Society of the Antiquaries of Ireland* 34 (1904): 41–64.

Ware, James. *De Praesulibus Lageniae, sive Provinciae Dubliniensis liber unus.* Dublin, 1628.

———. *De Scriptoribus Hiberniae.* 1639. Reprint, Farnborough: Gregg Press, 1966.

———. *The Whole Works of Sir James Ware.* Edited by Walter Harris. Vol. 1. Dublin: E. Jones, 1746.

Warner, Marina. *Alone of All Her Sex.* New York: Knopf, 1976.

Warren, W. L. "Church and State in Angevin Ireland." *Chronicon* 1 (1997): 1–17.

Watt, J. A. *The Church and the Two Nations in Medieval Ireland.* Cambridge: Cambridge University Press, 1970.

———. *The Church in Medieval Ireland*. 1972. Reprint, Dublin: University College Dublin Press, 1998.

———. "*Laudabiliter* in Medieval Diplomacy and Propaganda." *Irish Ecclesiastical Record* 87 (1957): 420–32.

———. "Negotiations between Edward II and John XXII Concerning Ireland." *Irish Historical Studies* 10 (1956): 1–20.

Watt, J. A., J. B. Morrall, and F. X. Martin, eds. *Medieval Studies Presented to Aubrey Gwynn, S.J.* Dublin: C. O. Lochlainn, 1961.

Waugh, Scott, and Peter Diehl. *Christendom and Its Discontents: Exclusion, Persecution, and Rebellion, 1000–1500.* Cambridge: Cambridge University Press, 1996.

Weltecke, Dorothea. "Beyond Religion: On the Lack of Belief During the Central and Late Middle Ages." In *Religion and Its Other: Secular and Sacral Concepts and Practices in Interaction,* edited by Heike Bock, Jörg Feuchter, and Michi Knecht, 101–14. Frankfurt: Campus Verlag, 2008.

Williams, Bernadette. "The Annals of Friar John Clyn—Provenance and Bias." *Archivium Hibernicum* 47 (1993): 65–77.

———. "The Dominican Annals of Dublin." In *Medieval Dublin II: Proceedings of the Friends of Medieval Dublin Symposium 2000,* edited by Seán Duffy, 142–68. Dublin: Four Courts Press, 2001.

———. "Heresy in Ireland in the Thirteenth and Fourteenth Centuries." In *Princes, Prelates and Poets in Medieval Ireland: Essays in Honour of Katharine Simms,* edited by Seán Duffy, 339–51. Dublin: Four Courts Press, 2013.

———. "The Heretic's Tale: Adam Duff O'Toole." Tales of Medieval Dublin Lunchtime Lecture Series, Presented by Friends of Medieval Dublin. October 19, 2010. http://www.dublinheritage.ie/media/heretics_tale.html.

———. "The Kilkenny Chronicle." In Barry, Frame, and Simms, *Colony and Frontier in Medieval Ireland,* 75–95.

———. "'She Was Usually Placed with the Great Men and Leaders of the Land in the Public Assemblies': Alice Kyteler, a Woman of Considerable Power." In Meek, *Women in Renaissance and Early Modern Europe,* 67–83.

———. "The Sorcery Trial of Alice Kyteler." *History Ireland* 2 (1993): 20–24.

Wood, Herbert. "The Templars in Ireland." *Proceedings of the Royal Irish Academy* 26C (1906–7): 327–77.

Woodcock, Brian. *Medieval Ecclesiastical Courts in the Diocese of Canterbury.* London: Oxford University Press, 1952.

Yeats, William Butler. *Selected Poems and Two Plays of William Butler Yeats.* Edited by M. L. Rosenthal. New York: Collier Books, 1962.

Zimmer, Heinrich. *Pelagius in Irland: Texte und Untersuhungen zur patristischen Litteratur.* Berlin: Weidmannsche Buchhandlung, 1901.

❧ INDEX

As last names were in the process of being established during this time, but varied significantly in spelling and were not universally used, the organizational system I follow is somewhat artificial.[1] In the case of patronymics (Irish names beginning with Mac or O', fitz for Anglo-Irish individuals), people are listed by the patronymic signifier first (e.g., Richard fitz Ralph is listed under f, as fitz Ralph, Richard). In some families, the patronymic changed with each generation; for example, the father of Geraldine Maurice fitz Thomas was Thomas fitz Maurice (as Maurice's grandfather was also named Maurice), and his sons were Maurice fitz Maurice and Gerald fitz Maurice; all could be classified under the name Fitz Gerald (representing the Geraldine family), but I do not follow this later convention here. A place name that uses "de" (e.g., de Midia) is treated as a last name listed alphabetically according to the place (so de Midia is under M, de Valence under V). A place name that is rendered "of" (e.g., Bernard of Clairvaux) is listed in the index alphabetically according to the first name (so Bernard of Clairvaux is listed under B, Isabella of France under I). Place names that have become the functional equivalent of last names (e.g., Aquinas, Eriugena) are treated as such for indexing purposes. Last names that begin with an independent "le" or "la" (e.g., le Poer, la Warr, but not Ledrede) are listed according to the primary part of their last name (so le Poer under P and la Warr under W, but Ledrede under L).

For more information about individuals who held religious or secular office, participated in the heresy trials, or were members of prominent families, please see the "Guide to Groups," at http://www.cornellpress.cornell.edu/book/?GCOI=80140100398210; click on "Assets."

absenteeism, 16–17, 97, 105, 148, 226; of Richard de Haverings, 50, 71, 97, 142
absolution: in Kyteler case, 131, 133, 135, 137, 145; for Ledrede, 179, 181, 184; in Templar trial, 45, 47–48, 53–56, 58–59, 61, 63
Acre, 33, 39–40, 53, 75
Adam and Eve, 20, 96, 115, 191
Adrian IV (Nicholas Breakspear), 5, 7, 10, 208, 212–13, 218
Albigensians. *See* Cathars
Alexander III, 5, 8, 10, 21, 200
All Hallows' Priory (Dublin), 66, 205
Amaury of Bene, 196, 199
Andrew, William, 235–36
Annals of Inisfallen, 32, 68, 91n68, 221n156
apostasy, 29–30, 89; of Adducc Dubh O'Toole, 18–19, 204–5, 207–11, 219,

229, 231–32, 240; among Irish generally, 1, 10, 24, 200, 207–8, 211, 219, 231–32; in Kyteler case: 85, 105, 162; of Templars, 37, 53, 61, 77
Aquinas, Thomas, 26, 109, 111n159
ard rí (high king), 10, 217
Arles, Council of, 192, 196
Armagh, 73, 216; archbishops of, 15, 68, 118n2. *See also* fitz Ralph, Richard; Malachy of Armagh
Armeston, Richard de, 154, 184n172
Augustine, St., 191–92, 196
Avignon, 106; Ledrede in, 78, 82, 92, 169, 171–72, 175, 177, 179; O'Kelly and fitz Ralph in, 180–81, 228, 230

babies and young children: in unholy activities, 85, 108, 111

---

1. The Irish adopted patronymics perhaps as early as 900 (Curtis, *History of Medieval Ireland*, xxvii), however.

Bacheler, Walter le, 37–38, 47, 57, 59, 60
Badlesmere, Margaret, 99n104, 151, 153
Balybyn, Richard de, 60–61, 64
barbarians, 5, 7–8, 11, 190, 196–98, 200, 215
Barber, Malcolm, 44n45, 58, 65n127, 75
Becket, St. Thomas, 8–11, 101–2, 124, 138, 148, 213
Benedict XII (Jacques Fournier), 6, 90, 147, 177–79, 185
Bermingham, John de, 155–56, 158–61, 167–68, 173, 175–76
Bermingham, Peter de, 213
Bermingham, William de, 155, 158–61, 167, 173, 176–77
Bernard of Clairvaux, 1, 4–5, 7, 28, 39, 53–54, 197, 239
Béziers, 23
Bible, 22, 125, 137, 155, 192; denial of, 188, 204, 207; as judge of heresy, 194–95, 197, 199–200
Bicknor, Alexander de, 13, 68, 70, 119, 130, 202, 212; and feud with Ledrede: 101, 149–50, 155, 167–76, 178–83, 187, 189, 219, 240–42; as treasurer, 49, 204
blasphemy, 30; of Arnold le Poer, 162–63, 174; of Irish and Adducc Dubh O'Toole, 208–10; of MacConmaras, 18, 219, 227–29; of Templars, 53, 57, 67, 77
Blund, Adam le, 88, 98, 102–4, 120
Blund, Margaret le, 99
Boneville, John de, 158, 169
Boniface, St., 195–96
Boniface IV, 194, 199
Boniface VIII, 41, 43, 73, 89, 128, 131, 214n124
Botiller (Butler), James le, 155, 159–61, 173, 176
Botiller, Thomas le, 155, 161, 173
Bradeley, Ralph de, 53, 56
Bras, Michael de, 65–66, 75
Braybrook, Philip de, 17–18, 29, 32–33, 50, 70–76, 78, 174, 205, 209, 233, 239
Broghton, Thomas de, 58n105, 64–67
Bruce, Edward, 141, 152, 155, 157, 203, 214, 216, 221; as king of Ireland, 129, 189, 217–18
Bruce, Robert, 152, 158, 217–18
Bruce invasion, 119, 155, 172, 227; Irish involvement in, 91, 141, 201, 216, 221
Bunratty Castle, 153–54, 213, 220–25; and execution of MacConmaras, 77, 219, 227–29, 233
Burgh, Katherine de, 152

Burgh, Richard de, 152, 221
Burgh, Walter fitz William de, 160
Burgh, William de, 156, 160, 176, 223–24
Burghs (Burkes), 16, 152–53, 156, 159–60, 173, 176, 220–24
Bustlesham, Richard de, 51–52, 55–57, 61–62

Caithréim Thoirdhealbhaigh, 14, 16, 221–22, 224
Callan (Co. Kilkenny), 98, 156n32
Callan, battle of (Co. Kerry), 16
Canon *Episcopi*, 107–8
Canterbury, 5, 7–8, 46, 48
Carmelites, 90, 230. *See also* O'Kelly, Ralph
Carretto, Enrico del, 90, 92
Cashel, archbishops of, 9, 24, 68, 91, 99, 216, 231, 235. *See also* fitz John, William; O'Kelly, Ralph
Cashel, First Synod of (1101), 4
Cashel, Second Synod of (1172), 10, 124
Castledermot, 216, 227
Catalonia, 59–60
Cathars, 20–22, 58, 76, 108
cats, 47, 86, 108
Caunton, Robert de, 101, 149–50, 155, 160–61, 167–77, 179–81, 240
Celtic Christianity, 1, 3, 8, 12, 39, 81, 189–200, 237–41; fourteenth-century references to, 69, 212
Chaddesworth, Thomas de, 18, 32–33, 50–51, 70–76, 200, 209, 233, 239
Charnells, William, 139, 184–86
cin comfocuis (native Irish system of kin accountability), 106, 130, 153
Cistercians, 4, 9, 15, 147, 214–15, 235. *See also* Bernard of Clairvaux; Malachy of Armagh
Clapdale Castle, 113–14
Clare, Gilbert de (lord of Kilkenny), 97
Clare, Richard de (second lord of Thomond), 152–53, 155n28, 221–23
Clare, Richard de (Strongbow, lord of Leinster), 5, 6, 16
Clare, Thomas de (first lord of Thomond), 213, 220
Clares, 16, 220–23
Clemens, 195–97, 199, 232
Clement V, 42–46, 48, 68, 73, 74, 89
Clement VI, 170, 179–83, 230
clerical arrest, 41, 89, 135; Ledrede's 1320 arrest, 122, 169; Ledrede's 1324 arrest, 79, 117, 124–26, 131, 133, 141, 151, 157,

163, 179–80, 240; warrant for Ledrede's
1329 arrest, 171, 174, 178
clerical marriage, 8–10, 118–19
Clontarf, 34n13, 49, 64
Cloyne, 68, 235
Clyn, Friar John, 31–32, 70, 85, 111–12,
159, 179, 202, 212
Columbanus, St., 193–200, 232, 238
Connacht Irish, 12, 212, 223
cords (Templar), 57–58, 63
Cork, 60, 68n136, 84n26, 161, 165, 215
Counter-Remonstrance, 204, 207–12, 218,
232–35, 241
Cradock, Roger, 27, 184n172, 189, 219,
228–31, 233–34, 241
Crumpe, Henry, 235–36
crusade: Albigensian, 20, 22–24; in Holy
Land, 38–40, 75; in Ireland, 2, 19, 25,
28, 143, 188–89, 205, 207–12, 219, 229,
232–33, 235, 240
Cummian, 193, 197–99, 238
Curragh, Peter, 231, 235
curses, 86–87, 121
Cusack, Nicholas, 215–16
Cyprus, 59, 64–67

Danet, Henry, 50, 52–53, 55–64, 67,
69–70
Darcy, John, 126–27, 131–32, 139, 143–44,
154, 170, 172–73, 208–11
Despenser, Hugh, 150–51, 156, 161, 169
diabolism: English, 93–94; French, 40,
77, 89–90; in Kyteler case, 80, 85–86,
113–14, 140, 163, 177; and witchcraft,
106–11. See also necromancy
diversity, 3, 28, 198–200, 237–38
dogs, 15, 78, 86, 164, 185n178, 189, 214
Dominicans, 146–48, 230; in Ireland, 12,
43, 60–61, 66–67, 126, 141. See also
Balybyn, Richard de; Charnells, William;
O'Scannell, Maol Pádraig; Pembridge,
John de; St. Saviour's Priory
Drogheda, 49n69, 165, 214, 216
Dublin, 4, 8–9, 17, 133, 159, 201–3, 225,
227; Alice Kyteler in, 103, 123; Castle,
150, 165, 167, 176, 205, 224; heretics
in, 2, 177, 180, 182; sheriff of, 36, 82,
102–4, 122. See also Bicknor, Alexander
de; Braybrook, Philip de; Chaddesworth,
Thomas de; Haverings, Richard de;
Holy Trinity Cathedral; John of St.
Paul; Nottingham, William de; O'Toole,
Adducc Dubh; parliament; Pembridge,
John de; Rodyerd, William de;

St. Patrick's Cathedral; St. Saviour's
Priory; Templar trial in Ireland
Dunbrody Abbey, 36–37, 204n78
Dysert O'Dea, Battle of, 152–53, 155n28,
222–23

Easter, 3, 83, 159, 192–95, 198, 204
Edward I of England, 36, 99, 102, 118,
215–16, 220, 226
Edward II of England, 91, 119, 141, 155–56,
169, 215–16; deposed, 150, 157, 167; and
Irish Remonstrance, 69, 208, 217–19; and
Ledrede, 124–26, 129–30, 172; and trial
of Templars, 33, 44–46, 48–50, 62, 233
Edward III of England, 156, 159, 188, 208,
212, 225; and Ledrede, 19, 92, 100, 138,
148–50, 162–64, 168, 171–72, 175–78,
182–86
Emly, 68, 131
England, 17–19, 69, 125, 139–41, 236–38;
and Desmond-le Poer feud, 154, 159–60;
heresy in, 93–94, 106, 140; and invasion
of Ireland, 4–8, 14–16, 29, 33, 200, 208;
and Kyteler case, 87, 113–14, 124, 127,
129, 136, 162–64, 240; Ledrede in, 78,
167–68, 172, 175, 177, 182, 185; and
Mortimer-Despenser feud, 150–52,
158–59, 161; Norman Conquest of, 3, 6,
39; Templars and, 31, 33–38, 44–50, 52,
54, 61–63, 67–68, 85
Enquede, Galharda, 90
Eriugena, John Scottus, 196–97, 199–200
ethnic tensions: between Anglo-Irish
and English, 117, 127, 129–130, 225;
between Irish and English/Anglo-Irish,
15–17, 34, 78, 91, 141, 180, 202. See also
MacConmaras; O'Toole, Adducc Dubh;
Remonstrance of Irish Princes
Eton (Heton), Roger de, 31n4, 60
eucharist, 5, 71, 74, 208, 235–36; Ledrede's
use of, 125–27, 139, 162–63, 174,
177, 187, 239–40; perversions of, 108,
112–13; and Templars, 37, 59, 64. See also
sacraments
excommunication, 21, 35, 37, 45, 73,
139–40, 194, 212, 218, 231; of Bicknor,
169–70, 181; by Kilkenny witches,
87, 107; by Ledrede, 85, 103, 119–31,
133–36, 143–44, 163–66, 172, 183; of
Ledrede, 174, 179, 184

Faciens misericordiam, 43, 45, 48
fama (common opinion, public rumor), 65,
103–4, 127–28, 139–40

fautors, 24, 29, 43, 209, 211; Bicknor as, 171, 178, 240; Ledrede as, 170; Roger Outlaw as, 79, 82, 135, 165; William Outlaw as, 83, 127, 144–45

female inheritance, 97–99, 105, 116

Ferns (bishops of), 9n26, 68n136, 131, 139, 178–79, 184–85

fitz Gerald, Maurice (Geraldine), 14–15

fitz John, Thomas (second earl of Kildare, Geraldine), 151–52, 154–56, 159–60, 165, 172, 204

fitz John, William, 91–92, 118–19, 148

fitz Maurice, Gerald (third earl of Desmond, Geraldine), 17, 115–16

fitz Ralph, Richard, 15, 179–83, 216, 230, 241

fitz Thomas, Maurice (first earl of Desmond, Geraldine), 17, 115–16, 142, 223, 224, 233; and conspiracy to become king of Ireland, 154–57, 161, 176, 182, 203, 224; and feud with Arnold le Poer, 142, 149–60, 162, 164–65, 167–69, 173, 176, 187

Flanders, 105, 114

fosterage, 16–17, 96, 113–14, 226, 241

Frame, Robin, 151, 156–57, 165, 176n129

France, 6, 8, 40–41, 45, 68, 95, 121; heresy in, 20–23, 77, 89–92, 109, 146, 151; Ledrede in, 78, 93, 106; trial of Templars in, 17, 33, 38, 41–46, 49, 53–54, 57–58, 61, 63, 67, 76, 93, 233

Franciscans, 20–21, 32, 91–92, 111, 126, 132, 180, 227–28; and ethnic tensions in Ireland, 15, 141–42, 210, 214–16; suspicions of, 180, 230, 236; and Templar trial, 43, 60, 66–67. *See also* Clyn, Friar John; Cradock, Roger; Eton, Roger de; Ledrede, Richard de; Mac Lochlainn, Michael; Mercer, Simon le

Francis of Assisi, 20–21, 91, 121

Free Spirit, 25, 196–97

free will, 191–92, 196

Freyne, Fulk de la, 102, 105–6, 112, 138

Freyne, Fulk de la, the younger, 112, 138

gaelicization, 16–17, 96–97, 106, 143, 157, 201, 211, 225

Gaelic Resurgence, 16, 97n95, 239, 241

Gaul, 190–94

gender: in colony, 95–102; in *Narrative*, 2, 80, 83, 86–87, 110, 128; in witch trials, 109, 115–16

Geraldines, 16–17, 70, 99, 152, 157, 212, 220, 238. *See also* fitz Gerald, Maurice; fitz John, Thomas; fitz Maurice, Gerald; fitz Thomas, Maurice

Gerald of Wales, 7–16, 39

Glenmalure, 200–201, 205n83

grace, 138, 191, 193

Grace, James, 113, 204

Gregorian Reform, 3–4, 6, 10

Gregory I (the Great), 192, 194

Gui, Bernard, 90, 146–48

Guglielma of Milan, 242

hagiography, 4–5, 81, 237–38

Haselakeby, Henry de, 60, 62

Haverings, Richard de, 50–51, 71, 73–74, 97, 239

hell, 85, 111, 195, 197, 222

Henry II, 21, 33, 93; and invasion of Ireland, 1, 5–11, 39, 69, 124, 200, 208, 212–13, 218

Henry VIII, 17, 30

Hereford, Robert de, 65–66

heresy (defined), 19–20, 25–29, 90, 105, 242

Hincmar, 196, 199

Holy Land, 22–23, 33, 38–41, 53, 64, 66, 75, 137

Holy Trinity (Christ Church) Cathedral (Dublin), 2, 17–18, 32, 40, 64, 71–76, 102, 166

Honorius III, 15, 229

Hospitallers, 35–38, 50, 65, 68–70, 95, 201. *See also* Outlaw, Roger

Hothum, William de, 50, 60

immaculate conception, 111n159, 227, 230

Inistioge Priory, 184–86

Innocent III, 21–22

Innocent VI, 92, 138, 184–85

interdict, 35, 45, 125–26, 137, 163, 165, 181, 212

intermarriage, 6, 16, 96, 226, 241

Iona, 197–98

Ireland: invasion of, 1, 5–18, 24–25, 33, 38–39, 69, 124, 200; fourteenth-century discussions of, 208, 210, 212–13

Isabella of France (queen of England), 45, 115, 150, 157, 161–62, 167–70

Islip, Walter de, 84, 125, 131–33, 139, 143–44, 164, 169, 172

Jerome, St., 191–92, 194–96, 200

Jerusalem, 24, 38

Jesus Christ, 12, 20, 25, 38, 92, 190, 195, 199, 204, 207, 227–28, 242; denial of, 41–42, 47, 59, 64–65, 85, 204; Ledrede on, 101, 125, 127, 130, 141, 148, 163, 174, 186, 240

Jews, 40–41, 89, 120n15, 192–93

Johannes Teutonicus, 24, 190

John of England, 11, 16, 39, 241

John of Salisbury, 7, 108

John of St. Paul, 119, 182, 230

John XXII, 25, 78, 106, 141, 147–48, 177, 228; and Counter-Remonstrance, 188, 207–212, 241; and Irish Remonstrance, 218–19, 232; and Ledrede, 82, 102, 116, 122, 169, 171–72, 175, 185; and sorcery prosecution, 89–93, 109

Judaizing, 193–95, 198

Kells in Ossory, 123–24

Kerkyom, Stephen de, 184, 187

Kieckhefer, Richard, 80, 94–95, 106n139, 109

Kildare, 17, 60, 131, 151, 158, 179, 200–201, 215

Kilkenny, 78–88, 94–106, 110–13, 117–128, 131–45, 163, 178–79, 183, 185, 204, 225, 237; Castle, 125, 151; and Maurice fitz Thomas's conspiracy, 155–56, 159, 174, 176, 224. See also Kyteler, Alice; Ledrede, Richard de; Outlaw, Roger; Outlaw, William; parliament; Poer, Arnold le

Kilkenny, Statute of, 15, 17, 96, 225–26, 231, 234, 241

Kilkenny Chronicle, 31, 41, 226–29, 239

Killaloe, 2, 68, 219, 229

Kilmainham, 83, 117

Kilros, William de, 51, 53–55, 57–59, 61–63, 67, 75

Kiteler (Kyteler), William le, 102–3, 105, 136n76

Kyteler, Alice, 1–2, 79–88, 102–16, 117, 120–23, 126–29, 131–35, 143–48, 161–62; and fellow accused, 84; stepchildren of, 77, 83, 86, 88–89, 95, 139–40, 174; wealth of, 92, 97–99, 102, 105, 185. See also Midia, Petronilla de; Outlaw, William

Langeport, Adam de, 52, 60

Langton, Walter, 93–94

Lateran II (1139), 120, 124

Latimer, Adam le, 64, 66

Laudabiliter, 5–7, 11, 39; and fourteenth century, 18–19, 69, 124, 205, 208, 211, 216–19, 232, 241

law, Brehon (Irish), 12, 16–17, 96–98, 130, 226, 241

law, canon, 46, 90, 118–20, 171, 228; and conflict with civil law, 101, 103, 117, 127, 139–45; in Kyteler case, 124–26, 128, 132–38

law, English common (civil), 15, 37, 93, 97, 164, 226; Irish protection under, 202, 208, 213; in Kyteler case, 122–33; prohibits torture, 45–46, 62, 134. See also law, canon

Lea, Henry Charles, 61, 63, 76

Ledrede, Richard de, 1–2, 18–19, 73, 76–78, 89–96; author of Narrative, 2, 79, 82; collaboration with fitz Thomas, 149–57, 167–76; compared to other inquisitors, 145–48; conflict with common law, 139–45; conflict with king, 19, 149–50, 183–86; feud with Bicknor, 178–82, 240–41; and gender, 100–102, 105–6, 110–11, 115–16; heresy accusations for personal gain, 27–28, 92, 98–99, 138, 148; influence on others, 33, 204–11, 230–32, 241–42; Kyteler case, 78–88, 122–39; ongoing feud with Roger Outlaw and Arnold le Poer, 149–55, 160–66, 239–40; synod and constitutions, 103, 118–21. See also Caunton, Robert de; clerical arrest; fitz Thomas, Maurice; John XXII; Kyteler, Alice; Narrative; Outlaw, Roger; Outlaw, William; Poer, Arnold le; Red Book of Ossory

Leinster Irish, 130, 142, 202–3, 211–12, 225–26, 233–34

Limerick, 4, 156, 165, 168, 220, 224, 226, 231

Lindsey, Thomas de, 50, 52

Lismore, 68, 131, 161, 178–79, 228, 231; cleric of, 4–5, 28, 197, 238

Lollardy, 93, 181n154, 207, 236n2, 236n6

London, 37, 82, 94, 119, 134

Louth, 17, 155, 176

Lovetot, John, 93–94

Lucifer. See Satan (Lucifer)

MacConmaras (MacNamaras): control of Thomond, 155, 220–24; and heresy case, 2, 18–19, 27–29, 77, 189, 205, 209–10, 219, 226–34, 239–41

Mac Lochlainn, Michael, 142n97, 216

MacMurroughs, 201

MacMurrough, Aífe (daughter of Diarmaid MacMurrough), 6, 16

MacMurrough, Art and Muirchertach (Diarmaid's grandsons, Dónal's father and uncle), 213

MacMurrough, Diarmaid (king of Leinster), 6, 16, 200

MacMurrough, Dónal mac Airt, 202, 205, 211

MacThomas's Rout, 70, 100, 157, 159, 162, 164, 184, 187

magic, 27n91, 29, 160–61, 238n12; and Iberian Peninsula, 60n110, 95; and witchcraft, 80–81, 85, 88, 106–9, 112–15, 132, 237n10, 239–40. *See also* diabolism; necromancy

Magna Carta, 118, 129–30, 142

Malachy of Armagh (Máel-máedóc Ó Morgair), St., 4–5, 28, 215, 238–39

Maleficia, 29, 83–86, 89–90, 93, 103, 106–9, 116, 139, 148, 151

Map, Walter, 21, 108

Marshall, John le, 49n67, 60

martyrdom, 9, 24, 76, 207; Ledrede's aspirations to, 101–2, 124–25, 138, 148, 193. *See also* Becket, St. Thomas

Mary, Blessed Virgin, 110–11; denial of, 47, 64, 204, 208–10, 219, 227–28, 233; veneration of, 57, 76, 121, 207, 240–41

Meath, 17, 235

Mercer, Simon le, 214, 216

Midia, Petronilla de, 77; confession of, 27, 82, 84–88, 107, 110–12; execution of, 80, 84, 103, 117, 134, 142–43, 146, 148, 210, 219

Midia, Sarah de, 84, 104n132

Molay, Jacques de, 42–43, 61, 64

Montpellier, 13, 42

More, William de la, 34n12, 48, 52, 54

Mortimer, Roger, 150–51, 156–60, 162, 169–70, 221

Munster, 157–60, 221, 226

Muslims (Saracens), 22–23, 39, 41, 57–58, 63, 75, 119–20

Narrative of the Proceedings against Dame Alice Kyteler, 2, 79–88, 98–12, 115, 122–45, 162–64, 168, 240; and Desmond–le Poer conflict, 153, 157; foreshadowing Adducc Dubh O'Toole's case, 210–11

nationalism, 13–14, 117, 129–30, 236–37

Neary, Anne, 79, 80n2, 84n26, 157, 186, 205

necromancy, 89–96

Nicholson, Helen, 32, 52, 57–59, 64

Nogaret, William de, 41–42

Normans: Anglo-Normans, 29, 33; Norse, 4, 6. *See also* England: and invasion of Ireland; Ireland: invasion of

Nottingham, William de, 101n118, 104, 128, 142–43, 207–12, 232

obedience: and heresy, 20–21, 28, 195; Ireland's to Rome, 23–24, 212; and Kyteler case, 127, 129, 132, 137–39; and original sin, 191; and Templars, 38, 53, 61–62

O'Brien, Brian Bán, 153, 155, 220–24

O'Brien, Brian Ruad, 213, 220

O'Brien, Diarmait, 222, 224

O'Brien, Donnchad, 221

O'Brien, Muirchertach, 153, 221–24

O'Brien, Tairdelbach, 220–21

O'Briens, 4, 16, 219–24, 227, 234

Ó Cróinín, Dáibhí, 193, 198

O'Heney, Muirges, 9, 24

O'Hogan, Tomás, 219, 229, 233

O'Kelly, Ralph, 27, 180–83, 189, 228, 230–31, 234, 241

O'Neill, Dónal, 188, 212–19, 232

original sin, 111n159, 191, 227

Orpen, Goddard Henry, 153, 157

O'Scannell, Maol Pádraig, 12, 236

Ossory, 122, 133, 143, 155, 159–64, 175, 179, 184, 225; bishop of, 18, 76, 78, 91, 94, 113, 118, 141, 169; heretics in, 2, 82, 120–21, 130–31, 177, 180, 188; under interdict, 125–26, 137, 165. *See also* Kyteler, Alice; Ledrede, Richard de; Outlaw, Roger; Outlaw, William; parliament; Poer, Arnold le

O'Toole, Adducc Dubh (Adam), 2, 18–19, 25, 77, 105, 188–89, 203–7, 219, 229, 231–34, 240–41; and Counter-remonstrance, 207–11; ties with Kyteler case, 142–43, 166, 174

O'Toole, David, 203, 205–7

O'Toole, Laurence, St. (Lorcán Ó Tuathail), 4, 200

O'Toole, Walter, 202, 204

O'Tooles, 70, 189, 200–203, 205, 211, 234, 240

Outlaw, Roger, 80, 98, 118, 159–60, 176, 204, 208, 210–11; and assistance to William Outlaw, 133, 135–38; as fautor, 82, 241; and resistance to Ledrede, 83–84, 101, 117, 122–23, 125–26, 129, 131–32, 139–45, 164–65, 171–74; trial of, 146, 148, 149–50, 165–66, 168

Outlaw, Rose, 88n46, 102

Outlaw, William, 80n4, 100–104, 109n155, 120, 143; confession, imprisonment, and penance of, 92, 114, 132–39, 144–45,

148, 182, 185, 210; among Kilkenny
accused, 77, 84, 110, 127, 141; and
Petronilla's accusation, 87–88, 112–13;
and resistance to Ledrede, 83, 98, 122–26,
129
Oxford, 13, 93, 236n2, 238

paganism, 81, 107–8, 119–20, 177, 195, 222,
229–30, 238, 240; alleged of Irish, 1, 4, 8,
11–13, 18
Palladius, 190–92, 200
parliament: in 1310 (Kilkenny and Kildare),
118, 153, 158, 214; in 1317 (Dublin),
221–22; in 1324 (Dublin), 117, 129–31,
142–43, 149, 153, 170n103, 185, 210;
in 1328 (Kilkenny), 159, 161; in 1329
(Dublin), 165–66, 169–70, 172–73; in
1333 (Dublin), 202; in 1421 (Dublin),
210; in 1447 (Trim), 81, 236; in 1541
(Dublin), 17
Passover, 192–93, 195n32
Pastoralis praeeminentiae, 43–44
Patrick, St., 189–91, 198–200
Paul, St., 121, 192, 194
Pelagianism, 93, 190–93, 195–96, 199
Pelagius, 191–92, 196, 198, 200
Pembridge, John de, 31, 41, 70, 152, 173;
on Arnold le Poer, 157, 159, 161; on
Kyteler case, 87, 112–13, 116n181, 122,
134, 137; on O'Tooles, 202–4, 207
penitentials, 81, 197
Peter, St., 121, 136, 194
Philip IV of France, 40–45, 68–69, 75, 89,
147, 233, 239
pilgrimage, 38, 40, 64, 125, 137, 193, 238
Poers (Powers), 106, 126, 166, 168, 176; and
Desmond-le Poer feud, 152–60, 164, 173,
182, 184, 186
Poer, Arnold le, 131–33, 143–44, 210; and
feud with Maurice fitz Thomas, 16,
150–60, 176; and Irish patriotism, 14,
69, 129, 142, 236–37; Ledrede's vendetta
against, 82, 120, 146, 148, 149–50,
160–69, 172–74, 180, 185, 187, 208,
239–41; and opposition to Ledrede, 77,
83, 100–101, 117, 122–30, 139, 141
Poer, Eustace le, the elder (uncle of Arnold
le Poer), 102, 166
Poer, Eustace le, the younger (son of Arnold
le Poer), 176
Poer, John le (baron of Dunoyl), 154, 159,
173
John le Poer (brother of Arnold le Poer),
83, 88, 102, 106n138, 153, 155, 160, 176

Poer, Stephen le (bailiff), 124, 133
Ponthieu, 46, 63
Pourbriggs, Robert de, 57, 62
Publicans, 93, 108
purgation, 137–38, 144–45, 161, 165, 182

quartodecimanism, 193

Raphoe, 12, 236
Red Book of Ossory, 109, 118–19, 148, 186
Regnans in coelis, 43, 67
Remonstrance of Irish Princes, 8, 14–16, 19,
24, 69, 129–30, 188–90, 212–20, 232
Robert or Robin son of Art (Alice's
demon), 80, 85–86, 138
Rodyerd, William de, 13n41, 126, 130–31,
135, 141–43, 165–66, 204–5; and
Counter-Remonstrance, 207–11, 229,
232–33
Rokeby, Thomas de, 183, 219, 225–28,
233–34
Roman Empire, 3, 7, 10, 190, 199–200
Rome: and papacy, 1, 4, 6, 21, 39, 191–93,
197–99, 212, 228

sacraments, 35, 60, 163, 177, 188; baptism,
85, 89, 125; confession, 37, 53–56, 88,
185–86; ordination, 21, 125. See also
eucharist
Satan (Lucifer), 20, 24, 96, 99, 105, 107,
115, 135
Sayles, G. O., 155n29, 157, 167–68, 203
Scotland, 6, 36, 68, 102, 203, 225; Templar
trial in, 45, 67; and ties with Ireland,
14n45, 129, 152, 217
Ségéne, abbot of Iona, 197–99
sexual allegations, 89, 227; against Irish, 10,
12, 209, 236; and Kyteler case, 80, 84, 86,
106–11, 113–14; against Templars, 36,
41–42, 47, 53, 57–61, 64–67
Significavit, 143–44
Simms, Katharine, 11–13
Si quis suadente (Canon 15 of the Second
Lateran Council), 120, 124–25, 141
Stappelbrugge, Stephen de, 47–49, 52
St. Canice's Cathedral (Kilkenny), 79,
92n69, 112, 118–19, 121, 133, 136,
138
St. Mary's (Kilkenny), 112, 132, 138
Stoke, John de, 47–48, 65
St. Patrick's Cathedral (Dublin), 236;
Bicknor's attack on Ledrede in, 170–71,
173–74; and feud with Holy Trinity, 18,
32, 71–73; Templar trial in, 51, 64,

St. Patrick's Cathedral (*continued*)
  66n130. *See also* Bicknor, Alexander de;
  Chaddesworth, Thomas de; Islip, Walter
  de; Nottingham, William de; Rodyerd,
  William de; Wylyby, Peter de
St. Saviour's Priory (Dublin), 31, 112, 166,
  177n133
St. Thomas the Martyr Abbey (Dublin),
  66, 166
syncretism, 28, 237
Syria, 59–60, 67

Tallaght, 202, 212
Templars: arrest of, 31, 42, 44–45, 49–50; as
  chaplains, 34, 42, 53–55, 58–59, 61–62,
  63; execution of (in France), 44, 73;
  history in Ireland of, 33–38; inquisitors
  of, 18, 32, 41–42, 45–52, 59–62, 64–65,
  67, 70, 73, 75–77, 147, 233, 239; outside
  witnesses of, 18, 31, 36, 38, 40, 45, 51–52,
  55, 63–67, 69, 233, 239; property of, 49,
  69, 95, 102, 136, 169; rules of, 53–55;
  suppression of, 25, 67–70; torture of, 27,
  32, 38, 42–44, 46–50, 59–63, 75–76, 85,
  147; trial of, 2, 17–18, 26–29, 31–33,
  39–48, 48–67, 71–77, 78, 89, 93, 107,
  109, 134, 147–48, 174, 177, 207, 233,
  239, 242
Theudelinda and Agilulf of Lombardy, 194,
  199
Thomond (north Munster), 153–54, 220–24,
  226–27, 229, 234
Three Chapters controversy, 194, 199
Torrington, Philip, 231, 235
torture, 20, 89–90, 93, 126, 134, 145–47,
  236n5; of Petronilla de Midia, 77, 80,
  84–85, 117; of Templars, 27, 32, 38,
  42–44, 46–50, 59–63, 75–76
Tuam (archdiocese), 68, 230, 241

Ua Máel Muaid, Ailbe, 9
Ulster, 152, 188, 212, 217, 220–21

Ut inquisitionis, 73, 128, 131–33, 139,
  142–44

Valdès of Lyon (founder of Waldensianism),
  20–21, 23
Valence, Agnes de, 99
Valle, Richard de, 88, 97, 105
Victorius of Aquitaine, 192–93, 199
Vienne, Council of, 19, 25, 27, 32, 67–70,
  75, 125, 213n120
Vikings, 3, 6, 205
Virgil (Fergal) of Salzburg, St., 196
visitations, 56, 72, 82, 105, 113, 124, 127,
  179, 231
vita apostolica (apostolic life), 20
Vox in excelso, 68, 75

Waldensians, 20–23, 105, 108, 242
Wales, 6, 45, 231
Walter of Guisborough, 68, 75
Warenne, William de, 40, 51–52, 64, 67
Warr, Henry la, 74, 239
Waterford, 4, 95, 156, 159, 165, 178,
  230–31; bishops of, 142, 161, 184. *See also*
  Cradock, Roger
Wexford, 4, 158
Wicklow, 142, 200–203, 211
William of Paris, 41–42, 147
Williams, Bernadette, 70, 79–80, 112, 114,
  205, 226–27
witchcraft, 2, 27n91, 29, 79–81, 85–87,
  95–96, 99–100, 103, 105–16, 222,
  235–37, 239; and witch craze, 26, 80,
  115–16, 148
Wogan, John, 49–50
Worship of idols, 12, 41–42, 47, 53, 57,
  59–61, 75–76, 90, 236
Wyclif, John, 93, 181n154, 207,
  236n6
Wylyby (Willeby), Peter, 60, 66, 166

York, 45–46, 48, 52, 61, 63, 113–14